THE A & C BLACK
COLOUR BOOKS

Colour photography for the Kate Greenaway frontispiece was provided by A. C. Cooper Ltd., London W1; the complete set of the 20 shilling series reproduced on the jacket and facing page 20, by Mike Woolley, Market Harborough. All other colour plates by Mark Payne-Gill, Piddington, High Wycombe.

A & C Black's Soho Square headquarters: a pencil sketch by Joseph Pike

Callender, who was to become a partner ten years later and who, incidentally, during his 52 years of employment with the firm did not take one single day off as a result of illness. Soon after the move south McGlashen died and Adam William Black was forced by ill health to retire at the early age of 55.

The directors of A & C Black during the 'colour book' period:
Adam Black (left), photographed during the 1920s, and
W. W. Callender, a portrait painted in 1926.

The remaining partners, James Tait and Francis, now brought into partnership their own sons: Adam, thirty one, son of James Tait, and Adam Rimmer, twenty six, son of Francis Black. By now sales of the ninth edition of *Britannica* were slowing down, and the loss of Adam William's enterprise was beginning to show. To add to the problems Francis Black died in 1892, which placed an added burden on the two young Adams. A welcome boost came from publication of the Dryburgh edition of Scott in twenty five volumes, profusely illustrated with wood and steel engravings. The edition was the result of the collating of earlier editions with the interleaved *Magnum Opus*, which was a prized possession of the firm at this time and for many years afterwards but which was sold to an American buyer in mysterious circumstances, probably in 1929. Apart from this edition, which cost £20,000 to produce, the catalogue in 1892 included the ninth edition of the *Britannica* at £37 for a set in cloth, Black's *General Atlas of the World* at 3 guineas, over forty home and fifteen foreign guide-books, a set of Poe and a short-lived fiction list; also over 100 books on science, history and theology.

Later in the 1890s work started on the production of Sir Walter Besant's massive *Survey of London*, in which he was assisted by Miss G. E. Mitton, who joined the firm in 1899 and who was to go on to write a number of colour plate books. The *Survey* was published in ten volumes during 1908-12, remaining in print until the 1930s.

James Tait Black retired in 1899 and his son decided not to continue in the business; A & C Black was thus left in the hands of two young directors: Adam (Rimmer), whose middle name no longer had to be used to distinguish him from other members of the family, and W. W. Callender. The *Britannica* was sold to two Americans, James Clarke and Horace Everett Hooper, at the turn of the century, but much of the money received from its sale went to pay off James Tait Black and his son when they left the business.

The ownership of *Who's Who* was acquired when its owners, Simpkin Marshall, put it up for sale at Hodgson's auction rooms. Adam Black and George Whitaker, who published *Whitaker's Almanac*, were both interested in the title but agreed not to bid against each other. They tossed a coin: Adam won and secured *Who's Who* for a mere £30. Its later success, which continues to this day, owes much to Adam's diligence in developing the work over the next thirty years.

The partners, now thirty four and thirty seven years old, also found themselves saddled with another large and expensive venture, the *Encyclopaedia Biblica*. This huge scholarly work was published between 1899 and 1903 at 80s (£4) a set. It contained over five million words, much setting in Hebrew and Greek, many engravings and maps, and was edited by Professor T. K. Cheyne of Oxford assisted by the Hebrew scholar J. Sutherland Black. However, on publication of the second volume, as Newth writes: '... it began to be hinted in senior common rooms, that Cheyne was unsound. His colleagues had realised ... that the editor was growing more extreme in his views, increasingly intolerant of moderate theologians.' Criticism grew with publication of the other volumes, by which time, according to the *Dictionary of National Biography*, Cheyne's textual criticism had 'crossed at last the boundary beyond which sanity ceases.'

Although the first printing eventually sold out, the resulting loss to A &

C Black on the *Encyclopaedia Biblica* was over £10,000, a huge sum at the time, equivalent to several hundred thousand pounds today.

It was in these unpromising financial circumstances that the partners, motivated especially by Callender's enthusiasm, accepted Mortimer Menpes' suggestion for a book on his Boer War experiences, profusely illustrated by the new three-colour process, and thus embarked on the publication of the Twenty Shilling series of colour plate books.

1

War Impressions

On May 23 1901 the firm of Adam & Charles Black of London and Edinburgh published *War Impressions*. A smallish fat volume, it contained in its 63,000 words of text reminiscences by the Australian artist Mortimer Menpes of the months he spent in South Africa during the Boer War, acting as war artist for the weekly magazine *Black and White*, during which time he 'did not hesitate to press upon the heels of our advancing armies'. More important, however, it included 99 full page illustrations in colour and tint of watercolour drawings made by Menpes, depicting the scenes of battle and portraying the leaders and participants on both sides in the war.

The book was a landmark in a number of ways: it is generally accepted that it was the first to make use of the potential of the recently invented three-colour process, which enabled the printing of adequate quality colour illustrations at a reasonable cost, it set the pattern for the publication of hundreds of colour plate books by A & C Black over the next thirty years and it marked a change of direction for the firm itself.

The firm's young partners, Adam Black and W. W. Callender, responded promptly and favourably to Menpes' initial proposal for *War Impressions* and deserve credit for committing themselves to the production of a book that broke new ground in British publishing.

They accepted Menpes' offer on 23 November 1900, and by December 1 were able to tell him that to produce an edition of 3,000 ordinary plus 300 large paper copies would cost £900, a figure which included £100 for advertising but nothing for royalties. The intention was to charge 15s (75p) for the trade edition and 30s (£1.50) for the large paper limited edition. By February 1901, however, the decision had been taken to raise the selling price of the trade edition to 20 shillings (£1), a price that was to be maintained for this series for the next twenty years. Menpes was offered 2s 6d (12½p) per ordinary copy sold, 10s (50p) per large paper copy and £3 10s each for copies Nos 1-25 of the limited edition, each of which was to contain an original watercolour bound in as frontispiece. These terms were extraordinarily generous to Menpes and reflect the fact that the copies containing the original watercolours were sold by subscription, thus cutting out any bookseller's commission.

The provisional costings for the book are worth setting out:

Setting and printing 3,000 copies of 350 pages text	£60
Making 96 sets of illustrations, mostly three-colour blocks	£210
Printing illustrations	£120
Paper	£130
Binding	£140
Advertising	£100
300 large paper copies	£140
Total	£900

These figures show clearly that it was the large number of illustrations that made the biggest contribution to the book's high cost. And one should be in no doubt that it was a bold venture to publish a book costing £1 in 1900; today's equivalent price would be over £40. A weekly wage of £1 in the first decade of the century was average reward for a skilled labourer. A farmworker was paid only about 10s a week and domestic servants less than this, while a reasonably prosperous family owning their own home might have had an income of £150—£200 a year — a sum which would have been sufficient for them to employ one or more domestic staff.

Even to professional people of this sort £1 would have been a large sum to pay for a book: one can hardly imagine anyone today being prepared to pay the equivalent of a skilled craftsman's weekly wages (say £200) for such a book. But comparison of the relevant prices in 1900 and the 1980s shows that all books were expensive relative to income compared with those of the present day.

By January 1901 the manuscript of *War Impressions* was in the hands of W. Earl Hodgson, the firm's reader, who was asked to alter as little as possible but was also told: 'If there are any attacks on people in South Africa you might soften them as much as possible'.

Hodgson obviously made some alterations, for on January 30 Adam wrote to him: 'Mr Menpes would like to see in places his ideas more clearly expressed ... First with regard to Lord Kitchener he does not think him the animal that the description suggests, but rather a man, machine-like and with his mind pigeon-holed. Such a machine that his smile suggested a grin. I said I got the impression from the passage that Lord Kitchener was a

And there's capital tomes that are filled with fly hooks,
And I've frequently found them the best kind of books.
ANDREW LANG.

SALMON FISHING

By W. EARL HODGSON

AUTHOR OF 'TROUT FISHING'

WITH EIGHT FULL-PAGE PLATES IN COLOUR; INCLUDING, AS
FRONTISPIECE, THE FAMOUS PICTURE "SALMON FISHING ON
THE DEE," BY JOSEPH FARQUHARSON, A.R.A., AND A MODEL
BOOK OF **74** VARIETIES OF SALMON FLIES. ALSO TEN PAGE
ILLUSTRATIONS IN BLACK AND WHITE, AND A SKETCH PLAN
OF MODEL SALMON PASS

Post Free **7/10.**   *Price* **7/6** *net.*   *Post Free* **7/10.**

PUBLISHED BY A. & C. BLACK, SOHO SQUARE, LONDON, W.

*W. Earl Hodgson, the firm's Reader for many years, seen here on a
prospectus for his book* Salmon Fishing.

man of animal passion, at which Mr Menpes was horrified & said he meant
no such thing, & that Lord K. was not animal in that sense.'

The publisher's advance publicity for *War Impressions* was a success
because copies 1-25 of the limited edition were sold by February 8 1901
and the rest of this edition by February 27, well ahead of its publication in
May.

The printing of the letterpress was carried out by R & R Clark of
Edinburgh, who were responsible for the majority of A & C Black's
printing work at the time and for many years afterwards. The engraving
and printing of the illustrations, however, were entrusted to Carl
Hentschel, who had more experience of this sort of work than any other
printer, but who nonetheless caused the publisher great anxiety because of
his constant inability to meet deadlines. However serious this may have
seemed to A & C Black at the time, records show that the time from
Menpes' first approach to the publisher to the day of publication of *War
Impressions* was a mere six months, an amazingly swift achievement.

*   *   *

Carl Hentschel was born in Lodz in Russian Poland in 1864 and came to
Britain with his family when he was four. Like his father he became a
process engraver, and in his thirties invented the Hentschel Colourtype
process for the reproduction of colour illustrations. He was a notable
figure in Edwardian London and is said to be the original of Harris in
Jerome K. Jerome's *Three Men in a Boat*. He was a founder member of the
O. P. Club and the Playgoers' Club and, in his own words in his *Who's
Who* entry, 'initiated the innovation of having no speeches at a public city
dinner at the Bartholemew Club, 1904'. He also edited the one and only
number of *The Half-Tone Times,* and among his publications was one
entitled *The Necessity of Trams across the Bridges.* An entertaining character, his name crops up regrettably infrequently in A & C Black's correspondence: 'Hentschel has been in a lawsuit with people who have a private
house next to his works & who said the works caused "stinks" & that the
engines made a great noise' is a typical example of a passing reference made
to him in a letter from Adam Black to Mortimer Menpes.

Hentschel was not the inventor of the three colour half-tone process,
though he was closely involved in its development. The process itself
seems to have originated simultaneously with two Frenchmen working
independently, Louis A. Ducos du Hauron and Charles Cros in 1867, but
it was an American, Frederick E. Ives, who developed the method of

Carl Hentschel (left), *process engraver and man-about-town, and
Edward Clark, head of the printer R & R Clark who carried out most of
A & C Black's letterpress work.*
Photo: Courtesy National Portrait Gallery

breaking up the half-tones into dots and translating the picture into a relief
surface that could be inked, though he did not regard his work as
important enough to warrant taking out a patent. Further refinement of
the process took place during the latter years of the 19th century: a
comprehensive account can be found in *Colour Printing and Colour Printers*
by R. M. Burch (Sir Isaac Pitman and Sons, 1910; reprinted in facsimile by
Paul Harris Publishing, 1983).

A contemporary account of the process is given in *English Coloured
Books* by Martin Hardie (Methuen, 1906): 'Once the principle is accepted
that any combination of colours, say in a painting, can be resolved into its
primary elements, it remains only for the photographer to obtain three
negatives, which, as it were, automatically dissect the original, making
three distinct photographic records of the reds, yellows and blues which
enter into the composition. This result is obtained by the use of trans-
parent screens of coloured pigment or liquid, 'light filters,' as they are
technically termed, placed in front of the lens. These filters admit any two
of the primary colours and absorb the other one. Three separate screens are
employed, each with the lines ruled at a different angle, and when the

negative records of the colour analysis are obtained, the three photographs are converted into printing surfaces, exactly as in the ordinary half-tone process. On the metal printing surface the separate colours are impressed in ink and transferred to paper. The block representing the yellow tones of the original is printed first with yellow ink; over this picture the block representing red is accurately registered and printed in red; while the final block representing blue is printed over the combinations of the first two, with blue ink. The result is a complete picture containing all the shades of the original, no matter whether the original is a natural object, an oil-painting, or a water-colour, an object of art or of commerce.'

Hardie goes on to point out that although these three colours should be sufficient, occasionally, and especially where the original is deep in tone, a fourth plate, inked with grey or black, may be used. He also warns that the printer can ink the plates with colours materially different from what they should be, so that there is no necessarily true reproduction.

It is this omission of the fourth colour that led to much of the criticism of the process as applied in A & C Black's colour books. *The Studio* complained regularly that the three colour process could not be relied on to reproduce the original colours faithfully, and that it was apt to lose all the greys in a prevailing tone of puce; on another occasion it declared that it was 'never successful in the interpretation of green'. In the case of *War Impressions*, the originals for which had recently been exhibited in London, it considered that many of the original drawings had 'lost much of their force and value in the reproductions'. But it also admitted that in some instances 'remarkable verisimilitude' had been obtained.

To the modern eye the colour plates in *War Impressions* do appear pallid, hardly more than lightly tinted sketches in some cases. But the process was to show steady improvement over the next ten years, reaching a particularly high standard in reproducing the detailed watercolours of such artists as Sutton Palmer.

As Hardie points out, 'the great value of the three-colour process lies in the speed and cheapness with which the prints can be produced. As an artistic method of reproducing water-colours, or natural objects such as butterflies or leaves, it is sometimes wonderfully successful, but the results are very uneven. At its best the three-colour process produces excellent results; at its worst it is a positive conflagration of crude blues and greens and oranges that coalesce without harmony.'

The speed of the process was an undoubted advantage. As Hardie says: '. . . in connection with a recent law-suit, Mr Carl Hentschel, to show before some barristers his process at Norwood, executed colour-prints from a water-colour drawing of Lincoln's Inn within four hours from start to finish'. Hardie — whose excellent book is not easy to find but which is due to be reissued by Batsford in 1990 — goes on to give full credit to A & C Black for pioneering the development of this method of book illustration. And he points out that the process produced the paradoxical result whereby the plates make the book, while the text merely illustrates.

*   *   *

Another central figure in the development of the books was the designer Albert Angus Turbayne. Born in America in 1866 of Scottish parents and educated in Boston and Canada, Turbayne and his colleagues at the Carlton Studio were responsible for the majority of the cover designs for A & C Black's colour books and also for overall design of the series. His scarab monogram does not appear on *War Impressions* but it can be found on many of the covers: in the tail of the sea-horse on *The Clyde*, at bottom left on the front of *Kent*, at bottom right on the front of *George Morland*, *Germany* and *Bonnie Scotland*, while the Carlton Studio monogram of an S within a C can be seen on *Birket Foster* and *Cambridge*.

The absence of the monogram does not mean that the design was not carried out by Turbayne: it does not appear, for instance, on one of his most splendid designs, that for the Motor Routes series.

It is hard to disagree with Callender, who wrote in 1903 that Turbayne: '... stands first in this country in this class of work ... his great forte is lettering'. There have been times over the recent past when these designs, in three or more colours and with liberal use of gilt, may have seemed, in Newth's words, ornate and over-lavish. But they reflect the exuberance of the age, and Turbayne was always careful to relate the design closely to the subject of the book. Newth quotes Turbayne's notes on his design for *India:* 'The centre panels on the spine and front are meant to suggest one of the carved stone lattice windows of the Mosque of the Palace of Ahmedabad, one of the most delicate and beautiful specimens of Indian ornament. The narrow border is based on a border on a stone screen round a tomb at Gwalior, 17th century work. The treatment of the peacock was suggested by some old Indian embroidery.'

The link between cover design and subject matter is much more obvious in many of the books: the hops on *Kent*, the eagle on *Germany*, the grapes on *The Italian Lakes*, the palette and brushes on *John Pettie*.

Turbayne was himself influenced by William Morris, an influence which shows most clearly in the layout of the pages, where a relatively small area of type is surrounded by wide margins. Morris rebelled against the drabness of many Victorian books by introducing exuberant decoration of covers and title pages, brightly coloured boards, heavy typefaces and thick paper. He saw the double page of text as a unit in two columns and aimed to make the inner margin of a page half the width of the outer and the bottom margin deeper than the top. In a typical example of one of A & C Black's 20s series books the inner margin is 1″ (25mm) wide, the outer 1½″ (38mm); the top margin 1″ and the bottom 1¾″ (44mm). Text area on each page is thus no more than 5½″ × 3¾″ (137 × 93mm), a marked departure from the closely-set text and narrow margins of a typical Victorian product. Combined with a large typeface, the small text area also helped to disguise the fact that the books comprised fewer than 40,000 words, although they still had to contain over 200 pages to accommodate the interleaving of the plates, often at intervals of only two pages.

*   *   *

The book that started the 20s series was published on May 23 1901 in an edition of 3,000 copies — a figure that was to become standard for most of A & C Black's colour books — plus a limited large paper edition of 350 copies signed by Mortimer Menpes. Size of the trade edition was quoted as 8¼″ × 6″ (210 × 153mm) and of the limited edition 11″ × 8¼″ (280 × 210mm).*

The trade edition was about 1¾″ thick and contained 99 full page illustrations printed on coated art paper with captions on the protecting tissues. Most of the illustrations were three colour but a number were in black and one colour only. The 63,650 words of text — Menpes' reminiscences as 'transcribed' by his seventeen year old daughter Dorothy — occupied 254 pages and also included was a folding chart of a Boer plan of the battle of Magersfontein.

The cover was in mid-green cloth with a design by Turbayne in white, with titling in gilt, while the design for the white vellum cloth of the limited edition was a variant of that for the trade edition.

At the back of the book Menpes printed a number of letters written to him by the war leaders. One, from Brigadier General Pole-Carew was withdrawn before publication, but a few copies were printed at Menpes'

---

* Book size rather than paper size is quoted throughout this book.

request for his own twelve copies of the book. One of these can be found in the large paper copy in A & C Black's Historic Library. It reads:

'Dear Mr Mempes [sic]

I do not hold with the present mode of conducting affairs in this country — the Boer is now nothing but a brigand, and should be treated as such.

I should put a price on the heads of the leaders — sell their farms and do a little hanging — every life we lose now is wasted and it seems to me that to permit any unnecessary prolongation of the struggle is unkind to the country and unwise.

I hope to be on my way home before you get this.'

Pole-Carew's letter requesting the removal of the above is one of those included in the book, and must have baffled readers who were not given the opportunity to see the original.

Copies including the first letter, which are likely to number no more than twelve, may therefore be regarded as having originated from the Menpes family. The publisher's records do not indicate whether Menpes' twelve copies were of the large paper or trade edition; however, since the copy of the letter inserted in the Historic Library's copy is printed on the hand-made paper used for the limited editions, it is likely that these twelve copies would likewise have been the large paper version. It is hard to imagine Menpes being satisfied with anything less.

Menpes provided three watercolours too many for the first twenty five copies of the limited edition (Lord Roberts, Cecil Rhodes and General Macdonald). One of these was placed in the copy for Edward Clark of the Edinburgh printer R & R Clark, whose financial guarantee had helped the series to get off the ground. Copy No. 1, the frontispiece of which portrayed Sir Hector Macdonald, went to Mr Broadley of The Knapp, Bradpole, Bridport, who was also offered copy No. 1 of *Japan*. The publisher's letters do not record why this gentleman was so favoured.

One of the editors at A & C Black in 1901 was Miss G. E. Mitton, a faithful employee of the firm for many years, who assisted Sir Walter Besant with the *Survey of London*, edited *The Englishwomen's Year Book* and worked on *Who's Who* as well as writing a number of the colour books. In 1920 she married Sir George Scott, who had just retired as political officer of the Shan States of Burma. Her own large paper copy of *War Impressions*, unnumbered and marked Editor's Copy, was presented by Lady Scott to the London Library in 1943, where it is available for members to borrow to this day.

* * *

The first reviews of *War Impressions* were fairly enthusiastic. *The Studio* had reservations about the reproduction of some of the illustrations, but on the text it said: 'Mr. Menpes' experiences are detailed with much graphic power, his reflections display no little acumen, while his anecdotes are given with all the art and telling force which his reputation as a raconteur would lead us to anticipate. The book is eminently readable from cover to cover.' Today's reader would hardly be so generous: the Menpes' text is a series of fairly sycophantic portraits of the British leaders, with occasional outbursts against the Boers. But Menpes' original dispatches from South Africa, used as the basis for the book, were inspected by the army censors.

Reviews of Menpes' books also drew attention to the curiosity whereby his thoughts were 'transcribed' by his daughter. The result is that although the text is said to be 'by' Dorothy, the 'I' is Menpes himself. *The Studio* wrote of *Venice:* 'It is Mr Menpes' whim to attribute the text to his daughter, but he often forgets he has done so, as in the chapters in the present volume, called "A Glimpse into Bohemia" and "Gondolas and Gondoliers", neither of which could possibly have been penned by a young girl ... The personal pronoun also changes constantly from I to you, one to they, in a confusing manner ...'

Born 'inartistically' in Australia, probably in 1856, Mortimer Menpes moved to England in the 1880s. His biography in *Who's Who* — written by himself — says that he was 'nominally educated at a grammar school in Port Adelaide, but really on a life scheme of his own. His career as a painter began when he was one year old'. He neglects to make any mention of his marriage at the age of nineteen to Rose Grosse or of his six children, and describes himself as 'painter, etcher, raconteur and rifle-shot.'

For a time he was studio assistant to James McNeill Whistler, his experiences during this time being entertainingly described in *Whistler as I Knew Him,* and he also fell under the influence of Japan, which he visited more than once. The artistic results of his first visit were shown at the Dowdeswell Galleries in Bond Street in 1888: '... paintings and etchings, hung in a room with walls draped in pale heliotrope satin, the frames of these small fan-suggestive offerings in varied shades of gold. Everything intended to reproduce the true atmosphere of Japan. Even a girl in full Japanese dress ...' Among the guests — all wearing sprays of orange

'*Stand still. I am making a little sketch of you on copper.*'

'*Some results of that kind of work are shown in my latest book,* The World's Children.'

'*But enough of shop, let me show you some of my Japanese treasures.*'

'*What a wonderful nation! I am passionately fond of their work.*'

Mortimer Menpes: four photographs (from a page of nine) showing Menpes at home and in his studio; they accompanied an article in The Sketch, *February 21 1906.*

blossom — were Forbes Robertson, Miss Du Maurier, Oscar Wilde and his wife and Robert Browning as well as Whistler. The Prince of Wales attended later. The pictures sold quickly, for a total of over £2,000.

Soon afterwards Menpes and Whistler fell out, it is said over a remark about the latter's treasured lock of white hair, but Menpes' career continued to prosper. Some of Whistler's eccentricity seems to have rubbed off, however: C. R. W. Nevinson records in *Paint and Prejudice* that Cezanne, Gauguin and Van Gogh had presented canvases to Menpes, who, considering them the work of 'ardent bunglers' had put them aside and lost them!

Menpes' association with A & C Black, which started in 1900, lasted only a few years; his last book for the firm appeared in 1915, though his involvement with the Menpes Series of Great Masters — colour reproductions of well known paintings intended for framing — continued for longer. During this ten year period Menpes produced well over 900 watercolours for A & C Black publications, plus a large number of simpler drawings to be inserted as frontispiece in (usually) the first 50 copies of the limited editions. In addition, together with his daughter Maud, who had studied colour printing in Germany, he set up and ran his own process engraving firm, The Menpes Press, which carried out much of the process work for his own and other books.

The effect of this workload often shows in the rather skimpy pictures he produced: there is frequently little variation between subjects in many of Menpes' drawings, especially in the landscape views. Some of his portraits, however, were excellent, and well regarded at the time.

Among his other accomplishments Menpes claimed to have had more one-man exhibitions in London than any other living artist. He lived for some years in a remarkable house in Cadogan Gardens, just off Sloane Square, which was decorated in the Japanese style. A detailed description of this house, which was designed by A. H. Mackmurdo, appeared in Vol 17 of *The Studio* in 1899 under the title *An Experiment in the Application of Japanese Ornament to the Decoration of an English House*. Among its features a small mirror was angled above one of the upper windows so that Menpes could scrutinise would-be visitors before deciding whether to be 'at home' to them.

Today only the facade of the house remains as it was, and it is neatly incorporated into the north west corner of the Peter Jones department store at Sloane Square.

In his later years Menpes founded and ran the Menpes Fruit Farm at

Pangbourne, Berkshire, which also included the Carnation Nurseries at Purley near Reading. He died on April 1 1938 and was buried at Pangbourne, where a memorial can be found in the churchyard. His death certificate gives his age as 83, which means that he was born in 1855 or 1856, at least four years before the date given in most reference books.

The Times obituary of Menpes of April 5 1938 summed him up well: 'Menpes', it said 'made a much greater impression as a personality than as an artist, being alert, resourceful and opportunist — never at a loss for a retort in argument.'

However, it is likely that without Mortimer Menpes' energy and enthusiasm, A & C Black's colour books would never have enjoyed such resounding success.

2

From Japan to Oxford

A & C Black were quick to capitalise on the success of *War Impressions:* Menpes and his daughter were immediately despatched to Japan, returning, as Newth wrote, 'in an incredibly short time with seventy-five paintings'. *Japan* was published on December 7 1901, and adopted the 9″ × 6¼″ format (228 × 159mm) that was to be used for the bulk of the books in this series and for many others.

With the single exception of *Belgium, Japan* is the easiest title in the 20s series to find today. A note in the Historic Library copy shows that 3,210 copies were printed in 1901, 2,080 in 1902, 2,100 in 1903, 2,080 in 1904, 3,120 in 1905, 3,420 in 1911 and 3,120 in 1914; a total of 19,130.

As first issued *Japan* contained 100 illustrations, not the 75 referred to by Newth; the 1902 reprint also has 100, as have those of 1903 and 1904, while copies dated 1905 can be found with 100, 75 and 50 illustrations.

The illustrations for *Japan* were engraved by the Hentschel process and printed at the Menpes Press, although Georg Buxenstein of Berlin was also asked to quote, being found to be far too expensive. The letterpress remained in the hands of R & R Clark, and the cover design — blue cloth with decoration in pink and gilt — was again by Turbayne.

At this time A & C Black considered abandoning the tissues protecting the plates, at least in the trade editions of the books. The 1902 reprint of *Japan* has no tissues and the captions are printed on the back of the plates, but this omission was not repeated, except in *World Pictures* and one or two later books, and a letter to Menpes of May 17 1902 confirms the publisher's decision: 'We have come to the same conclusion as you about the tissue papers but unfortunately too late for the *Japan* reprint.'

A limited large-paper edition of 600 copies of *Japan* was produced, priced now at £2-2s, the first 100 of which carried an original watercolour as frontispiece and were sold at £10-10s, a price that proved to be more than the market would bear; subsequent volumes were sold for £5-5s.

Several attempts were made to publish the book in other languages.

The 20 shilling series, arranged in approximate order of scarcity

A selection of 20 shilling books in dust wrappers: books were published with wrappers from 1905, and wrappers may have been produced retrospectively for books published earlier

Brockhaus of Leipzig considered a German translation, as did a Stuttgart publisher, and Hachette and Octave Uzanne both wanted to produce the book in French: all, however, were frustrated by Menpes' adamant refusal to allow any other text than his own to accompany his pictures. Macmillan of New York, who were closely associated with A & C Black at this time, were offered sets of illustrations at £190 for 1,500 or £240 for 2,000 plus a 10% royalty to Menpes. Menpes' own royalty was 4s per copy on the first edition, 6s on the second, and the publisher estimated the net profit per copy on the first edition to be 6d, prompting the comment to Menpes that 'your books have been sold at far too low a price'.

Japan was generally well received, although *The Studio* still suggested that the publisher should 'reproduce fewer illustrations by a process that would do fuller justice to them . . . But as the general public prefer quantity to quality, it might not pay so well'.

Three more books came from the pen and brush of the Menpes family in 1902 and 1903: *World Pictures, World's Children* and *The Durbar*. The first, *World Pictures*, published in September 1902, contained fifty colour and fifty wash illustrations plus 400 line drawings in the text, and was produced in large quantity. The text recounts some of the Menpes' experiences in nineteen countries and has its entertaining passages, as in the description of Dorothy falling down a well. It is most commonly found in a version bearing no date at all; the 1902 and 1903 impressions are dated on the title page.

The book was produced in an edition of 8,200 copies, 5,000 of which were the US edition, which was published jointly with Collier. The text — using English spelling — was set and printed in the US, flat sheets being sent to England. Similarly, the colour blocks were made and printed in the UK, sheets being sent to the US, and the wash blocks and line drawings were both printed in the US. UK copies, however, are described only as being printed by Ballantyne & Company.

Again the decision was taken to leave out the tissues and place the captions on the back of the plates. Later issues, however, have the captions below the illustrations or on tissue guards. The 1915 reprint was produced to sell at 7s 6d, as were many other reprints at that time.

520 large paper copies were printed, the first 50 with an original watercolour. The British Museum demanded one of these, causing Adam Black to write to Menpes: 'Many thanks for the charming sketch. It is far too good for the BM & will be given to a favoured customer.'

The originals of the illustrations were exhibited and put on sale for £10-

£50 each, though later some were offered to the trade for £7-7s each, to be sold for not less than £10-10s, Menpes to get £6-6s. Unusually the limited edition was issued in the same red cloth as the trade edition, rather than the white vellum cloth normally used.

In this instance *The Studio* preferred the line illustrations, regretting that the three colour process was 'ill-adapted for reproduction of serious work', and The Times Book Club pointed out that the American continent was represented in the book only by Mexico.

World's Children similarly described the children of roughly the same list of countries, and is interesting for containing a picture of Dorothy, looking winsome. (According to her daughter-in-law — who as far as is known is the one surviving member of the Menpes family — this was not a trait that followed her into later life.) The book's elaborate cover — and that of *World Pictures* — bears two monograms showing MM and DM, probably the work of Menpes, but the cover design was carried out by Turbayne, although his own scarab monogram does not appear on any of Menpes' books.

The Durbar, published in September 1903, described the Menpes' visit to the Delhi Durbar of 1902, where they were the guests of Lord Curzon, the Viceroy. The pictures were exhibited at the Dowdeswell Galleries in June 1903 and highly praised in *The Studio,* which said they 'gave an excellent impression of his skill as an oil-painter and water-colourist ...'

A large limited edition of *The Durbar* was published, 1,000 copies, no fewer than 100 of which contained an original watercolour.

By this time A & C Black had realised that a successful series could not be built on the work of one man (and his daughter), and at the end of 1901 they approached the artist John Fulleylove to provide 100 drawings and Professor George Adam Smith to write the text of a book on the Holy Land.

The publisher's practice was always to approach the artist first, then to commission the letterpress. Most authors were paid a flat fee, ranging from £50 upwards for the letterpress, while the artists were paid a fee for the reproduction of each picture in colour, often £2 but sometimes as much as £6. No expenses were paid, although the publisher often went to great lengths to obtain free rail passes and sea passages from the railway and shipping companies, not always successfully. (The first few paragraphs of *Burma*, a paean of praise of Bibby Lines and their vessels, suggests that this sort of arrangement was made with the company for the book's artist/ author Talbot Kelly.)

After processing, the pictures were returned to the artist, who could then use publication of the book to help with their sale. Simultaneous exhibitions were often arranged, sometimes with A & C Black's help, usually at the Fine Art Society or Leicester galleries, occasionally the Dowdeswell.

Authors received fairly clear instructions, which were not always carried out: 'In this series of books the text is not closely associated with the illustrations, author and artist each give their impressions independently. It would not therefore be necessary for you to 'write up' to the illustrations but we send you proofs of these as they were engraved. The text we like is of a bright readable description not overloaded with statistics. There are so many illustrations that the reader would find it difficult to hold the thread of a serious argument.' This letter was written to Wilfred Campbell some years later (June 1906), by which time texts had varied between superficial and thoroughly serious. Sometimes author and artist seem to have worked closely together, usually to the book's advantage, but often they hardly seem to have contacted each other.

George Adam Smith declined the Holy Land offer because he was too busy, but recommended a friend and travelling-companion, John Kelman, the first of a number of travelling clerics to appear in the series.

Kelman's text was of the serious variety, as would be expected of a distinguished Presbyterian minister; he later became Pastor of the Fifth Avenue Presbyterian Church in New York. His balanced and well written book was favourably reviewed at the time and still reads well today. The publisher obviously thought highly of him since he was paid £100 for *The Holy Land* and £200 for *From Damascus to Palmyra*, which was written a few years later. John Fulleylove was not treated as generously, being offered only £100 for the right to reproduce the 100 (actually 92) illustrations. But Fulleylove went on — at higher fees — to illustrate *Greece* and *Oxford* in the 20s series and a number of other books before his early death in 1908 just before he started work on *Eton*. He is one of the few A & C Black artists to achieve the distinction of an entry in the *Dictionary of National Biography*.

The cover of *The Holy Land*, based on the Menorah, the seven branched candlestick, was the work of Miss E. E. Gillespy 'under the supervision of John Fulleylove.' It should be noted that the first issue contains 92 illustrations, while all reprints have 93, the drawing of 'Syrian Women at a Fountain', which was used in the prospectus for the book, having at first been omitted in error.

The limited edition of 500 was signed not by the author or artist but *A & C Black* in the forward-sloping handwriting of Adam Black, a practice which was used when artist or author were either unavailable or dead. Occasionally Callender's rounder hand can be detected.

Work on the books now began to be spread more widely, though Hentschel continued to be responsible for most of the engraving work. The printing of the illustrations for *The Holy Land*, for instance, was shared between Hentschel, R & R Clark, Stoddart & Malcolm, Geo Jones and The Menpes Press.

Egypt was painted and written by R. Talbot Kelly, who during his twenty years in Egypt had 'lived the life of the Arab in all its primitive surroundings ... so studying the subject from the inside.' The book was the first to bear Turbayne's monogram (bottom right on the front). It was much reprinted, on most occasions with corrections to the text, between 1903 and 1918, and appears in a number of different shades of blue cloth, none of which is crucial in identification since the publishing history is well charted on the title versos. An index and glossary were included from 1904 onwards. In many ways Talbot Kelly was the ideal author/artist: a readable text not too encumbered with facts accompanied by pleasant, airy watercolours which would not have been too difficult for the printer to reproduce and which did not call for the addition of a fourth colour.

As with many of the books in this series gilt titling was used only on the spine in later issues. It was the practice when a book had stopped selling at full price to sell off sets as quires — folded and collated sheets, unbound — usually to John Grant, the Edinburgh bookseller, or to H. B. Claflin of Manchester and New York. The books were then issued at remainder price, normally 7s 6d or 8s, but obviously the use of expensive gilt in these reissues had to be limited. A number of titles were reprinted as 'instant remainders', to sell at a comparable price, also without much gilt.

A serious disagreement broke out in 1907, when Talbot Kelly accused Clive Holland, author of A & C Black's *Warwickshire* and *Wessex*, of plagiarism in his book *Things seen in Egypt* published by Seeley Service. Holland denied having read Kelly's book but admitted that he might have looked at it in shops or seen it serialised in magazines. The row rumbled on and was undoubtedly responsible for the non-appearance of a projected volume by Holland on Stratford-upon-Avon.

Egypt contained 75 colour plates, a figure that was to become standard for most of the rest of the series. Kelly went on to write and illustrate *Burma*, which has a particularly fine and intricate cover design by

Turbayne and which is one of the more difficult books to find in good condition because of the cloth's proneness to fading.

Happy England, illustrated by Helen Allingham and written by Marcus B. Huish, director of the Fine Art Society, was the first of a few books on artists to be published in the series, an area which one might expect A & C Black to have exploited more extensively. Later volumes dealt with the work of Kate Greenaway, Birket Foster, George Morland and John Pettie, a somewhat arbitrary selection of subjects, while a further volume, *Cruikshank's Water-Colours*, published in December 1903, combined George Cruikshank's illustrations with extracts from books by Dickens, William Harrison Ainsworth and W.H. Maxwell.

Happy England was first published in dark blue cloth in 1903 in an edition of 5,000, and reprinted in 1904. Edition dates are clearly indicated on title page and its verso, but there are also differences in the text on pages 118-130 as the result of a complaint by Batsford that some of the material used in the first edition fell under their copyright. Some three pages of new text were provided. Arthur Chamberlain's name replaced that of Sir J. Kitson as owner of The Donkey Ride in copies from late 1906 onwards.

The book was reissued in larger format ($9\frac{1}{2}$" × 7"; 241 × 178mm) in 1909 bound in red cloth, omitting the frontispiece photograph of Mrs Allingham. The reason for the reprint was explained in a letter from Adam Black to Huish: 'This is merely a reissue rushed out to compete with a new book illustrated by Mrs Allingham. This new book [*The Cottage Homes of England*, Edward Arnold, 1909] is larger than the current edition of *Happy England* & as the booksellers say they prefer the larger size we were compelled to follow suit.' However, copies bound in red cloth in the usual 9" × $6\frac{1}{4}$" format can also be found dated 1909; these are the 1913 reprint.

A limited edition of 750 copies, signed by Mrs Allingham, was produced, one of which was accepted by the Queen in December 1903.

Helen Allingham's affectionate depiction of the sunnier aspects of rural England — no winter scenes cast a chill over the pages of this book — is highly regarded and *Happy England* is rarely to be found cheaply.

The reissue in 1903 of *War Impressions* — now made uniform in format with the rest of the series — prompted Adam Black to comment to Menpes: 'I hope that purchasers of the 1st edition will not discover the superiority of the 2nd or they will want to exchange.' Examination shows him to be right: the three colour process showed steady improvement during the first decade of the century.

Another war book, *War Sketches in Colour* by Captain S. E. St Leger, was published at the end of 1903, in an edition of only 2,150, plus a limited edition of 250. It does not seem to have sold well, being remaindered at the end of 1906, and can be considered scarce today. St Leger served with the mounted infantry attached to General French's 1st Cavalry Brigade, and thus had better opportunities than Mortimer Menpes for depicting the heat of battle, but he had no outstanding ability as an artist.

Oxford was published at this time and introduces one of the few writers of real distinction to the series, Edward Thomas.

Henry W. Nevinson, literary editor of *The Daily Chronicle* and a champion of 'causes', had been approached for the text, but suggested the twenty five year old Thomas as a substitute. The fee paid for what was to prove an uncongenial task was £100, vital earnings for the perennially hard-up writer. But Thomas did not skimp the task, although he regarded it as hack work. There are passages of what his biographer R. George Thomas, calls his worst 'colour book' style but also much humorous and observant writing in *Oxford*, which includes affectionate composite portraits of dons and undergraduates, among them, Raymond Asquith, F.E. Smith and Hilaire Belloc, 'presented in thin disguises'. *The Studio*, however, accused Thomas of flippancy, suggesting that 'more dignified treatment should have been meted out to the Alma Mater'. But the magazine seems to have been accustomed to more solemn texts than this. In their way this book and Thomas's *Beautiful Wales* reach greater depths than any in the series and, indeed, than any of the fashionable 'colour books' of the time.

The first issue of *Oxford* and the large paper edition (300 copies, signed *A & C Black*), are captioned on the tissue rectos, except for the frontispiece which is printed on the tissue verso. In at least one later issue (advertisements at the back dated autumn 1904) this arrangement is reversed.

Robert P. Eckert in *Edward Thomas: A Biography and a Bibliography* (J. M. Dent, 1937) refers to the statement in the Popular series reprint of the book (1922) that *Oxford* was reprinted in 1911, but says that 'a continued search has revealed no copy of this edition'. The publisher's ledger shows that 3,200 copies were produced 'for America' — a reprint carried out specifically for Claflin — in 1911, though of the total 6,570 copies printed only 1,460 copies actually went to Claflin, while 2,419 were sold off to the trade at 4s 6d. Two pages of titles are recorded as having been newly set, which means that the correct 1911 date should be shown; but the continued absence of copies dated 1911 must arouse suspicion as to whether the date was altered.

Eckert also refers to the second issue of the trade edition as saying simply BLACK at the bottom of the spine rather than the A & C BLACK on the first issue. His authority for this is given as the publisher's statement; examination of a number of copies confirms this point.

Fulleylove's illustrations for *Oxford* included both oils and water-colours. While watercolours made up by far the majority of those used in the colour books, oils could be used, provided, as the publisher explained in a letter to Augustine FitzGerald in 1903, there were not too many ridges of paint present. Others to use oils, apart from FitzGerald, included Francis Walker in *Ireland*, T. Mower Martin in *Canada* and Nico Jungman in *Holland*. Warwick Goble also used some pastels in his drawings for *Constantinople*.

3

Venice to Tibet via London

Venice, the Menpes' next book, published in May 1904, follows the same pattern as previous volumes, with 100 illustrations in the first impression and the 1906 reprint, reducing to 75 by 1912. The blue cloth cover design, 'based on a well known Venetian ornament', is partly the work of Menpes, partly of Turbayne: 'Mortimer Menpes' front had more gold than we had bargained for', the publisher wrote.

The *Venice* watercolours were exhibited at the Leicester Galleries, causing Adam Black to write to Earl Hodgson: 'I had a view of the exhibition yesterday & it is first rate & I only wish the letterpress was one tenth as good!' But it was to be another two years before Adam could bring himself actually to reject one of Miss Dorothy's manuscripts. *The Studio* complained that 'the author or authoress has also an irritating habit of jumping abruptly from one subject to another, as when he or she says: "In San Giorgio there is a wonderful entombment by Tintoretto. This is the place for red mullet from the Adriatic," as if the painting — which, by the way has not even the dignity of a capital letter — and the fish were of quite equal importance.'

A new text for *Venice* was eventually provided by The Rev Canon and Mrs Lonsdale Ragg but not until 1916; their effort, however, was not much better than Dorothy's. For this reissue the Menpes' monograms had of course to be removed from the cover design of the book, leaving two unfilled spaces.

Other books dealing with foreign parts published during 1904 were *The Alps, Naples, Holland* and *Morocco*. The first of these was written by Sir Martin Conway, later Lord Conway of Allington, and illustrated by A.D. McCormick, though *The Studio* reviewed the book as if Conway had painted and McCormick written! It was, according to Conway in 1910, 'produced in a hurry as you will remember to provide a job for McCormick'. Conway was well known as art historian and mountaineer (what a splendid conjunction of interests!) and his early books such as

Woodcutters of the Netherlands in the Fifteenth Century (1884) are very
scarce. His book *Episodes in a Varied Life* (Country Life, 1932) can be
recommended to connoisseurs of unstructured autobiographies.

Two more husband-and-wife teams were employed for *Naples* and
Holland. Sybil FitzGerald raised the publisher's hackles during the production of the former. To Earl Hodgson he wrote: 'Mrs FitzGerald, who
I fancy is a foreigner, complains that her text is being tampered with!' To
Mrs FitzGerald: 'We cannot agree with your criticism of the work of our
reviser and in the case you quote prefer his version.' And to Hodgson
again: 'Mrs FitzGerald is a nuisance . . . I shall write to her husband to use
his influence.' And finally in two letters to Augustine FitzGerald: 'It is a
matter of indifference to our reader whether his corrections and suggestions are adopted or not but to the author it is of the utmost importance that
a first book should be as good as possible . . . we must leave it to your
goodsense to consider duly the corrections and suggestions made by a
brilliant literary man on the work of, we understand, a beginner.' This
acrimonious correspondence, coupled with the fact that the artist had
managed to negotiate himself a royalty rather than the usual flat fee, may
explain why the FitzGeralds were not approached for any more books.

No such troubles arose with the other couple Nico and Beatrix
Jungman, whose name was variously spelt Jungman (by Black's) and
Jungmann (in a number of other publications). Beatrix (Beatrice) was
English, Nico Dutch; their book adopts the Menpes convention of being
'by' Nico (in gilt), with text by Beatrix (no gilt, smaller type). Beatrix later
divorced Nico Jungman and married The Hon Richard Guinness; known
as Gloomy Guinness, she became a well-known society hostess.

Nico's illustrations, with their strongly drawn line, do not appeal to all
tastes and are perhaps more successful in the portraits than the landscapes.
Beatrix's texts, both for *Holland* and *Norway* (1905) are delightful. In the
words of *The Studio* review of *Norway* she 'jotted down with charming
naivete every incident, however trivial, which happened on the journey,
so that the reader gets from her a far more vivid idea of the country and its
people than from her husband's drawings.' Especially to be savoured are
the references in *Holland* to the Dutch habit of washing everything in sight
except themselves and the description of the St Nicholas treat for children
which resulted in everyone getting comprehensively soaked; also the
delicacy with which she refers to mixed saunas in *Norway*.

Beatrix seems to have been in charge of the family's finances. In January
1902 Adam Black wrote to her: 'We are going to have the *Holland* account

made up, and if we find the book has paid, would be inclined to fall in with your request to make pounds guineas but, if it has not, you will find us stony hearted. Will you kindly tell your husband that whatever your portrait in the "International" may be as a work of art in my humble opinion as a likeness it is a libel.'

The covers of both Jungman books were by Nico himself; that of *Norway*, with its blood-stained swords and axe, is especially fine.

Morocco, by Samuel Levy Bensusan, a journalist and prolific author, and illustrated by A.S. Forrest was another of the many books that described a journey through a country that was little known at the time.

It was followed in September 1904 by *British Water-Colour Art*, a joint publication with the Fine Art Society. This reproduced the 61 drawings presented to King Edward VII by the Royal Society of Painters in Water Colours on the occasion of his coronation. The book's publication was intended to mark the society's centenary. The blue cloth cover has an unusually large amount of gilt in its design (by Turbayne), and the book also includes a facsimile reproduction of the address presented to the King and Queen. It was first advertised as *English Water-Colour Art*, a title which was changed in deference to a number of Irish and Scottish artists whose work was included.

It is interesting to note that of the artists commissioned by A & C Black for their colour books, only Helen Allingham, Rose Barton and Herbert Marshall appear in the list of painters in this volume. The sum of 100 guineas (£105) was paid to the King's Hospital Fund for permission to reproduce the illustrations.

Three more books on British subjects concluded the proceedings for 1904: *The Channel Islands* by Edith F. Carey and painted by Henry B. Wimbush, who was best known as a postcard painter. *The Studio* complained that the artist had forgotten to temper the topography with a measure of atmospheric charm; and there is much inadequate colour reproduction in the illustrations as well as faulty register: this is strange because the illustrations were engraved by Hentschel and printed by Geo W. Jones, who between them carried out much of the process work on the various colour book series. An index and (folding) sketch map were provided for the first time in this book, and became standard for most of the series.

Bonnie Scotland introduced Harry Sutton Palmer to the colour books series; he was to go on to illustrate several more books for the publisher, and today his magnificently detailed romantic landscapes fetch high prices.

In 1905 an enquirer was offered originals by Sutton Palmer for £10-£25 each, but this was regarded as too expensive. Sutton Palmer produced over 300 illustrations for A & C Black during the next twenty years.

Bonnie Scotland was written by A. R. Hope Moncrieff, otherwise known as Ascott R. Hope, another immensely productive author, whose name crops up with regrettable frequency in the lists of A & C Black and other publishers. Hope Moncrieff has an extremely large amount of information to impart and a somewhat dull way of imparting it. But *Bonnie Scotland* is a fine book, easy to find in one of its many reprints.

Familiar London was the first of four books on London published during 1904 and 1905, none of which was reprinted. Rose Barton, an Irish watercolourist who lived and worked mostly in Dublin and London, was responsible for both text and illustrations, though there were some reservations about her ability as a writer, the publisher promising to put the book into the hands of an expert reviser. In spite of relying heavily on quotations, her text is valuable for giving her own views on art and on her own manner of working. The paintings were borrowed from their owners for reproduction: the publisher proposed sending an ordinary copy of the book to all who had lent pictures, though Miss Barton suggested that a prospectus might be sufficient! A large paper copy, however, was presented to the Princess of Wales.

The other three London books appeared in June and July 1905, *London to the Nore* by W. L. Wyllie and his wife and *London Vanished and Vanishing* by Philip Norman being published on the same day, while *The Scenery of London* by Herbert Marshall with text by Miss Mitton appeared a couple of weeks later.

The Wyllie's book is a delightful production as well as being a rare instance of a wife being admitted into full partnership: for while William painted and Amy wrote, the book is said to be 'Painted and described by W. L. Wyllie and Mrs Wyllie'. He deserves the admiration of posterity for this, when so many other painters were prepared to relegate their spouses' names to smaller type. The book's brown cloth bears a fine pictorial design by Turbayne, and its 60 illustrations faithfully depict the teeming life of the lower Thames, while Mrs Wyllie weaves into her narrative the daily experiences on the barge from which she and her husband worked as well as a vivid eye-witness account of the opening of Tower Bridge in 1894. A further merit of the book is that text and illustration complement each other, the illustrations being placed as close as possible to the text reference to their subjects. William Wyllie was an established painter in his fifties

William Wyllie and his wife, the artist and author of London to the
Nore, *with an unidentified friend on a sailing holiday.*
Photo: Courtesy Chris Beetles Ltd

when the book was produced and was paid the high fee of £300 for the 60 illustrations. So it is hard to understand why it did not sell well, fewer than 1,000 copies having been moved by January 1906. Over half of the edition was sold off to John Grant at remainder price, as were substantial numbers of the other three London books.

London Vanished and Vanishing is a workmanlike production by an artist/author who spent many years chronicling the disappearance of London buildings, and whose drawings were kept in the South Kensington Museum, now the Victoria and Albert. This is a valuable record of the disappearing buildings of the capital and a reminder of the depredations made by developers even in turn-of-the-century London. The book has the unusual distinction of being the only one in the series with an undecorated cover; perhaps someone was trying to make the point: vanished London, vanished decoration! The prospectus for *London Vanished and Vanishing* includes the splendid disclaimer: 'If it be objected that houses of entertainment have had too much attraction for him, he would point out that those which he knew best were of rare beauty and interest; besides it was their outward appearance, not the interiors, with which he was oftenest familiar.'

A French version of this book may exist: Octave Uzanne was offered 500 sets of illustrations for £50 in December 1905 and was told to contact the author regarding translation.

The Scenery of London was painted by a London devotee, Herbert Menzies Marshall, another artist to command a generous fee, £350 for 75 illustrations in this case. The commissioning letter to Marshall is worth quoting in full:

Dear Sir,

Mr Brown of the Leicester Galleries has kindly informed us that you intend to bring out a work on London, with coloured illustrations reproduced from your drawings, & that he suggested our name to you as publishers. May we say that we shall be very pleased to publish your book on the terms mentioned (£350) & propose to include it in our colour series. We trust you will pardon our saying that we believe the public prefers bright colours in these books & we hope, therefore, you will include a fair number of drawings with bright colouring. Among your exhibits in the R.W.S. Gallery we find only one (Chartres), which we should say had bright colouring, all the rest have, we think, a somewhat dark atmosphere. A number of dark drawings in a book

might prove monotonous & we therefore venture to make the above request.
Believe us, dear Sir,
Yours very truly (sgd) A & C Black

*Herbert Marshall (*left*), who illustrated* The Scenery of London *in the
20 shilling series, and George Flemwell, photographed while painting
an Alpine scene.*

Slavish adherence to such instructions was no doubt responsible for much 'chocolate box' art, and certainly Marshall seems to have taken the advice partly to heart since most of the illustrations are fairly bright. The publisher, however, may well have been remembering that dark drawings are more difficult and expensive to reproduce, usually requiring the addition of black to the three colours normally used!

This was the only book of the four not to be simultaneously issued in a large paper limited edition. Up to 1904 a limited edition accompanied each title; of the fifteen published in 1905, however, only seven were so favoured, and from then on they appeared only very occasionally. The publisher explained this in a letter to Alfred Austin, the Poet Laureate, in March 1905: '. . . the market has persistently refused for some time to take editions de luxe of our colour books. When we first issued colour books each one had an edition de luxe now — with one or two exceptions arranged some time ago — not one has such an edition.'

Large paper editions were published of thirty five of the 20s series, plus a further nine from other series.

Yet another husband and wife team was introduced in *Florence and Some Tuscan Cities* by Colonel R. Goff (who painted) and his wife Clarissa (who wrote), while Forrest and Henderson followed up their *Morocco* with *The West Indies*. Henderson's text, which deals largely with people rather than places, is in parts as relevant today as it was then, while Forrest's limpid watercolours suit the subjects well.

The first edition of *The West Indies* was of only 2,000 copies; 600 of these were specially bound for the Elder Dempster shipping line and carry a dedication to Sir Alfred Jones, the company's owner. Elder Dempster bought a total of 1,300 copies of the edition.

Rome, published in April 1905, was written by two ladies, M. A. R. Tuker and Hope Malleson, and illustrated by Alberto Pisa, an Italian artist who lived in London. *Rome* was reprinted in 1911, 1913 and 1915, but all copies are dated 1905. The advertisements at the back and the presence or absence of gilt on the front must therefore be used as a guide to date of issue. Of the first impression of 3,000 the very earliest copies have the interleaves to pages 154 and 224 (very similar captions) interchanged. This was put right soon after publication.

Of *Rome* Adam Black wrote to Miss Tuker: 'Messrs Dent have to some extent 'scored' by appearing first but if their Rome is like their recently published Paris, we shall eventually win easily.'

Edward Thomas's *Wales* also appeared in 1905, painted by Robert Fowler. *The Studio* again preferred artist to author, accusing Thomas of 'meandering on from topic to topic, indulging in all manner of irrelevant dissertations.'

The Menpes' next book was *Brittany*, whose mauve cloth is particularly prone to fading, with the result that although the book is not especially scarce, copies in very good condition are hard to find. Menpes' illustrations for this book are among his best: his many years' residence in Brittany aroused in him a respect and liking for the Breton which is reflected in his work and the book benefits from portraying people, Menpes' forte, rather than landscapes, although the publisher had indicated that there were too many character studies at the expense of landscape views. Many of the drawings display a stronger line than Menpes usually employed.

Dust wrappers began to appear at about this time. Writing to an enquirer in 1905 the firm said: '. . . we shall be glad to supply new wrappers, as far as possible, for your stock of Colour Books . . . some of the earlier volumes in the series were without wrappers, but all those published during the current year had them specially printed on stout paper. It is our intention to print wrappers for certain of the earlier volumes of the Colour Series and in future to have a stout wrapper on all cloth-bound volumes published by us.'

Books carrying dust-wrappers can still be found occasionally, but they are fairly drab affairs intended only to protect the book until it arrived on the purchaser's shelf. Few purchasers will have wished to hide Turbayne's colourful designs behind the sober dust wrappers, though in terms of preventing fading it is a pity they did not.

A typical example of a wrapper is that of Brittany: light mauve paper, lettering in black with a similar design to that on the cover of the book in dark red and maroon.

Fortunately the market does not demand the presence of a wrapper on these books in the same way that it does on modern first editions. Pray that it never does!

With the publication of *The English Lakes* one of A & C Black's most faithful artists, Alfred Heaton Cooper, was introduced to the series. From 1905 to the late 1920s he painted several hundred watercolours for the firm, which appeared in some thirty different books, many of which recycled the same pictures again and again.

Heaton Cooper was struggling to make a living when the publisher approached him and his career was transformed by the commission for the book. His family, led by his son William, have continued to paint in the Lake District to this day. William Heaton Cooper does not regard the work for A & C Black as the best of his father's painting, many being more an attempt to reproduce what the publisher wanted, 'a visual description of a particular place.' But this is a purist point of view and Heaton Cooper is hardly to be blamed if many of his landscapes are no more than workman-like. 'Careful' was how one review described them. They were particularly well suited to reproduction by the three-colour process.

The text by W. T. Palmer, editor and writer of several popular guides and books about the Lake District, is notable for the number of little known onomatopoeic words it contains: sloom, glish, siss, benks, cluthering, dowly, etc.

Richard Bagot, better known as a novelist, wrote the text for *The Italian Lakes*, which was painted by Ella Du Cane, who was later to illustrate several more books in this and other series. Her brightly coloured illustrations catch the warmth and charm of the scenery, without perhaps

*Alfred Heaton Cooper, a regular A & C Black artist, at
work on a Lake District scene.*

capturing its grandeur. Bagot's text is notable for a number of attacks on Germans and German-Swiss: 'To those fresh from a journey from Basle through the St. Gothard Pass, the change from a stuffy railway carriage, very likely shared in the company of a German couple on their voyages de noces, embarrassing enough to any but Teutonic spectators — triflings of which the sucking of the same orange is not an uncommon, and a comparatively delicate example — to the little steamer which conveys travellers from Lugano to Porlezza and Italy, is grateful enough.' The German-Swiss, he writes, are 'probably the most disagreeable race in Europe.' However, the book's prejudices do not seem to have deterred purchasers and it was much reprinted.

Kate Greenaway, published at the end of October, was a genuine attempt at a serious biography, written by Marion Harry Spielmann and George Somes Layard. Spielmann was editor of the *Magazine of Art* and a disciple of John Ruskin, with whom Miss Greenaway had a relationship whose precise nature is still the subject of debate. Spielmann published a number of articles in his magazine about the work of Kate Greenaway, and after her death at the age of 55 in 1901, he was approached by her brother John to write her biography. According to Rodney Engen in his book about the artist (*Kate Greenaway: A Biography* Macdonald, 1981) Spielmann requested access to all Kate Greenaway's correspondence, placing particular importance on that with Ruskin. Her cousin Joan Severn, however, protective of the artist's reputation, insisted on censoring the letters by indicating sections that he might not quote. The result was to make it 'almost impossible for Spielmann to piece together Ruskin's role in his subject's life.' The book that emerged, while commendably detailed, was disjointed and confusing and was, according to Engen, deeply disappointing to the family.

Faults or not, however, it has remained in demand by both collectors and researchers to the present day, and even copies in truly dreadful condition still manage to command a substantial price. Fading of the spine is particularly common.

Production of the book's 51 colour illustrations was supervised, shortly before his death, by Edmund Evans, the famous colour printer and engraver, who had published much of Kate Greenaway's work. The engraving was carried out by Mortimer Menpes, while the decorative endpapers were printed from a wallpaper design produced by Mr Walker of Manchester. The 1913 reprint is dated 1905 but has plain endpapers. The limited edition of Kate Greenaway consisted of 500 copies numbered and signed by John Greenaway, but a further 100 (unnumbered) were printed as presentation copies and 'over' copies. Nos 16-500, priced at £2-2s, each contain an original pencil sketch, selected from the large amount of unfinished work left at Miss Greenaway's death. Copies 1-15, however, were priced at £10-10s each; Nos 5-15 each contain a small original watercolour as frontispiece; No. 4 is thought to contain two such watercolours and No. 3 three, while No. 2 has four, one of a young lady, two of young girls and one of a boy in a red hat. Copy No. 1 contains five small circular watercolours of girls' heads, one of 3" diameter surrounded by four of $1\frac{1}{4}$" diameter. The front is blocked in gilt whereas the covers of the bulk of the limited edition are blind stamped, and a fawn dust wrapper with green and brown decoration and brown titling is present. A book-plate bears the name Charles Hesketh Fleetwood-Hesketh.

Copies of the limited edition are usually highly priced, though whether the sums asked can be justified must depend on an individual collector's regard for Miss Greenaway's work and valuation of the often rather skimpy pencil sketches included in each volume. But A & C Black collectors will here find themselves in competition with the army of Kate Greenaway collectors, and prices are bound to be high.

Two books on Asian countries followed, *India* and *Tibet and Nepal*. For the text of the former the publisher decided to approach Flora Annie Steel, who was already well known as a novelist and writer about India. Thus Adam Black wrote to Menpes on May 24 1905: 'On thinking over the best author for India Flora Annie Steel naturally took first place. We wrote to her on the off-chance enclosing a few proofs and rather to our surprise she replies as follows: 'I should like to do the book much; but it is a question of pay. What do you propose as I have a lot of work on hand and should have to set some aside to get this done. The drawings are quite charming.' Now we do not think it is worth offering less than £250, which is a good deal more than we can give. If, however, you will contribute £100 we shall rise to the remaining £150. We do not mean that you should hand over money but that we should deduct the amount from the "India" royalties. After reading this you will think all the world is "getting at" you but, what you have to decide is, if text by such an authority will raise the sale to an extent to recoup the £100. Personally I think it will, & in any case the literary will approach the artistic level & form an irresistible combination.'

This unusual proposal seems to have been accepted, though the publisher had to resist an attempt by Miss Steel to push the fee even higher.

Anyone who wishes to find out more about this admirable and endearing lady may be recommended to read *Flora Annie Steel: Novelist of India* by Violet Powell (Heinemann, 1981), in which, however, Menpes is spelt Mempes and Dorothy is referred to as Menpes' wife.

India was published without a large paper limited edition, partly because of the failure of that of *Brittany* to sell well.

Tibet and Nepal, which was published in January 1905, is possibly the most unusual and entertaining book in the whole of the A & C Black oeuvre. The *Who's Who* biography of its author and artist A. Henry Savage Landor, grandson of the author Walter Savage Landor, is a catalogue of exploits around the world, many of which were subsequently recounted in books whose contents would have been described as too fantastic if presented as fiction.

Savage Landor despised the Alpine Club traditions of mountaineering, and preferred to wear city clothes and ordinary shoes or light boots, even in the Himalayas. The adventures described in *Tibet and Nepal* met with some scepticism when the book was published, especially as regards the greatest height reached by the author, and it would be a very naive reader who would take at face value the illustration of 'An awkward Moment' facing page 22: not so much awkward as fatal! 'A Moment of Suspense' facing page 34 presents an equally improbable scene, while 'A perilous Crossing' facing page 86 and 'A balancing Feat' opposite page 100 depict ridges of impossible sharpness above nearly vertical slopes! The illustration facing page 92 shows the boater-wearing Savage Landor dangling his feet over a 6,500 foot drop; that opposite page 98 shows him — boater still in place — being suspended one-handed by one of his men after the cornice on which he had been sitting fell away. This incident is described on pages 94-96; both text and illustrations stretch the reader's credulity beyond its limits. There may be collectors who do not bother to read the A & C Black volumes parked on their shelves: an exception should be made in this instance.

One more amazing fact about *Tibet and Nepal* is the speed with which it was printed and published. On December 14 1904 the publisher wrote to R & R Clark: 'We are to receive the manuscript of this book next Tuesday & are anxious to publish early in January as several books on the subject are announced. Could you arrange to set it up & print 3,000 copies before you shut for the New Year?' This was duly carried out.

However, the book did not sell well, and in September 1907 it was decided to remainder it. In October 1905 A & C Black turned down

Savage Landor's offer of a book on Soudan and Abyssinia.

No record exists of who designed the unusual cover, which has titling in black on a background gilt design of the ancient symbol of prosperity and creativity revered by Buddhists, Hindus and others, a symbol which was later transmuted into the swastika. The sketch map at the back of the book is, unusually, protected by a flimsy tissue guard.

4

The County Books

The books in the 20s series that deal with the English counties would make up a worthy collection on their own; and they can be supplemented by a number of titles from other series.

There are nine county books in this series (including the old county of Wessex), to which could be added from the 20s series *The English Lakes*, which deals with parts of Cumberland and Westmorland. In addition the collection could include *Cornwall*, *Worcestershire* and *Middlesex* and *Isle of Man* and *Isle of Wight* from the 7s 6d series; *North Devon*, *South Devon* and *The Peak Country* from the 6s series; and *Derbyshire*, *Devon*, *Dorset*, *Durham*, *Gloucestershire*, *Northumberland*, *Somerset* and *Wild Lakeland* from the Popular series published during the 1920s.

A similar if smaller collection could comprise the colour plate books on the various parts of Scotland; assembling either as a complete set would be an enjoyable and rewarding pursuit — and not an excessively expensive one.

First to be published in the 20s series was *Wessex*, the text of which, by Clive Holland, deals in conventional manner with the history and topography of the parts of Devon, Somerset, Wiltshire, Dorset and Hampshire that made up the Saxon kingdom of Wessex. The illustrations, however, mostly depict the places and scenes referred to in Thomas Hardy's Wessex Novels. To the Hardy lover the book therefore forms a fascinating adjunct to the novels.

A first impression of only 2,000 copies of *Wessex* was produced, though it is fairly easily found, especially in the 1912 reprint; it is a rare instance of a book where the cloth hardly ever fades.

The publisher sent a copy of the book to Hardy, who replied on 24 March 1906: 'I owe you many thanks for the copy of your handsome volume Wessex today received. It is the sort of book that will serve admirably for a present, either on birthdays, at weddings or any other occasion by people concerned with this part of England to those who live elsewhere.' To those, he was probably thinking, who were unfortunate enough to live elsewhere.

Warwickshire followed in July 1906, painted by Fred Whitehead, who was himself best known as a painter of Hardy's Wessex. A fulsome description of Whitehead's work appeared in *The Studio* in 1904, which told how the artist and his wife were accustomed to spend the summer months travelling through Wessex, living out of doors in caravan and tent so that he could make the best use of the daylight hours.

Warwickshire was also produced in an edition of 2,000, as if A & C Black were not yet quite convinced of the likely demand for books on English counties; even Turbayne seems to have passed on some of the cover designs to his colleagues, since both *Warwickshire* and *Surrey* bear the symbol of the Carlton Studio, while *Hampshire* and *Yorkshire* share the same design. *Warwickshire* is probably the most difficult of these books to find in good condition; it too was reprinted in 1912, and the advertisements at the rear may have to be used to confirm the date of a particular copy since all bear the 1906 date. Text was again by Holland, prolific and reliable, but who was soon to fall out of favour as a result of the plagiarism row over *Egypt* referred to above.

The appearance of *Sussex* in July 1906, with the words 'Painted by Wilfrid Ball' on the cover but with no mention of any author, must have puzzled its buyers — not least because it would have been obvious to readers that the author was Hilaire Belloc. The liberal sprinkling of typical Belloc enthusiasms — the quality of the port at the George Inn, Robertsbridge, for instance — and prejudices — his dislike of rich 'incomers' and artists' colonies such as that at Rottingdean — would have been enough to give the game away.

The facts of the matter, as far as they can be ascertained, are these: early in 1904 Wilfrid Ball was asked to provide the illustrations for a book on Sussex. In April the publisher approached E. V. Lucas for the text, offering £100 for 40,000 words, with no restriction on the use of the material serially before publication. A later letter confirmed that there was no objection to a first person narrative but Lucas' request for a royalty rather than a flat fee was refused.

Lucas eventually declined the offer and matters seem to have rested there until July 1905 when W. H. Hudson was asked for a text. He too refused and on 28 July A & C Black wrote to Belloc, offering either £100 on publication or a royalty of 5% on the first 1,000 copies sold and 15% on the second 1,000, 'the copyright then to become our property'.

Belloc accepted but stipulated in a letter of September 1 1905 that his name should not be used on the book, to which the publisher replied: 'An unsigned text presents a difficulty but not we hope an insuperable one ... Does it alter the case that our book would not be published until the spring of 1906 — say seven or eight months hence, and that the price will be 20/- net.' The letter goes on to suggest the use of a pseudonym, to which Belloc initially agreed before later changing his mind. He accepted the flat fee offer — not surprisingly since he was perennially short of money — and he promised to deliver the text by the end of January 1906.

On February 1 1906 A & C Black asked him whether his election to Parliament 'does not affect your decision not to place your name on the title page'. No reply is recorded. In April Belloc delivered the manuscript — which was short by 7,000 words — and telephoned to suggest that the fee should be paid there and then. The publisher agreed to pay half at the time and the other half when the final proof was passed for publication, provided that Belloc allowed his name to be used on any subsequent editions. Belloc returned the cheque and restated even more firmly his wish to stick to the original arrangement; later the same month he complained that A & C Black had acted in bad faith by putting the words 'By an anonymous writer' in the prospectus for the book — though readers can hardly have been expected to think that the book wrote itself!

More words had to be squeezed out of Belloc, until on 6 June he was asked to 'round off what you are engaged on at present ... We should like to publish this month if possible'.

Even in 1911 Belloc was still annoyed that his name appeared as author of *Sussex* in the British Museum catalogue, and the publisher was unable to explain why this was so since their receipt bore only Ball's name: today's British Library catalogue makes no mention of Belloc. And the matter obviously still rankled in 1924 when the book was being prepared for reissue in the Popular Series and Belloc wrote: 'By all means make any changes you like in the book. I have no say in the matter. I do not acknowledge it. (You know the circumstances under which you got the manuscript at half price), nor have I any property or interest in it.'

The whole affair is curious because Belloc was one of the least anony-mous people of his age — his booming voice and strident opinions were familiar at social and political gatherings throughout the country; and he must have realised that his style of writing would be recognised. Nor was he under contract to any one publisher at the time.

It is of course possible that he was annoyed at being third choice as author; or that he wished to avoid making too much of a reputation as an author of topographical pot-boilers; or that writing this sort of book was not a suitable activity for a newly elected MP — he was elected as the Liberal member for Salford in January 1906.

But the most probable explanation — and this is the view of Belloc's most recent biographer A. N. Wilson — is simply that he wished to recycle the material elsewhere. Belloc had been brought up in the expectation that he would always be well off; this turned out not to be the case and he was constantly beset by financial problems. Many of his papers, like those of so many other British authors, reside with an American university; the crucial letter of September 1 1905, which might finally settle this matter, is not among them.

Sussex was a success, being reprinted in 1907 and 1913 (while Belloc himself eventually reworked the text for reissue by Cassell in 1936). Belloc's text is admirably set off by Wilfrid Ball's splendid (small) watercolours, which capably depict the charm of the English village. An affectionate memoir of Ball by C. Lewis Hind appeared in *The Studio* in May 1917 after the artist's death from heat stroke while serving as an army accountant in Khartoum.

Ball also painted *Hampshire* (1909), a task to which he was less suited because of the necessity for a number of illustrations of Winchester, which was to be published as a separate volume in the 7s 6d series. Ball obviously had an aversion to painting interiors: neither *Sussex* nor *Hampshire* contain any at all, even of Chichester or Winchester cathedrals, and the effect is to make *Winchester* a somewhat unbalanced production, since the text refers in detail to the splendour of the interior of the cathedral, which is nowhere depicted.

Text of *Hampshire* was by Rev Telford Varley, a teacher at Peter Symonds School, Winchester, who also wrote a book called *Progressive Chemistry* for A & C Black. He starts from the premise that Hampshire is heaven on earth — a fair supposition according to those who live there — and proceeds in a very readable and informative manner. *Winchester* was written first, and its text cut down for inclusion in the county volume. *Hampshire* was reprinted in 1915 (to sell at 7s 6d), though all copies are dated 1909.

Surrey, published in September 1906, benefits from better reproduction of the illustrations than in either *Sussex* or *Hampshire*; but this is at least partly because Sutton Palmer produced much larger pictures — many of them were painted before the book was commissioned — and was thus able to include more detail. The artist was paid the remarkably high sum of £500 for the illustrations, the publisher to keep ten. The reproductions in this book show both artist and the three colour process at the peak of their achievement, and there is a welcome absence of the excess of orange and pink that disfigures some of the illustrations in *Sussex*, *Hampshire* and *Kent*. (A good example of this is 'The Close of a Stormy Day, Deal Castle', facing page 140 of *Kent*; no sky in Britain, except perhaps during the war, can have looked like this.)

Kent (1907) is notable for one of Turbayne's finest cover designs, a pattern of interwoven hops. Its author, the journalist and novelist W. Teignmouth Shore, and artist, W. Biscombe Gardner, do not appear to have colluded much: on page 126 Fort House is stated not to be the original of Dickens's Bleak House; the caption opposite page 124 says that it is. Also the publisher seems to have got into a collation problem, since eighteen plates are grouped together in twos towards the end of the book; there is no apparent reason for this since the plates were tipped in individually rather than being wrapped round the sections of text as occurred later.

Biscombe Gardner submitted too many illustrations (sixteen) of Maidstone, while omitting Greenwich, Tunbridge Wells, Ashford, Chatham, Rochester, Deal, Herne Bay, Westerham, Ramsgate, etc. He was asked to remedy this. The large number of Canterbury drawings was acceptable because of the intention to publish a book on the city separately in the 7s 6d series. This appeared first, *Kent* six months later.

Yorkshire, which appeared in August 1908, comprised both text and illustrations of three books in the 7s 6d series — *Coast and Moorland Scenes* (1904), *Dales and Fells* (1906) and *Vales and Wolds* (1908), though with the curious omission of the illustration of the Typical Yorkshire farmer that faces page 120 of *Coast and Moorland*. Gordon Home, as both author and artist, was offered a royalty of 10% on 3,000 copies, 15% thereafter. He went on to write and illustrate a number of other colour books and for a time was employed by A & C Black as an editor.

Yorkshire was produced in an impression of only 1,500, but was reprinted in 1913 and 1918.

Essex (May 1909) has acquired the reputation of being among the scarcer of the county books, though it was published in the usual edition of 3,000; no reprint was called for, however.

Essex was, surprisingly, the only book illustrated by L. Burleigh Bruhl, who later became president of the British Watercolour Society, since his work seems ideally suited to the three-colour process. He also offered to write the text, but after inspecting a sample chapter the publisher declined his offer. Instead it was left to Hope Moncrieff, who at least made up in reliability what he lacked in excitement.

Finally, *Buckinghamshire and Berkshire*, published in 1920 and priced at 25 shillings (£1-25): a purist might wish to exclude this as not belonging to a 20 shilling series, but in every other respect it does. Giltless on its front, a sign of more difficult times economically, this is nonetheless a fine book, Sutton Palmer's illustrations admirably complemented by Miss Mitton's text, which was written just before she married Sir George Scott and left the firm.

To many collectors the 20s series books have become known as the 'county' books of A & C Black. It therefore comes as a surprise to find that only nine are so titled, though there are many others that deal with areas and cities of the British Isles. But a very fine nine they are.

5
Ireland to Insect Life

The 20 shilling series reached a peak in 1905, when fifteen books were published; eleven appeared in 1906, ten in 1907, nine in 1908 and eight in 1909, after which there was a swift decline.

Of the non-county books of 1906 the first was *Ireland*, from the pen of Frank Mathew, a writer of historical novels and a barrister, and painted by Francis S. Walker, who, unusually for this series, used oil paints (some of the illustrations were taken from small paintings on wood). This may well be the reason for the decision to commission Alfred Heaton Cooper to provide new illustrations for the 1916 reprint. The cover of *Ireland* is in green cloth with shamrock decorations in lighter green, harp and titling in gilt; the 1912 reprint is in olive green cloth, shamrocks in mid-green. The illustration Emigrants facing page 154 was specially requested by the publisher as representing 'a phase of Irish life only too common during the last generation'.

Walker also illustrated *Poet's Country*, published by the curiously similarly named T.C. & E.C. Jack; this has a fine decorated cover designed by Turbayne and bearing his monogram, and can easily be mistaken for an A & C Black book. But it is a measure of Black's success in developing its own style of colour plate book that only rarely are they likely to be confused with those from other publishers.

Another artist to use another medium than watercolour was Warwick Goble, who included a number of pastels in his illustrations for *Constantinople*, published in May 1906. Goble had travelled widely in Europe and Asia in the years before he received the commission for this book, but Constantinople was still sufficiently unknown for him to ask the Foreign Office whether he would need protection while working in the open, 'for he fears he will be interfered with'.

In December 1904 the publisher wrote '... there can be no doubt about the excellence of Mr Goble's work but how the public will like it when reproduced is unfortunately uncertain ... we should like to wait before giving Mr Goble a further commission'. In the event the public did not like the book well enough to warrant another commission, although it was reprinted in 1915 to sell at 7s 6d.

More surprising is the absence of any reprint of *Greece*, painted by John Fulleylove and written by Rev J. A. McClymont, which received excellent reviews on its publication in the same month. *Greece* is one of the more elusive volumes in the series; records show that over 1,700 copies were sold off at remainder price, all of which may not have been bound up for sale. However, *Greece* is easier to find than *Algeria and Tunis*, written and painted by Frances E. Nesbitt, which appeared in the same year. This — for the benefit of collectors who have never seen a copy — is in blue cloth with decoration in orange and yellow.

If any pattern at all can be detected in the relative scarcity of certain volumes in the 20s series, it is that the books dealing with the more exotic locations — less likely to be visited except by the more intrepid traveller — sold in smaller numbers than those describing places nearer to home or more accessible. The quality of the book itself seems to be a secondary consideration: for who could say, for instance, that *Southern Spain* or *Algeria and Tunis* are finer books than several others more easily found?

Northern Spain, published in October 1906, provokes admiration for the stamina of its author and illustrator Edgar (later Sir Edgar) Wigram, who covered the country on a bicycle. How, one wonders, did he and his unnamed companion carry the painting materials? No mention is made of any servants. The book's publication was intended to coincide with the marriage in Spain of King Alfonso XIII to Princess Ena of Battenberg, a niece of King Edward VII, in May 1906.

A further addition to the select group of books on artists was made with the publication of *Birket Foster*. The text was written by H. M. Cundall, at the time senior keeper at the Victoria and Albert Museum, although Marcus B. Huish of the Fine Art Society had been approached first, in September 1904. Several reminders to Huish produced no result and the publisher therefore withdrew the offer at the start of 1906 and commissioned Cundall. Huish meanwhile had arranged for a biography with Foster's family and accused A & C Black of offering the book elsewhere while he was still involved. The letters show that this was not the case, but the affair still led to ill-feeling between A & C Black and one of their regular authors. Huish's projected book did not appear.

Birket Foster was reprinted in 1930 — the plates unguarded by tissues and with gilt titling on the spine only and still dated 1906; copies can be easily identified by the presence of advertisements for the New Series of colour books, which were first published in 1927.

Birket Foster was the only book published in 1906 to be accompanied by a large paper limited edition, of 500 copies.

Adam Black came to grips with one more difficulty in 1906: the inadequate quality of Dorothy Menpes' texts. Writing to Earl Hodgson, he said:

> I enclose Miss Dorothy Menpes's M.S. of 'The Thames' & should be obliged if you would answer the following queries quite frankly:
>
> 1. If printed as it is would it in your opinion damage the series.
> 2. Would your usual editing suffice to turn out a text that in your opinion would not damage the series.
> 3. Could you by rewriting or treating the M.S. as you please turn out a text that in your opinion would be up to the average of the other books in the series — (Miss D. Menpes's excluded) & if so, what honorarium would you suggest.
>
> This is between ourselves so we need not hesitate to discard the ancient fiction that Miss Dorothy is a talented authoress. What in the world do the critics mean by saying she is — it is disgusting! We tackled friend Hind on the point, who had buttered her up in the 'Chronicle' & he blushed!

No more texts from that quarter.

To Dorothy he wrote later in 1906:

> Dear Miss Dorothy,
> I should have written to you about this matter before. As I think you know we did not like your text for this book nearly so well as the work you had done for other volumes. As we have to face a considerable competition we decided to get another text written. It seems hard however that you should have laboured for nothing and I suggest we pay you £25 and resign all rights in the text. We return the manuscript herewith and you will see the editor has only worked over the first chapter. It might be worth your while treating the whole manuscript in the same way and publishing it in the form of magazine articles.

The new text was provided, predictably, by the faithful Miss Mitton.

The Thames is unusual in that in addition to the 55 full-page colour illustrations, it also contains twenty chapter headings in colour, the first time that such illustrations had appeared on the same page as text matter.

To accomplish this one side of the relevant sheets had to be coated since the three colour process was only successful on art paper. The result may be a small landmark in publishing history but is an uneasy compromise and the experiment was not repeated.

Topographical books published in 1907 included *Kent*, mentioned above, *Cambridge* and *The Clyde*. Of these *Cambridge* is notable for a splendid Carlton Studio cover design and excellent illustrations by William Matthison. The text by Miss Tuker is turgid, though she herself regarded it so highly that she tried to have the illustrations grouped at the back of the book, a request that was tersely refused. Miss Tuker can hardly have been A & C Black's most popular author, since the correction costs for the book amounted to 60% of the total setting costs; authors were usually charged for any amount above 25%.

The Clyde on the other hand was written by an author of genuine distinction, Neil Munro, the Scottish novelist and poet, who was paid the high fee of £250. Finding a suitable illustrator for the book proved a problem. William Wyllie was approached first but no agreement with him was reached; George Houston was then asked for some specimen illustrations but, in the publisher's words, 'the longer we kept Mr Houston's drawings the less we liked them'. Sutton Palmer was also considered, but eventually J. Young Hunter and his wife Mary, who had recently held an exhibition at the Leicester Galleries, were commissioned. The Young Hunters' painting style was very similar.

Foreign books in 1907 numbered only three: *The Riviera*, written and painted by William Scott, who was told that his text 'should be of a light and readable character, with nothing guidebooky about it and not too descriptive of the pictures'; *The Savage South Seas* — those of them, at any rate, that the author and artist managed to visit; and *Canada*, for which Canadians were commissioned as author and artist.

E. Way Elkington, author of *The Savage South Seas*, was a journalist whose early career had included the study of medicine, working on the stock exchange, gold digging and cattle driving. He had, according to the book's prospectus 'made a particular study of savage races'; this did not prevent the publisher from asking him to strengthen his material, which was regarded as somewhat thin. A & C Black's Historic Library copy of this book is in blue cloth; most others seen are in mid-green. In this case 2,289 copies were sold off as sheets to John Grant, and it is probably these that were published with a green cloth binding. The book made a loss of £381 for the publisher.

In the case of *Canada*, George Brett of Macmillan in New York was asked to find an author. Approaches were made to a Mr Fraser, Mr Bradley and Mr Willison before Brett lit upon the poet Wilfred Campbell, who used the opportunity to quote widely from his own work. On the evidence presented he would have made a good Poet Laureate!

Lord Strathcona, then Canadian high commissioner in Britain, was asked for a Preface, but objected to aspects of the text, including the first two paragraphs of the book, so the idea was abandoned; but his comments resulted in the rewriting of some paragraphs about Canada's adverse climate.

Arrangements were made with Macmillan of Toronto for a number of presentation copies of *Canada* to be produced containing thirty two illustrations only. These were to have gilt on the spine only and eight pages of prelims: title page and verso, two page preface, two pages of contents, two pages listing illustrations. No copy has been seen. Arrangements were also made for translation into French and Spanish.

George Morland was added to the list of books on artists, and was one of only two books published in 1907 (the other was *The Clyde*) to be accorded a large paper limited edition, of 250 copies, which were signed by Walter Gilbey, its joint author. *George Morland* is an excellent biography for its time but perhaps fails to do full justice to the rakishness of its subject's character.

The remaining three books of 1907 — *Birds of Britain, English Costume* and *The Royal Navy* — suggest that the publisher might have been looking to widen the scope of the series.

The first of these was written by J. Lewis Bonhote and included 100 illusrations by H. E. Dresser from his nine-volume *A History of the Birds of Europe*, which was published during 1871-96.

Complaints on publication suggested that the colours in some of the illustrations were inaccurate — a charge refuted by Dresser — and that the text plagiarised Saunders' *Manual of British Birds*. A comparison of texts by the publisher led them to the conclusion that there were more similarities between Newton's *Dictionary of British Birds* and the Saunders book than between Saunders and Bonhote.

Birds of Britain was much reprinted and was reissued as *Birds of Britain and Their Eggs* in 1923 with thirty three illustrations, including some of eggs; reissued again in 1927 with 82 illustrations in an edition of 1,000 copies; and reprinted in 1930 (3,000 copies). The two books bear similar covers, and care should be taken not to confuse the later title with the 1907 book, which contains 100 plates.

Dorothy Menpes as portrayed by her father in the pages of
World's Children

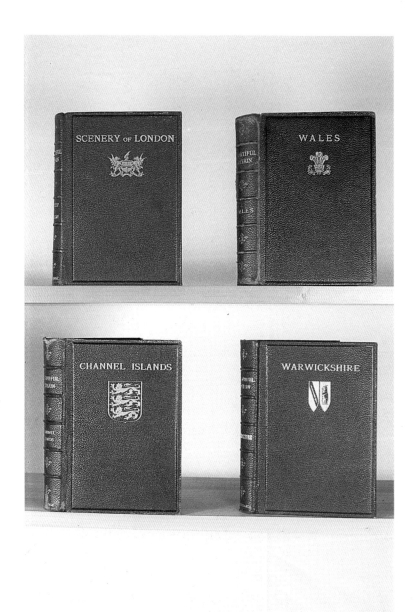

20 shilling books rebound in leather for the Royal Canadian Edition under the series title Beautiful Britain; at least 12 titles were published.

Only one other bird book appeared in the 20s series: *Egyptian Birds*, published in 1909, which was written and painted by Charles Whymper, the son of J. W. Whymper, the landscape artist, and brother of the alpinist Edward Whymper. Whymper illustrated many books on travel, sport and natural history during his long life; *Egyptian Birds* is a particularly fine example of them. As in other cases where the artist also provided the text, Whymper was offered a royalty of 15% on the first 2,000 copies, 20% thereafter, '13 as 12'.

(It was fairly common practice at the time for publishers to supply booksellers with thirteen copies of a book for every twelve that they paid for; booksellers therefore received one free copy in every thirteen, in addition to the usual trade discounts. In assessing the author's royalties, however, sales of a book were calculated only on the twelve copies paid for not on the total number supplied for sale.)

A large paper edition of only 100 copies of *Egyptian Birds* was published, signed by the artist.

English Costume was another venture into new fields in 1907, although in this case the four individual sections had been published as separate books in the 7s 6d series during 1906, and had sold well enough to justify production of the larger volume. The book was written and painted by Dion Clayton Calthrop, playwright, actor and artist, a member of a well known theatrical family: his father was the actor John Clayton, his mother Eve Boucicault.

His book received only lukewarm reviews, *The Studio* regarding his 'sartorial lore being far superior to his technical skill and knowledge of the anatomy of the human form'. But *English Costume* remained in print in one version or another until well into the 1950s, so must have served a useful purpose as a source of reference. The poor condition in which it is often found bears testimony to this. Calthrop's autobiography, *My Own Trumpet* (Hutchinson, 1935) is a record of a life packed with incident but in some curious way unfulfilled.

The Royal Navy also broke new ground. It was illustrated by Norman Wilkinson, who was only twenty six when he received the commission, receiving the high fee of £300 for 50-60 illustrations. Wilkinson became well known as a painter of naval scenes during a long and distinguished career and invented the concept of dazzle painting of ships during the first world war. His autobiography *A Brush with Life*, written in his late eighties, fails to mention the A & C Black commission; he died at the age of 92 in 1971. The book, which was written by H. Lawrence Swinburne, also contained notes on the costume of sailors of the past by Cdr. N. Robinson; these were illustrated by J. Jellicoe. A desirable volume, not easily found, almost two thirds of the 3,000 edition being sold off at remainder price.

A & C Black were not keen to produce too many books on military subjects, their attitude being outlined to William Wyllie in 1905 in reply to his proposal for a book on the Japanese war: the public, the publisher suggested, would 'prefer quiet & cheerful subjects to those depicting the reek of battle'. It may be, however, that this was a polite way of saying to Wyllie that they were not prepared to risk another book by him until they knew how well *London to the Nore* would sell.

Armies of India (1911) was the only other book of a military nature to appear in the series. Written by Major G. F. MacMunn (later Lt. Gen. Sir George Fletcher MacMunn) and beautifully illustrated by Col. A. C. Lovett, it depicts and records the history of the various regiments serving in India. A limited edition of 500 large paper copies was published, with the plates tipped on grey mounts. *Armies of India* is not especially difficult to find, but is usually highly priced, not least, one hopes, because it is a very fine book.

The nine books of 1908, apart from *Yorkshire*, referred to above, include some of the rarest in the series as well as the most commonly found — at least in terms of reprints.

It will come as no surprise to most collectors to learn that the scarcest title in the series as measured by the number of copies printed is *The Lake of Geneva* — at the most 1,000 copies and almost certainly a much smaller number. But what is surprising is that it is joined in this position by the first issue of *Belgium*.

Many collectors will have visited book fairs where almost every stall seems to have a copy of *Belgium* on its shelves. Almost all carry a shield printed in red on the title page; in the first issue, however, this shield is printed in black only.

Both *The Lake of Geneva* and *Belgium* comprise the text and illustrations of three books previously published in the 7s 6d and 10s series; these were published in an edition of 2,000 copies, though 3,000 sets of text and illustrations were printed. The remaining 1,000 sets were combined and issued in the 20s series. In the case of *The Lake of Geneva* 1,000 copies sufficed and the books remains scarce: indeed the infrequency with which copies appear on the market suggests that only a proportion of the 1,000 sets were bound and put on sale. Unfortunately no binders' records remain for the precise figure to be determined.

The illustrations for *The Lake of Geneva* were provided by J. Hardwicke Lewis and his daughter May: the list of illustrations in the 7/6 series *Geneva* and *Montreux* indicate who painted what: that in *Lausanne* does not, the inconsistency being carried over in the 20s volume which thus shows who painted two thirds of the illustrations but not the other third. In fact the Lewises' signatures can generally be discerned on the illustrations themselves. Gribble's text for the book is strictly historical and in no way relates to the subject matter of the illustrations.

The 1,000 copies of the 20s *Belgium*, however, proved insufficient and the book was soon and regularly reprinted, no doubt largely as a result of the upsurge of feeling towards the Belgians during the First World War. All copies of *Belgium* are dated 1908 so the bound in advertisements may have to be used as a guide to the date of a particular volume. Gilt should not be used as a guide since, although copies with gilt titling blocked on the front and with the top edge gilt have been seen, they are in a small minority and do not form part of the first issue.

A further caution should be issued here: many copies of *Belgium* and of other 20s series books include tipped in pages of advertisements listing books published up to and including 1912; but these lists refer to no books published after 1912 even when they are included in books published during 1913-1918. A copy of *Belgium* containing advertisements listing books published up to 1912 should thus be regarded as being issued in 1912 *or any later year up to 1918*.

The relative scarcity of two other 1908 books can be accounted for only by their failure to sell well on publication since each was published in an edition of 3,000. There is some evidence of this in the case of *Ancient Tales and Folklore of Japan*. The text of this book was selected by W. Earl Hodgson from the manuscript volumes of Richard Gordon Smith, who had been to Japan to collect items of interest for the British Museum. (Smith's name is correctly spelt without a hyphen but in later life he did not seem to mind whether one was used or not, with the result that his work is indexed under G in the British Library and elsewhere.) The illustrations were provided by Mr Mo-No-Yuki, a Japanese artist, based on Smith's ideas. The book was not well reviewed and by January 1909, two and a half months after publication, of the 3,120 copies printed 504 had been sold outside America, 250 sent to America and 86 had been given away. Smith protested that A & C Black were not doing enough to sell his book, which provoked the testy reply that 'You can have little idea of the stress of modern European competition if you think we can continue to exist without applying intelligence & attention to orders and advertisements'. Smith was being paid a royalty of 10% on 2,000 copies, 15% on the third and fourth thousand, 20% thereafter and therefore had a greater than usual interest in the matter.

Smith also complained that the publisher had failed to stick to the original binding because 'the squares ought by rights to be this

———————————
———————————
———————————
———————————

instead of

———————

———————

———————

———————

'This does not matter much as no Europeans probably notice it, but it has been noticed here just as much as if we were to reverse our doors & windows to lengthways instead of up & down.' It seems to have been one of Turbayne's rare lapses that he failed to reproduce correctly the shape of the Japanese Shoji blind, which is what Smith had intended to depict.

Three presentation copies bound in white vellum were produced for the author; other presentation copies were produced with the book in a box bearing one of the illustrations on the outside. However, no large paper edition was published of any of the 1908 books.

Southern Spain, another scarce volume, has a particularly fine cover design by Turbayne. The publisher had earlier turned down a cover design suggested by the author Frederick Calvert because in Callender's words: '... as we say in Edinburgh, it had the look of having been designed in Kirkcaldy'. Menpes had intended to produce a book on Southern Spain, but failed to do so in time.

An account of the work of Frank Wright in *The Studio* in 1905 led A & C Black to approach the artist for a book on New Zealand, which he illustrated jointly with his brother Walter; text was by William Pember Reeves, a distinguished New Zealand politician who from 1908 to 1917 was director of the London School of Economics. Reeves is best known for *The Long White Cloud*, a history of New Zealand.

Another book by Rev John Kelman, *From Damascus to Palmyra*, was illustrated by Margaret Thomas, a widely travelled artist and author. The book's textured white cloth means that copies are most often found in grubby condition or with a darkened spine. Like others at this time it failed to sell and recorded a loss to the publisher.

A further addition (the last) to the select list of books on artists was *John Pettie*, written by his nephew Martin Hardie, who persuaded the publisher to produce the book in spite of the latter's reservations: 'In London we find Pettie unknown or forgotten.'

The book is perhaps most frequently seen in grained mid-brown cloth, which is prone to come disbound; but the olive green smooth cloth version is the one that resides in A & C Black's Historic Library, and therefore the one that may be considered the true first; both are dated 1908. Evidence gleaned from individual copies suggests that the olive green version came first. Advertisements for other books in this case provide little help.

The final book of 1908 also suffers from colour confusion. Ella Du Cane favoured a white cover for her book *The Flowers and Gardens of Japan*, but was told that this was not popular with booksellers as it soiled so easily. Green, with darker green decoration, was chosen instead; but the book can be found in white cloth and in blue-grey cloth, all dated 1908. The artist was not keen on the cover and was told that although the design could not be changed, the colours could. Of the three versions that in white cloth seems to appear most frequently, closely followed by the green version.

Miss Du Cane was also told that the book would be sent out to shops in a 'handsome box with one of the illustrations on the outside'. No such copy has been seen.

Text was by Miss Du Cane's sister Florence, who according to *The Studio* 'made liberal use of Mr Conder's great work on Landscape Gardening in Japan'.

Kashmir and *Hungary*, published in September and November 1909, are further examples of the series at its finest. The former, written by the explorer and mystic Sir Francis Younghusband, proved popular and was reprinted in 1911 and 1917. In the words of his biographer, George Seaver: 'Two years later he poured forth all the stores of his knowledge and love of natural lore and of native history in his book *Kashmir*, which is still the classic on the subject. It was written with all his accustomed thoroughness, poetic sensibility combined with scientific accuracy to form a perfect guide book, at the request of his friend Major Edward Molyneaux, DSO, who illustrated it with no less than seventy exquisite watercolour sketches, the beauty of which sacrifices nothing to the truth. Of these it must be said, as Younghusband gratefully acknowledged, that their artistry excels his own word painting.'

Another husband and wife team, Marianne and Adrian Stokes (both painted, he wrote) were responsible for *Hungary*, then a very 'foreign' country to British readers. A lovely book, whose white cloth again puts fine copies at a premium. Some of Mrs Stokes's portraits are particularly successful.

Another fine production is *The Rivers and Streams of England*, painted by Sutton Palmer and written by A. G. Bradley, a text that is well worth reading today. Bradley was a prolific and competent author, who was also responsible for a number of volumes in the Highways and Byways of England series. Sutton Palmer's splendidly detailed landscapes are beautifully reproduced. The publisher, however, found it impossible to sell the originals for £15 each!

Finally in 1909, the long-delayed appearance of the Menpes' 20s *Paris*. This was first advertised in autumn 1904, the prospectus indicating that as usual the first fifty copies of the large-paper edition would include an original watercolour; the book is also listed in the Times Book Club catalogue of 1905. No book appeared at this time, however, and by 1906 arrangements had been made to cancel Dorothy Menpes' text for the book. But in the event it was her text that was used in 1907 when the book appeared as part of the 6s series, with twenty four illustrations (of the 75 that Menpes had painted). It may be that the publication by Dent of *Paris and its Story* by Thomas Okey in 1904 led the publisher to stay his hand, and there is a note of urgency in a letter of December 1903 which indicates that 'a rival has been announced and we must put our book in hand at once and publish as soon as possible'. On September 22 1904 Adam Black wrote to Menpes: 'Miss Dorothy promised the complete M.S. last Saturday, you promised it yesterday, but it has not yet come to hand. This means the book cannot be published at soonest before November & Dent announces his book as almost ready. One can only hope that Dent is not so far advanced as he makes out & that by making a big effort he can yet be forestalled.' But this sort of thing had not bothered A & C Black in the case of books such as *Venice*, and it would probably not have been a great concern in this case had the text been better.

In the end Adam Black was almost certainly unwilling to pitch Dorothy's text against Okey's. But Menpes himself may also have brought pressure to bear by being unwilling to accept a new text to accompany his paintings. The only reference in the publisher's correspondence is to 'retrieving an unfortunate situation' in a letter to Menpes in which Adam Black suggests setting up the Menpes Crown Series.

It is in situations like this that the researcher comes to regret deeply the invention of the telephone, which meant that much correspondence is one-sided or otherwise incomplete.

In March 1909 A & C Black wrote to John Grant of Edinburgh: 'In reply to your letter of today we have 3,000 each and over copies of 51 illustrations [those not used in the 6s *Paris*], which we are prepared to let you have for £100. This would include the right to print an impression of 3,000 copies of the letterpress but, if you wished to print up the 24 illustrations already published, we feel sure Mr Menpes would insist on printing them himself.' A letter of two days later shows that one copy of each of the 51 had been sent to Grant, and that the cost of printing 3,000 of the twenty four would be £62. 5s. Two days later again the publisher writes that Menpes has refused to allow his blocks to be printed elsewhere: 'In any case we can assure you they cannot be printed in Edinburgh sufficiently well for a book with our imprint.' A somewhat sweeping statement from a publishing house which had only recently vacated its Scottish base.

A further letter of September 23 says that A & C Black 'are not prepared to accept your offer & we would remind you that the offer to sell the plates did not emanate from us. What we offered you for £100 cost us almost three times as much'. Finally in this correspondence a letter of April 28: 'In reply to your letter of yesterday if you will pay the £162-5s on Nov 1st we will put your order in hand at once and deliver by the end of May.'

In the event *Paris* was eventually published by Grant but under the A & C Black imprint; it was printed by Oliver & Boyd in February-June 1909 in an edition of 3,050 copies, with a limited large paper edition of 500 copies (numbered but unsigned and without the original watercolour in copies nos 1-50). At no point was the book advertised by A & C Black, nor does it appear in any of the publisher's catalogues; there was no copy in the Historic Library until 1987. The American edition was published by Charles L. Bowman and Company of New York and is in white cloth decorated in red and gilt; the British edition in red cloth decorated in black and gilt and with titling in gilt. The standard of reproduction of both text and illustrations is much higher in the limited edition than in the trade edition.

By now the poor sales of some of the volumes had led the publisher to stop commissioning many further books for this series. Only one was published in 1910, *Australia*, by the Australian painter Percy F. S. Spence and Frank (later Sir Frank) Fox, an Australian journalist, and just two in 1911: *Armies of India*, mentioned earlier, and *Sicily*, where Alberto Pisa was approached only after Ella Du Cane had turned down the commission in spite of being offered the high fee of £4 a picture. Adam Black had obviously changed his mind since 1904 when he wrote to Marion Spielmann: 'I find we are debarred from bringing out a book on Sicily & have written to tell Mrs Waterfield so. I am sorry that she & you have been led to take so much trouble in vain but, in any case, I am afraid the lady exaggerates the importance of Sicily as a tourist resort. There is never likely to be a boom in Sicily (such accomplished 'boomers' as Mrs Tweedie & Mr Sladen have attempted it without success), as the journey is too tedious & expensive.'

Germany and *South America* were published in 1912, the former illustrated by the father and son team of E. T. Compton and E. Harrison Compton, both of whose work has a lovely airy quality which sometimes steps over into the 'chocolate box' school of art. The text, by the Reverend Dickie, another travelling cleric, is pallid; Turbayne's cover design, on the other hand, is magnificent.

South America was painted by A. S. Forrest, who had earlier proposed a book on Mexico with John Henderson, his collaborator on *The West Indies*.

Two books were added to the list in 1913: *The Banks of the Nile* by Ella Du Cane with text by Professor John Aiton Todd, a lawyer and academic who worked for a time in Cairo; and *Russia*, which once again combined the text and illustrations of three books from the 7s 6d series: *St Petersburg* (1910), *Moscow* (1912) and *Provincial Russia* (1913). Half of the illustrations were reproduced in colour, half in black and white. The publisher, writing in 1905, was cautious about making a firm commitment to all three books. To de Haenen, the artist, he wrote: '... we should of course like to complete the book but it would be foolish were we to undertake to do so, as the taste of the public may entirely change. We will meet you so far that we undertake to pay for the Moscow drawings (£100) though not to publish them. If the St. Petersburg portion recoups expenses we shall publish Moscow & if the Moscow part recoups expenses, we shall publish The Russian Provinces & the complete Russia.'

In his choice of subjects and the variety of their treatment de Haenen comes closer than most of the A & C Black artists to capturing the character of the country he is painting and the life of its people. It is regrettable that he was not afforded the opportunity for all his illustrations to be reproduced in colour. A fine artist about whom little is known.

Texts were by H. M. Grove, then British Consul in Moscow, H. Stewart and George Dobson, the latter a journalist whose entry in *Who's Who* and *Who Was Who* records almost every detail of a life crowded with incident.

The only other book to deal with South America appeared in 1914: *Argentina Past and Present*, with 96 illustrations, only thirty two of them in colour, painted by E. W. Christmas, and the remainder from photographs. The author in both cases was W. H. Koebel. *Argentina* is oversize at $10 \times 6\frac{1}{2}$ inches and only just creeps into the series. The text is a reprint of the book of the same title published in 1910 by Kegan Paul.

Southern India is a lovely book, written by F. E. Penny, otherwise Mrs Fanny Emily Penny, a novelist who lived in India for many years, and beautifully illustrated by Lady Lawley, whose privileged position as the wife of Sir Arthur Lawley, Governor of Madras during 1906-11, allowed her to persuade all manner of unwilling Indians to sit for her. The resultant illustrations of Indian people of all ranks and castes are charmingly painted and well printed.

The year 1915 brought only one book, *Plant Life*, another curious departure from the usual coverage of the series, while 1916 saw the reappearance of *Venice* with its new text by the Raggs, and another oversize book ($9\frac{1}{2}'' \times 7''$), *Royal Palaces and Gardens*, painted by Mima Nixon. The introduction was written by Dion Clayton Calthrop, the remainder of the text by a variety of authors who receive mention only at the end of their contributions. The illustrations are tipped in on the same paper as used for the text of the book, and there are no tissue guards. The standard of reproduction is not high. A limited edition of 200 copies was published.

Ireland, too, reappeared in 1916, its illustrations newly painted by Alfred Heaton Cooper (blue cloth, shamrocks green, harp yellow).

London was the first of five books published during and just after the First World War containing illustrations recycled from others in the series.

London was first issued in the 7s 6d series, while the rest were published at 10s with thirty two illustrations under the title The Fascination of Europe, and swiftly reduced to 7s 6d. Their reissues, with 60-64 illustrations, were made uniform with the 20s series. The purist might wish to omit these from the series on the grounds that all the material except for the covers had been published before, but there is a strong case to be made for their inclusion. The other titles are *Switzerland, Italy, France* and *England.* Somewhat ungraciously on the part of the publisher, the artists' names are given scant mention. Tissues are present in these books but they have gilt on the spines only, and the top edges were no longer gilt.

Two further books published in The Fascination of Europe series, *Bulgaria* and *Austria/Hungary*, were not reissued uniform with the 20s series.

After the war the economic situation obviously made it impossible to publish this sort of book for 20s, and the final two volumes, honorary members of the series at the very least, were published at 25s (*Buckingham-shire and Berkshire*) and 30s (*Insect Life*) in 1920 and 1921. Sutton Palmer was still painting, Turbayne was still designing (*Buckinghamshire and Berkshire*), while *Insect Life* makes a fair ending for a fine series.

Collectors can make up their own minds about which books comprise the 20s series. My own list would include one version of *War Impressions*, two of *Ireland*, two of *Venice*, one of *Happy England* (1903); it would omit *Stained Glass* (oversize and published at 25s) and a number of books such as *The Basque Country, Lancashire* and *Belgium Past and Present / The Cockpit of Europe* which were issued at 20s but are not uniform with the remainder and which are listed under the Miscellaneous section.

*   *   *

The size of the 20s books meant that they always presented a problem to the binder; shaken and loose bindings and cracked hinges are commonly found, as are loose plates, though this problem was overcome once plates were folded in pairs round sheets of eight pages, which occurred from about 1909. Many of the colours used for the covers had proved prone to fading when exposed to sunlight: some (*Kate Greenaway, Burma, Brittany*) have suffered more than others in this respect, and the blues used are particularly fugitive. Heads of spines are liable to split, corners to fray and the cloth to bubble and lift. The difficulty of finding the books in very good condition becomes ever harder, but this makes it all the more rewarding to the collector who finds an immaculate copy.

Copies that have been broken so that the prints can be framed further increase the rarity of some titles. Breaking of the books occurred as early as 1909, though the dealer in this case was only interested in illustrations by Helen Allingham and Sutton Palmer. Most modern collectors will take the view that the breaking of books in extremely poor condition is just about acceptable but that applying the same process to volumes in good or better condition is akin to a criminal act. And they will, of course, treat dealers who do this with contempt.

*   *   *

A Royal Canadian Edition of a number of titles was published, bound in leather. The publisher's records show that 300 such copies were shipped of the following titles: *Happy England, Oxford, The Channel Islands, Familiar London, Bonnie Scotland, Ireland, London to the Nore, London Vanished and Vanishing, Beautiful Wales, The Scenery of London, Warwickshire* and *Wessex*. This is not a comprehensive list, but certain of A & C Black's ledgers are missing. Curiously the only copies so far seen state that they were limited to 1,000 sets.

*   *   *

A final word on scarcity: the lists in this book show the number of copies printed of each title, including reprints (all of which were produced from moulds of the pages taken on publication; no book was reset for a reprint). The number of copies printed of any title therefore ranges from 1,000 copies (*Lake of Geneva*) to around 20,000.

One of A & C Black's ledgers gives sales and destination figures for some of the books. Thus of the 3,150 copies of *Greece*, 512 were sent to Macmillan in New York, 17 to Macmillan in Toronto, 13 to Macmillan in India, 46 to Australia, 864 were sold to the trade, while 1,692 were sold at remainder price (2s 7d) to Claflin & Co. Similarly 1,051 copies of *The Channel Islands* were sold off to John Grant as quires (folded sheets, unbound), as were 1,653 of the first impression of *Morocco*, 1,601 of *London to the Nore*, 1,935 of *The Royal Navy*, 2,247 of *From Damascus to Palmyra* and 2,289 of *The Savage South Seas*; while Claflin took 883 copies (of 2,000) of *Algeria and Tunis*, 1,390 of *The Scenery of London*, 1,834 of *Constantinople* and 931 of *Familiar London*. There is no evidence that all of these copies were ever bound up and sold, though it should be remembered that a number of titles were specially reprinted for Claflin in 1911 and 1912, and there was obviously a market for these at reduced prices. The cheaper reprints, of course, bear less gilt on their covers and only rarely are accurately dated.

6

Other Series

A & C Black were inclined to group all books published at a particular price in a 'series' regardless of whether the books bore any resemblance to each other. Here, however, books that form series uniform in style and content are separated from those that do not; the latter are discussed and listed under an admittedly somewhat arbitrary Miscellaneous section.

THE 12s 6d SERIES

Four books here form a small series: *Rembrandt*, *Romney*, *Reynolds* and *Velasquez*. The first is described as 'by' Mortimer Menpes, which in this case means that he contributed the preface and was responsible for the reproduction of the sixteen illlustrations; C. Lewis Hind wrote the text and might have been less than pleased at receiving, so to speak, second billing. The other three books were written by Randall Davies. The publisher lists them as $11'' \times 9\frac{1}{2}''$ or $8\frac{1}{4}''$; measurement shows them to be $11\frac{1}{2}'' \times 9''$ (292×228mm). By comparison with other Black books they are worthy but somewhat dull. They do not immediately stand out as A & C Black publications — a fact which itself shows how successful the firm was in creating its own 'house style' for the colour books. The reproduction of the illustrations in these books, however, is excellent, four colours having been used in reproducing many of the illustrations, necessary because of the large amounts of dark tones present.

THE 10s SERIES

One volume, the album-shaped *The Light Side of Egypt*, is listed under Miscellaneous. The other four appear to be refugees from the 7s 6d series, but with more illustrations than was common in those books, and therefore issued at a higher price. *Bruges and West Flanders* is one of the three books that were later combined to make up the 20s *Belgium*, while *The Highlands and Islands of Scotland* complements *The Heart of Scotland* and *Bonnie Scotland*; these three volumes plus *The Clyde* in the 20s series mean that most of Scotland was described and depicted in the colour book series. *Normandy* is in the distinctive style of Nico Jungman, while *From Sketch Book and Diary* was written and painted by the popular military painter Lady Elizabeth Butler.

THE 7s 6d SERIES

Next to the 20s series the bulk of A & C Black's colour plate books were issued at 7s 6d (37½p). The same format was used, but the cover decoration was generally less elaborate, often consisting only of gilt titling within printed borders, and the books contained twenty, twenty four or thirty two full page illustrations in colour, the plates in most instances protected by tissues. Of the series of 73 one is not a book but a portfolio of drawings and at least one other volume must be considered rare. Reprints of these books were much less frequent than in the 20s series.

The series opened in 1903 with *Letters from the Holy Land* by Lady Butler, the text consisting of letters she wrote to her mother when she accompanied her husband Lt General Sir William Butler on a tour of Palestine while he was based at Alexandria.

Lady Butler, who before her marriage painted as Elizabeth Thompson, was offered either half the profits on the book or a 10% royalty rising to 15% after 2,000 copies had been sold or a payment of £50 on the day of publication. Diligent negotiation enabled her to push the offer up to £50 on publication plus 10% royalty rising to 15% after the sale of 2,000, generous terms. As was usual with books in the 20s series at this time, a limited large paper edition of 250 copies was published, to sell at one guinea (21s).

The publisher, Lady Butler wrote in her autobiography, 'reproduced the water-colour illustrations very faithfully', and she recorded her delight at being numbered 'among the authors'. The shell that forms part of the cover decoration was an emblem of St James of Compostella.

The second book, *The Vicar of Wakefield* by Oliver Goldsmith, was a curiosity since, with the notable exception of the works of Sir Walter Scott, A & C Black have never been noted as publishers of adult fiction.

Only two other such books appeared in this series: *Aucassin and Nicolete*, if this twelfth century fable can be regarded as such, and Mrs Craik's *John Halifax Gentleman*.

The Vicar of Wakefield was also unusual in that its illustrations were by John Massey Wright (Masey according to the *Dictionary of National Biography*), who lived from either 1773 (A & C Black) or 1777 (DNB) to 1866, and not by a contemporary artist. The 'recent discovery' of these beautifully delicate watercolours, however, would have been reason enough for their publication.

It is not easy to discern any particular theme in the choice of books for the 7s 6d series. Many depicted towns or cities in Britain and abroad, subjects which would not have justified the 75 or so illustrations used in the 20s series; others dealt with counties and sections of counties, the component parts eventually being combined to form a 20s volume.

An example is *Yorkshire* where three 7s 6d books (*Coast and Moorland, Vales and Wolds, Dales and Fells*) were later combined in the 20s *Yorkshire*. The 20s books *Russia* and *The Lake of Geneva* also comprised the contents of three 7s 6d volumes, and similar arrangements occurred with *English Costume* and *Belgium*. The usual practice was for a full edition of 3,000 copies to be printed, 2,000 of these being prepared for the 7s 6d series; if the individual parts sold out, the remaining 1,000 were bound for sale as the composite volume in the 20s series.

As well as this a number of books were written for the smaller series and then either cut down or used intact for the larger volumes: an example of the former is *Winchester*, the abridged text of which appeared as part of *Hampshire*, and of the latter *Canterbury*, where the full text and illustrations are incorporated into *Kent*.

The New Forest, which appeared in 1904, was the work of Mrs Willingham Rawnsley, who resolutely refused to agree to the publisher's suggestion that the book appear under her own name (Alice Julia). A large paper edition of only 100 copies of the book was produced, suggesting that the publisher's confidence in such editions was waning: only nine of the 7s 6d series were favoured with such large paper editions, usually of 250 copies.

Mrs Rawnsley submitted her own idea for the cover design, as a result of which A & C Black wrote to her on February 17 1904: 'As the volume will appear in the same series as Lady Butler's *Holy Land* and others, it has been thought fit to use the same idea for the design, but the leaves and the blossom emblematic of the Forest have been adopted from your sketch.

The russet colour of the cloth may be taken to suggest autumn.' Her own design had involved too much (expensive) gold.

Mrs Rawnsley's other contribution to the series, *Country Sketches for City Dwellers* (1908), was a rare instance of 'vanity' publishing, A & C Black having declined to take the risk on the book. Mrs Rawnsley was quoted a sum of £180 for the production of 1,500 copies, excluding the cost of author's and publisher's corrections, the net proceeds then to be paid to her. In fact an edition of 2,000 was printed and Mrs Rawnsley must have remained heavily out of pocket since the book was sold off in 1910 when 1,800 copies remained in stock. This is almost certainly a record low figure for the publisher's sales of any of these books.

Westminster Abbey and *Edinburgh* were both illustrated by John Fulleylove, the former written by Mrs A. Murray Smith, a daughter of George Bradley, Dean of Westminster, and sister of the author A.G. Bradley, and the latter by Rosaline Masson, author and historian, and daughter of Professor David Masson, Historiographer Royal for Scotland. Miss Masson has the distinction of winning an entry in *Who's Who* in her own right; many of the A & C Black female authors (authoresses as they were usually called) appear in reference books only as the wives or daughters of the male subject entries. In some cases this was justified since the lady's only function was to provide text to fill the spaces between her husband's illustrations; but often the works of reference are silent on highly competent authors and artists.

Miss Masson tried to stipulate that the text should not be in any way altered without her consent; the publisher, not surprisingly, refused to agree to this.

Adventures among Pictures reproduced more or less unaltered a number of essays by C. Lewis Hind that had appeared in *The Academy*, of which he was editor from 1896 to 1903. *The Studio* in its review of the book regarded the result as too idiosyncratic to be of general interest and also criticised the reproduction of the illustrations. Hind went on to write *Days with Velasquez* (1906), which was published in an edition of only 2,000 copies.

Scottish Life and Character by H.J. Dobson, a well known painter of the 'homely and pathetic', and William Sanderson, editor of *The Border* magazine, was another book that fell into no particular category; first published in 1903 with twenty illustrations, the 1914 reprint has only sixteen, while the 1919 reprint reverts to twenty.

The variety of the series can be seen in the books published during

1905: *Nuremberg* by A. G. Bell and his wife, a prolific author who up to 1882 wrote as N. D'Anvers; *The Homes of Tennyson* illustrated by Helen Allingham and written by her brother Arthur Paterson, a book that was criticised for depicting only summer scenes and giving no hint of the storm and stress in which Tennyson delighted; *Abbotsford* (Sir Walter Scott's home) by Rev W. S. Crockett and William Smith Jr; and *The Garden that I Love*, by Alfred Austin. It was the success of this work, first published in 1894, that was partly responsible for Austin being made Poet Laureate in 1896. The DNB says of Austin (in a gentle and beautifully phrased demolition by Henry Buckley Charlton) that he probably 'is best in his prose "garden-diaries", casual but often pompous jottings, half reverie, half autobiography, mainly devoted to the charm of his Kentish home or of his Italian holidays: they are not as solemnly sentimental as his poems.' But Austin, who was always treated with great deference by A & C Black, was one author whose works usually ran to reprints, and both this book and *Lamia's Winter Quarters* (1907) were illustrated by a fine painter of gardens, George S. Elgood, who was able to command the high fee of over £5 a picture. It is a pity that these were the only two books that he illustrated for A & C Black. *Haunts of Ancient Peace* (1908), the third Austin book, was the only one not to be accompanied by a large paper limited edition.

Also published in 1905 was *The Beautiful Birthday Book*. This book, in blue cloth and with decorated endpapers, contained twelve illustrations by Gertrude Demain Hammond, including a frontispiece of a splendidly voluptuous young lady, and decorative borders by Turbayne. Its purpose was for the owner to record the birth dates of friends and relations (A & C Black's Historic Library copy contains those of many of the firm's authors and artists).

Many copies will have been destroyed at the deaths of their owners, and this book must be regarded as rare. Even rarer would be one of the first copies bound up: Miss Hammond's name was omitted entirely from the proofs of the books and only finally appeared on the page listing the illustrations, but not until the first copies had been sent out; the newly printed replacement page had to be inserted in already printed copies. In addition to this the firm's correspondence records that: 'Several book-binders have purchased unbound copies with intention of binding them specially.' The publisher's records show that of an edition of 3,000 copies, 209 went to Macmillan in New York, 28 to India, 20 to Australia, 676 were sold to the trade at 5s 8d, 740 to the trade at prices varying from 1s 2d

Left: *Henry Elford Luxmoore, Eton schoolmaster, creator of Lux-*
moore's Garden and painter of the Eton from a Backwater *portfolio.*
Right: *John Fulleylove, who illustrated* Oxford, The Holy Land *and*
Greece *in the 20 shilling series and who was engaged on more work for*
A & C Black at the time of his death in 1908.
Photo: *Courtesy National Portrait Gallery*

to 5s and the rest were sold off to John Grant in quires at 3d each. If the
Beautiful Birthday Book is found at all today there is no guarantee what
colour cloth it will be clad in.

The next couple of years saw publication of several of the books that
were later combined to make up 20s volumes: the three Yorkshire books
(only one of which was issued in a large paper limited edition), the four
volumes of *English Costume*, three that combined to make up *Belgium*, and
the three component parts of *The Lake of Geneva: Montreux, Geneva* and
Lausanne.

British Dogs at Work was another oddity in this series, but in style and
content belongs here rather than with the books for sportsmen; while *Our
Life in the Swiss Highlands* by John Addington Symonds and his daughter

Margaret combined an earlier text (Symonds lived from 1840 to 1893) with illustrations by J. Hardwicke Lewis, who was commissioned simultaneously for this book and *The Upper Engadine* in the 6s series, the two books bearing a number of illustrations in common.

John Fulleylove's final contributions were *Middlesex* (1907) and *The Tower of London* (1908) before his untimely death the same year. Fulleylove had been asked for illustrations for a book on Eton, to form one of a number on Britain's main public schools and the towns that housed them. *Eton* and *Winchester* were published and *Harrow* and *Rugby* were planned but did not appear.

H. E. Luxmoore, an Eton housemaster who retired at Easter 1908, had offered watercolours for a book on Eton in 1906, at which time Fulleylove already had the commission; on the latter's death, however, Luxmoore was asked to provide some sample drawings. He was keen to avoid the more usual views of college and town, but the publisher was less enthusiastic about this 'backwater' idea: '. . . it must be remembered that the stock views are not hackneyed in colour & it would be a pity to confine the sale solely to Etonians.' In addition to the views he had submitted Luxmoore was asked to provide five popular subjects; as an alternative it was suggested that he might be prepared to co-operate with Miss Edith Brinton, sister of another Eton master, each providing a number of drawings. By early August 1908, however, Luxmoore had decided to pull out and the publisher wrote to him that they: '. . . regret your decision that your drawings are unsuited to Mr Stone's text, and we are all the more sorry as in this series of books we encourage artist & author to work independently.' Author of *Eton* was Christopher Stone, whose name was suggested by A. C. Benson, who had been approached first.

Miss Brinton's illustrations were the ones eventually used in the book, which was not published until November 1909. Luxmoore, however, decided to publish his drawings as a portfolio at his own expense as his contribution to the Eton Memorial Building Fund. Luxmoore was quoted £3 for each set of blocks and £2 per subject for a printing of 250 copies, £3 each for 500, £4 each for 1,000; A & C Black confirmed that they would be happy to produce the portfolio for him, eventually quoting him a total cost of £75 for 1,000 copies, which they expected to sell at 2s 6d each. By November, however, it had been decided to sell at 7s 6d, and in January 1909 the publisher confirmed that 1,000 copies had been printed and 500 of these made ready for sale. Publisher's selling commision was the usual 15 per cent.

In 1910 the remaining 200 copies were bought back from Luxmoore for £50 (a strangely high figure) with an agreement that they should not be used without his consent. Later some of the drawings were used in *Windsor and Eton* in the Beautiful Britain series, which provoked a mild complaint from Luxmoore. Most of these, however, would have had to be newly printed from the original blocks, since 5,000 copies of *Windsor and Eton* were printed. The majority of Luxmoore's watercolours depict Tangier Island and other lesser known parts of the college.

Eton from a Backwater was regularly advertised as part of the 7s 6d series, though there may be those who will say that because it is not a book it should not be included. Book or not, however, it forms an integral part of the series, one that many collectors will have to resign themselves to doing without. Since the drawings were intended for framing many copies will have been broken up, and it must now be considered a rare item. Most, for obvious reasons, were sold to Etonians and Old Etonians.

British towns and cities continued to form one focus for the series during the next few years, which saw the publication of *Windsor* (permission to paint inside the castle was requested and refused), *Chester*, *Winchester* (with no interior views of the cathedral), *Bath and Bristol* and *London*; the latter was an oversize book with text by Hope Moncrieff and illustrations selected from earlier volumes; it was later reissued with 60 illustrations in the 20s series.

Books on gardens remained popular and included *Gardens of England* by E. T. Cook and painted by Beatrice Parsons; *Dutch Bulbs and Gardens*, whose orange cloth makes it a difficult book to find in good condition; *The Charm of Gardens*, with illustrations plucked from various sources and text by the versatile Dion Clayton Calthrop, a book which appeared over the years in a range of variations, with and without gilt titling; *Flowers and Gardens of Madeira* by the Du Canes; *Alpine Flowers and Gardens*, beautifully illustrated by George Flemwell; and *The Herb Garden*, with fine illustrations by Florence Amherst, one of the seven daughters of Baron Tyssen-Amherst of Hackney, and Isabelle Forrest, an elusive book. The plates in both this and Benger and Morrah's *Highways and Hedges* are shown off to advantage by being tipped in on grey mounts. It is regrettable that A & C Black did not do this more often.

An addition to the small number of books on artists came with the publication of the 'autobiography' (put together by H. M. Cundall) of the watercolourist William Callow, who died in 1908. The publisher's reservations about the wisdom of producing the book were justified: only

522 copies had been sold by the end of 1910, and it was sold off at 4s (retail) with a balance of £200 remaining against it.

Alfred Heaton Cooper visited the Isles of Man and Wight for the series, text for the former being written by W. Ralph Hall Caine, brother of Hall Caine and a writer on history, religion and anthropology. Other areas of Britain covered included *The Wye* (extracted from *The Rivers and Streams of England* in the 20s series); *The Inns of Court*; *Deeside*, another oversize book, as is *British Castles*; *Ayrshire Idylls*, also oversize, written by the Scottish novelist Neil Munro; and *Worcestershire*. The artist commissioned for *Worcestershire* was Thomas Tyndale, who should not be confused with Walter, painter of Wessex, though they may have been related. There were problems with Thomas Tyndale: '... we find you have included a drawing of Child's Wickham which is in Gloucestershire. Would it not be well to substitute for it a drawing of the Teme valley?' And to A.G. Bradley, the author, the publisher wrote: 'We quite agree with your criticisms on the *Worcestershire* drawings but what can be done? We select the best artist we can find for a district & he disappoints us!' There were so many complaints about the drawing of Worcester Cathedral that Tyndale was asked to repaint it.

Two books published in 1910, *A Short History of the Church of England* and *British Floral Decoration* provide early examples of colour illustrations reproduced from colour photographs, 'autochromes' as they were called. They look crude to modern eyes. The Church of England book is often said to be the first book illustrated in this way, but *British Floral Decoration* came first by seven months and should therefore surely win the prize. *A Short History of the Church of England*, however, included illustrations taken from colour photographs of moving subjects rather than static ones.

Among the 'foreign' books *St Petersburg* (with a fine cover design on vulnerable yellow cloth), *Moscow* and *Provincial Russia* were later combined as *Russia* (20s). Alberto Pisa reappeared as painter of *Pompeii*, while Vittorio Boron from Turin painted *Malta*, another book that is not easily found and which, like many others in this series, was not reprinted. *The Dolomites* proved that Reginald Farrer was a naturalist of the first rank. This book can be found both with and without gilt titling, dated 1913.

The Canary Islands, however, comes in a quite bewildering variety of styles: white, blue, red, grey-blue and green cloths have been noted, containing twenty or sixteen illustrations. The 'benchmark' version housed in A & C Black's Historic Library contains twenty illustrations and is in white cloth with gilt titling on front and spine; plates are guarded by tissues, which bear the captions. Although all other copies are dated 1911, the book was reprinted in the early 1930s for W. H. Smith and Son, and it is these that form the bulk of those most commonly found; they are slightly larger than the white cloth version.

The Cape Peninsula with text by Réné Juta was produced by Juta Publishing of South Africa, to whom A & C Black paid a 15% commission on sales. It is also found under the Juta imprint.

The Spirit of Paris, published in 1913, has a lovely Art Nouveau cover design by G. Riom and includes colour illustrations by six French artists, among them Raphael Kirchner, Lucien Gautier and Gustave Fraipont. If one is allowed favourites in the series, then this is mine.

Last to appear was *Around St Malo* in 1917, itself a retitling of *La Côte d'Emeraude* (1912). The latter was published in an edition of 3,000 and the unsold stock used for *Around St Malo*, only the title pages being altered.

Six books from the 7s 6d series were reprinted in the 1920s at 6s with sixteen illustrations at $8\frac{1}{4}'' \times 5\frac{1}{2}''$. Titles reissued were *Ayshire Idylls*, *Gardens of England*, *Flowers and Gardens of Madeira*, *The Wye*, *Chester* and *Edinburgh*. These volumes should not be confused with the 6s series (see below), which were issued only during 1906-08.

THE FASCINATION OF EUROPE

As mentioned above, these six books were published nominally at 10s but immediately reduced to 7s 6d. *England, France, Italy* and *Switzerland* were reissued in the 20s series with decorated covers. *Switzerland*, however, was also reprinted in 1930 in its thirty two illustration form in red or blue cloth. Publication dates are printed in the book.

Austria-Hungary and *Bulgaria* were not reissued, probably because it was impossible to assemble enough illustrations from stock — and certainly impossible in 1914 to despatch an artist!

Bulgaria can be found in red as well as brown cloth.

THE 6s SERIES

This is an attractive small series of just thirteen books on topographical subjects published during 1906-08. Size is quoted as $7\frac{1}{2}'' \times 5\frac{1}{4}''$: this is the paper size; overall book size is $8'' \times 5\frac{1}{2}''$ (202 × 137mm). Only the frontispiece plate has a flimsy tissue guard, which is often absent.

The texts for the series were newly commissioned with the exceptions of *Ireland*, *Jamaica* and *Paris*; the illustrations, however, were taken from earlier colour plate books. *Ireland* contains the whole text and thirty two of the illustrations from the 20s *Ireland* and was made up from the unused stock of that volume; *Jamaica* comprises that section of *The West Indies*; and *Paris* is the whole text and twenty four illustrations from the 20s *Paris*, which was supposed to appear in the 20s series in 1904 but was not published until 1909 (see above).

North Devon makes no mention of its painter Henry B. Wimbush, perhaps because the illustrations had been bought from Raphael Tuck, the postcard publishers, who were paid 50 guineas for them. It was agreed that Tuck would submit all their drawings in the same way, while A & C Black would submit colour books to Tuck. Certainly Tuck published many postcards taken from illustrations in A & C Black colour plate books, though there is little evidence that Tuck supplied many illustrations for the colour books.

Liverpool was written by Dixon Scott, a young leader writer on the *Liverpool Courier*, whose real name was Walter Scott but who was unwilling for his work to appear under that illustrious name. An author of great promise, he died of dysentery during the first world war. An appreciation was printed in the Christmas 1915 issue of *The Bookman*, which regarded his death as 'at least as great a loss to literature as was the death of Rupert Brooke'.

Kew Gardens was produced in green cloth decorated in black and light green (gilt on the spine only) as well as the standard grey cloth with green and gilt decoration; *The Peak Country* appears in fawn cloth with black, pink and light blue decoration (gilt on spine only) as well as the standard navy blue cloth and gilt decoration.

THE 5s SERIES

One series of four books, one of three and a number of Miscellaneous volumes:

Motor Routes
More was promised here than actually achieved. The A & C Black oeuvre contains few 'ghosts', but advertisements refer to three projected Motor Routes books that were not published. The four that were are *England: Southern Section*; *England: Western Section and Wales*; *France Part I*; and

Germany. Described as 'in active preparation' were *England: Eastern and Northern Sections*; *France Part II*; and *Scotland*. The outbreak of the first world war put an end to these plans, and the publication of *Germany* in May 1914 was a particularly unfortunate piece of timing since few travellers can have found it useful for some years to come!

Highlight of the books is Turbayne's magnificent cover design, depicting the motor car as winged chariot complete with goggled driver and passenger: gilt and bright red on *England: Southern*; gilt and light green on *England: Western*; gilt and pink on the others. The colour illustrations (24 or 16) were taken from previously published volumes, and there is a plentiful supply of maps and town plans; also a few commercial advertisements.

The books were also published at 7s 6d bound in grained leather, with the cover design in gilt only. There is an excellent coloured map at the end of each book.

The 'People' books

Only three books were published: *The People of Egypt* by Lance Thackeray; *The People of India* by Mortimer Menpes; *The People of Holland* by Nico Jungman. These are lovely books whose short introductory text is followed by thirty two illustrations tipped on grey mounts; captions on the protective guards face the plates, while the rectos of the interleaves carry pencil drawings in black and white. The introductions to *Holland* and *Egypt* were written by Gordon Home, who also contributed the pencil sketches to *Holland*, a fact which was not recorded on the title page, to Jungman's annoyance; possibly Home was annoyed too! The standard of reproduction of the plates is as high as any produced by A & C Black. Size is $9\frac{1}{2} \times 7$ inches rather than the $9 \times 7\frac{1}{2}$ indicated in the prospectuses.

THE MENPES CROWN SERIES

This is a series of one book! In 1907 Mortimer Menpes was busy with another venture for A & C Black, the publishing of the Menpes Series of Great Masters — reproductions of masterpieces in British and European galleries which were sold in moulded old gold frames. On January 9 Adam Black wrote to Menpes:

To put great things before small, the great masters before books, it seems to me the important question is can you or may I say we, afford to let things drift. The campaign is beginning in earnest: our one traveller is en route to the United States another to Australia. Our own two travellers start next week, a third begins canvassing the country print sellers at once and today we have practically arranged for the really first rate man to visit the London print sellers ...

You have sometime expressed a desire to have a colour series of books entirely your own and the present seems a good time to start it. If the series were quite distinctive we should of course reserve it entirely for your books. This however puts the six shilling series out of court as it was our idea and several volumes have already been issued in it, but why not a 6s series, the Menpes Crown Series with 50 illustrations, 18 full page in colour and the rest in black and white. The format, binding, type of paper etc would all be distinctive and reserved for you but I think it would be a pity to start it with any of the countries you mention. Our experience is that these far away places, Japan excepted, do not sell as well as the countries nearer home and we may say that Mr Forrest's Mexico is to be published only if he secures a large order in that country. [it was not]

The series should be opened by a strong and popular book such as Italy or Spain, and of these two I prefer the former. Paris should stand as at present arranged as the circumstances are exceptional and we are all united in attempting to retrieve a bad situation.

Menpes' view obviously prevailed since the book that appeared was *China* with text by Sir Henry Arthur Blake, a former Governor of Hong Kong and Ceylon. Sixteen colour plates were incorporated, together with 64 line drawings in a book $10\frac{1}{4}" \times 7\frac{1}{2}"$ bound in blue cloth, published in 1909.

And that was it: no further book appeared in this series and no correspondence remains to tell us why this was the case.

BEAUTIFUL BRITAIN SERIES

Twenty nine books, $9" \times 6\frac{1}{4}"$ (228 × 159mm), bound at first in blue boards and later in blue cloth with one of the twelve illustrations — which were largely taken from earlier books — onlaid on the cover. The artists' names were not mentioned. The texts, around 11,000 words, were newly written for the series or cut down from earlier volumes, and the books had pictorial endpapers, with the frontispiece plate tipped on a grey mount.

The series was published during 1910-16; subjects were largely conventional and at 1s 6d these books would have been good value for money. The prospectus described them as 'a pioneer among books at a low price containing illustrations equal in all respects to those hitherto only obtainable in expensive volumes'. The publisher's records show that titles published in 1914 and 1915 — eight in all — were enclosed in boxes, as were books produced at this time in the Artist's Sketch Book and Water-Colour series. There is no example of a box in A & C Black's Historic Library and none has yet been seen.

A first impression of 5,000 copies of the Beautiful Britain titles was printed. Many titles were reprinted from 1920 onwards, with eight or twelve illustrations, the cover picture being incorporated inside the book and a crude alteration made to the list of illustrations showing its new position. The fact that this alteration can be found in books with eight illustrations — which had newly printed title pages — suggests that late decisions were made not to have a pictorial cover. The books were clad in brown decorated dust wrappers.

The oddity in this series is *Girton College*, which contains eight colour illustrations and seven from photographs, with text by E.E. Constance Jones, who was Mistress of Girton. The publisher agreed to go ahead with the book provided the college bought 2,000 copies. Half of the profit was to go to Miss Jones after deduction of a 15% publisher's commission.

BEAUTIFUL EUROPE SERIES

These seven books in the style of the above were published between 1914 and 1924, four in boxes. In this series also no mention is made of the artists' names: most will be recognised from previously published books, especially those in the 20s series. A & C Black might be considered to have made good use of the illustrations whose right of reproduction they had purchased, sometimes for as little as £2: some illustrations can be traced through six or more different incarnations.

A few titles in this series can be found with the background to the titling on the front and spine printed or blocked in a darker shade of blue; close examination shows that the darker blue was used to cover a previously printed title *The Lake of Geneva*. The existing records are silent about whether a printer's error resulted in a huge over-run of *Lake of Geneva* covers, which then had to be turned to some other purpose. Among copies seen with two-tone boards are *The Engadine* and *Norwegian Fjords*.

An advertisement in an A & C Black catalogue for books in boxes to be sent as Christmas cards; books from the Water-Colour series were later added to the list. The publisher's ledgers show that only some of the titles advertised here were produced in boxes.

BLACK'S WATER-COLOUR SERIES

A very attractive series of 46 titles, each containing reproductions of sixteen or twenty watercolours and published between 1913 and the mid-1930s. Costing 1s, later 1s 6d and 2s 6d, they were bound in cloth or brown-paper covered boards, with one of the illustrations onlaid on the cover. Four titles plus the 1914 reprint of *Hampshire* were issued in boxes during 1914 and 1915. Book size was the usual 'square demy octavo', although *The Nile* by Ella Du Cane was issued both at this size and album shaped, $6\frac{1}{4}'' \times 9''$. The series was much reprinted, the reprints during the 1930s containing only sixteen illustrations. Tissue guards accompany three 1930s reprints: this sort of short-lived departure from standard format seems almost a deliberate attempt by the publisher to confuse the collector of the future.

Two albums of Henry Wimbush's illustrations for *Jersey* and *Guernsey*, containing twenty plates tipped on green paper, were published in 1908 under the title Water-Colour Views; no further titles were added.

BRITISH ARTISTS SERIES

Four books (*Birket Foster, Kate Greenaway, George Morland, John Pettie*), consisting of a 5,000 word introduction and sixteen colour plates tipped on Vandyke brown mounts. One of the illustrations is onlaid on the cover. These are attractive and well designed books, not easy to find. A further volume, on Helen Allingham, was planned but did not appear. The curiously arbitrary choice of subjects would have been dictated by the existence of blocks from earlier books on the same artists. A fifth book, *Rembrandt*, appeared under the series title Great Artists, of which it forms the sole component.

QUOTATION AND PICTURE SERIES

In the words of the prospectus: 'Sixteen coloured views with descriptions by poets or well-known authors arranged opposite views to which they refer.'

Only four books were issued, three in 1915 and *Sussex* in 1928; though a similar volume is *A Few Flowers of the Italian Riviera*. The books, $8\frac{3}{4}'' \times 6''$ (224 × 152mm) were bound in paper boards with a patterned decoration and title label stuck on the front, within white wrappers bearing a captioned illustration in colour. The artists' names are not mentioned.

The illustrations in *Sussex* consist of twelve by Wilfrid Ball of Sussex views and four by Sutton Palmer, three of them of places in Surrey. Thus Belloc's poem *The South Country* is placed opposite a picture of Evening on the Moors, Hindhead, which first appeared in *Surrey* (20s); Conan Doyle's text on Crowborough appears opposite a view of Milford Common. Instance of carelessness of this sort are happily rare in A & C Black books.

BRUSH PEN AND PENCIL SERIES

These books depict the life and work of six contemporary artists and illustrators. Published in 1907-13, they were bound in fawn cloth with a caricature on the cover on a red, yellow or green background. However, this colour background was absent from the covers of the most commonly found 1930 reprints. The books contain between four and eight colour illustrations with a large number in black and white, with text by A.E. Johnson, the literary agent.

THE WAR FRONT SERIES

Four books published in 1920 and written and illustrated by former military officers, among them Donald Maxwell and Martin Hardie. Bound in blue cloth blind stamped with a military motif, they contained either thirty two or fifty illustrations and were published at 25s, an increase in price that showed that copiously illustrated books could no longer be produced to sell at 20s.

Of the authors and artists, the Sheldon-Williams brothers (*The Canadian Front in France and Flanders*), sons of the artist Alfred Sheldon-Williams, accompanied the Canadian army, while Captain Martin Hardie (*Our Italian Front*) was Head Censor in Italy and Lieutenant Donald Maxwell (*The Naval Front*) served with the navy during the war; A.J. Mann and William T. Wood (*The Salonika Front*) were members of the Salonika Balloon Company.

BEAUTIFUL BOOKS FOR SPORTSMEN

A & C Black has for many years produced books for fishermen and those who shoot — and does so to this day. During the early years of the century those containing a number of colour plates cost 7s 6d, while the large number with only the frontispiece in colour or illustrated in black and white were priced at 3s 6d.

The high prices that are demanded for many of these books reflects the collecting interest in hunting, shooting and fishing books.

Particularly worth looking out for are *Grouse and Grouse Moors*, illustrated by Charles Whymper, *Partridges and Partridge Manors* and *Pheasants and Covert Shooting*, while the books of G. E. M. Skues, not listed here, include the splendidly named *Minor Tactics of the Chalk Stream and Kindred Studies*, and are much sought after today.

W. Earl Hodgson, who wrote books on salmon and trout fishing, was for many years the Principal Reader for A & C Black. According to the history of the firm, he 'worked successfully in a back room at Soho Square in charge of a large and expanding fishing list until he died of an excess of nicotine'. Listed here are only books with colour plates by named artists.

PORTRAIT BIOGRAPHIES

Three books by Mortimer Menpes, one on (Sir) Henry Irving, the actor, published in 1906, and the others on the war leaders Kitchener and Roberts, which were published in 1915. These small volumes in dark blue cloth are not immediately recognisable as A & C Black books, although the Menpes' monogram appears on the front of each.

THE ARTISTS' SKETCH BOOK AND CHARM SERIES

This is perhaps a good point to insert a number of books that strictly have no place in a discussion of colour plate books: for the Artists' (or Artist's; A & C Black spelt the title of the series both ways) Sketch Books contain only black and white illustrations (usually sixteen or twenty four) from pencil sketches, as did the larger format Charm series.

The bulk of the forty five volume Artists' Sketch Book series depicted British towns and cities, with a few excursions into foreign parts; plus one

THE
"ARTIST'S SKETCH BOOK" SERIES.
Edited by MARTIN HARDIE, A.R.E.

Square Demy 8vo., with artistic cover, bearing a label designed by the artist. Containing 24 reproductions from pencil drawings.

SKETCH BOOKS IN THE SERIES.

BATH AND WELLS
BRIGHTON
CAMBRIDGE
CANTERBURY
DURHAM
EDINBURGH
FLORENCE
GLASGOW
HARROW
HARROGATE
HASTINGS
ISLE OF WIGHT
LIVERPOOL
LONDON
LONDON AT NIGHT
RIVERSIDE LONDON
NEWCASTLE-UPON-TYNE
NORWICH
OXFORD
PARIS
ROCHESTER
ROME
SCARBOROUGH AND WHITBY
STRATFORD-ON-AVON
VENICE
WINCHESTER
WINDSOR AND ETON
ZOO, THE

Published by A. & C. BLACK, LTD.,
4, 5 & 6 SOHO SQUARE, LONDON, W.1.

Black's Beautiful Postcards
OF BRITISH DESIGN & MANUFACTURE

Price 9d. net per packet of Six Cards.

THE subjects have been selected, in most cases, from volumes in "Black's Beautiful Books" and the "Artist's Sketch Book" Series, and they meet the demand, often expressed by possessors of these volumes, for separate pictures to be framed or sent away to friends.

IN COLOUR.

Series 2, 3 and 4. THE CHANNEL ISLANDS
  „   5, 6 and 7. THE ENGLISH LAKES
  „   8 and 9. BELGIUM
  „   10 and 11. BANKS OF THE NILE
  „   12 and 13. PEOPLE OF EGYPT
  „   14. EDINBURGH
  „   15. CANTERBURY
  „   16. NORFOLK BROADS
  „   17. THE TROSSACHS
  „   18 and 19. ENGLISH GARDENS
  „   20. BRITISH DOGS
  „   21, 22 and 23. OUR INDIAN ARMIES
  „   24. THE PEOPLE OF INDIA
  „   25. ALPINE FLOWERS
  „   27. RUBAIYAT OF OMAR
  „   31. RUSSIA   [KHAYYAM
  „   33, 34 and 35. JAPAN
  „   36. DEVON
  „   37, 38 and 39. SURREY
  „   40. THE WYE
  „   41 and 42. SUSSEX
  „   43. ENGLISH CHILDREN
  „   44 and 45. ENGLISH NURSERY
            RHYMES (with Music)
  „   46 and 47. BIRDS OF BRITAIN
  „   48. GARDENS OF ENGLAND
  „   49 and 50. MADEIRA, Flowers and
                              Gardens

IN PENCIL AND TINT.

Series 51. OXFORD
  „   52 and 59. CAMBRIDGE
  „   53. WINDSOR AND ETON
  „   54 and 55. HARROW
  „   56. CANTERBURY.
  „   57. STRATFORD-ON-AVON
  „   58. LONDON
  „   60. THE ZOO
  „   62. BOURNEMOUTH
  „   63 and 64. CHESTER.

Published by A. & C. BLACK, LTD.,
4, 5 & 6 SOHO SQUARE, LONDON, W.1.
                              [P.T.O.

*Bookmarks advertising the Artists' Sketch Book series and
Black's Beautiful Postcards.*

or two oddities such as *The Zoo* and *Alpine Sport*. Artists included Joseph Pike, Walter M. Keesey, Lester G. Hornby, Katharine Kimball and Fred Richards, and the series was edited by Martin Hardie. Brown-paper or cloth-covered boards were used, and a pictorial label was onlaid on the front. Brown wrappers with a sketch on the front accompanied the books, but examples of these are only rarely seen.

Again several titles — those published or reprinted in 1913-1915, seventeen in all — were issued in semi-transparent plain tissue wrappers and contained in a box. The box is made of white card with a variant of the title page on the cover. Two different types have been seen: one with the pictorial title label printed on the box cover, the other with it stuck on the box cover: the latter has the words 'With the Season's Greetings' at the top and a space for the donor's name at the bottom.

Copies of these books in A & C Black's Historic Library have no boxes and no wrappers; *Bournemouth* and *Bristol* are clad in soft covers.

A few of the books were reissued in the 1930s with fifteen illustrations and greatly expanded captions and notes, and some titles were still being reprinted in the 1950s.

Being thin, these books are easily overlooked in the search for the more obtrusive colour plate volumes.

St Andrews — poems by Rudyard Kipling and Walter de la Mare — with etchings and drawings by Malcolm Patterson is in the style of the series and is listed with a small series of larger format sketch books and the six volumes in the Charm series. Of the latter *The Charm of Cambridge* is oversize, having been first published by Simpkin Marshall, who for many years were A & C Black's wholesalers. Simpkin Marshall's *The Charm of Oxford*, however, did not appear under the A & C Black imprint.

POPULAR AND NEW SERIES

Many of the books published at 20s and 7s 6d were reprinted during the 1920s and early 1930s in the Popular and New series. These were bound in blue cloth with a repeated armorial design blind stamped on the front and spine and the publisher's logo blind stamped on the back cover, $8\frac{1}{4}" \times 6"$, titling in black; the white dust wrappers were printed with a colour illustration on front and spine. Thirty two illustrations was usual, though a few had only twenty four. Title page design was by R. S. Austin. A number of new titles appeared in these series, however, as well as some

Prospectus for the Artists' Sketch Book series.

other new material. The new titles in the Popular series were *Dalmatia, Denmark, Derbyshire, Devon, Dorset, Durham, Gloucestershire, Northumberland, Somerset, Sweden* and *Wild Lakeland*; most of the illustrations for these were specially commissioned. Also *Ireland, Japan* and *Spain* (from *In Spain* by John Lomas, 1908) were given new texts, while that of *India* was increased by 5,000 words and *Cornwall* acquired extra illustrations and an extra chapter; material was added to *The Italian Lakes*. Several other texts were reduced by up to one third. Belloc's name is still absent from *Sussex*: his testy reply to the publisher's inquiry whether he wished to make any changes for this edition is quoted above (p 44).

The New series reprinted most of the Popular series titles but added *Austria* (by J.D. Newth, author of the firm's history), *England, Germany* and *Norway*, all with illustrations culled from earlier volumes. Several of the New reprints are indistinguishable from their Popular equivalents.

Among the artists to provide new paintings for these series were Sutton Palmer (*Devon*) and Alfred Heaton Cooper, who contributed to several titles.

MISCELLANEOUS BOOKS

Included in this section are colour plate books that fall into no particular series but which will still be of interest to the A & C Black collector. The firm's list always consisted of several hundred books: colour books, children's books, educational books, guide books and so on. To draw the line between the colour books and other categories is an almost impossible task, and the list is necessarily a compromise. Most of the volumes listed, however, would be desirable additions to any collection. Books without colour plates or with only the frontispiece in colour have largely been omitted, as have works of fiction.

Several books listed were published at 20s but fall outside the compass of the 20s series. Among these are *The Basque Country* (1921) by Katharine and Romilly Fedden, which although ostensibly published at 20s was swiftly reduced to 5s; *The Cockpit of Europe* (1920), which was reissued the same year from the existing stock under the title *Belgium Past and Present* included a number of illustrations of places in France and Germany as well as Belgium, thus making the original title the more logical one; and *Lancashire* (in the style of the Fascination of Europe series, containing thirty two illustrations).

Other books in more or less the style of the 20s series are *Stained Glass of the Middle Ages in England and France*, published at 25s, illustrated by Lawrence B. Saint, an American who made a lifetime study of stained glass and who also painted murals; *The Essential Kafir* (18s) by Dudley Kidd, illustrated by 100 black and white photographs and therefore not listed here; and *California* (18s).

The illustrations for *California* were carried out by Sutton Palmer while visiting his wife's family, who lived there. He also recommended the book's author, Mary Hunter Austin, a very strange lady. Her parents, a civil war captain and a feminist (and rigid puritan) made it clear that she was an unwanted child. Her only child was mentally retarded and was placed in an institution; when her husband failed in farming Mary Austin took his place while he did the housework. Later, separated from her husband, she spent many years studying the Indians in the Mojave Desert and began to make a living from writing. According to Sutton Palmer 'she takes the first place among American writers'. *California* has a pictorial dustwrapper, and the book was issued in a pictorial box. However, A & C Black's Historic Library affords the only complete example seen.

Boulogne: A Base in France reproduces thirty two drawings by (Captain) Martin Hardie, eight of them in colour, and is unusual among the books discussed here in having an untitled spine.

Oriental Carpets, Runners and Rugs, and some Jacquard Reproductions introduced not only the longest title of any of the books but also a new dimension to the book's preparation. Letters from the publisher to Sydney Humphries, the author, reveal that for the purposes of reproduction a number of carpets were transported from Kidderminster to Watford and back. It was reckoned that this process would take four days.

A further letter to Humphries indicates that common practice was to keep the type of colour books for two months and then decide whether to keep it longer with a view to another edition or to take papier mache moulds. With *Carpets*, the publisher suggested that since a large edition was being prepared the best course would be 'to disperse the type and let the book if possible become rare'. This is curious since the records show that it was in any case the practice to take moulds of almost every book published.

Carpets was poorly reviewed: *The Studio* said that it was 'an olla podrida of rambling notes and observations relating to painting, scupture, history, biography, literature, politics, travel and other matters which have no bearing whatever on the subject upon which the book is supposed to treat'.

The book's publication was underwritten by Humphries, who published most of his books at his own expense.

A Century of Sea Trading (1824-1924), another book to adopt the style of the 7s 6d series, was produced at the behest of The General Steam Navigation Co. Ltd, who bought half the edition at 7s a copy. It can be found in the trade edition blue cloth or as white cloth presentation copies.

The Light Side of Egypt was produced as an album shaped volume, 9" × 12", and contained thirty six illustrations by Lance Thackeray. Advertisements for this book in *The People of Egypt* refer to forty eight illustrations: this was the original intention. But the error is a curious one since the latter was published two years after *The Light Side of Egypt*. A later (1928) revision is $11\frac{1}{4}$" × $8\frac{3}{4}$" and contains only twenty four illustrations, tipped in.

Gainsborough has the distinction of being the largest book listed here (in size rather than number of pages). An imperial quarto of 15" × 11", its fifteen illustrations were engraved by Menpes, while the text was written by James Greig, who was upset by the relative weight given to his and Menpes' names on the title page. The publisher replied to this complaint that what was acceptable to Flora Annie Steel, Sir Henry Blake and C. Lewis Hind would surely be acceptable to him.

Commendatore Formilli's *The Castles of Italy* will appeal to collectors of dedications since it is dedicated to Mussolini, while Paul Vernon's in *Morocco from a Motor* is worth quoting: 'To my father whose early poems possessed a merry rhythm and whose commercial letters were examples of clearness.' Was this, one wonders, some sort of joke?

Heaton Cooper added *Norfolk and Suffolk* (1921) to the long list of books that he illustrated, while *A Book of Porcelain* by Bernhard Rackham is meticulously illustrated by William Gibb. *War Posters* reproduced in colour and black and white 80 posters 'issued by belligerent and neutral nations 1914-19'. It can be found in red cloth decorated in black with gilt titling on the spine; in fawn cloth decorated in black and red with no gilt; in green cloth decorated in black and red with no gilt; all dated 1920. It has not been possible to assign an order of precedence to these, though the version with gilt must be a clear leader.

Mortimer Menpes' reminiscences of his time with James McNeill Whistler appeared as *Whistler as I Knew Him* in 1904. A quarto of 11" × $8\frac{1}{4}$" it contained 125 illustrations in colour and tint, many of them representing successive phases in a picture's preparation; an edition of 2,000 was published to sell at £2, while the limited edition of 500 copies contained as frontispiece 'an original etching never before published. This etching has been printed direct from the copper by Mr Menpes himself and the plate has now been presented to the British Museum'. The etching depicts four of Menpes' six children; the limited edition sold for the high figure of £5-5s.

Macmillan arranged for the copy for *Whistler* to be set in the USA, while the illustrations were processed and printed in Britain; plates and sheets were then swapped. Macmillan, who published an edition of 1,000, shared the production costs and paid Menpes a 15% royalty; in the case of the limited edition Menpes received the whole return after deduction of costs and a 15% publisher's commission.

Turbayne provided the cover design, having been told that 'Whistler was fond of the check pattern & the Japanese wave pattern & also liked straight lines and simplicity'.

W. Earl Hodgson, the Reader, reckoned that the chapter 'Whistler the Exaggerated' should come out, but in the event it remained as the book's introduction. In spite of the generally fulsome nature of Menpes' reminiscences, there are comments in the book that would have raised Whistler's ire; but Whistler had died the year before and was in no position to object.

The *Annals of Hampstead* by Thomas J. Barratt in three volumes was limited to 550 copies to sell at £5-5s, later raised to £8 8s. These elaborately produced volumes were published at the author's own expense.

Another elaborate production on a smaller scale — some would say over-ornamented — is Gray's *Elegy in a Country Churchyard*, illustrated by G. F. Nicholls. This was designed and printed by W. W. Curtis Ltd at the Cheylesmore Press, Coventry. This book, no part of which remains undecorated, is somewhat at variance with A & C Black's 'house style'. No other such books were published.

THE PEEPS

These were, in the words of the publisher, 'little 1/6 books for young people of 2 to 14 years of age ... in which a feature is made of the work and play of children of the land under description & the general way of life among the people forms another special point'. Nearly 200 different Peeps were issued in fourteen series from 1907 to the 1930s. Twelve or thirteen full-page illustrations in colour were incorporated, one being onlaid on the

A window of a Great Yarmouth bookshop photographed in 1907:
on display are the first Peeps at Many Lands and Cities books and a
selection of the Menpes Great Masters framed reproductions.

cover; sometimes this cover picture was included in the list of illustrations, sometimes it duplicated one of the illustrations in the book.

The idea for the Peeps germinated in April 1906 when John Finnemore was asked for a trial volume for a series called 'Peeps at Other Lands'; but the publisher inquired: 'How would the title suit if England or Wales were one of the countries?' The result was that eventually Finnemore's suggestion of 'Peeps at Many Lands' was accepted.

Finnemore was offered a royalty of 5% on the published price of the first 10,000 copies of the books that he contributed to the series, 7½% on the next 10,000, 10% thereafter. Later this offer was raised to 7½% on the first five titles, the intention being to publish twelve books initially, six by Finnemore and six others; Finnemore's sixth was Japan, where he was offered only 5% because original illustrations had been commissioned from Ella Du Cane for £4 each. This did not happen often: the bulk of the illustrations were taken from earlier colour books, and in the later Peeps there is an increasing use of photographs.

A & C Black also admitted that it would be difficult to use some of the illustrations (from earlier books) 'unless we employ the artists' wives to write the letterpress, e.g. Mrs Jungman for *Holland* and *Normandy*' (the latter did not appear). Mrs Jungman was duly offered £10 for 20,000 words for *Holland*, a level of payment that became the norm for the series. One lady who had demanded more was told curtly: '... in this country one pound per 1,000 words is considered moderately good pay, & only a Kipling or a Caine would aspire to £5'. However, when Menpes appeared in the series he was offered half the profits of the relevant books, a further example of the special treatment he was accorded by A & C Black.

Editions of 5,000 copies were published in most cases, but high sales in the colonies ensured regular reprints. In 1908, for example, in reply to a letter from Madras, the publisher says that Japan and Italy had been prescribed for the matriculation examination of December 1909 '... several thousand copies have already been despatched'. To Finnemore they wrote: 'The Peeps are being widely adopted as Readers ... our intention is to prepare an edition more suitable to schools with a plainer binding, 6 or 8 illustrations instead of 12 & a published price of 1/6 ordinary instead of 1/6 net. This intention was not carried out.

The books, however, had swiftly acquired a royal imprimatur, for in June 1908 Adam Black writes that the Princess of Wales (later Queen Mary) had called and expressed approval of the series; all her family, she said, read the Peeps and 'Eddy' (later Prince of Wales and King Edward VIII) had read all those published up to that time.

Reprints of many of the Peeps were frequent; cloth colours were apt to change for new editions, and in some instances different illustrations were used; later reprints and some of the later titles had no cover picture and only eight illustrations, while titles published and reissued in the 1920s had to incorporate the changes in the map of Europe brought about by the first world war. *England*, to give an example, was published in September 1908, reprinted in October 1908, December 1909, August 1910, 1912, 1913, 1917 and 1926; and the publishing history of *Bird Life of the Seasons*, published in 1911, shows reprints in 1912, 1917, 1920, 1923, 1926, 1930, 1935, 1939, 1940 and 1944. *Scotland* appeared in September 1907 and was reprinted in 1907, 1908, 1910, 1918 (with some new illustrations), 1920 (with 8 illustrations) and revised in 1927; while *Belgium* saw its cloth change from navy blue in 1909 to black in 1915 and its cover illustration replaced by one of the King (more patriotic in wartime) with shields added to the endpapers.

Of the eight books in the Peeps at Great Railways series three were retitled reissues caused by the renaming of certain railway companies.

During the first world war a number of titles were produced with a pocket at the back containing six outline drawings taken from illustrations in the book; these were intended for colouring in by the young readers and were also sold separately at 2d a set. Not surprisingly the drawings are only rarely found to be present in such copies, and even less frequently are they untouched.

French publishers, among them Lafitte and John M. Raphael, showed interest in publishing the Peeps in French, though Hachette opined that there would be no market for them in France. The twelve that were produced in France under the series title Les Beaux Voyages included new texts rather than translations, and were written by French authors who included among their number Judith Gautier, who had a close relationship with Richard Wagner in the 1870s.

In addition three Peeps titles were produced in Spanish, using the text written for the French editions; and a further eight or nine in Portuguese, the bulk of these being sold to A. Moura of Rio de Janeiro. Neither the Historic Library nor the British Library contain copies of these titles. One Peep (*India*) was also translated into Welsh, and a further translation into French, of *The South Seas (Melanesia)* under the title *Un Tour en Mélanésie*, turns up in a series called Contes et Nouvelles, also published by Les Art Graphiques but looking exactly like an oversize Peep. The other four books in this series, translations of A & C Black children's books, were published on a joint profits basis with the French publisher. None is present in the Historic Library, and details are based on copies in the British Library.

Tales of English Minsters (eight titles published during 1910 and 1911) is similar in format to the Peeps, but contains fewer illustrations; they were written by Elizabeth Grierson.

PICTURES OF MANY LANDS

The colour books make a distinct overlap with the firm's educational activities in the large format ($9\frac{3}{4}'' \times 7''$) Pictures books, published during 1910-16, which combined photographs and colour illustrations on the same sheet in a rather unattractive manner. Most of the seventeen titles were written by H. Clive Barnard or Clothilde von Wyss and combined

5,000-10,000 words of simple description of the country or countries concerned with up to 60 illustrations, around half of them in colour. The standard of colour printing in these books is distinctly below par; but then some of the colour blocks had by this time had many outings.

One further use of many of the colour blocks was made in a series of portfolios called Travel Pictures; these too combined colour and black and white illustrations on the same sheet in the same way as the Pictures series. They were intended purely for educational purposes with questions and problems listed for children to solve.

BLACK'S BEAUTIFUL POSTCARDS

These were 'Of British Design and Manufacture', so stated the prospectus firmly.

A & C Black published over 90 series of postcards using material from the colour plate books. Most were issued in sets of six contained in a buff envelope. Around twenty of these sets were reproduced from drawings used in the Artists' Sketch Book Series.

In addition to those published by A & C Black themselves, a large number were also issued by Raphael Tuck. Over 90 series of postcards from A & C Black books have been identified as issued by Tuck, while among other postcard publishers to reproduce A & C Black illustrations were J. Salmon, J. Henderson & Sons, Pictograph Publishing Co., Robert Peel Postcard Company, Wrench, G. Ajelli and E. F. Rochat.

* * *

Other bindings
Almost every collector will possess one or more A & C Black books in a binding other than the publisher's standard one. Among these are books produced in the USA and normally issued by Macmillan but sometimes by other publishers such as Charles H. Bowman; books rebound by the Times Book Club in plain cloth but whose title pages retain the A & C Black imprint; books, among them *Oriental Carpets*, which appeared under the London Press Exchange imprint; and books rebound in a variety of forms by such major stores as the Army and Navy. A few examples of the latter are shown in the Army and Navy Stores catalogue of 1907 reissued a few years ago by David & Charles under the title *Yesterday's Shopping*. This illustrates *Egypt* rebound in half-polished levant morocco with vellum sides and an Egyptian flag in colour on the front with a specially

designed hand worked spine, which was priced at £3 3s; the same style of binding without the inlaid design on the spine cost £2 2s. Copies of books were also specially bound for W. H. Smith, for Burns & Oates and for other publishers and bookshops.

Foreign editions

In addition to instances mentioned earlier, books that may have been translated into other languages include the following: *Morocco* in French (Hachette); *Japan* in French (Hachette or Uzanne); *Tibet and Nepal* in German (Brockhaus, Leipzig); *Japan* and *The Holy Land* in German (Deutsche Verlags-Anstalt, Stuttgart); *India* and *Egypt* in German; *Canada* in French and Spanish; *London Vanished and Vanishing* in French (Uzanne).

Rejections

Among the books that were turned down by the publisher during the first years of the century were: *London Churches* by Ernest Thesiger; a book on the Japanese war by William Wyllie; *Bridges over the Thames* by H. Sandham; *Mexico* by Henderson and Forrest; *The Thames* by A. R. Quinton (this was published by Dent in 1907); *Norfolk* by Nico Jungman or Waterfield; *Surrey* by a Mr Gregory; *Cathedral Cities of England* by Mr Collins. Also rejected was a suggestion for a book of ghost stories by Algernon Blackwood and for a book called *Dudley Jones* by P. G. Wodehouse (A & C Black, of course, published most of Wodehouse's early work). A book on gardens by Mortimer Menpes, containing 100 illustrations was advertised in 1904 but did not appear.

The usual rejection letter to artists was carefuly calculated not to offend: 'We have examined your pictures but regret to say that we do not find them quite suitable for our process.'

The publisher's judgment on this seems to have been careful and sound. Weighing up the possibility of the book on Mexico, Adam Black wrote to George Brett of Macmillan, New York, that Forrest and Henderson had returned from Mexico wanting to do a 20s book when a 7s 6d book had been arranged before they left: 'They say Mexico is full of wealthy people & that an edition de luxe at 2 pounds could be sold in hundreds. Never having sold a single book in Mexico I could only doubt & say nothing but luckily remembered you would know all about it so they departed to await your answer. It must be remembered that Mr Forrest is not an absolutely first-class artist.' The Mexico project did not go ahead.

Front and back of a Scottish Widows' Fund bookmark of a type still frequently found in A & C Black colour books

Scottish Widows

It is still quite common to find Scottish Widows' Fund Assurance book-marks in copies of A & C Black colour books. The clue to why the insurance company made such widespread use of this form of publicity may lie in a letter from Adam Black in December 1906 to A. H. Turnbull of Edinburgh. Addressed to 'My dear Uncle', Adam suggests that he might write a book as 'late manager of the Scottish Widows' Fund Life Assurance Society'.

Bibliography

BY COLIN INMAN AND HUGH CLOOSTERMAN

Notes

This bibliography lists the colour plate books produced by A & C Black between 1901 and about 1930. Where a series was first published before 1930, titles issued during the 1930s have been listed, but not those published later. Books first published without colour plates but which acquired them in reprints have largely been omitted. For this reason the Black's Guides are not included: they would in any case be better listed as part of a bibliography of travel guides. Books with only the frontispiece in colour are also omitted.

The many children's fiction and fairy tale books are not included: these would form a suitable subject for a separate bibliography. The various Peeps series, however, are listed here: they include many of the illustrations first used in other series, and many of the authors of books in the major series also produced texts for the Peeps. The general aim has been to record books which made further use of the illustrations first published in the 20s and 7s 6d series.

SOURCES
A & C Black's Historic Library at Eaton Socon has been used as the basis for the bibliography. A copy of most of the books listed was deposited in this library at the time of publication, a bookplate stuck to the front endpaper giving basic details such as price, print number, size, etc. These are not invariably accurate.

Where the Historic Library contains no copy, other collectors' libraries or copyright libraries have been consulted. (Information on the two series of books in French is based on copies in the British Library.) Other major sources used are the publisher's Publication Book, which runs from the 1890s to 1925, and a number of ledgers, which give information about the publication of some titles. These ledgers cover the period from 1910, in greater or less detail depending, it seems, on which member of staff was making the entries.

The records of the printer R & R Clark, which are held in the National Library of Scotland, have also been consulted.

NUMBERING
The numbering of the books is not continuous to enable each series to begin at a number ending in 1; thus the 20s series is numbered 1-92, the 12s 6d series 101-104, the 10s series 111-114, etc. The gaps created will give readers who wish to disagree with the author's assignment of books to particular series the opportunity to make their own rearrangement; and will afford the opportunity for similar books to be appended to the lists.

TERMINOLOGY
The modern use of the term 'edition' refers to all copies of a book printed from the same typesetting and plates. Using this definition only a few of the books listed here reached a second edition, since almost all reprints were taken from moulds made from the original type. 'Impression' refers to all copies bound from sheets printed at one time; thus what A & C Black referred to as a second edition we would today call a second impression. 'Issue' has been taken to refer to copies of a book bound at the same time and in the same style.

TITLES
Books are listed alphabetically within series in a style roughly corresponding to that used by the publisher. Thus *The Scenery of London* will be found under L rather than S.

AUTHORS AND ARTISTS
It was A & C Black's practice to print the artist's name before the author's — perhaps justifiably since it was the illustrations that were responsible for the books' popularity, the texts being regarded as necessary but secondary. However, in the lists that follow the author's name is placed first, largely because listing by author is standard practice among libraries and booksellers; to list by artist would cause unnecessary confusion.

Artists' and authors' names are given only when they appear on the book's title page or in the list of illustrations. In instances where a book is illustrated by a known artist whose name is not mentioned in the book — for instance in the Beautiful Britain series — the name is printed within square brackets. Where numerous artists' illustrations are used in a book their names have been omitted.

DATES
The publication date of a book has been taken as that given on the bookplate in the Historic Library copy; the lists indicate where this varies from the date printed in the book. Dates of reprints have been obtained from the publisher's ledgers and from the books themselves.

COPIES PRINTED
To A & C Black an 'edition' was 3,000 copies and the bulk of the books listed here were produced in a first printing of 3,000. The bookplates in the Historic Library copies have been regarded as the primary source, except in instances where the Publication Book and ledgers show them to be wrong.

It was common practice for 40 'over' copies per 1,000 to be produced, to allow for wastage, but this figure has only been quoted where the ledgers show that the full 3,120 rather than 3,000 copies were bound up for sale.

In the frequent cases where the ledgers cite different figures for the number of copies printed of text, illustrations, wrappers, tissues, etc, the lowest number is used.

BOOK SIZES

The sizes given for the books are book sizes in millimetres, with the height given first. Minor variations within a series have been ignored: thus the standard size for the 20s books is 228 × 159 mm, the average size for this series, despite the fact that a few (*Kent, John Pettie*, etc.) are usually found to be a few millimetres oversize.

A & C Black's publicity referred to this standard size as 'square demy octavo'. However, a demy sheet of 17½″ × 22½″ would produce an octavo page size of 8¾″ × 5⅝″, not the 8¾″ × 6⅛″ that results from measuring a 20s series book.

PAGINATION

The expression +1, +2 etc after the figure for a book's pagination refers to advertisements that are bound in as part of the collation. Advertisements printed on different paper (usually thinner and whiter) are not referred to; in any case these did not appear in first issues.

MAPS

The word 'map' has been used to refer to a single page map printed on a page of the book; 'folding map' refers to maps glued in at the end of many books.

CLOTHS AND COLOURS

The colour of a book's cloth is rarely itself a determinant of a particular state, which is more easily identified by such factors as the absence of gilt titling on the front. The cloth colours have therefore only been broadly described in the lists. Where possible relation has been made to Winsor and Newton's oil and water-colour charts, but these charts have been defeated by many of the colours used, particularly the wide range of blues. But in most instances where slight variations occur — as in *Egypt* — a book's title pages record the relevant issue.

DECORATION AND TITLING

Details of the colours used in the cover designs have been broadly indicated, but only in a few instances in the major series has the precise nature of the designs themselves been described. To have done so, as the *India* example quoted in the text shows, would have required access to Turbayne's notes.

Titling and decoration are described as 'blocked' where there is clear evidence of an indentation, indicating that a blocking press using either gold or coloured foil has been employed. Where this is not the case (and in cases of doubt) the word 'printed' has been used.

ILLUSTRATIONS

In the 20s series the plates were normally printed on rectos, the frontispiece on the verso. The captions might be either recto or verso, but were uniform throughout a book, with the frontispiece caption printed on the opposite leaf to those in the rest of the book. In a few instances the positioning of the captions can be used to identify a particular issue, so this information has been included. In other series the plates were often printed left and right alternately or randomly.

REPRINTS
The dates and numbers of reprints are stated where known. Where it is known that
the title pages were altered to show a reprint date, this fact is stated. In some cases,
however, the only apparent difference between the first issue and a reprint is the
absence of gilt from the front cover of the reprint. The Claflin reprints referred to
usually consisted of 3,000 copies specially ordered for the American market.

DUST WRAPPERS
Dust wrappers accompanied most of the books published from 1905 onwards; they
are occasionally seen but are not referred to in the lists.

Books in the Beautiful Britain, Water-Colour and Artists' Sketch Book series
were issued in boxes during 1914 and 1915 only; the lists indicate the relevant titles.

COMMON FACTORS
Where aspects of a series (book size, edition number, etc.) are common to a whole
series, this information is printed at the top of the relevant list rather than being
repeated for each entry.

The 20 Shilling Series

1. Algeria and Tunis painted and described by Frances E. Nesbitt. June 1 1906;
2,000 copies.
228 × 159mm; ix, 229pp +2.
Blue cloth with a design printed in orange, green and cream on the front and spine;
titling blocked in gilt on the front and spine; top edge gilt.
70 full page illustrations in colour captioned on the tissue versos.

2. The Alps by Sir Martin Conway; painted by A. D. McCormick. June 7 1904;
3,200 copies.
228 × 159mm; x, 294pp.
Blue grey cloth with pictorial designs printed in light green and white on the front
and spine; titling blocked in gilt on the front and spine; top edge gilt.
70 full page illustrations in colour captioned on the tissue rectos.
Reprinted 1911 (3,000 copies; a Claflin reprint).
Note: The text was reissued in 1910 at 3s 6d, illustrated with photographs taken by
L. Edna Walter.

3. Argentina Past and Present by W. H. Koebel; painted by E. W. Christmas. Nov 6
1914; 3,000 copies.
254 × 165mm; xx, 465pp +2; index; folding map in colour.
Brown cloth with a design printed in blue, brown and cream on the front and spine;
titling blocked in gilt on the spine; top edge gilt.
32 full page illustrations in colour and 64 in black and white from photographs.
Note: This book is a reprint of *Argentina Past and Present* published by Kegan
Paul Trench, Truebner & Co in 1910, which was illustrated only by photographs.

4. Australia by Frank Fox; painted by Percy F. S. Spence. Nov 11 1910; 3,000 copies.
228 × 159mm; xii, 219pp; index; folding map.
Blue cloth with a design blocked in gilt and printed in green on the front and spine; titling blocked in gilt on the front and spine; top edge gilt.
75 full page illustrations in colour captioned on the tissue versos.

5. Belgium by G. W. T. Omond; painted by A. Forestier. Aug 28 1908; 1,000 copies.
228 × 159mm; ix, 390pp; index; folding map.
Black cloth with a heraldic design printed in yellow on the front within yellow and orange borders and a design printed in yellow and orange on the spine; titling blocked in gilt on the spine.
77 full page illustrations in colour captioned on the tissue versos.
Reprinted 1914 (twice, 3,000 copies each, the second reprint to sell at 7s 6d); 1915 (5,000 copies to sell at 7s 6d); 1916 (2,000 copies to sell at 8s); 1918 (3,200 copies).
Note: The shield on the title page is in black in the first impression, in red in all reprints.

6. Birds of Britain by J. Lewis Bonhote; painted by H. E. Dresser. Dec 13 1907; 3,000 copies.
228 × 159mm; xii, 405pp; index.
Brown cloth with a pictorial design printed in magenta, olive green and black on the front and spine; titling blocked in gilt on the front and spine.
100 full page illustrations in colour, taken from Dresser's *Birds of Europe*, captioned on the tissue versos.
Reprinted April 1912 (3,000 copies); June 1912 (3,200 copies); Dec 1912 (3,000 copies); 1914 (3,000 copies); 1917 (3,000 copies).

7. British Water-Colour Art by Marcus B. Huish; illustrated by drawings presented to King Edward VII and Queen Alexandra at their coronation by the Royal Society of Painters in Water Colours. Sept 23 1904; 3,000 copies.
228 × 159mm; xv, 218pp; index.
Blue cloth with a design blocked in gilt and printed in red on the front and spine; titling blocked in gilt on the front and spine; top edge gilt.
60 full page illustrations in colour captioned on the tissue rectos; one in black and white from a photograph; and a folding facsimile of the address to the presentation.
The Fine Art Society appears on the title page as joint publisher.

8. Brittany by Dorothy Menpes; painted by Mortimer Menpes. July 12 1905; 3,000 copies.
228 × 159mm; ix, 254 pp.
Mauve cloth with a fishing and agriculture motif blocked in gilt on the front and printed in olive and light green on the front and spine; titling blocked in gilt on the front and spine; top edge gilt.
75 full page illustrations in colour captioned on the tissue versos.
Reprinted 1912 (3,000 copies dated 1912).

Note: One of a number of books also issued in plain cloth binding by the Times Book Club, an arrangement which was discontinued when the latter was found to be undercutting the publisher's price.

9. Buckinghamshire and Berkshire by G.E. Mitton; painted by Sutton Palmer. Feb 11 1920; 3,000 copies; published at 25s.
228 × 159mm; ix, 232pp; index; folding map.
Chrome green cloth with a pictorial design printed in olive green, light green and black on the front and spine; titling blocked in gilt on the spine.
60 full page illustrations in colour captioned on the tissue versos.

10. Burma painted and described by R. Talbot Kelly. Nov 10 1905; 3,000 copies.
228 × 159mm; xv, 261pp; index; folding map.
Maroon cloth with a pictorial design blocked in gilt and printed in red and light green on the front and spine; titling blocked in gilt on the front and spine; top edge gilt.
75 full page illustrations in colour captioned on the tissue versos.
Reprinted 1912 (3,200 copies, dated 1912).

11. Cambridge by M.A.R. Tuker; painted by William Matthison. May 3 1907; 3,000 copies.
228 × 159mm; xx, 396pp; two indexes; folding town plan.
Blue cloth with a design blocked in gilt and printed in pale green and brown on the front and spine; titling blocked in gilt on the front and spine; top edge gilt.
77 full page illustrations in colour captioned on the tissue versos.
Reprinted 1912 (3,150 copies, dated 1907).

12. Canada by Wilfred Campbell; painted by T. Mower Martin. May 8 1907; 3,000 copies.
228 × 159mm; xviii, 272pp; index; folding map.
Purple cloth with a design blocked in gilt and printed in green and light purple on the front and spine; titling blocked in gilt on the front and spine; top edge gilt.
77 full page illustrations in colour captioned on the tissue versos.
Reprinted 1911 (3,000 copies); 1912 (3,000 copies). It is likely that both reprints bear the 1907 date.

13. The Channel Islands by Edith F. Carey; painted by Henry B. Wimbush. Oct 20 1904; 3,000 copies.
228 × 159mm; xiii, 294pp; index; folding map.
Prussian blue cloth with a design blocked in gilt on the front and printed in green and orange on the front and spine; titling blocked in gilt on the front and spine; top edge gilt.
76 full page illustrations in colour captioned on the tissue rectos.

14. The Clyde by Neil Munro; painted by Mary Y. Hunter and J. Young Hunter. Dec 5 1907; 3,000 copies.

228 × 159mm; xi, 206pp; index; folding map.
Cyanine blue cloth with a design of seahorses, trident and agricultural motifs blocked in gilt and printed in pale green, blue and brown on the front and a design printed in pale green, blue and brown on the spine; titling blocked in gilt on the front and spine; top edge gilt.
67 full page illustrations in colour captioned on the tissue versos.
Reprinted 1915 (3,000 copies, dated 1907, to sell at 7s 6d).

15. Constantinople by Professor Alexander van Millingen; painted by Warwick Goble. May 8 1906; 3,000 copies.
228 × 159mm; ix, 282pp; index; folding map.
Fawn cloth with a design blocked in gilt and printed in green and brown on the front and spine; titling blocked in gilt on the front and spine; top edge gilt.
63 full page illustrations in colour captioned on the tissue versos.
Reprinted 1915 (3,200 copies, dated 1906, to sell at 7s 6d).

16. Cruikshank's Water-Colours with an introduction by Joseph Grego; illustrated by George Cruikshank. Dec 15 1903; 3,000 copies.
228 × 159mm; xxvii, 328pp.
Brown cloth with a design printed in light brown on the front and spine; titling blocked in gilt on the front and spine; top edge gilt.
67 full page illustrations in colour captioned on the tissue rectos and one woodcut.
Note: The text consists of extracts from *Oliver Twist* by Charles Dickens, *The Miser's Daughter* by William Harrison Ainsworth and *The History of the Irish Rebellion in 1798* by W. H. Maxwell.

17. From Damascus to Palmyra by Rev. John Kelman; painted by Margaret Thomas. Nov 4 1908; 3,000 copies.
228 × 159mm; xvi, 368pp; index; folding map.
White textured cloth with a design printed in green, blue and brown on the front and spine; titling blocked in gilt on the front and spine; top edge gilt.
70 full page illustrations in colour captioned on the tissue versos.

18. The Durbar by Dorothy Menpes; painted by Mortimer Menpes. Sept 29 1903; 5,000 copies.
228 × 159mm; xii, 210pp.
Brown cloth with a design blocked in gilt and printed in orange and blue on the front and spine; titling blocked in gilt on the front and spine; top edge gilt.
100 full page illustrations in colour captioned on the tissue rectos.

19. Egypt painted and described by R. Talbot Kelly. Nov 10 1902; 3,000 copies.
228 × 159mm; xiii, 240pp.
Cobalt blue cloth with a design blocked in gilt and printed in yellow ochre and green on the front and spine; titling blocked in gilt on the front and spine; top edge gilt.
75 full page illustrations in colour captioned on the tissue rectos.

Reprinted Feb 1903 (3,200 copies); with slight corrections Feb 1904 (xvi, 246pp; index; glossary); with additional corrections Oct 1906 (4,000 copies); with new preface July 1910 (2,000 copies); March 1912 (3,200 copies); 1918 (3,000 copies). A number of shades of blue cloth were used for the reprints; all are clearly dated.

20. Egyptian Birds painted and described by Charles Whymper. Oct 22 1909; 3,000 copies.
228 × 159mm; x, 221pp; index.
Fawn cloth with a design blocked in gilt and printed in red and green on the front and spine; titling blocked in gilt on the front and spine; top edge gilt.
51 full page illustrations in colour captioned on the tissue versos and 11 line drawings in the text.

21. England by Sir Frank Fox; [painted by various artists]. Aug 15 1919 (book dated 1918); 3,000 copies.
228 × 159mm; xiii, 206pp; index; map.
Red cloth with a design printed in dark red and green on the front and spine; titling blocked in gilt on the spine.
64 full page illustrations in colour captioned on the tissue versos.
Note: First published with 32 illustrations as part of the Fascination of Europe series; the illustrations were taken from earlier volumes in the colour book series.

22. Happy England by Marcus B. Huish; painted by Helen Allingham. Sept 29 1903; 5,000 copies.
228 × 159mm; xi, 204pp.
Prussian blue cloth with a floral design printed in green and red on the front and spine; titling blocked in gilt on the front and spine; top edge gilt.
80 full page illustrations in colour captioned on the tissue rectos; frontispiece portrait in black and white.
Reprinted as follows:
Nov 1904 (3,000 copies, dated on title page and verso; plates captioned on tissue versos; alterations were made to pp118-130 in this and subsequent reprints).
Dec 1909 (2,150 copies); 241 × 178mm; dark red cloth with a design in red and green printed on the front and spine; titling blocked in gilt on the front and spine; top edge gilt; 80 full page illustrations in colour captioned on the tissue versos; the photograph of Mrs Allingham has been omitted. This reprint, to a larger size than standard for the series, was hurriedly issued to compete with *The Cottage Homes of England* by Stewart Dick and Helen Allingham which had just been published by Edward Arnold.
Dec 1913 (5,520 copies, bearing the 1909 date).
Note: Reprints in red cloth dated 1909 can be found in both larger and standard formats; in the absence of evidence to the contrary, it seems probable that the 1913 reprint was bound in red cloth at the standard 228 × 159mm size.

23. The Rivers and Streams of England by A. G. Bradley; painted by Sutton Palmer. Nov 26 1909; 3,000 copies.
228 × 159mm; xiii, 287pp; index; folding map.

Prussian blue cloth with a design blocked in gilt and printed in green and white on the front and a similar design printed in green and white on the spine; titling blocked in gilt on the front and spine; top edge gilt.
75 full page illustrations in colour captioned on the tissue versos.
Reprinted Sept 1914 (3,000 copies, dated 1909).

24. English Costume painted and described by Dion Clayton Calthrop. May 8 1907; 1,000 copies.
228 × 159mm; xvi, 463pp.
Plum cloth with a pictorial design printed in blue, olive green and tint on the front and spine; titling blocked in gilt on the front and spine; top edge gilt.
70 full page illustrations in colour captioned on the tissue versos; 32 half-tone reproductions (on 8 pages) of engravings by Wenceslaus Hollar; 60 half-tone reproductions in black and white (on 15 pages) of wash drawings, 48 by Calthrop and 12 by Robert and Denis Dighton; and numerous line drawings by Calthrop throughout the text.
Reprinted 1913 (3,000 copies); 1917 (3,000 copies); 1923 (3,000 copies; 225 × 143mm; 61 illustrations in colour); 1926 (3,000 copies); 1931 (3,000 copies); 1937 (3,000 copies); also 1941; 1946; 1950.
Note: The contents of this book were first published in four volumes in the 7s 6d series in 1906. It was reprinted in smaller format and with fewer illustrations on a number of occasions up to the 1950s.

25. The English Lakes by W. T. Palmer; painted by A. Heaton Cooper. Aug 2 1905 (book dated July 1905); 3,000 copies.
228 × 159mm; ix, 232pp; index; map.
Blue grey cloth with a design blocked in green and printed in orange and white on the front and spine; titling blocked in gilt on the front and spine; top edge gilt.
75 full page illustrations in colour captioned on the tissue versos.
Reprinted 1905; 1908; 1911 (3,900 copies); 1913 (twice, 3,090 and 3,200 copies); 1918 (3,000 copies).

26. Essex by A. R. Hope Moncrieff; painted by L. Burleigh Bruhl. May 12 1909; 3,000 copies.
228 × 159mm; xii, 262pp; index; folding map.
Vandyke brown cloth with a design printed in red, green and white on the front and in red and green on the spine; titling blocked in gilt on the front and spine; top edge gilt.
75 full page illustrations in colour captioned on the tissue versos.

27. Florence and some Tuscan Cities by Clarissa Goff; painted by Colonel R. C. Goff. Feb 23 1905; 3,000 copies.
228 ×159mm; xii, 262pp; index.
Carmine cloth with a design printed in light brown, white and black on the front and in light brown and black on the spine; titling blocked in gilt on the front and spine; top edge gilt.

75 full page illustrations in colour captioned on the tissue versos.
Reprinted June 1911 (3,000 copies; a Claflin reprint); Aug 1912 (3,200 copies). All copies bear the 1905 date.

28. Birket Foster by H. M. Cundall; illustrated by Birket Foster. Nov 29 1906; 3,000 copies.
228 × 159mm; xx, 216pp; index.
Blue cloth with a design blocked in gilt and printed in green, orange and white on the front and spine; titling blocked in gilt on the front and spine; top edge gilt. 73 full page illustrations in colour captioned on the tissue versos; 20 full page illustrations in black and white; 58 smaller illustrations throughout the text, mostly from pencil drawings, two by F. S. Walker.
Reprinted Sept 1930 (3,000 copies); all copies are dated 1906 but advertisements for the New series — and the absence of gilt on the front — enable reprints to be dated.

29. France by Gordon Home; painted by Mortimer Menpes and others. Feb 24 1919 (book dated 1918); 3,000 copies.
228 × 159mm; ix, 219pp; index; map.
Red cloth with a design printed in pink on the front and spine; titling blocked in gilt on the spine.
64 full page illustrations in colour captioned on the tissue versos.
Note: First published with 32 illustrations as part of the Fascination of Europe series; the illustrations were taken from earlier volumes in the colour book series.

30. The Lake of Geneva by Francis Gribble; painted by J. Hardwicke Lewis and May Hardwicke Lewis. Sept 15 1909; 1,000 copies.
228 × 159mm; x, 360pp; index; folding map.
Blue cloth with a design printed in green on the front and spine; titling blocked in gilt on the front and spine; top edge gilt.
60 full page illustrations in colour captioned on the tissue rectos.
Note: The three sections of the book were also published as separate volumes in the 7s 6d series.

31. Germany by Rev. J.F. Dickie; painted by E.T. Compton and E. Harrison Compton. Oct 15 1912. 3,000 copies.
228 × 159mm; x, 227pp; index; folding map.
Light brown cloth with a design based on the Prussian eagle printed in black, brown and white and blocked in gilt on the front and a design based on the iron cross printed in black, brown and white on the spine; titling blocked in gilt on the spine.
75 full illustrations in colour captioned on the tissue versos.

32. Greece by Rev. J.A. McClymont; painted by John Fulleylove. May 8 1906; 3,000 copies.
228 × 159mm; xii, 235pp; index; map.

Navy blue cloth with a design blocked in gilt and printed in brown and white on the front and spine; titling blocked in gilt on the front and spine; top edge gilt. 75 full page illustrations in colour captioned on the tissue versos.

33. Kate Greenaway by M.H. Spielmann and G.S. Layard. Oct 30 1905; 3,000 copies.
228 × 159mm; xx, 301pp; index.
Deep blue cloth with a design printed in light blue, green and orange on the front and spine; titling blocked in gilt on the front and spine; top edge gilt.
52 full page illustrations by Kate Greenaway in colour captioned on the tissue versos; 34 full page illustrations in black and white from photographs and line drawings; and 56 thumbnail and other sketches throughout the text; Kate Greenaway endpapers from a wallpaper design.
Reprinted Dec 1905 (with Greenaway endpapers); Oct 1913 (3,000 copies, dated 1905 but without Greenaway endpapers).

34. Hampshire by Rev. Telford Varley; painted by Wilfrid Ball. April 1909, 3,000 copies.
228 × 159mm; xi, 316pp; index; folding map.
Green cloth with a design printed in light green, pink and black on the front and spine; titling blocked in gilt on the front and spine; top edge gilt.
75 full page illustrations in colour captioned on the tissue versos.
Reprinted 1915 (3,000 copies, dated 1909, to sell at 7s 6d).

35. Holland by Beatrix Jungman; painted by Nico Jungman. Aug 19 1904; 3,000 copies.
228 × 159mm; ix, 212pp +4.
Pale blue cloth with a pictorial design blocked in gilt and printed in orange and green on the front and spine; titling blocked in gilt on the front and spine; top edge gilt.
75 full page illustrations in colour captioned on the tissue versos.
Reprinted May 1911 (3,200 copies; a Claflin reprint); 1912 (3,120 copies).

36. The Holy Land by Rev. John Kelman; painted by John Fulleylove. Oct 3 1902; 3,000 copies.
228 × 159mm; xv, 302pp +2; index.
Prussian blue cloth with a design blocked in gilt and printed in green on the front and spine; titling blocked in gilt on the front and spine; top edge gilt.
92 full page illustrations (77 in colour, 15 in black and white) captioned on the tissue versos.
Reprinted 1904 (2,000 copies); June 1911 (3,450 copies; a Claflin reprint); Sept 1912 (3,200 copies); Nov 1913 (3,000 copies); Feb 1917. All reprints contain 93 illustrations, No. 93, Syrian Women at a Fountain, having been added. This was used in the prospectus for the book but omitted in error from the first impression.
Note: The text only was published separately in 1909 at 3s 6d.

37. Hungary by Adrian Stokes; painted by Adrian and Marianne Stokes. Nov 19 1909; 3,000 copies.
228 × 159mm; xix, 320pp; index; folding map.
White cloth with an armorial design blocked in gilt and printed in green and red on the front and a design printed in green and red on the spine; titling blocked in gilt on the front and spine; top edge gilt.
75 full page illustrations in colour captioned on the tissue versos.

38. India by Flora Annie Steel; painted by Mortimer Menpes. Dec 1 1905 (book dated November); 3,000 copies.
228 × 159mm; xii, 216pp; index.
Crimson cloth with a peacock design blocked in gilt on the front and an ornamental design printed in green and yellow ochre on the front and spine; titling blocked in gilt on the front and spine; top edge gilt.
75 full page illustrations in colour captioned on the tissue versos.
Reprinted Feb 1912 (3,000 copies); 1916 (1,000 copies, to sell at 8s); 1917 (2,000 copies).

39. The Armies of India by Major G. F. MacMunn; painted by Major A. C. Lovett; with a foreword by Field-Marshal Earl Roberts. Oct 6 1911; 3,000 copies.
228 × 159mm; xiv, 224pp; index.
Blue cloth with designs blocked in gilt and blind on the front and spine; titling blocked in gilt on the front and spine; top edge gilt.
72 full page illustrations in colour captioned on the tissue versos; and 20 small line illustrations.
Reprinted 1915 (3,000 copies to sell at 7s 6d).
Note: Later variants may have the titling in yellow on the front; the plates tipped on grey mounts (as in the large paper edition); and red cloth with decoration in blind on the front and spine.

40. Southern India by F. E. Penny; painted by Lady Lawley. Nov 10 1914; 3,000 copies.
228 × 159mm; xi, 257pp +2; index; folding map.
Orange grained cloth with an ornamental design blocked in brown and printed in black and yellow on the front and printed in black and yellow on the spine; titling blocked in gilt on the front and spine; top edge gilt.
50 full page illustrations in colour captioned on the tissue versos.

41. Insect Life by C. A. Ealand. Feb 15 1921; 3,000 copies; published at 30s.
228 × 159mm; xii, 340pp; index.
Fawn cloth with a pictorial design blocked in brown and printed in green and cream on the front and spine; titling blocked in brown on the front and in gilt on the spine.
74 full page illustrations, 50 in colour from nature and 24 from photographs taken by the author; also numerous line drawings throughout the text.

42. Ireland by Frank Mathew; painted by Francis S. Walker. May 5 1906; 3,000 copies.
228 × 159mm; xix, 212pp; index.
Green cloth with a harp blocked in gilt on the front and a shamrock design printed in lighter green on the front and spine; titling blocked in gilt on the front and spine; top edge gilt.
79 full page illustrations in colour captioned on the tissue versos.
Reprinted 1911 (1,000 copies); 1912 (3,240 copies) in light green cloth with the shamrock design in darker green.
Note: Only 1,300 copies of the 1906 impression were sold, the remaining 1,700 being cut down to produce the 6s series *Ireland.*

43. Ireland by Frank Mathew; painted by A. Heaton Cooper. June 27 1916; 3,000 copies; published at 8s.
228 × 159mm; xix, 212pp; index.
Dark blue cloth with a harp and shamrock design printed in green and yellow; titling blocked in gilt on the spine.
50 full page illustrations in colour captioned on the tissue versos.
Note: Text the same as No. 42.

44. The Italian Lakes by Richard Bagot; painted by Ella Du Cane. Oct 30 1905; 3,000 copies.
228 × 159mm; xi, 201pp; index.
Light blue cloth with a design blocked in gilt and printed in green, mauve and yellow on the front and spine; titling blocked in gilt on the front and spine; top edge gilt.
68 full page illustrations in colour captioned on the tissue versos.
Reprinted 1908 (2,000 copies); 1911 (3,000 copies; a Claflin reprint); 1912 (3,200 copies); 1913 (3,000 copies); 1916 (3,000 copies to sell at 8s). The publication date was not changed on the 1913 and 1916 reprints; thus copies are most often found bearing the 1912 date.

45. Italy by Frank Fox; painted by Alberto Pisa and others.
Sept 2 1918; 3,000 copies.
228 × 159mm; xi, 207pp; index; map.
Light blue cloth with a design of vines and grapes printed in purple, green and yellow on the front and spine; titling blocked in gilt on the spine.
64 full page illustrations in colour captioned on the tissue versos.
Note: First published with 32 illustrations as part of the Fascination of Europe series; illustrations by Alberto Pisa, George Flemwell, Mortimer Menpes, Mima Nixon, Col R. C. Goff, William Scott, Ella Du Cane, etc. were taken from earlier colour plate books.

46. Japan by Dorothy Menpes; painted by Mortimer Menpes. Dec 7 1901; 3,200 copies.
228 × 159mm; xiv, 207pp.

Blue cloth with a design blocked in gilt and printed in pink on the front and spine; titling blocked in gilt on the front and spine; top edge gilt.
100 illustrations in colour captioned on the tissue rectos.
Reprinted 1902 (2,080 copies); Feb 1903 (2,100 copies); 1904 (2,080 copies); 1905 (3,000 copies); 1911 (3,000 copies; a Claflin reprint); 1914 (3,120 copies).

Notes:
1. The number of illustrations was reduced to 75 in 1905, though copies dated 1905 can be found with 100, 75 and 50 illustrations.

2. The 1902 reprint has no tissues, the plates being captioned on the back. This practice was soon abandoned.

47. Ancient Tales and Folklore of Japan by Richard Gordon Smith; [painted by Mo-No-Yuki from sketches by Richard Gordon Smith]. Nov 4 1908; 3,000 copies.
228 × 159mm; xv, 361pp.
Grey cloth with a design blocked in gilt on the front and printed in yellow, white and black on the front and spine; titling blocked in gilt on the front and spine; top edge gilt.
60 full page illustrations in colour (62 subjects) captioned on the tissue versos.

48. The Flowers and Gardens of Japan by Florence Du Cane; painted by Ella Du Cane. Oct 2 1908; 3,000 copies.
228 × 159mm; x, 249pp.
Green cloth with a pictorial design printed in dark green on the front and spine; titling blocked in gilt on the front and spine; top edge gilt.
50 full page illustrations in colour captioned on the tissue versos.
Reprinted June 1911 (3,000 copies; a Claflin reprint); Feb 1914 (3,000 copies to sell at 7s 6d); all copies are dated 1908.
Notes: The reprints were bound in white cloth with the decoration printed in green; and in blue grey cloth. It was intended to market the book in 'a handsome box with one of the illustrations on the outside'. No copy has been seen to verify this.

49. Kashmir by Sir Francis Younghusband; painted by Major E. Molyneaux. Sept 24 1909; 3,000 copies.
228 × 159mm; xv, 283pp; index; folding map in colour.
Dark red cloth with a design printed in blue, orange and yellow on the front and spine; titling blocked in gilt on the front and spine; top edge gilt.
70 full page illustrations in colour captioned on the tissue versos.
Reprinted 1911 (3,000 copies, dated 1909; a Claflin reprint); 1917 (3,000 copies).

50. Kent by W. Teignmouth Shore; painted by W. Biscombe Gardner. Oct 11 1907; 3,000 copies.
228 × 159mm; x, 240pp; index; folding map.
Green cloth with a hop design blocked in black and printed in light and olive green on the front and spine; titling blocked in gilt on the front and spine; top edge gilt.
73 full page illustrations in colour captioned on the tissue versos.

51. London by A. R. Hope Moncrieff; [painted by various artists.] Dec 1916; 3,000 copies.
228 × 159mm; viii, 312pp; index; folding plan.
Red cloth with a design printed in yellow on the front and spine; titling printed in yellow on the front and spine.
60 full page illustrations in colour captioned on the tissue versos.
Note: Text first published in the Fascination of Europe series; illustrations by J. H. Hartley, John Fulleylove, W. L. Wyllie, L. Deller, Herbert Marshall, Gordon Home, Rose Barton, Mima Nixon and Allan Stewart were taken from earlier colour plate books.

52. Familiar London painted and described by Rose Barton. Nov 22 1904; 3,000 copies.
228 × 159mm; xii, 208pp.
Dark red cloth with a design printed in red, green and yellow on the front and spine; titling blocked in gilt on the front and spine; top edge gilt.
61 full page illustrations in colour captioned on the tissue rectos.

53. London to the Nore painted and described by W. L. Wyllie and Mrs Wyllie. June 23 1905; 3,000 copies.
228 × 159mm; ix, 260pp; index.
Brown cloth with a pictorial design blocked in gilt and black on the front and in black on the spine; titling blocked in gilt on the front and spine; top edge gilt.
60 full page illustrations in colour captioned on the tissue versos and 28 chapter head- and tailpieces in black and white.

54. London Vanished and Vanishing painted and described by Philip Norman. Dec 1 1905; 3,000 copies.
228 × 159mm; xvi, 294pp +2; index.
Blue grey cloth with titling blocked in gilt on the front and spine; top edge gilt.
75 full page illustrations in colour captioned on the tissue versos.
Note: Most of the illustrations were borrowed from the South Kensington Museum.

55. The Scenery of London by G. E. Mitton; painted by Herbert M. Marshall. July 4 1905; 3,200 copies.
228 × 159mm; xiii, 223pp; index.
Grey cloth with a design printed in green, orange and black on the front and spine; titling blocked in gilt on the front and spine; top edge gilt.
75 full page illustrations in colour captioned on the tissue versos.

56. George Morland: His Life and Works by Sir Walter Gilbey and E. D. Cuming. Nov 30 1907; 3,000 copies.
228 × 159mm; xix, 290pp +2; index.
Blue green cloth with a pictorial design printed in olive and light green on the front and spine; titling blocked in black on the front and in gilt on the spine; top edge gilt.

50 full page illustrations in colour by George Morland captioned on the tissue versos.

Reprinted Aug 1912 (3,000 copies, dated 1907).

Note: The description of this book is based on the copy in A & C Black's Historic Library; on other copies the titling on the front is blocked in gilt.

57. Morocco by S. L. Bensusan; painted by A. S. Forrest. Sept 13 1904; 3,000 copies.

228 × 159mm; xv, 231pp.

Beige cloth with a design printed in blue, green and red on the front and spine; titling blocked in gilt on the front and spine; top edge gilt.

74 full page illustrations in colour captioned on the tissue rectos.

Reprinted June 1911 (3,000 copies; a Claflin reprint).

58. Naples by Sybil FitzGerald; painted by Augustine FitzGerald. June 21 1904; 2,000 copies.

228 × 159mm; xii, 235pp.

Maroon cloth with a design blocked in red and printed in green and orange on the front and spine; titling blocked in gilt on the front and spine; top edge gilt.

80 full page illustrations in colour captioned on the tissue rectos.

Reprinted June 1911 (3,000 copies; a Claflin reprint).

59. The Royal Navy by H. Lawrence Swinburne; painted by Norman Wilkinson. Nov 28 1907; 3,000 copies.

228 × 159mm; xx, 378pp; index.

Blue cloth with a design printed in brown and cream and border blocked in gilt on the front and spine; titling blocked in gilt on the front and spine; top edge gilt.

61 full page illustrations in colour captioned on the tissue versos, 51 by Wilkinson and 10 (of costumes) by J. Jellicoe.

60. New Zealand by The Hon W. P. Reeves; painted by F. and W Wright. Oct 2 1908; 3,000 copies.

228 × 159mm; ix, 241pp; index; folding map.

Brown cloth with a design based on Maori carvings printed in green, white and black on the front and in white and black on the spine; titling blocked in gilt on the front and spine; top edge gilt.

75 full page illustrations in colour captioned on the tissue versos.

Reprinted 1915 (3,000 copies to sell at 7s 6d).

61. Banks of the Nile by Prof. John A. Todd; painted by Ella Du Cane. Oct 10 1913; 3,000 copies.

228 × 159mm; xv, 282pp; index; two folding maps.

Fawn cloth with a pictorial design printed in blue, brown and green on the front and spine; titling blocked in gilt on the front and spine; top edge gilt.

60 full page illustrations in colour with captions by Florence Du Cane on the tissue versos.

62. Norway by Beatrix Jungman; painted by Nico Jungman. April 14 1905; 3,000 copies.
228 × 159mm; x, 199pp; index.
Green cloth with a pictorial design blocked in gilt and printed in red and black on the front and spine; titling blocked in gilt on the front and spine; top edge gilt.
75 illustrations in colour captioned on the tissue versos.
Reprinted 1911 (3,150 copies; a Claflin reprint).
Note: Some copies contain four extra prelim pages not counted in the roman numeral pagination; one blank leaf before the half title and one leaf following the title, the recto being an 'alternative' title page: it consists of the title information in a decorative design by Nico Jungman printed in red. It is not possible to state with certainty that copies with the extra pages are those of the 1911 reprint.

63. Oxford by Edward Thomas; painted by John Fulleylove. Dec 15 1903; 3,200 copies.
228 × 159mm; xii, 265pp.
Blue cloth with a design blocked in gilt and printed in black on the front and spine; titling blocked in gilt on the front and spine; top edge gilt.
60 full page illustrations in colour captioned on the tissue versos.
Reprinted 1911 (3,200 copies; a Claflin reprint); 2pp titles were altered for this reprint, which is the one referred to in Eckert's bibliography but not seen by him. The text only was reprinted in 1932 (196 × 128mm; 2,000 copies; 3s 6d).

64. Paris by Dorothy Menpes; painted by Mortimer Menpes. June 1909; 3,000 copies.
228 × 159mm; xii, 186pp.
Red cloth with a design printed in red on the front and spine; titling blocked in gilt on the front and spine; top edge gilt.
75 full page illustrations in colour captioned on the tissue rectos.
Note: The UK edition was published by John Grant, the booksellers, of Edinburgh while retaining the A & C Black imprint; the US edition bears the joint imprint of Adam and Charles Black and Charles L. Bowman and Company and is also dated 1909. See text pp 58-60.

65. John Pettie by Martin Hardie. Nov 13 1908; 3,000 copies.
228 × 159mm; xxiv, 278pp; index.
Olive green cloth with a palette and laurel wreath design blocked in gilt and printed in green and pink on the front and spine; titling blocked in gilt on the front and spine; top edge gilt.
50 full page illustrations in colour by Pettie captioned on the tissue versos and eight small illustrations in black and white.
Note: The book is also found in mid-brown grained cloth. No reprint is recorded so it must be assumed that both variants were bound from the first printing of 3,000 copies.

66. Plant Life by Charles A. Hall; painted by C.F. Newall. June 18 1915; 3,000 copies.

228 × 159 mm; xi, 380pp; index.
Blue green cloth with a design printed in pink and yellow on the front and spine; titling blocked in gilt on the front and spine; top edge gilt.
50 full page illustrations in colour by Newall, 24 in black and white from photographs taken by Hall and 80 line illustrations in the text.

67. The Riviera painted and described by William Scott. Oct 11 1907; 3,000 copies.
228 × 159 mm; xii, 236pp; index; folding map.
Blue cloth with a shield design blocked in gilt on the front and a floral design printed in red and green on the front and spine; titling blocked in gilt on the front and spine; top edge gilt.
75 full page illustrations in colour captioned on the tissue versos and 16 head and tailpieces in black and white.
Reprinted June 1911 (3,000 copies; a Claflin reprint).

68. Rome by M. A. R. Tuker and Hope Malleson; painted by Alberto Pisa. April 7 1905; 3,000 copies.
228 × 159 mm; xi, 267pp; index.
Cyanine blue cloth with a design blocked in gilt and printed in green and black on the front and spine; titling blocked in gilt on the front and spine; top edge gilt.
70 full page illustrations in colour captioned on the tissue versos.
Reprinted June 1911 (3,000 copies; a Claflin reprint); Dec 1913 (3,000 copies); April 1915 (3,000 copies to sell at 7s 6d). All copies are dated 1905.
Note: The first issue has the interleaves to the plates opposite pp 154 and 224 interchanged. The reference to the Nuns' Church should face p 154.

69. Royal Palaces and Gardens with an introductory essay by Dion Clayton Calthrop; painted by Mima Nixon. June 22 1916; 3,000 copies.
246 × 180 mm; xii, 317pp.
Red cloth with a design blocked in white on the front and spine; titling blocked in gilt on the spine.
60 full page illustrations in colour tipped on the text paper.
Note: The text was written by a number of authors who are either anonymous or are accorded only a sign-off at the end of their contributions.

70. Russia by G. Dobson, H. M. Grove and H. Stewart; painted by F. de Haenen. Nov 5 1913; 1,500 copies.
228 × 159 mm; x, 479pp; index; folding map.
Brown cloth with pictorial designs printed in yellow, black and white on the front and spine; titling blocked in gilt on the front and spine; top edge gilt.
48 full page illustrations in colour captioned on the tissue versos and 48 in black and white.
Reprinted 1915 (3,000 copies to sell at 7s 6d; gilt on spine only; no tissues).
Note: Comprises the combined text and illustrations of three volumes in the 7s 6d series.

71. Bonnie Scotland by A. R. Hope Moncrieff; painted by Sutton Palmer. Nov 10 1904; 3,000 copies.
228 × 159mm; xi, 255pp.
Blue cloth with a thistle design printed in olive green, light green and pink on the front and spine; titling printed in gilt on the front and spine; top edge gilt.
75 full page illustrations in colour captioned on the tissue rectos.
Reprinted Dec 1905 (3,000 copies); April 1912 (3,200 copies); March 1913 (3,330 copies); July 1914 (3,000 copies); Dec 1917 (3,120 copies). Reprints are only dated up to 1912.

72. Sicily by Spencer C. Musson; painted by Alberto Pisa. Nov 24 1911; 3,000 copies.
228 × 159mm; xii, 312pp; index; folding map.
Blue green cloth with a vines and grapes design printed in pink, green and yellow on the front and spine; titling blocked in gilt on the front and spine; top edge gilt.
48 full page illustrations in colour tipped on grey mounts and captioned on the tissue versos.

73. South America by W. H. Koebel; painted by A. S. Forrest. Oct 24 1912; 3,000 copies.
228 × 159mm; viii, 230pp +2; index; folding map.
Light green cloth with a design printed in dark green and yellow on the front and spine; titling blocked in gilt on the front and spine.
75 full page illustrations in colour captioned on the tissue versos.

74. The Savage South Seas by E. Way Elkington; painted by Norman H. Hardy. June 18 1907; 3,000 copies.
228 × 159mm; xii, 211pp; index; folding map.
Blue cloth with a design printed in black and white on the front and spine; titling blocked in gilt on the front and spine; top edge gilt.
68 full page illustrations captioned on the tissue versos.
Note: The book is more often found in green cloth, with similar decoration. Of the 3,000 copies printed, over 2,400 were sold off to John Grant at remainder price.

75. Northern Spain painted and described by Edgar T. A. Wigram. Oct 19 1906; 2,100 copies.
228 × 159mm; xvi, 311pp +4; index; folding map.
Yellow ochre cloth with a design printed in brown and yellow on the front and spine; titling blocked in gilt on the front and spine; top edge gilt.
75 full page illustrations in colour captioned on the tissue versos.
Reprinted May 1911 (3,000 copies dated 1906).

76. Southern Spain by A. F. Calvert; painted by Trevor Haddon. Oct 23 1908; 3,000 copies.
228 × 159mm; xii, 210pp +2; index; folding map.

Purple lake cloth with a design printed in orange and lemon on the front and spine; titling blocked in gilt on the front and spine; top edge gilt.
75 full page illustrations in colour captioned on the tissue versos.

77. Surrey by A. R. Hope Moncrieff; painted by Sutton Palmer. Sept 11 1906; 3,000 copies.
228 × 159mm; xi, 252pp; folding map.
Blue green cloth with a bramble design blocked in gilt and printed in purple and light green on the front and spine; titling blocked in gilt on the front and spine; top edge gilt.
75 full page illustrations in colour captioned on the tissue versos.
Reprinted 1909 (2,000 copies); 1912 (3,000 copies; a Claflin reprint); 1915 (3,000 copies to sell at 7s 6d).

78. Sussex [by Hilaire Belloc]; painted by Wilfrid Ball. July 6 1906; 2,000 copies.
228 × 159mm; ix, 197pp; index; folding map.
Oriental blue cloth with a design printed in light green and brown on the front and spine; titling blocked in gilt on the front and spine; top edge gilt.
75 full page illustrations in colour captioned on the tissue versos.
Reprinted April 1907 (2,130 copies); Aug 1913 (3,000 copies); 1917. No reprint is dated later than 1907.
Note: See text pp 43-45.

79. Switzerland by Frank Fox; painted by J. and M. Hardwicke Lewis, A. D. McCormick and others. June 1917; 3,000 copies.
228 × 159mm; xii, 203pp; index; map.
Fawn cloth with a pictorial design printed in blue, white and black on the front and spine; titling blocked in gilt on the spine.
64 full page illustrations in colour captioned on the tissue versos.
Note: First published with 32 illustrations as part of the Fascination of Europe series; the illustrations were taken from earlier colour plate books.

80. The Thames by G. E. Mitton; painted by Mortimer Menpes. July 27 1906; 3,000 copies.
228 × 159mm; xii, 248pp +2; index; folding map.
Grey cloth with designs printed in light blue, green and white on the front and spine; titling blocked in gilt on the front and spine; top edge gilt.
55 full page illustrations in colour captioned on the tissue versos and 20 chapter headings in colour.
Note: See text pp 50-51.

81. Tibet and Nepal painted and described by A. Henry Savage Landor. Jan 13 1905; 3,000 copies.
228 × 159mm; x, 233pp; index; folding sketch map, tissue guarded.
Light blue cloth with a design blocked in gilt and printed in blue on the front and spine; titled in black on the front and spine; top edge gilt.

Above: *Some large paper limited editions: these numbered and signed editions ranged from 100 copies (*The New Forest, Egyptian Birds) *to 1,000 (*The Durbar). Below: *Talbot Kelly's* Egypt *rebound by the Army & Navy Co-operative Society: half polished levant morocco, vellum front and back with the Egyptian flag in colour on the front and a specially designed hand-worked spine; in this form the book cost £3 3s.*

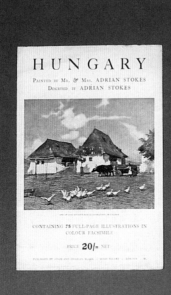

Four prospectuses for books in the 20 shilling series

50 full page illustrations in colour and 25 in black and white captioned on the tissue rectos.
Reprinted June 1911 (2,000 copies; a Claflin reprint). The reprint is captioned on the tissue versos.

82. Venice by Dorothy Menpes; painted by Mortimer Menpes. May 17 1904; 3,000 copies.
228 × 159mm; x, 222pp.
Blue cloth with a design blocked in gilt on the front and printed in white on the front and spine; titling blocked in gilt on the front and spine; top edge gilt.
100 full page illustrations in colour captioned on the tissue rectos.
Reprinted 1906; 1912 (3,000 copies; 75 illustrations).

83. Venice by Rev. Canon and Mrs Lonsdale Ragg; painted by Mortimer Menpes. Feb 28 1916; 1,000 copies; published at 7s 6d.
228 × 159mm; xiii, 208pp; index.
Blue green cloth with a design printed in white on the front spine; titling blocked in gilt on the spine; top edge gilt.
75 full page illustrations in colour captioned on the tissue versos.
Reprinted Dec 1916 (2,000 copies).

84. Beautiful Wales by Edward Thomas; painted by Robert Fowler. May 31 1905; 3,200 copies.
228 × 159mm; xi, 213pp.
Dark green cloth with a design printed in red on the front and spine; titling blocked in gilt on the front and spine; top edge gilt.
74 full page illustrations in colour captioned on the tissue versos.

85. War Impressions transcribed by Dorothy Menpes; painted by Mortimer Menpes. May 23 1901; 3,000 copies.
216 × 153mm; xiv, 254pp; folding chart.
Green cloth with a design printed in white on the front and spine; titling blocked in gilt on the front and spine; top edge gilt.
99 full page illustrations in colour captioned on the tissue rectos.
Note: See text pp 7-19.

85a War Impressions Transcribed by Dorothy Menpes; painted by Mortimer Menpes. Dec 9 1903 (book dated Oct 1903); 1,500 copies.
228 × 159mm; xiv, 254pp; folding chart.
Green cloth with a design printed in white on the front and spine; titling blocked in gilt on the front and spine; top edge gilt.
99 full page illustrations in colour captioned on the tissue rectos.
Note: No. 85 reissued in the standard format for the series.

86. War Sketches in Colour painted and described by Captain S. E. St Leger. Dec 4 1903; 2,150 copies.

228 × 159mm; xiii, 274pp.
Navy blue cloth with a design printed in red and yellow on the front and spine; titling blocked in gilt on the front and spine; top edge gilt.
50 full page illustrations in colour and 15 in black and white captioned on the tissue rectos, and 100 sketches in the text.

87. Warwickshire by Clive Holland; painted by Fred Whitehead. July 4 1906; 2,000 copies.
228 × 159mm; xi, 365pp; folding map.
Blue cloth with a design blocked in gilt and black and printed in green and white on the front and spine; titling blocked in gilt on the front and spine; top edge gilt.
75 full page illustrations in colour captioned on the tissue versos.
Reprinted 1912 (3,150 copies); later copies include an index, raising the pagination to 372.

88. Wessex by Clive Holland; painted by Walter Tyndale. March 13 1906; 2,000 copies.
228 × 159mm; xii, 280pp; index; folding map.
Dark green cloth with a design blocked in gilt and printed in yellow and black on the front and spine; titling blocked in gilt on the front and spine; top edge gilt.
75 full page illustrations in colour captioned on the tissue versos.
Reprinted 1912 (3,000 copies).

89. The West Indies by John Henderson; painted by A. S. Forrest. May 5 1905; 2,000 copies, 600 of which include a 2 page dedication to Sir Alfred Jones.
228 × 159mm; x, 272pp; index.
Cerulean blue cloth with a design blocked in gilt and printed in yellow and dark green on the front and spine; titling blocked in gilt on the front and spine; top edge gilt.
74 full page illustrations in colour captioned on the tissue rectos.
Reprinted June 1911 (3,000 copies, 2,137 of which were sent to Claflin).

90. World's Children by Dorothy Menpes; painted by Mortimer Menpes. June 19 1903; 3,200 copies.
228 × 159mm; x, 246pp.
Light blue cloth with a design blocked in gilt and blind and printed in green and ochre on the front and spine; titling blocked in gilt on the front and spine; top edge gilt.
100 full page illustrations in colour captioned on the tissue rectos.

91. World Pictures by Dorothy Menpes; painted by Mortimer Menpes. Sept 2 1902; 8,200 copies, 5,000 of which were the USA edition.
228 × 159mm; x, 332pp.
Red cloth with a design blocked in gilt and black on the front and spine; titling blocked in gilt on the front and spine; top edge gilt.
50 full page illustrations in colour and 50 in black and white captioned on the back;

400 small illustrations in the text. Reprinted 1903; 1912 (3,200 copies); 1915 (3,000 copies to sell at 7s 6d).
Notes:
1. A joint production with Collier of the USA. The text was set in America and flat sheets shipped to Britain. The illustrations were engraved and printed in Britain and similarly shipped to the USA. Wash blocks and line drawings were made and printed in the USA.
2. The 1902 printing is dated MCMII at bottom right of the title page.
3. The 1903 reprint is dated MCMIII in the same position; the illustrations are tissue guarded.
4. All later reprints bear no date; the wording on the title page reads [WORLD] [PICTURES] [BEING A RECORD] [IN COLOUR BY etc]; captions are printed below the illustrations.

92. Yorkshire painted and described by Gordon Home. Aug 28 1908; 1,500 copies.
228 × 159mm; xi, 464pp; index; folding map.
Olive green cloth with a design blocked in gilt and printed in green and white on the front and spine; titling blocked in gilt on the front and spine; top edge gilt.
71 full page illustrations in colour captioned on the tissue versos.
Reprinted 1913 (3,000 copies); 1918 (3,200 copies).
Note: Comprises the text and illustrations (minus one) of the three 7s 6d series books on Yorkshire.

The 12s 6d Series

Of the few books listed by A & C Black under this heading four are uniform and are listed here. The remainder appear in the Miscellaneous category.

101. Rembrandt by Mortimer Menpes; with an essay on the life and work of Rembrandt by C. Lewis Hind. Nov 10 1905; 3,000 copies.
292 × 228mm; xii, 50pp +2.
Light brown cloth with a design printed in brown and orange on the front and spine; titling blocked in gilt on the front and spine; top edge gilt.
16 full page illustrations in colour captioned on the tissue versos.

102. Reynolds by Randall Davies. Dec 22 1913; 3,000 copies.
292 × 228mm; vii, 56pp; index.
Light brown cloth with a design printed in brown and orange on the front and spine; titling blocked in gilt on the front and spine.
16 full page illustrations in colour captioned on the tissue versos.

103. Romney by Randall Davies. April 1 1914; 3,000 copies.
292 × 228mm; vii, 56pp; index.

Light brown cloth with a design printed in brown and orange on the front and spine; titling blocked in gilt on the front and spine.
16 full page illustrations in colour captioned on the tissue versos.

104. Velasquez by Randall Davies. April 1 1914; 3,000 copies.
292 × 228mm; vii, 52pp; index.
Light brown cloth with a design printed in brown and orange on the front and spine; titling blocked in gilt on the front and spine.
16 full page illustrations in colour captioned on the tissue versos.

The 10s Series

111. Bruges and West Flanders by G. W. T. Omond; painted by A. Forestier. Jan 23 1906; 2,000 copies.
228 × 159mm; x, 187pp; index.
Dark blue cloth with a design printed in light blue and green on the front and spine; titling blocked in gilt on the front and spine; top edge gilt.
37 full page illustrations in colour captioned on the tissues.

112. The Highlands and Islands of Scotland by A. R. Hope Moncrieff; painted by William Smith Jr. April 6 1906; 2,000 copies.
228 × 159mm; x, 232pp; folding map.
Purple brown cloth with a design blocked in gilt on the front and printed in green and light green on the front and spine; titling blocked in gilt on the front and spine; top edge gilt.
40 full page illustrations in colour captioned on the tissues.
Reprinted July 1907 (2,000 copies).

113. Normandy by G. E. Mitton; painted by Nico W. Jungman. Sept 29 1905; 2,000 copies.
228 × 159mm; xii, 192pp.
Blue cloth with a design printed in black and white on the front and spine; titling blocked in gilt on the front and spine; top edge gilt.
40 full page illustrations in colour captioned on the tissues.

114. From Sketch Book and Diary painted and described by Lady Elizabeth Butler. Nov 19 1909; 3,000 copies.
228 × 159mm; x, 177pp +2; index.
Blue cloth with a design blocked in gilt on the front; titling blocked in gilt on the front and spine; top edge gilt.
28 full page illustrations in colour captioned on the tissues and 21 chapter head- and tailpieces in black and white.

Note: Burns & Oates bought 550 copies for publication under their own imprint.

Burns & Oates' name appears alone on the spine, both firms' names on the title page but with Adam & Charles Black printed in smaller type.

Note: *The Light Side of Egypt,* which is not uniform with the four books listed here, can be found under Miscellaneous.

The 7s 6d Series

121. Abbotsford by Rev. W. S. Crockett; painted by William Smith Jr. July 21 1905; 3,000 copies.
228 × 159mm; xii, 224pp; index.
Green cloth with a design blocked in gilt on the front and spine; titling blocked in gilt on the front and spine; top edge gilt.
20 full page illustrations in colour captioned on the tissues.

122. Adventures among Pictures by C. Lewis Hind. March 3 1904; 3,000 copies.
228 × 159mm; xxii, 302pp +2.
Blue cloth with a design blocked in gilt and printed in black on the front and spine; titling blocked in gilt on the front and spine; top edge gilt.
8 full page illustrations in colour and 16 in black and white captioned on the tissues.

123. Alpine Flowers and Gardens painted and described by G. Flemwell. May 10 1910; 3,000 copies.
228 × 159mm; xiv, 167pp; index.
Green cloth with a floral design printed in white on the front and spine; titling blocked in gilt on the front and spine; top edge gilt.
20 full page illustrations in colour captioned on the tissues.
Reprinted 1916 (3,000 copies to sell at 3s 9d).

124. Aucassin and Nicolete translated and with an introduction by H. H. Child; painted by Miss A. Anderson. Nov 8 1911; 3,000 copies.
254 × 190mm; xliii, 132pp.
White cloth with a floral and border design printed in light blue and brown on the front and spine; titling blocked in gilt on the front and spine; top edge gilt.
6 full page illustrations in colour captioned on the tissues.

125. Ayrshire Idylls by Neil Munro; painted by George Houston. Nov 30 1912; 3,000 copies.
241 × 178mm; x, 139pp.
Grey green cloth with a design blocked in gilt on the front and printed in pink on the front and spine; titling blocked in gilt on the front and spine; top edge gilt.
20 full page illustrations in colour tipped on white mounts.

126. Bath and Bristol by Stanley Hutton; painted by Laura Happerfield. Sept 15 1915; 3,000 copies.

228 × 159mm; xiv, 167pp; index.
Green cloth with a floral design printed in white on the front and spine; titling blocked in gilt on the front and spine; top edge gilt.
20 full page illustrations in colour captioned on the tissues.

127. The Beautiful Birthday Book painted by Gertrude Demain Hammond. Sept 22 1905; 3,000 copies.
228 × 159mm; 210pp; index; pictorial endpapers.
Blue cloth with a design blocked in gilt on the front and spine; titling blocked in gilt on the front and spine; top edge gilt.
12 full page illustrations in colour captioned on the facing pages and decorative borders by A. A. Turbayne.
Note: First issue omits Miss Hammond's name; in most copies it appears on the same page as the list of illustrations.

128. Brabant and East Flanders by G. W. T. Omond; painted by A. Forestier. Aug 21 1907; 2,000 copies.
228 × 159mm; vii, 127pp; index.
Red cloth with a design printed in pink and brown on the front and spine; titling blocked in gilt on the front and spine; top edge gilt.
20 full page illustrations in colour captioned on the tissues.

129. British Castles painted and described by Charles H. Ashdown. Oct 18 1911; 3,000 copies.
241 × 178mm; xx, 208pp; index.
Green cloth with a design printed in grey on the front and spine; titling blocked in gilt on the front and spine; top edge gilt.
32 full page illustrations in colour and many line drawings in the text.

130. British Dogs at Work by A. Croxton Smith; painted by G. Vernon Stokes. Nov 9 1906; 3,000 copies.
228 × 159mm; xii, 123pp +2.
Fawn cloth with a pictorial design printed in blue and brown on the front and spine; titling blocked in gilt on the front and spine; top edge gilt.
20 full page illustrations in colour captioned on the tissues; 20 line drawings.

131. British Floral Decoration by R. Forester Felton. May 6 1910; 3,000 copies.
228 × 159mm; xvii, 194pp.
Blue cloth with a design printed in green and mauve on the front and spine; titling blocked in gilt on the front and spine; top edge gilt.
12 full page illustrations in colour captioned on the tissues and 14 full page illustrations in black and white.
Note: The book is also commonly found in white cloth decorated in green and mauve. An unusually large number of author's copies seem to exist.

132. William Callow by H. M. Cundall. Dec 4 1908; 3,000 copies.
228 × 159mm; xxiv, 181pp +2; index.

Green cloth with a design printed in black and orange on the front and spine; titling blocked in gilt on the front and spine; top edge gilt.
22 full page illustrations by Callow in colour captioned on the tissues, 9 full page in black and white and numerous line drawings in the text.

133. The Canary Islands by Florence Du Cane; painted by Ella Du Cane. Nov 8 1911; 3,000 copies.
228 × 159mm; vii, 172pp +4; folding map.
White cloth with a design blocked in gilt on the front and in blind on the spine; titling blocked in gilt on the front and spine; top edge gilt.
20 full page illustrations in colour captioned on the tissues.
Reprinted 1933 (3,000 copies for W. H. Smith, 16 illustrations).
Note: The book can be found in red, grey-blue and green cloths, slightly oversize. All are dated 1911 and the plates have no tissue guards; these are the reprint listed above.

134. Canterbury by W. Teignmouth Shore; painted by W. Biscombe Gardner. May 3 1907; 3,000 copies.
228 × 159mm; ix, 122pp; folding map.
Blue cloth with a design blocked in gilt on the front and spine; titling blocked in gilt on the front and spine; top edge gilt.
20 full page illustrations in colour captioned on the tissues.

135. The Cape Peninsula by Réné Juta; painted by W. Westhofen. Dec 20 1910; 3,000 copies.
228 × 159mm; xi, 118pp.
Red cloth with a design blocked in gilt and printed in black on the front and spine; titling blocked in gilt on the front and spine; top edge gilt.
25 full page illustrations in colour captioned on the tissues.
Note: The book was produced by Juta Publishing of South Africa, to whom A & C Black paid a 15% commission on sales. It is also found under the J. C. Juta imprint.

136. Chester by Francis Duckworth; painted by E. Harrison Compton. May 18 1910; 2,000 copies.
228 × 159mm; xi, 183pp; index; folding map.
Dark red cloth with a design blocked in gilt on the front and printed in light blue on the front and spine; titling blocked in gilt on the front and spine; top edge gilt.
20 full page illustrations in colour captioned on the tissues.
Reprinted 1913 (1,000 copies).

137. A Short History of the Church of England by J. F. Kendall. Dec 13 1910; 2,000 copies.
228 × 159mm; viii, 208pp; index.
Blue cloth with a design blocked in gilt on the front and spine; titling blocked in gilt on the front and spine; top edge gilt.
16 full page illustrations in colour captioned on the tissues and 8 full page in black

and white; the illustrations are from autochromes of the church pageant taken by Ernest C. Elliott (Elliott & Fry).

Reprinted 1912 (text only; 197 × 134mm; 3s 6d).

Note: The preface claims that it is the first book to be illustrated by colour photographs; however, *British Floral Decoration*, which also reproduces autochromes, was published a few months earlier.

138. Cornwall by G. E. Mitton; painted by G. F. Nicholls. Nov 12 1915; 3,000 copies.

228 × 159mm; vii, 149pp; index; double page map.

Blue grey cloth with a design blocked in gilt on the front and printed in black on the front and spine; titling blocked in gilt on the front and spine; top edge gilt.

20 full page illustrations in colour captioned on the tissues.

139. La Côte d'Emeraude by S. C. Musson; painted by J. Hardwicke Lewis. Dec 13 1912; 3,000 copies.

228 × 159mm; viii, 176pp; index; folding map.

Blue green cloth with a design printed in light green on the front and spine; titling blocked in gilt on the front and spine; top edge gilt.

20 full page illustrations in colour captioned on the tissues.

Reissued in 1917 under the title *Around St Malo* (No. 178).

140. Country Sketches for City Dwellers painted and described by Mrs Willingham Rawnsley. June 30 1908; 2,000 copies.

228 × 159mm; x, 166pp.

Green cloth with a design blocked in gilt on the front and spine; titling blocked in gilt on the front and spine; top edge gilt.

16 full page illustrations in colour captioned on the tissues.

141. Deeside by Robert Anderson; painted by William Smith Jr. Oct 11 1911; 3,000 copies.

241 × 178mm; ix, 176pp; folding map.

Green cloth with a design blocked in gilt and black and printed in white on the front and spine; titling blocked in gilt on the front and spine; top edge gilt.

20 full page illustrations in colour.

142. The Dolomites by Reginald Farrer; painted by E. Harrison Compton. Oct 10 1913; 3,000 copies.

228 × 159mm; vii, 207pp; folding map.

Blue grey cloth with a pictorial design printed in green, black and orange on the front and spine; titling blocked in gilt on the front and spine; top edge gilt.

20 full page illustrations in colour captioned on the tissues.

Note: 14 illustrations were new, while 6 were taken from *The Tyrol* (6s series).

143. Dutch Bulbs and Gardens by Una Silberrad and Sophie Lyall; painted by Mima Nixon. June 4 1909; 3,000 copies.

228 × 159mm; xii, 176pp; index.
Orange cloth with a design blocked in gilt on the front; titling blocked in gilt on the front and spine; top edge gilt.
24 full page illustrations in colour captioned on the tissues.
". . . . . and we fear *Bulb Idylls* would not appeal to the public." (Adam Black to Mima Nixon, Dec 1 1908).

144. Edinburgh by Rosaline Masson; painted by John Fulleylove. Dec 1 1904; 3,000 copies.
228 × 159mm; viii, 176pp +4; index.
Blue cloth with a design blocked in gilt on the front and spine; titling blocked in gilt on the front and spine; top edge gilt.
21 full page illustrations in colour captioned on the tissues.
Reprinted July 1907 (3,300 copies); May 1912 (3,466 copies); Dec 1914 (3,000 copies).

145. English Costume: I Early English painted and described by Dion Clayton Calthrop. April 11 1906; 2,000 copies.
228 × 159mm; viii, 80pp.
Blue cloth with a design blocked in gilt on the front and spine; titling blocked in gilt on the front and spine; top edge gilt.
18 full page illustrations in colour captioned on the tissues.

146. English Costume: II Middle Ages painted and described by Dion Clayton Calthrop. June 7 1906; 2,000 copies.
228 × 159mm; vii, 142pp.
Blue cloth with a design blocked in gilt on the front and spine; titling blocked in gilt on the front and spine; top edge gilt.
15 full page illustrations in colour captioned on the tissues.

147. English Costume: III Tudor and Stuart painted and described by Dion Clayton Calthrop. Oct 23 1906; 2,000 copies.
228 × 159mm; viii, 142pp.
Blue cloth with a design blocked in gilt on the front and spine; titling blocked in gilt on the front and spine; top edge gilt.
19 full page illustrations in colour captioned on the tissues.

148. English Costume: IV Georgian painted and described by Dion Clayton Calthrop. Dec 21 1906; 2,000 copies.
228 × 159mm; x, 99pp.
Blue cloth with a design blocked in gilt on the front and spine; titling blocked in gilt on the front and spine; top edge gilt.
19 full page illustrations in colour captioned on the tissues.

149. Eton by Christopher Stone; painted by E. D. Brinton. Nov 25 1909; 2,000 copies.

228 × 159mm; xi, 174pp +2; index; folding plan.
Blue grey cloth with a design blocked in gilt on the front and spine; titling blocked in gilt on the front and spine; top edge gilt.
20 full page illustrations in colour captioned on the tissues.
Note: See text p 71.

150. Eton from a Backwater A portfolio painted by H. E. Luxmoore. Jan 4 1909; 1,000 copies.
A fawn folder 279 × 197mm quarter bound in black cloth, which houses a black paper folder with three flaps; this contains a four page paper folder bearing a list of contents; the 12 illustrations in colour printed on white art paper are housed within this folder.
Note: The portfolio is dated MCMVIII. It was sold in aid of the Eton Memorial Building Fund. See text pp 71-72.

151. The Garden that I Love by Alfred Austin; painted by George S. Elgood. Sept 25 1905; 3,000 copies.
228 × 159mm; xiii, 146pp +2.
Green cloth with a design printed in black and grey on the front and spine; titling blocked in gilt on the front and spine; top edge gilt.
16 full page illustrations in colour captioned on the tissues.
Reprinted July 1906 (2,000 copies); Nov 1913 (3,000 copies).

152. The Charm of Gardens by Dion Clayton Calthrop; [painted by various artists]. Oct 7 1910; 3,000 copies.
241 × 178mm; xii, 240pp +4.
Green cloth with a design blocked in gilt and printed in white on the front and spine; titling blocked in gilt on the front and spine; top edge gilt.
32 full page illustrations in colour.
Reprinted 1911 (3,000 copies); 1917 (3,000 copies); 1931 (3,000 copies, 16 illustrations); 1933 (3,000 copies, 32 illustrations).

153. Gardens of England by E. T. Cook; painted by Beatrice Parsons. June 19 1908; 3,000 copies.
228 × 159mm; ix, 199pp.
Dark green cloth with a design printed in white on the front and spine; titling blocked in gilt on the front and spine; top edge gilt.
20 full page illustrations in colour captioned on the tissues.
Reprinted 1910; Dec 1911 (3,200 copies; a Claflin reprint); Oct 1913 (3,000 copies); 1916 (3,000 copies to sell at 3s 9d).

154. Geneva by Francis Gribble; painted by J. Hardwicke Lewis and May Hardwicke Lewis. Oct 23 1908; 3,000 copies.
228 × 159mm; x, 135pp; index.
Blue cloth with a design blocked in gilt and printed in fawn on the front and spine; titling blocked in gilt on the front and spine; top edge gilt.

20 full page illustrations in colour captioned on the tissues.
Note: It is probable that this edition was of 2,000 copies only, the remaining 1,000 copies being used for *The Lake of Geneva* (No. 30).

155. John Halifax Gentleman by Mrs Craik (Dinah Maria Mulock); painted by Oswald Moser and G. F. Nicholls. Dec 15 1912; 3,000 copies.
228 × 159mm; xii, 464pp.
Brown cloth with a design printed in white on the front and spine; titling blocked in gilt on the front and spine; top edge gilt.
20 full page illustrations in colour.

156. Haunts of Ancient Peace by Alfred Austin; painted by Agnes Locke. Oct 23 1908; 3,000 copies.
228 × 159mm; vi, 169pp.
Blue grey cloth with a design printed in black on the front and spine; titling blocked in gilt on the front and spine; top edge gilt.
20 full page illustrations in colour captioned on the tissues.
Reprinted Aug 1908 (2,000 copies).
Note: The plates of a Macmillan edition of the book were used instead of fresh setting.

157. The Herb Garden by Frances A. Bardswell; painted by The Hon Florence Amherst and Isabelle Forrest. March 31 1911; 3,000 copies.
228 × 159mm; viii, 173pp +2.
Mauve cloth with a floral design printed in white and green on the front and spine; titling blocked in gilt on the front and spine; top edge gilt.
16 full page illustrations in colour tipped on grey mounts captioned on the tissues.
Reprinted June 1930 (3,000 copies; edited by E.T. Ellis. xi, 173pp+4; index; white cloth; 16 illustrations).

158. Highways and Hedges by Herbert A. Morrah; painted by Berenger Benger. June 27 1911; 3,000 copies.
228 × 159mm; xv, 144pp.
Brown cloth with a floral design printed in green and white on the front and spine; titling blocked in gilt on the front and spine; top edge gilt.
20 full page illustrations in colour tipped on grey mounts and captioned on the tissues.
Reprinted March 1915 (3,000 copies to sell at 3s 6d); also reprinted March 1925 (3,000 copies; 191 × 121mm; xv, 144pp; 16 illustrations; published at 5s).

159. Inns of Court painted and described by Cecil Headlam. May 18 1909; 3,000 copies.
228 × 159mm; viii, 211pp; folding plan.
Red cloth with a design blocked in gilt on the front and spine; titling blocked in gilt on the front and spine; top edge gilt.
20 full page illustrations in colour captioned on the tissues.

160. Isle of Man by W. Ralph Hall Caine; painted by A. Heaton Cooper. Nov 5 1909; 3,000 copies.
228 × 159mm; xvi, 240pp; index; two folding maps.
Dark red cloth with a design blocked in gilt on the front and spine; titling blocked in gilt on the front and spine; top edge gilt.
20 full page illustrations in colour captioned on the tissues.

161. Isle of Wight by A. R. Hope Moncrieff; painted by A. Heaton Cooper. Aug 28 1908; 3,000 copies.
228 × 159mm; viii, 176pp; folding map in colour.
Blue cloth with a design blocked in gilt on the front; titling blocked in gilt on the front and spine; top edge gilt.
24 full page illustrations in colour captioned on the tissues.

162. Lamia's Winter Quarters by Alfred Austin; painted by George S. Elgood. Oct 24 1907; 3,000 copies.
228 × 159mm; xviii, 164pp.
Red cloth with a design printed in black and orange on the front and spine; titling blocked in gilt on the front and spine; top edge gilt.
16 full page illustrations in colour captioned on the tissues; 13 head and tail pieces by William Scott.

163. Lausanne by Francis H. Gribble; painted by J. Hardwicke Lewis and May Hardwicke Lewis. March 19 1909; 3,000 copies.
228 × 159mm; viii, 110pp.
Dark red cloth with a design blocked in gilt on the front and spine; titling blocked in gilt on the front and spine; top edge gilt.
24 full page illustrations in colour captioned on the tissues.
Note: See note to No. 154.

164. Letters from the Holy Land painted and described by Lady Elizabeth Butler. March 24 1903; 3,200 copies.
228 × 159mm; x, 84pp.
Blue cloth with a shell design blocked in gilt and printed in white on the front and spine; titling blocked in gilt on the front and spine; top edge gilt.
16 full page illustrations in colour captioned on the tissues.
Reprinted July 1906 (2,000 copies, with alterations); June 1912 (3,350 copies).
Note: 500 copies of the first impression were produced with a Burns and Oates imprint.

165. Liège and the Ardennes by G. W. T. Omond; painted by A. Forestier. June 5 1908; 2,000 copies.
228 × 159mm; viii, 125pp +2.
Blue cloth with a design printed in green and yellow on the front and spine; titling blocked in gilt on the front and spine; top edge gilt.
20 full page illustrations in colour captioned on the tissues.

166. London by A. R. Hope Moncrieff; painted by various artists. Sept 23 1910; 3,000 copies.
241 × 184mm; viii, 312pp; index.
Red cloth with a design blocked in gilt on the front and spine; titling blocked in gilt on the front and spine; top edge gilt.
32 full page illustrations in colour captioned on the tissues.

167. The Tower of London by Arthur Poyser; painted by John Fulleylove. June 24 1908; 3,000 copies.
228 × 159mm; xiv, 220pp; index; folding plan.
Red cloth with a design blocked in gilt and printed in brown on the front and spine; titling blocked in gilt on the front and spine; top edge gilt.
20 full page illustrations in colour captioned on the tissues.

168. Flowers and Gardens of Madeira by Florence Du Cane; painted by Ella Du Cane. Nov 5 1909; 3,000 copies.
228 × 159mm; vii, 150pp +2.
White cloth with a design blocked in gilt and blind on the front and blocked in blind on the spine; titling blocked in gilt on the front and spine; top edge gilt.
24 full page illustrations in colour captioned on the tissues.

169. Malta by Frederick W. Ryan; painted by Signor V. Boron.
Nov 11 1910; 3,000 copies.
228 × 159mm; xii, 184pp; index; folding map.
Green cloth with a design printed in red, blue and white on the front and spine; titling blocked in gilt on the front and spine; top edge gilt.
20 full page illustrations in colour captioned on the tissues.

170. Middlesex by A. R. Hope Moncrieff; painted by John Fulleylove. Oct 11 1907; 3,000 copies.
228 × 159mm; ix, 160pp; folding map.
Dark blue cloth with a design blocked in gilt and printed in brown on the front and spine; titling blocked in gilt on the front and spine; top edge gilt.
20 full page illustrations in colour captioned on the tissues.

171. Montreux by Francis H. Gribble; painted by J. Hardwicke Lewis and May Hardwicke Lewis. April 9 1908; 2,000 copies.
228 × 159mm; viii, 112pp.
Blue cloth with a design blocked in gilt and printed in red on the front and spine; titling blocked in gilt on the front and spine; top edge gilt.
20 full page illustrations in colour captioned on the tissues.

172. Moscow by Henry M. Grove; painted by F. de Haenen. Oct 15 1912; 3,000 copies.
228 × 159mm; viii, 142pp +2; index; map.
Blue cloth with a design blocked in gilt on the front and printed in light blue and

yellow on the front and spine; titling blocked in gilt on the front and spine; top edge gilt.
16 full page illustrations in colour captioned on the tissues and 16 in black and white.

173. The New Forest painted and described by Mrs Willingham Rawnsley. March 29 1904; 3,000 copies.
228 × 159mm; vii, 134pp.
Red brown cloth with a design blocked in gilt and printed in brown on the front and spine; titling blocked in gilt on the front and spine; top edge gilt.
20 full page illustrations in colour captioned on the tissues.

174. Nuremberg by Mrs A. G. Bell; painted by Arthur George Bell. April 11 1905; 2,000 copies.
228 × 159mm; ix, 177pp; index.
Blue cloth with a design blocked in gilt and printed in dark blue on the front and spine; titling blocked in gilt on the front and spine; top edge gilt.
20 full page illustrations in colour captioned on the tissues.

175. The Spirit of Paris by Frankfort Sommerville; painted by Parisian artists. May 9 1913; 3,000 copies.
228 × 159mm; xii, 170pp +2.
Brown cloth with a pictorial design blocked in gilt and printed in pink, green and black on the front and spine; titling blocked in gilt on the front and spine; top edge gilt.
20 full page illustrations in colour captioned on the tissues. [Illustrations by G. Fraipont, Raphael Kirchner, G. Riom, Lucien Gautier, Maurice de Lambert, A. Marcel-Clement.]

176. Pompeii by W. M. Mackenzie; painted by Alberto Pisa. May 30 1910; 2,000 copies.
228 × 159mm; xii, 180pp; index; folding plan.
Blue cloth with a design blocked in gilt on the front and printed in light blue on the front and spine; titling blocked in gilt on the front and spine; top edge gilt.
20 full page illustrations in colour and 4 in black and white from photographs captioned on the tissues.
Reprinted 1913 (3,000 copies).

177. Provincial Russia by Hugh Stewart; painted by F. de Haenen. Oct 10 1913; 2,000 copies.
228 × 159mm; viii, 172pp; index; folding map.
Maroon cloth with a design blocked in gilt on the front and printed in pink on the front and spine; titling blocked in gilt on the front and spine; top edge gilt.
16 full page illustrations in colour captioned on the tissues and 16 in black and white.

178. Around St Malo by S. C. Musson; painted by J. Hardwicke Lewis. 1917.
viii, 176pp; index; folding map.
Blue cloth with a design and titling printed in pale green on the front and spine.
20 full page illustrations in colour captioned on the tissues.
Note: First published in 1912 as *La Côte d'Emeraude* and made up from the unused stock of that volume.

179. St Petersburg by G. Dobson; painted by F. de Haenen. June 22 1910; 2,000 copies.
228 × 159mm; xii, 167pp; index; folding map in colour.
Yellow cloth with a design blocked in gilt on the spine and printed in black on the front and spine; titling blocked in gilt on the front and spine; top edge gilt.
16 full page illustrations in colour captioned on the tissues and 16 in black and white.

180. The Heart of Scotland by A. R. Hope Moncrieff; painted by Sutton Palmer.
March 19 1909; 3,000 copies.
260 × 190mm; x, 206pp +2.
Dark blue cloth with a design printed in pink and green on the front and spine; titling blocked in gilt on the front and spine; top edge gilt.
24 full page illustrations in colour captioned on the tissues.

181. Scottish Life and Character by William Sanderson; painted by H. J. Dobson.
Nov 3 1904; 3,000 copies.
228 × 159mm; x, 159pp.
Red cloth with a design blocked in gilt and blind on the front and spine; titling blocked in gilt on the front and spine; top edge gilt.
20 full page illustrations in colour captioned on the tissues.
Reprinted Dec 1905 (2,100 copies); 1914 (3,000 copies, 16 illustrations); 1919 (3,200 copies, 20 illustrations).

182. Our Life in the Swiss Highlands by John Addington Symonds and his daughter Margaret; painted by J. Hardwicke Lewis. Oct 11 1907; 2,000 copies.
228 × 159mm; xxii, 278pp; folding map.
Dark green cloth with a design blocked in gilt and printed in red on the front and spine; titling blocked in gilt on the front and spine; top edge gilt.
20 full page illustrations in colour, some on dark brown mounts, captioned on the tissues; 1 photograph; 1 pencil sketch by Symonds.

183. The Homes of Tennyson by Arthur H. Paterson; painted by Helen Allingham.
Nov 16 1905; 3,000 copies.
228 × 159mm; x, 98pp +2.
Green cloth with a design blocked in gilt and printed in pink and dark green on the front and spine; titling blocked in gilt on the front and spine; top edge gilt.
20 full page illustrations in colour captioned on the tissues.

184. Days with Velasquez by C. Lewis Hind. Jan 18 1906; 2,000 copies.
228 × 159mm; xii, 160pp; index.
Grey cloth with a design blocked in gilt and printed in black on the front and spine; titling blocked in gilt on the front and spine; top edge gilt.
8 full page illustrations by Velasquez in colour captioned on the tissues and 16 in black and white.

185. The Vicar of Wakefield by Oliver Goldsmith; painted by J. Massey Wright; with an introduction by Joseph Grego and including John Forster's essay on the story. Nov 5 1903; 3,000 copies.
228 × 159mm; xli, 260pp.
Dark green cloth with a design blocked in gilt on the front and printed in light green on the front and spine; titling blocked in gilt on the front and spine; top edge gilt.
13 full page illustrations in colour captioned on the tissues.
Reprinted Sept 1911 (3,000 copies, 222 × 146mm, 8 illustrations, to sell at 3s 6d); 1919 (3,000 copies); 1927 (3,800 copies); 1930 (3,000 copies).

186. Westminster Abbey by Mrs A. Murray Smith; painted by John Fulleylove. Aug 30 1904; 3,000 copies.
228 × 159mm; viii, 147pp; index.
Blue cloth with a design blocked in gilt and printed in white on the front and spine; titling blocked in gilt on the front and spine; top edge gilt.
21 full page illustrations in colour captioned on the tissues.
Reprinted March 1906 (2,000 copies).

187. Winchester by Rev Telford Varley; painted by Wilfrid Ball. June 28 1906; 2,000 copies.
228 × 159mm; xi, 201pp +2; index; plan.
Blue cloth with a design blocked in gilt on the front and printed in green on the front and spine; titling blocked in gilt on the front and spine; top edge gilt.
24 full page illustrations in colour captioned on the tissues.

188. Windsor by Sir Richard Rivington Holmes; painted by George M. Henton. Feb 13 1908; 3,000 copies.
228 × 159mm; vii, 117pp +2; index.
Red cloth with a design blocked in gilt and black on the front and spine; titling blocked in gilt on the front and spine; top edge gilt.
20 full page illustrations in colour captioned on the tissues.

189. Worcestershire by A. G. Bradley; painted by Thomas Tyndale. June 4 1909; 3,000 copies.
228 × 159mm; viii, 181pp; index; folding map.
Blue cloth with a design blocked in gilt on the front and spine; titling blocked in gilt on the front and spine; top edge gilt.
24 full page illustrations in colour captioned on the tissues.

190. The Wye by A. G. Bradley; painted by Sutton Palmer. April 21 1910. 3,000 copies.
228 × 159mm; ix, 180pp; index; folding map.
Blue grey cloth with a design blocked in gilt on the front and printed in green and white on the front and spine; titling blocked in gilt on the front and spine; top edge gilt.
20 full page illustrations in colour captioned on the tissues.

191. Yorkshire: Coast and Moorland Scenes painted and described by Gordon Home. April 26 1904; 3,000 copies.
228 × 159mm; x, 148pp; index; folding map.
Green cloth with a design of shields of arms blocked in gilt and printed in black on the front and spine; titling blocked in gilt on the front and spine; top edge gilt.
32 full page illustrations in colour captioned on the tissues.
Reprinted May 1907 (3,000 copies).

192. Yorkshire: Dales and Fells painted and described by Gordon Home. July 27 1906; 3,000 copies.
228 × 159mm; ix, 180pp; index; folding map.
Red cloth with a design of shields of arms blocked in gilt and printed in brown on the front and spine; titling blocked in gilt on the front and spine; top edge gilt.
20 full page illustrations in colour captioned on the tissues.

193. Yorkshire: Vales and Wolds painted and described by Gordon Home. May 29 1908; 3,000 copies.
228 × 159mm; xi, 188pp; index; folding map.
Blue cloth with a design of shields of arms blocked in gilt and blind on the front and spine; titling blocked in gilt on the front and spine; top edge gilt.
20 full page illustrations in colour captioned on the tissues.

7s 6d books second impression

Six books were reissued as follows:
209 × 140mm; 3,000 copies; published at 6s.
16 illustrations in colour.

201. Ayrshire Idylls by Neil Munro; painted by George Houston. Sept 13 1923. x, 139pp.
Green cloth with a design blocked in black and printed in pink on the front and spine.

202. Chester by Francis Duckworth; painted by E. Harrison Compton. May 18 1927. xi, 183pp; plan.
Blue cloth with a design printed in light blue on the front and spine; titling blocked in gilt on the spine.

203. Edinburgh by Rosaline Masson; painted by John Fulleylove. 1931. ix, 203pp.
Blue grey cloth with a design printed in blue on the front and spine; titling blocked
in gilt on the spine.

204. Gardens of England by E. T. Cook; painted by Beatrice Parsons. Oct 12 1923.
ix, 199pp.
Green cloth with a design printed in light green and white on the front and spine.

205. Flowers and Gardens of Madeira by Florence Du Cane; painted by Ella Du
Cane. Sept 1 1926. vii, 150pp.
Grey cloth with a design printed in brown on the front and spine; titling blocked in
gilt on the spine.

206. The Wye by A. G. Bradley; painted by E. Harrison Compton. Sept 1 1926.
ix, 189pp +2; index; folding map.
Grey green cloth with a design printed in black on the front and spine; titling
blocked in gilt on the spine.

The Fascination of Europe

Six books published at 10s in 1913-15. The 32 illustrations were mostly taken from
previously published 20s series books. Apart from the first two they were reissued
with 60 or 64 illustrations to form part of the 20s series, where they are also listed.

   The price of the books was reduced to 7s 6d shortly after publication: 'instant
remainders'.

211. Austria-Hungary by G. E. Mitton; painted by Mr and Mrs Adrian Stokes.
Sept 25 1914; 3,000 copies.
228 × 159mm; viii, 214pp; index; folding map.
Red cloth with a design blocked in gilt on the front and spine; titling blocked in gilt
on the front and spine; top edge gilt.
32 full page illustrations in colour.
Note: The illustration facing p105 is of Schubert's birthplace not Mozart's house.

212. Bulgaria by Frank Fox; painted by Jan V. Mrkvitchka and Noel Pocock.
March 9 1915; 3,000 copies.
228 × 159mm; viii, 208pp; index; folding map.
Brown cloth with a design blocked in gilt and blind on the front and spine; titling
blocked in gilt on the front and spine.
32 full page illustrations in colour.
Note: The book also appears bound in red cloth, also dated 1915.

213. England by Frank Fox; painted by various artists. Dec 22 1913; 3,000 copies.
228 × 159mm; ; xii, 206pp; index; map.

Red cloth with a design blocked in gilt and blind on the front and spine; titling blocked in gilt on the front and spine.
32 full page illustrations in colour.

214. France by Gordon Home; painted by various artists. Jan 13 1914; 3,000 copies.
228 × 159mm; viii, 219pp; index; map.
Red cloth with a design blocked in gilt on the front and spine; titling blocked in gilt on the front and spine; top edge gilt.
32 full page illustrations in colour.

215. Italy by Frank Fox; painted by various artists. Feb 10 1914; 3,000 copies.
228 × 159mm; x, 206pp; index; map.
Red cloth with a design blocked in blind on the front and in gilt and blind on the spine; titling blocked in gilt on the front and spine.
32 full page illustrations in colour.

216. Switzerland by Frank Fox; painted by various artists. Feb 24 1914; 3,000 copies.
228 × 159mm; xi, 204pp; index; map.
Red cloth with a design blocked in gilt and blind on the front and spine.
32 full page illustrations in colour.
Reprinted 1930 (3,000 copies).

Limited Editions

Large paper copies, numbered and signed, of books from the 20s and 7s 6d series.
275 × 205mm. Published at 2 guineas (£2-2s) except where stated.

221. The Alps by Martin Conway; painted by A. D. McCormick. June 7 1904; 300 copies, signed *A. & C. Black*.
x, 294pp.
White vellum cloth with a pictorial design printed in green, white and orange on the front and spine; titling blocked in gilt on the front and spine; top edge gilt, others uncut; blue silk marker.
70 full page illustrations in colour captioned on the tissue rectos.

222. British Water-Colour Art by Marcus B. Huish; illustrated by drawings presented to King Edward VII and Queen Alexandra at their coronation by the Royal Society of Painters in Water Colours. Sept 23 1904; 500 numbered copies and 100 unnumbered presentation copies, all signed *Marcus B. Huish*.
xv, 218pp; index.
White vellum cloth with a design printed in green and red on the front and spine; titling blocked in gilt on the front and spine; top edge gilt, others uncut; blue silk marker.

60 full page illustrations in colour captioned on the tissue rectos; one in black and white from a photograph; and a folding facsimile of the address to the presentation.

223. Brittany by Dorothy Menpes; painted by Mortimer Menpes. July 13 1905; 350 copies, signed *Mortimer Menpes.*
ix, 254pp.
White vellum cloth with a design blocked in gilt on the front and printed in green and dark green on the front and spine; titling blocked in gilt on the front and spine; top edge gilt, others uncut; green silk marker.
75 full page illustrations in colour captioned on the tissue versos.
Note: Copies Nos. 1-50, with an original watercolour bound in as frontispiece, were priced at £5-5s.

224. Burma painted and described by R. Talbot Kelly, Nov 10 1905; 300 copies, signed *R. Talbot Kelly.*
xv, 261pp; index; folding map.
White vellum cloth with an elaborate design blocked in gilt and printed in green, blue and red on the front and spine; titling blocked in gilt on the front and spine; top edge gilt, others uncut; red silk marker.
75 full page illustrations in colour captioned on the tissue versos.

225. The Channel Islands by Edith F. Carey; painted by Henry B. Wimbush. Oct 20 1904; 300 copies, signed *Henry B. Wimbush.*
xiii, 294pp; index; folding map.
White vellum cloth with a coat of arms design blocked in gilt and printed in green on the front and decoration and borders printed in green and brown on the front and spine; titling blocked in gilt on the front and spine; top edge gilt, others uncut; maroon silk marker.
76 full page illustrations in colour captioned on the tissue rectos.
Note: The author's copy is in the London Library.

226. The Clyde by Neil Munro; painted by Mary Y. Hunter and J. Young Hunter. Dec 10 1907; 400 copies, signed *Neil Munro, J. Y. Hunter.*
xi, 206pp; index; folding map.
White vellum cloth with a design blocked in gilt and printed in brown, green and blue on the front and spine; titling blocked in gilt on the front and spine; top edge gilt, others uncut; blue silk marker.
67 full page illustrations in colour captioned on the tissue versos.

227. Cruikshank's Water-Colours with an introduction by Joseph Grego; illustrated by George Cruikshank. Dec 15 1903; 300 copies, signed *A. & C. Black.*
xxviii, 328pp.
White vellum cloth with a design printed in brown and orange on the front and spine; titling blocked in gilt on the front and spine; top edge gilt, others uncut; maroon silk marker.
68 full page illustrations in colour captioned on the tissue rectos.

228. The Durbar by Dorothy Menpes; painted by Mortimer Menpes. Sept 18 1903; 1,000 copies, signed *Mortimer Menpes.*
xii, 210pp.
White vellum cloth with a design blocked in gilt and printed in blue and orange on the front and spine; titling blocked in gilt on the front and spine; top edge gilt, others uncut; light blue silk marker.
100 full page illustrations in colour captioned on the tissue rectos.
Note: Copies Nos. 1-100, with an original watercolour bound in as frontispiece, were priced at £5-5s.

229. Edinburgh by Rosaline Masson; painted by John Fulleylove. Dec 5 1904; 250 copies signed *A & C Black*; published at £1-1s.
viii, 180pp +4; index.
White vellum cloth with a design blocked in gilt and printed in green on the front and spine; titling blocked in gilt on the front and spine; top edge gilt, others uncut; blue silk marker.
21 full page illustrations in colour captioned on the tissue rectos.

230. Egypt painted and described by R. Talbot Kelly. Nov 10 1902; 500 copies signed *R. Talbot Kelly.*
xiii, 246pp.
Fawn grained cloth with a design blocked in brown and gilt and printed in light blue and orange on the front and spine; titling blocked in gilt on the front and spine; top edge gilt, others uncut; maroon silk marker.
75 full page illustrations in colour captioned on the tissue rectos.

231. Egyptian Birds painted and described by Charles Whymper. Oct 22 1909; 100 copies, signed *Charles Whymper.*
x, 221pp; index.
White vellum cloth with a design blocked in gilt on the front and spine; titling blocked in gilt on the front and spine; top edge gilt, others uncut; blue silk marker.
51 full page illustrations in colour tipped on grey mounts, captioned on the tissue versos.
Note: 'It was not our intention to have a large paper edition of the book, but if you have good reason to believe that even one hundred people might want it, it would be worth our while to do it. Originally we published large paper editions of nearly every book in the series in which Egyptian Birds will appear but the interest in them declined so we stopped them.' (Adam Black to Charles Whymper, March 23 1909).

232. Happy England by Marcus B. Huish; painted by Helen Allingham. Sept 18 1903; 750 copies, signed *Helen Allingham.*
xi, 204pp.
White vellum cloth with a design printed in green, pink and red on the front and spine; titling blocked in gilt on the front and spine; top edge gilt, others uncut; blue silk marker.

80 full page illustrations in colour captioned on the tissue rectos, and a frontispiece photograph of Mrs Allingham.

233. The English Lakes by W. T. Palmer; painted by A. Heaton Cooper. Aug 2 1905; 250 copies, signed *A. Heaton Cooper.*
ix, 232pp; index; map.
White vellum cloth with a design blocked in silver and printed in green and orange on the front and spine; titling blocked in gilt on the front and spine; top edge gilt, others uncut; maroon silk marker.
75 full page illustrations in colour captioned on the tissue versos.

234. Birket Foster by H. M. Cundall; illustrated by Birket Foster. Dec 6 1906; 500 copies, signed *A. & C. Black.*
xx, 216pp; index.
White vellum cloth with a design printed in green and pink on the front and spine; titling blocked in gilt on the front and spine; top edge gilt, others uncut; green silk marker.
73 full page illustrations in colour captioned on the tissue versos; 20 full page illustrations in black and white; 58 smaller illustrations throughout the text, mostly from pencil drawings, two by F. S. Walker.
Note: Copies Nos. 1-30, with an original pencil sketch bound in as frontispiece, were priced at £5-5s; copies Nos. 31-500, at £2-2s, each contained an etching by Birket Foster.

235. The Garden that I Love by Alfred Austin; painted by George S. Elgood. Oct 3 1905; 250 copies, signed *Alfred Austin*; published at £1-1s.
xiv, 146pp +2.
White vellum cloth with a design blocked in gilt and printed in green on the front and spine; titling blocked in gilt on the front and spine; top edge gilt, others uncut; green silk marker.
16 full page illustrations in colour captioned on the tissue versos.

236. Kate Greenaway by M. H. Spielmann and G. S. Layard. Nov 8 1905; 500 copies signed *John Greenaway*, plus a number of presentation copies. Copies Nos. 1-15, priced at £10-10s, contain at least one original watercolour sketch bound in as frontispiece; Nos. 16-500, published at £2-2s, each contain an original pencil sketch.
xx, 301pp; index.
White vellum cloth with a floral and border design blocked in blind on the front and spine; titling blocked in gilt on the front and spine; top edge gilt, others uncut; maroon silk marker; Kate Greenaway endpapers.
52 full page illustrations by Kate Greenaway in colour captioned on the tissue versos, 34 full page in black and white from photographs and line drawings; and 56 thumbnail and other sketches throughout the text.
Note: Copy No. 1 contains as frontispiece five small circular watercolours of girls' heads, one of 76mm diameter surrounded by four of 32mm diameter. The cover design is blocked in gilt and the book has a fawn dust-wrapper with green and

brown decoration and titling. A bookplate is of Charles Hesketh Fleetwood Hesketh.

Copy No. 2 has four watercolours similarly bound in: one of a young lady 51 × 38mm, two of young girls, 89 × 76mm and 38mm diameter, and one of a boy, 63mm diameter.

It is probable that copy No. 3 contains three watercolours and copy No. 4 two, while Nos. 5-15 contain one each.

237. John Halifax Gentleman by Dinah Maria Mulock (Mrs Craik); painted by Oswald Moser and G. F. Nicholls. Dec 15 1912; 250 copies signed *A. & C. Black*; published at 15s.

260 × 190mm; xii, 464pp.

White vellum cloth with a design printed in black and brown on the front and spine; titling blocked in gilt on the front and spine; top edge gilt, others uncut; brown silk marker.

20 full page illustrations in colour tipped on Vandyke brown mounts, captioned on the tissue versos.

238. Holland by Beatrix Jungman; painted by Nico Jungman. Aug 19 1904; 300 copies, signed *A. & C. Black*.

xi, 301pp.

White vellum cloth with a pictorial design blocked in gilt and printed in blue and orange on the front and spine and printed in green on the front; titling blocked in gilt on the front and spine; top edge gilt, others uncut; blue silk marker.

75 full page illustrations in colour captioned on the tissue rectos.

239. The Holy Land by Rev John Kelman; painted by John Fulleylove. Nov 14 1902; 500 copies, signed *A. & C. Black*.

xv, 302pp +2; index.

White vellum cloth with a design blocked in gilt and printed in green on the front and spine; titling blocked in gilt on the front and spine; top edge gilt, others uncut; blue silk marker.

77 full page illustrations in colour and 15 in black and white captioned on the tissue versos.

240. The Armies of India by Major G. F. MacMunn; painted by Major A. C. Lovett; with a foreword by Field-Marshal Earl Roberts. Oct 25 1911; 500 copies, signed *A. & C. Black*.

xiv, 224pp; index.

White vellum cloth with a design blocked in gilt and blind on the front and spine; titling blocked in gilt on the front and spine; top edge gilt, others uncut; navy blue silk marker.

70 full page illustrations in colour tipped on grey mounts, captioned on the tissue versos, and 20 small line illustrations.

241. Japan by Dorothy Menpes; painted by Mortimer Menpes. Dec 7 1901; 600 copies, signed *Mortimer Menpes.*
xiv, 207pp.
White vellum cloth with a design blocked in gilt and printed in green and red on the front and spine; titling blocked in gilt on the front and spine; top edge gilt, others uncut; red silk marker.
100 full page illustrations in colour captioned on the tissue rectos.
Note: Copies Nos. 1-100, with an original watercolour bound in as frontispiece, were priced at £10-10s.

242. Lamia's Winter Quarters by Alfred Austin; painted by George S. Elgood. Oct 24 1907; 250 copies, signed *Alfred Austin*; published at £1-1s.
xviii, 164pp.
White vellum cloth with a design blocked in gilt and printed in brown and orange on the front and spine; titling blocked in gilt on the front and spine; top edge gilt, others uncut; green silk marker.
16 full page illustrations in colour captioned on the tissue versos.

243. Letters from the Holy Land painted and described by Lady Elizabeth Butler. April 1 1903; 250 copies, signed *Elizabeth Butler*; published at £1-1s.
x, 84pp.
White vellum cloth with a design blocked in gilt and printed in green on the front and spine; titling blocked in gilt on the front and spine; top edge gilt, others uncut; blue silk marker.
16 full page illustrations in colour captioned on the tissue rectos.

244. Familiar London painted and described by Rose Barton. Nov 22 1904; 300 copies, signed *Rose Barton.*
xii, 208pp.
White vellum cloth with a floral design printed in brown, green and red on the front and spine; titling blocked in gilt on the front and spine; top edge gilt, others uncut; red silk marker.
61 full page illustrations in colour captioned on the tissue rectos.

245. London to the Nore painted and described by W. L. Wyllie and Mrs Wyllie. June 26 1905; 250 copies, signed *W. L. Wyllie.*
ix, 260pp; index.
White vellum cloth with a pictorial design blocked in gilt and printed in brown on the front and printed in brown on the spine; titling blocked in gilt on the front and spine; top edge gilt, others uncut; maroon silk marker.
60 full page illustrations in colour captioned on the tissue versos.

246. London Vanished and Vanishing painted and described by Philip Norman. Dec 7 1905; 250 copies, signed *Philip Norman.*
xvi, 296pp; index.

White vellum cloth with titling blocked in gilt on the front and spine; top edge gilt, others uncut; blue silk marker.

75 full page illustrations in colour captioned on the tissue versos.

247. George Morland: His Life and Works by Sir Walter Gilbey and E. D. Cuming. 1907; 250 copies, signed *Walter Gilbey.*

xix, 290pp; index.

White vellum cloth with a design blocked in gilt and printed in brown and green on the front and spine; titling blocked in gilt on the front and spine; top edge gilt, others uncut; blue silk marker.

50 full page illustrations in colour by George Morland captioned on the tissue versos.

Note: Each copy was accompanied by a mounted reproduction of 'Gathering Sticks' (facing p108) at its original size (15 × 12 inches).

248. Morocco by S. L. Bensusan; painted by A. S. Forrest. Sept 13 1904; 250 copies, signed *A. & C. Black.*

xv, 231pp.

White vellum cloth with a design printed in blue, green and red on the front and spine; titling blocked in gilt on the front and spine; top edge gilt, others uncut; red silk marker.

74 full page illustrations in colour captioned on the tissue rectos.

249. Naples by Sybil FitzGerald; painted by Augustine FitzGerald. June 21 1904; 250 copies, signed *Augustine FitzGerald.*

xii, 235pp.

White vellum cloth with a design printed in brown, green and red on the front and spine; titling blocked in gilt on the front and spine; top edge gilt, others uncut; green silk marker.

80 full page illustrations in colour captioned on the tissue rectos.

250. The New Forest painted and described by Mrs Willingham Rawnsley. April 13 1904; 100 copies, signed *Alice Julia Rawnsley*; published at £1-1s.

vii, 134pp.

White vellum cloth with a design blocked in gilt and printed in green on the front and spine; titling blocked in gilt on the front and spine; top edge gilt, others uncut; blue silk marker.

20 full page illustrations in colour captioned on the tissue rectos.

251. Oxford by Edward Thomas; painted by John Fulleylove. Dec 11 1903; 300 copies, signed *A. & C. Black.*

xii, 265pp.

White vellum cloth with a design blocked in gilt and printed in dark blue on the front and spine; titling blocked in gilt on the front and spine; top edge gilt, others uncut; blue silk marker.

60 full page illustrations in colour captioned on the tissue rectos.

252. Paris by Dorothy Menpes; painted by Mortimer Menpes. June 1909; 500 copies, numbered but unsigned.
xii, 185pp.
White vellum cloth with a design blocked in gilt and printed in red on the front and spine; titling blocked in gilt on the front and spine; top edge gilt, others uncut.
75 full page illustrations in colour captioned on the tissue rectos.
Note: Both the large paper and trade editions were published by John Grant of Edinburgh under the A & C Black imprint (see text pp 58-60).

253. Rome by M. A. R. Tuker and Hope Malleson; painted by Alberto Pisa. April 20 1905; 250 copies, signed *A. & C. Black.*
xi, 267pp; index.
White vellum cloth with a design printed in pink on the front and spine; titling blocked in gilt on the front and spine; top edge gilt, others uncut; blue silk marker.
70 full page illustrations in colour captioned on the tissue versos.

254. Royal Palaces and Gardens with an introductory essay by Dion Clayton Calthrop; painted by Mima Nixon. June 22 1916; 200 copies, signed *Mima Nixon.*
xii, 317pp.
White vellum cloth with a design printed in red and black on the front and spine; titling blocked in gilt on the front and spine; top edge gilt, others uncut.
60 full page illustrations in colour tipped on white mounts.

255. Bonnie Scotland by A. R. Hope Moncrieff; painted by Sutton Palmer. Nov 10 1904; 500 copies, signed *A. R. Hope Moncrieff.*
xi, 255pp.
White vellum cloth with a design and printed in green and pink on the front and spine; titling blocked in gilt on the front and spine; top edge gilt, others uncut; maroon silk marker.
75 full page illustrations in colour captioned on the tissue rectos.

256. Venice by Dorothy Menpes; painted by Mortimer Menpes. May 17 1904; 500 copies, signed *Mortimer Menpes.*
x, 222pp.
White vellum cloth with a design blocked in gilt and printed in blue on the front and spine; titling blocked in gilt on the front and spine; top edge gilt, others uncut; blue silk marker.
100 full page illustrations in colour captioned on the tissue rectos.
Note: Copies Nos. 1-50, with an original watercolour bound in as frontispiece, were priced at £5-5s.

257. The Vicar of Wakefield by Oliver Goldsmith; illustrated by J. Massey Wright; with an introduction by Joseph Grego and including John Forster's essay on the story; Sept 5 1903; 250 copies, signed *A. & C. Black*; published at £1-1s.
xli, 260pp.
White vellum cloth with a clover leaf design blocked in gilt and printed in olive

green on the front and spine; titling blocked in gilt on the front and spine; top edge gilt, others uncut; maroon silk marker.
13 full page illustrations in colour captioned on the tissue rectos.

258. War Impressions transcribed by Dorothy Menpes; painted by Mortimer Menpes. April 23 1901; 350 copies, signed *Mortimer Menpes*; published at 15s.
xiv, 254pp; folding chart.
White vellum cloth with a design printed in green on the front and spine; titling blocked in gilt on the front and spine; top edge gilt, others uncut; green silk marker.
99 full page illustrations in colour captioned on the tissue rectos.
Note: Copies Nos. 1-25, with an original watercolour bound in as frontispiece, were priced at £5-5s.

259. War Sketches in Colour painted and described by Captain S. E. St Leger. Dec 15 1903; 250 copies, signed *Stratford E. St Leger*.
xiii, 274pp.
White vellum cloth with a design printed in blue and red on the front and spine; titling blocked in gilt on the front and spine; top edge gilt, others uncut; blue silk marker.
50 full page illustrations in colour and 15 in black and white captioned on the tissue versos, and 100 sketches in the text.

260. Westminster Abbey by Mrs A. Murray Smith; painted by John Fulleylove. Aug 30 1904; 250 copies signed *A. & C. Black*; published at £1-1s.
viii, 147pp; index.
White vellum cloth with a design blocked in gilt and printed in green on the front and spine; titling blocked in gilt on the front and spine; top edge gilt, others uncut; blue silk marker.
21 full page illustrations in colour captioned on the tissue rectos.

261. Whistler as I knew him by Mortimer Menpes. June 2 1904; 500 copies signed *Mortimer Menpes*; published at £5-5s.
xv, 153pp.
White vellum cloth with a design printed in brown and orange on the front and spine; titling blocked in gilt on the front and spine; top edge gilt, others uncut; blue silk marker.
123 full page illustrations in colour and tint by James McNeill Whistler and Mortimer Menpes, and two from photographs, captioned on the tissue rectos.
Note: Each copy contains 'an original etching never before published. This etching [of four of Menpes' six children] has been printed direct from the copper by Mr Menpes himself and the plate has now been presented to the British Museum'.

262. World's Children by Dorothy Menpes; painted by Mortimer Menpes. June 19 1903; 500 copies, signed *Mortimer Menpes*.
x, 246pp.
White vellum cloth with a design blocked in gilt on the front and printed in green,

pink and purple on the front and spine; titling blocked in gilt on the front and spine; top edge gilt, others uncut; red silk marker.
100 full page illustrations in colour captioned on the tissue rectos.
Note: Copies Nos. 1-50, with an original watercolour bound in as frontispiece, were priced at £5-5s.

263. World Pictures by Dorothy Menpes; painted by Mortimer Menpes. Oct 15 1902; 500 copies, signed *Mortimer Menpes.*
x, 332pp.
Red cloth with a design blocked in gilt on the front and printed in black on the front and spine; titling blocked in gilt on the front and spine; top edge gilt, others uncut.
50 full page illustrations in colour and 50 in black and white captioned on the tissue rectos, plus 400 line drawings in the text.
Note: Copies Nos. 1-50, with an original watercolour bound in as frontispiece, were priced at £5-5s.

264. Yorkshire: Coast and Moorland Scenes painted and described by Gordon Home. April 29 1904; 200 copies, signed *Gordon Home*; published at £1-1s.
x, 148pp; index; folding map.
White vellum cloth with a design blocked in gilt on the front and printed in dark green on the front and spine; titling blocked in gilt on the front and spine; top edge gilt, others uncut; blue silk marker.
32 full page illustrations in colour captioned on the tissue versos.

The 6s Series

202 × 137mm; 3,000 copies (except *Ireland*).

271. The Cotswolds by Francis Duckworth; painted by G. F. Nicholls. May 5 1908.
xii, 231pp; index; folding map.
Dark green cloth with a design blocked in gilt and printed in red on the front and spine; titling blocked in gilt on the front and spine; top edge gilt.
24 full page illustrations in colour.

272. North Devon by F. J. Snell; [painted by Henry B. Wimbush]. Sept 6 1906.
viii, 186pp +6.
Dark green cloth with a design blocked in gilt and printed in red on the front and spine; titling blocked in gilt on the cover and spine; top edge gilt.
26 full page illustrations in colour.
Note: Wimbush's name is not mentioned.

273. South Devon by Chas. R. Rowe; painted by C. E. Hannaford. Nov 6 1907.
viii, 214pp +2; index.

Red cloth with a design blocked in gilt on the front and in blind on the front and spine; titling blocked in gilt on the front and spine; top edge gilt.
24 full page illustrations in colour.

274. The Upper Engadine by Spencer C. Musson; painted by J. Hardwicke Lewis. Oct 11 1907.
xii, 212pp; index; folding map.
Blue grey pictorial cloth with decorative borders blocked in gilt on the front and spine; titling blocked in gilt on the front and spine; top edge gilt.
24 full page illustrations in colour.

275. Galloway by J. M. Sloan; painted by James Faed Jr. June 19 1908.
viii, 311pp; index.
Blue cloth with a design printed in black on the front and spine; titling blocked in gilt on the front and spine; top edge gilt.
24 full page illustrations in colour, one in black and white.

276. Ireland by Frank Mathew; painted by Francis S. Walker. March 20 1907.
xix, 212pp; index.
Green cloth with a design printed in light green on the front and spine; titling blocked in gilt on the front and spine; top edge gilt.
32 full page illustrations in colour.
Note: Text as in No. 42; illustrations taken from No. 42. This edition was made up from the 1,700 unused copies of the 20s series *Ireland.*

277. Jamaica by John Henderson; painted by A. S. Forrest. Jan 16 1907 (book dated 1906).
x, 179pp.
Blue cloth with a design blocked in gilt on the front and printed in dark green on the front and spine; titling blocked in gilt on the front and spine; top edge gilt.
24 full page illustrations in colour.
Note: Text and illustrations taken from the 20s series *The West Indies.*

278. Kew Gardens by A. R. Hope Moncrieff; painted by T. Mower Martin. June 24 1908.
x, 208pp; index.
Grey cloth with a design blocked in gilt and printed in green on the front and spine; titling blocked in gilt on the front and spine; top edge gilt.
24 full page illustrations in colour.
Note: The book can also be found in green cloth, with a design in black and light green; titled in gilt on the spine only.

279. Liverpool by Dixon Scott; painted by J. Hamilton Hay. Aug 1907.
xii, 168pp; index.
Dark blue cloth with a design blocked in gilt and printed in green on the front and spine; titling blocked in gilt on the front and spine; top edge gilt.
24 full page illustrations in colour.

280. The Norwegian Fjords painted and described by A. Heaton Cooper. Aug 13 1907 (book dated Sept).
xii, 178pp +2; index.
Blue cloth with a pictorial design printed in light blue and red on the front and spine; titling blocked in gilt on the front and spine; top edge gilt.
24 full page illustrations in colour.

281. Paris by Dorothy Menpes; painted by Mortimer Menpes. March 20 1907.
viii, 186pp +6.
Red cloth with a design printed in orange on the front and spine; titling blocked in gilt on the front and spine; top edge gilt.
24 full page illustrations in colour.
Note: See text pp 58, 75.

282. The Peak Country by A. R. Hope Moncrieff; painted by W. Biscombe Gardner, May 5 1908.
xii, 182pp +2; index.
Navy blue cloth with a design blocked in gilt and printed in lilac on the front and spine; titling blocked in gilt on the front and spine; top edge gilt.
24 full page illustrations in colour.
Note: The book can also be found in fawn cloth, with a design printed in black and light blue, titled in gilt on the spine only.

283. Tyrol by W. A. Baillie-Grohman; painted by E. Harrison Compton. June 12 1908.
x, 208pp; index.
Dark blue cloth with a design printed in green and light blue on the front and spine; titling blocked in gilt on the front and spine; top edge gilt.
24 full page illustrations in colour.

The Motor Routes Series

214 × 138mm; 3,000 copies. Published at 5s (leather 7s 6d).

291. The Motor Routes of England *Southern Section* by Gordon Home. Aug 27 1909.
x, 334pp +2; index; folding map in colour; inserted advertisements.
Black cloth with a pictorial design blocked in gilt and printed in red on the front; titling blocked in gilt on the front and spine; top edge gilt.
24 full page illustrations in colour by various artists, 42 sketch maps and plans.

291a. As above but bound in dark mauve leather; design on front and titling blocked in gilt; all edges gilt.

292. The Motor Routes of England *Western Section and Wales* by Gordon Home. Aug 18 1911.
xv, 337pp; index; folding map in colour; inserted advertisements.
Dark green cloth with a pictorial design blocked in gilt and printed in light green on the front; titling blocked in gilt on the front and spine; top edge gilt.
16 full page illustrations in colour by various artists, 42 sketch maps and plans.

292a. As above but bound in leather; design on front and titling blocked in gilt; all edges gilt.

293. The Motor Routes of France Part I *To the Chateaux of Touraine, Biarritz, The Pyrenees, The Riviera and the Rhône Valley* by Gordon Home. May 6 1910.
x, 444pp; index; folding map in colour; inserted advertisements.
Blue cloth with a pictorial design blocked in gilt and printed in pink on the front; titling blocked in gilt on the front and spine; top edge gilt.
16 full page illustrations in colour by various artists, 16 in black and white by Gordon Home and 60 sketch maps and plans.

293a. As above but bound in leather; design on front and titling blocked in gilt; all edges gilt.

294. The Motor Routes of Germany by Henry J. Hecht. May 27 1914.
xxiv, 456pp; folding map in colour; inserted advertisements.
Blue grey cloth with a pictorial design printed in pink on the front; titling blocked in gilt on the front and spine; top edge gilt.
16 full page illustrations in colour by various artists, 54 sketch maps and plans.

294a. As above but bound in leather; design on front and titling blocked in gilt; all edges gilt.

The following books were described as 'in active preparation':
The Motor Routes of England *Eastern Section.*
The Motor Routes of England *Northern Section.*
The Motor Routes of Scotland.
The Motor Routes of France Part II.
None was published.

The 'People' Series

245 × 178mm; 3,000 copies.
Fawn cloth with pictorial design; titling blocked in gilt on the front.
Published at 5s.

301. The People of Egypt Painted by Lance Thackeray; with an introduction by Gordon Home. Nov 11 1910.

vi, 10pp text.

32 full page illustrations in colour tipped on grey mounts, captioned on the interleaf versos; 35 illustrations in black and white on the interleaf rectos and two from photographs.

Reprinted 1916 (3,000 copies; 226 × 158mm, the plates not tipped in; titled in orange on the front, the photographs absent).

302. The People of Holland Painted by Nico Jungman; with an introduction by Gordon Home. Nov 11 1910.

iv, 12pp text.

32 full page illustrations in colour tipped on grey mounts, captioned on the interleaf versos; 32 illustrations by Gordon Home in black and white on the interleaf rectos.

303. The People of India Painted by Mortimer Menpes; with an introduction by G. E. Mitton. Nov 11 1910.

iv, 12pp text.

32 full page illustrations in colour tipped on grey mounts, captioned on the interleaf versos; 32 illustrations in black and white on the interleaf rectos.

Note: The book is also to be found with the plates tipped on Vandyke brown mounts.

The Menpes Crown Series

304. China by The Hon Sir Henry Arthur Blake; painted by Mortimer Menpes. Sept 24 1909; 3,000 copies; published at 5s.

260 × 190mm; vii, 138pp.

Blue cloth with a design blocked in gilt on the front and in blind on the spine; titling blocked in gilt on the front and spine.

16 full page illustrations in colour within frame surrounds and 64 line drawings in black and white.

Beautiful Britain Series

228 × 159mm; 64pp; index. 5,000 copies, except where stated. Paper boards with a picture in colour onlaid and a design of flower motifs within borders printed in black on the front; or cloth with a picture in colour onlaid and a decorative design either blocked in blind and black or printed in black on the front; titled in black. Pictorial endpapers. Brown decorated dustwrappers.

12 full page illustrations in colour; frontispiece tipped on grey mount.

Published at 1s 6d; 2s 6d from 1919.

Note: Titles published in 1914 and 1915 were issued in boxes during those years only (nos 317, 325, 328, 329, 334, 335, 339, 340, 344, 345 and possibly others); the word **Boxed** is printed by these titles. Some of these bear the wording 'With the

Examples of the 5 shilling Motor Routes books in leather (top left)
and cloth (top right), *and the 6 shilling series*

Above: *Books from the British Artists and 'People' series.*
Below: *Water-Colour series books in paper boards (left) and cloth (right), with an example of the Quotation and Picture series.*

Season's Greetings'. A few books have the background to the titling on front and spine in a darker shade of blue: see text p 78.

311. Abbotsford [by Rev W.S. Crockett; painted by William Smith Jr]. May 24 1912. No index.
Note: The text was abridged by Miss Mitton from the 7s 6d series *Abbotsford*.

312. The Isle of Arran by Rev Charles A. Hall; [painted by Allan Stewart]. May 24 1912.
Reprinted 1925 (3,000 copies).
Note: The illustrations were commissioned for this book, Stewart being paid £38 for the 12.

313. Cambridge by Gordon Home; [painted by William Matthison]. July 14 1911.
Reprinted 1920 (3,000 copies).

314. Canterbury by Gordon Home; [painted by W. Biscombe Gardner]. July 31 1911.
Reprinted 1920 (3,000 copies).

315. The Channel Islands by Joseph E. Morris; [painted by Henry B. Wimbush]. April 17 1911.
Reprinted 1920 (3,000 copies).

316. The Firth of Clyde by MacKenzie MacBride. June 12 1911.

317. The Cotswolds by Francis Duckworth; [painted by G.F. Nicholls]. July 17 1914. Boxed.

318. The English Lakes by Gordon Home; [painted by A. Heaton Cooper]. April 17 1911.
Reprinted 1914; 1921 (3,000 copies).

319. Girton College by E.E. Constance Jones; [painted by Miss Mary Clarke]. Oct 20 1913.
Eight illustrations in colour, seven in black and white from photographs, one line drawing; map.

320. The Isle of Man by Joseph E. Morris; [painted by A. Heaton Cooper]. July 14 1911.

321. The Isle of Wight by G.E. Mitton; [painted by A. Heaton Cooper]. April 17 1911. Map.
Reprinted 1920 (3,000 copies).

322. Killarney by Mary Gorges; [painted by Francis S. Walker]. March 29 1912.

323. The Romance of London by Gordon Home. April 17 1911. Folding map. Reprinted 1924 (3,000 copies).
Note: A reprint of the book of the same title (No. 668) published in 1910 at 2s 6d.

324. The Tower of London by Arthur Poyser; [painted by John Fulleylove]. Sept 7 1916; 3,000 copies.
Reprinted 1916 (3,000 copies).

325. The New Forest painted and described by Mrs Willingham Rawnsley. May 17 1915; 3,000 copies. Boxed.

326. North Wales by Joseph E. Morris; [painted by Robert Fowler and Sutton Palmer]. July 14 1911.

327. Oxford by Joseph E. Morris; [painted by John Fulleylove]. June 12 1911. Reprinted 1920 (3,000 copies).

328. The Peak Country by Joseph E. Morris; [painted by W. Biscombe Gardner]. March 27 1914. Boxed.

329. St Paul's Cathedral by G. E. Mitton; [painted by Lawrence Deller]. Sept 25 1914. Boxed.

330. Stratford-on-Avon, Leamington and Warwick by Dixon Scott; [painted by Fred Whitehead]. Sept 2 1911.
Reprinted 1923 (3,000 copies).

331. The Thames by T. H. Manners-Howe; [painted by Sutton Palmer, A.R. Quinton and others]. April 17 1911.

332. The Trossachs by G. E. Mitton; [painted by Sutton Palmer]. April 17 1911. Reprinted 1916 (3,000 copies); 1925 (3,000 copies).

333. Wessex by C. G. Harper; [painted by Walter Tyndale]. April 17 1911.

334. Westminster Abbey by Joseph E. Morris; [painted by John Fulleylove]. May 27 1914. Boxed.

335. Winchester by Rev. Telford Varley; [painted by Wilfrid Ball]. June 12 1914. Boxed.

336. Windsor and Eton by Beatrice Home. [painted by George A. Henton and E. D. Brinton]. June 12 1911.

337. The Wye by A. G. Bradley; [painted by Sutton Palmer]. April 10 1916; 3,000 copies.

338. Yorkshire: Coast and Moorland painted and described by Gordon Home. May 7 1915; 3,000 copies. Boxed.

Beautiful Europe Series

228 × 159mm; 64pp; index. 5,000 copies, except where stated. Cloth covered boards with picture in colour onlaid on the front bordered by a decorative design printed in black; titled in black.
12 full page illustrations in colour.
Published at 1s 6d.
Uniform with the Beautiful Britain series but with plain endpapers except where stated.

339. Belgium by Joseph E. Morris; [painted by A. Forestier and William Callow]. April 30 1915; 5,000 copies. Boxed.
Frontispiece tipped on grey mount.

340. The Lake of Como by Joseph E. Morris; [painted by Ella Du Cane]. April 30 1915; 5,000 copies. Boxed.
Frontispiece tipped on grey mount.

341. The Engadine by Spencer Musson; [painted by J. Hardwicke Lewis]. Oct 22 1924; 3,000 copies.
8 illustrations; 2 maps.
Note: The text was cut down from that used in the 6s series *The Engadine*.

342. The Lake of Geneva by Joseph E. Morris; [painted by J. Hardwicke Lewis]. Aug 19 1919; 5,000 copies.

343. The Lake of Lucerne by Joseph E. Morris; [painted by J. Hardwicke Lewis]. Aug 19 1919; 5,000 copies.

344. Norwegian Fjords painted and described by A. Heaton Cooper; June 12 1914; 5,000 copies. Boxed.
Pictorial endpapers; frontispiece tipped on grey mount.

345. Venice by Joseph E. Morris; [painted by Mortimer Menpes and others]. March 5 1915; 5,000 copies. Boxed.
Frontispiece tipped on grey mount.

Black's Water-Colour Series

226 × 154mm. 3,000 copies except where stated.
Fawn cloth or paper-covered boards with a colour illustration onlaid on the front.
16 or 20 full page illustrations in colour, including the cover picture.
Published at 1s, later 1s 6d and 2s 6d.
Notes:
1. Titles published in 1914 and 1915 (Nos. 368, 376, 378, 389 and reprint of 371) were issued in boxes.
2. The number of illustrations was reduced to 16 in reprints from 1931; the artist's palette was also removed from the title page.
3. Tissue guards bearing the captions are mentioned in connection with the 1935 reprint of *Cornwall*, and the 1932 reprints of *English Lakes* and *Scottish Highlands*, and can be confirmed in the case of *Scottish Highlands*.
4. A number of titles were reissued with fuller captions in the 1950s. These are not listed.

351. Berkshire by Sutton Palmer. Feb 17 1922.
16 illustrations.

352. Birket Foster. May 20 1921.
16 illustrations.

353. Buckinghamshire by Sutton Palmer. Feb 17 1922.
16 illustrations.

354. Burns Country by George Houston. 1920; 3,200 copies.
16 illustrations.

355. Cambridge by William Matthison. Nov 1 1916.
20 illustrations.
Reprinted 1919 (3,000 copies); 1925 (3,000 copies).

356. Channel Islands by H.B. Wimbush. Nov 6 1919.
20 illustrations.
Reprinted 1919 (3,000 copies); 1921 (3,000 copies).

357. Chester by E. Harrison Compton. 28 July 1916.
20 illustrations.

358. Cornwall by G.F. Nicholls. Oct 6 1919; 3,000 copies.
20 illustrations.
Reprinted 1920 (3,000 copies); 1923 (3,000 copies); 1927 (3,000 copies); 1931 (3,000 copies); 1935 (3,000 copies, the illustrations tissue-guarded).

359. Cotswolds by G.F. Nicholls. Mar 31 1920; 3,200 copies.
20 illustrations.
Reprinted 1928 (3,000 copies); 1933 (3,000 copies).

360. Cottages of England by Helen Allingham. 1923.
20 illustrations.
Reprinted 1933 (3,000 copies).

361. Deeside by William Smith. June 27 1926.
20 illustrations.
Reprinted 1932 (3,000 copies).

362. Devon by Sutton Palmer. 1926.
20 illustrations.
Reprinted 1931 (3,000 copies); 1936 (3,000 copies); 1937.

363. Dickens Country by W. Biscombe Gardner and others. Oct 12 1920.
20 illustrations.

364. Dorset by Walter Tyndale and A. Heaton Cooper. Spring 1936.
16 illustrations.

365. Edinburgh by John Fulleylove. June 14 1920; 3,200 copies.
20 illustrations.

366. Egypt by Ella du Cane. 1931; 3,200 copies.
20 illustrations.

367. English Lakes by A. Heaton Cooper. Nov 6 1919.
20 illustrations.
Reprinted 1921 (3,250 copies); 1927 (3,000 copies); 1932 (3,000 copies, the illustrations tissue-guarded); 1936 (3,000 copies).

368. Essex by L. Burleigh Bruhl. March 5 1915. Boxed.
20 illustrations.
Reprinted 1918 (3,000 copies).

369. Eton by E.D. Brinton. Oct 6 1919; 3,000 copies.
20 illustrations.

370. Galloway by James Faed Jun. July 9 1919; 3,000 copies.
20 illustrations.
Reprinted 1926 (3,000 copies); 1935 (3,000 copies).

371. Hampshire by Wilfrid Ball. May 9 1913.
20 illustrations.

Reprinted 1914 (3,000 copies, boxed, 500 with W.H. Smith imprint); 1915 (4,500 copies); 1916 (3,000 copies); 1919 (3,000 copies).

372. Hardy Country by Walter Tyndale. 1920; 3,200 copies.
20 illustrations.

373. Holy Land by John Fulleylove. Oct 12 1920.
20 illustrations.

374. Isle of Man by A. Heaton Cooper. April 1 1920.
20 illustrations.

375. Isle of Wight by A. Heaton Cooper. March 16 1916.
20 illustrations.
Reprinted 1918 (3,000 copies); 1925 (3,000 copies).

376. Kent by W. Biscombe Gardner and Sutton Palmer. June 9 1914. Boxed.
20 illustrations.
Reprinted 1916 (3,000 copies); 1919 (3,000 copies); 1927 (3,000 copies); 1936 (3,000 copies).

377. Liverpool by J. Hamilton Hay. Sept 6 1916.
20 illustrations.

378. London by Herbert Marshall, W.L. Wyllie, Mortimer Menpes, Rose Barton, etc; May 17 1915. Boxed.
20 illustrations.
Reprinted 1917 (3,000 copies); 1919 (3,000 copies); 1927 (3,000 copies); 1934 (3,000 copies).

379. Mesopotamia (Iraq) by Edith Cheesman. Nov 30 1922.
16 illustrations.

380. The Nile by Ella du Cane. June 11 1920.
20 illustrations.

381. The Nile by Ella du Cane. May 28 1931; album format, 159 × 229mm; 3,200 copies.
20 illustrations.
Note: The illustrations differ from those used in No. 380.

382. Norfolk by A. Heaton Cooper. Mar 2 1926.
20 illustrations.

383. North Wales by Robert Fowler. June 11 1920; 3,200 copies.
20 illustrations.

384. Oxford by John Fulleylove. Oct 28 1916.
20 illustrations.
Reprinted 1919 (3,000 copies); 1923 (3,000 copies).

385. Scott Country by William Smith, Jr, Sutton Palmer, John Fulleylove, etc.
Aug 17 1920.
20 illustrations.
Reprinted 1932 (3,000 copies).

386. Scottish Highlands by Sutton Palmer and William Smith Junr. 1920; 5,000
copies.
20 illustrations.
Reprinted 1926 (3,000 copies); 1932 (3,000 copies, the illustrations tissue-guarded).

387. Somerset by Walter Tyndale and A. Heaton Cooper. Spring 1936.
16 illustrations.

388. Suffolk by A. Heaton Cooper. Mar 2 1926.
20 illustrations.

389. Surrey by Sutton Palmer. June 11 1915; 5,000 copies. Boxed.
20 illustrations.
Reprinted 1916 (3,000 copies); 1917 (3,000 copies); 1919 (3,000 copies); 1921 (3,000
copies); 1931 (3,000 copies).

390. Sussex by Wilfrid Ball. April 9 1913; 5,000 copies, 250 with Barrett imprint.
20 illustrations.
Reprinted 1916 (3,000 copies, 350 with Barrett imprint); 1926 (3,000 copies); 1931
(3,000 copies).

391. Switzerland by various artists. Aug 17 1920.
20 illustrations.

392. Warwickshire by Fred Whitehead. Mar 16 1916.
20 illustrations.
Reprinted 1918 (3,000 copies); 1928 (3,000 copies).

393. Windsor by G.M. Henton. Feb 17 1922.
16 illustrations.

394. Worcestershire by Thomas Tyndale. Mar 16 1916.
20 illustrations.
Reprinted 1919 (3,000 copies).

395. The Wye by Sutton Palmer. April 1 1920; 3,200 copies.
20 illustrations.

Reprinted 1923 (3,000 copies).

396. Yorkshire by Gordon Home. Mar 2 1926.
16 illustrations.
Reprinted 1934 (3,000 copies).

Water-Colour Views

Green paper albums 260× 206mm bound with ribbon. May 14 1908; 5,000 copies.
20 colour illustrations by Henry B. Wimbush tipped in; advertisement for Fry's
Cocoa on the back.
Published at 1s 6d.

401. Guernsey

402. Jersey

British Artists Series

241 × 178mm; 3,000 copies.
Bound in cloth, with an illustration in colour onlaid on the front within decorative
borders; titling blocked in gilt on the front.
16 or 17 illustrations in colour tipped on Vandyke brown mounts. Published at
2s 6d.

411. Birket Foster with 12pp introduction by H. M. Cundall. Sept 18 1910.
Green cloth; 17 illustrations including the front.
Reprinted 1912 (3,000 copies).

412. Kate Greenaway with 12pp introduction by M. H. Spielmann. Sept 23 1910.
Dark green cloth; 16 illustrations including the front.
Reprinted Dec 1910; Feb 1911 (3,000 copies, illustrations slightly enlarged).

413. George Morland with 12pp introduction by E. D. Cuming.
Sept 23 1910.
Grey cloth; 16 illustrations including the front.
Reprinted 1912 (3,000 copies).

414. John Pettie with 12pp introduction by Martin Hardie.
Sept 23 1910.
Blue cloth; 16 illustrations including the front.

Also, uniform with the above:

415. Rembrandt with 12pp introduction by C. Lewis Hind. Oct 18 1911.
Fawn cloth; 16 illustrations including the front, engraved by Mortimer Menpes.
Note: A volume on Helen Allingham was planned but did not appear.

Quotation and Picture Series

'Sixteen coloured views with descriptions by poets or well known authors arranged
opposite the views to which they refer.'
224 × 152mm; 3,000 copies.
Grey decorated cloth with a title label onlaid on the front; white paper wrapper
with an illustration in colour on the front.
16 full page illustrations in colour with descriptive text and verses opposite. Series
edited by J. B. Reynolds. Published at 1s (first three) and 2s 6d (Sussex).

421. The English Lake District painted by A. Heaton Cooper. May 7 1915.
Reprinted 1919 (3,000 copies); 1927; 1933 (3,000 copies).

422. London painted by Gordon Home. May 7 1915.

423. Scotland. May 7 1915.

424. Sussex [painted by Wilfrid Ball and Sutton Palmer] March 15 1928.
Note: The illustrations on pp 7, 21 and 27 are from Sutton Palmer's *Surrey.*

A similar volume is:
425. A Few Flowers of the Italian Riviera: Some Notes & Sketches from my Diary by
Hilda G. Day. 1927; 1,000 copies; published at 2s 6d.
Blue decorated cloth with a title label onlaid on the front.
32 full page illustrations with captions facing.

Brush Pen and Pencil Series

220 × 152mm.
Fawn cloth with a drawing printed on the front, the background to which is in
colour in the first impression but not in the 1930 reprints; all reprints are dated.
Series written and edited by A. E. Johnson. Published at 3s 6d.
Note: These titles were offered in 1914-15 in boxes bearing a pictorial label and the
wording 'With the Season's greetings'.

431. Tom Browne March 19 1909; 2,000 copies.
viii, 59pp.
8 full page illustrations in colour, 34 in black and white (35 subjects), 15 sketches.
Reprinted 1930 (3,000 copies).

432. Dudley Hardy Dec 3 1909; 3,000 copies.
viii, 55pp.
7 full page illustrations in colour, 43 in black and white (46 subjects).
Reprinted 1930 (3,000 copies).

433. John Hassall Oct 30 1907; 2,000 copies.
viii, 44pp.
7 full page illustrations in colour, 21 in black and white, 22 sketches.
Reprinted 1913 (2,000 copies).

434. Frank Reynolds Oct 30 1907; 2,000 copies.
viii, 61pp.
4 full page illustrations in colour, 22 in black and white (23 subjects), 19 sketches.
Reprinted 1930 (3,000 copies).

435. W. Heath Robinson May 23 1913; 3,000 copies.
viii, 52pp.
7 full page illustrations in colour, 24 in black and white, 31 sketches.
Reprinted 1930 (3,000 copies).

436. Lawson Wood Oct 7 1910; 2,000 copies.
viii, 44pp.
8 full page illustrations in colour, 15 in black and white, 33 sketches.
Reprinted 1930 (3,000 copies).

The War Front Series

227 × 152mm; 3,000 copies; published at 25s.

441. The Canadian Front in France and Flanders by Ralf Frederic Lardy Sheldon-Williams; painted by Inglis Sheldon-Williams. Nov 19 1920.
xiv, 208pp; index; folding map.
Blue cloth with a gun motif and border blocked in blind on the front; titling blocked in gilt on the spine.
32 full page illustrations in colour captioned on the tissue versos.

442. Our Italian Front by Warner Allen; painted by Martin Hardie. Feb 11 1920.
ix, 203pp; index; folding map in colour.

Blue cloth with a gun motif and border blocked in blind on the front; titling blocked in gilt on the spine.
50 full page illustrations in colour captioned on the tissue versos.

443. The Naval Front by Lieut Gordon S. Maxwell; painted by Lieut Donald Maxwell. June 18 1920.
xxx, 203pp +1; index.
Blue cloth with a design printed in green on the front; titling blocked in gilt on the spine.
16 full page illustrations in colour captioned on the tissue versos and 16 in black and white.

444. The Salonika Front by A. J. Mann; painted by William T. Wood. Feb 11 1920.
xiii, 196pp; index; folding map.
Blue cloth with a gun motif and border blocked in blind on the front; titling blocked in gilt on the spine.
32 full page illustrations in colour captioned on the tissue versos and 8 in black and white.

Beautiful Books for Sportsmen

203 × 134mm. Published at 7s 6d.

451. The Book of the Dry Fly by George A.B. Dewar, with contributions by the Duke of Rutland and J.E. Booth. Aug 16 1910; 1,500 copies.
xxviii, 277pp +2; index.
Blue grey cloth with pictorial designs blocked in gilt on the front and spine; titling blocked in gilt on the front and spine; top edge gilt.
8 full page illustrations in colour [by Sutton Palmer, Wilfrid Ball and W. Biscombe Gardner].
Note: First published in 1897 without colour illustrations.

452. Fisherman's Weather. Edited by F. G. Aflalo; opinions and experiences by 100 well known anglers; painted by Charles Whymper. May 30 1906; 2,000 copies.
xv, 256pp.
Blue grey cloth with a design printed in black on the front and spine; titling blocked in gilt on the spine; top edge gilt.
8 full page illustrations in colour.

453. Grouse and Grouse Moors by George Malcolm and Captain Aymer Maxwell; painted by Charles Whymper. Aug 26 1910; 3,000 copies.
ix, 286pp +2; index.

Blue grey cloth with pictorial designs blocked in gilt on the front and spine; titling blocked in gilt on the front and spine; top edge gilt.
16 full page illustrations in colour.

454. Partridges and Partridge Manors by Captain Aymer Maxwell; painted by George Rankin. Aug 25 1911; 3,350 copies.
xii, 327pp +2; index.
Blue grey cloth with pictorial designs blocked in gilt on the front and spine; titling blocked in gilt on the front and spine; top edge gilt.
16 full page illustrations in colour.

455. Pheasants and Covert Shooting by Captain Aymer Maxwell; painted by George Rankin. Sept 12 1913; 2,000 copies.
ix, 332pp +8; index.
Blue grey cloth with pictorial designs blocked in gilt on the front and spine; titling blocked in gilt on the front and spine; top edge gilt.
16 full page illustrations in colour.

456. Salmon Fishing by W. Earl Hodgson. June 22 1906; 2,000 copies.
xiii, 314pp +2; index.
Blue green cloth with pictorial designs blocked in gilt on the front and spine; titling blocked in gilt on the front and spine; top edge gilt.
Frontispiece in colour by Joseph Farquarson and 7 plates of flies in colour captioned on the tissues; 10 full page in black and white.

457. Trout Fishing by W. Earl Hodgson. March 1 1904; 2,000 copies.
xxi, 276pp; index.
Blue grey cloth with pictorial designs blocked in gilt on the front and spine; titling blocked in gilt on the front and spine; top edge gilt.
Frontispiece in colour by H.L. Rolfe and seven plates of flies in colour captioned on the tissues.
Reprinted 1904 (2,000 copies); 1908 (2,000 copies); 1930 (1,180 copies).

Portrait Biographies

164 × 109mm.
Dark blue cloth with the Menpes' monograms blocked in gilt on the front and a design printed in lighter blue on the front and spine; titling blocked in gilt on the front and spine. Published at 2s.

461. Henry Irving by Mortimer Menpes. June 22 1906; 3,000 copies.
vii, 53pp +6.
12 portraits in colour on 8 pages and a facsimile reproduction of a letter from Irving.

Note: The book is titled as above on the title page but *Sir Henry Irving* on the front and spine.

462. Lord Kitchener by Mortimer Menpes. May 7 1915; 3,000 copies.
64pp.
8 full page portraits in colour.

463. Lord Roberts by Mortimer Menpes. May 7 1915; 3,000 copies.
64pp.
8 full page portraits in colour and a facsimile reproduction of a letter from Roberts.

The Artists' Sketch Book Series

Edited by Martin Hardie, R.E.
'Square demy 8vo (9 × 6¼in), with artistic cover and wrappers bearing a label designed by the artist. Containing 16 or more reproductions in facsimile from pencil drawings.'

226 × 154mm. 3,000 copies except where stated.
Fawn cloth or paper covered boards with a label designed by the artist. Fawn wrapper with a similar design.
16 or 24 full page illustrations from pencil sketches.
Published at 1s; 1s 6d in 1917; 2s 6d from 1919.
Notes:
1. Titles published or reprinted in late 1913, 1914 and 1915 were issued in cardboard boxes with a picture title label onlaid (Nos. 478, 479, 484, 486, 489, 490, 494, 496, 499, 501, 502, 505, 507, 510, 512, 513, 515 and possibly others). Some of these bear the wording 'With the Season's Greetings'.
2. A few titles can also be found bound in soft brown covers.

471. Alpine Sport by Reginald Cleaver. Jan 10 1922. 890 copies (the unused balance from *A Winter Sport Book*).
16 illustrations tipped on white mounts.

472. Ampleforth by Joseph Pike. Oct 20 1921.
16 illustrations.
Note: The artist bought 2,500 copies at 1s 1d each.

473. Bath and Wells by D.S. Andrews. Feb 11 1920.
24 illustrations.

474. Bournemouth and District by Dorothy E.G. Woollard. Feb 3 1921.
24 illustrations.

475. Brighton & Environs by H.G. Hampton and Dorothy E.G. Woollard. Dec 21 1919.
24 illustrations.

476. Bristol by Dorothy E.G. Woollard. Nov 3 1920.
24 illustrations.

477. Bruges by Joseph Pike. Mar 29 1922.
16 illustrations.

478. Cambridge by Walter M. Keesey. Oct 15 1913.
24 illustrations.
Reprinted 1914 (3,000 copies); 1916 (3,000 copies); 1917 (3,000 copies); 1918 (3,000 copies); 1920 (3,000 copies); 1925 (3,000 copies).

479. Canterbury by Walter M. Keesey. Mar 3 1915.
24 illustrations.
Reprinted 1922 (3,000 copies).

480. Cardiff by D.S. Andrews. Nov 19 1920.
24 illustrations.

481. Chester by Joseph Pike. Aug 28 1920.
24 illustrations.
Reprinted 1925 (3,000 copies).

482. Cornwall by Jasper Salwey. May 24 1922.
16 illustrations.

483. Durham by Robert J.S. Bertram. Mar 31 1920.
24 illustrations.

484. Edinburgh by Lester G. Hornby. May 1 1912.
24 illustrations.
Reprinted 1914 (3,000 copies); 1918 (3,000 copies); 1925 (1,000 copies).

485. English Lakes by Gordon Home. Mar 29 1922.
16 illustrations.

486. Florence by Fred Richards. June 19 1914.
24 illustrations.
Reprinted 1916 (3,000 copies); 1925 (2,500 copies).

487. Glasgow by John Nisbet. 9 May 1913.
24 illustrations.

488. Harrogate and District by R. Sharpley; May 15 1920; 3,200 copies.
24 illustrations.

489. Harrow by Walter M. Keesey. Nov 12 1914.
24 illustrations.
Reprinted 1917 (3,000 copies).

490. Hastings & Environs by H.G. Hampton. March 3 1915.
24 illustrations.

491. Isle of Wight by Dorothy E.G. Woollard; Nov 20 1919.
24 illustrations.

492. Lincoln by Jasper Salwey. Mar 1928.
24 illustrations.

493. Liverpool by Sam J.M. Brown. May 11 1917.
24 illustrations.

494. London by Lester G. Hornby. May 1 1912.
24 illustrations.
Reprinted 1913 (3,750 copies); 1915 (3,000 copies); 1917 (3,000 copies); 1924 (3,000 copies).

495. London by Dorothy E.G. Woollard. Aug 25 1924.
24 illustrations.
Note: 16 new illustrations, 8 from *Riverside of London* (No. 497).

496. London at Night by Frederick Carter. Sept 25 1914.
24 illustrations.

497. Riverside of London by Dorothy E.G. Woollard and P.N. Boxer; Feb 11 1920.
24 illustrations.

498. Malta by Gordon Home. Oct 20 1921.
16 illustrations.

499. Manchester by H.P. Templar. Aug 22 1928.
24 illustrations.

500. Newcastle-upon-Tyne by Robert J.S. Bertram. Nov 6 1914.
24 illustrations.
Reprinted 1916 (2,000 copies); 1919 (3,000 copies).

501. Norwich by E.V. Cole. April 15 1920.
24 illustrations.

Reprinted 1925 (3,000 copies).

502. Oxford by Fred Richards. Oct 10 1913.
24 illustrations.
Reprinted 1914 (3,000 copies); 1915 (3,000 copies); 1916 (3,000 copies); 1919 (3,000 copies); 1922 (3,000 copies); 1924 (3,000 copies); 1928 (3,000 copies).

503. Paris by Eugène Bejot. Oct 15 1912.
24 illustrations.
Reprinted 1915 (1,480 copies).

504. Rochester by K. Kimball. May 1 1912.
24 illustrations.
Reprinted 1920 (3,000 copies).

505. Rome by Fred Richards. May 28 1914.
24 illustrations.
Reprinted 1916 (3,000 copies); 1922 (3,000 copies).

506. Scarborough and Whitby by J.F. Greenwood. April 26 1920.
24 illustrations.

507. Stratford-on-Avon by Gordon Home. Nov 5 1913.
24 illustrations.
Reprinted 1917 (2,445 copies); 1920 (3,000 copies).

508. Surrey by R.S. Austin. May 24 1922.
24 illustrations.

509. The Thames by R. Sharpley. March 23 1921.
24 illustrations.

510. Venice by Fred Richards. May 2 1914.
24 illustrations.
Reprinted 1916 (3,000 copies); 1921 (3,000 copies).

511. Warwick, Leamington & Kenilworth by R.S. Austin; Nov 3 1920.
24 illustrations.

512. Winchester by Gordon Home. Feb 10 1914.
24 illustrations.
Reprinted 1916 (2,000 copies); 1918 (3,000 copies); 1923 (3,000 copies).

513. Windsor and Eton by Fred Richards. Nov 6 1914.
24 illustrations.
Reprinted 1917 (3,000 copies).

514. York by Gordon Home. Mar 31 1922.
16 illustrations.

515. The Zoo by A.W. Peters. Sept 16 1915.
24 illustrations.
Reprinted 1919 (3,000 copies).

New Artists' Sketch Book Series

These seven books are reissues of volumes from the earlier series, with only 15 illustrations but with expanded captions and notes. 3,000 copies.

516. Cambridge by Walter M. Keesey. April 1935.
15 illustrations with captions facing.

517. Edinburgh by Gordon Home. April 12 1933.
15 illustrations with captions facing.

518. Harrow by Walter M. Keesey. April 1933.
15 illustrations with captions and notes by Clement du Pontet facing.

519. Lincoln by Jasper Salwey. April 1934.
15 illustrations with captions and notes by J.W.F. Hill facing.

520. Norwich by E.V. Cole. April 1933.
15 illustrations with captions and notes by Geo. A. Stephen facing.

521. Oxford by Fred Richards. April 1935.
15 illustrations with captions facing.

522. Winchester by Gordon Home. April 1933.
15 illustrations with captions and notes by Rev. A.W. Goodman facing.

A Few Similar Books

523. Rugby: A Series of Pencil Sketches by Joseph Pike; with an introduction by H.C. Bradby. March 5 1930; 3,000 copies; published at 3s 6d; 6s in full imitation blue leather.
241 × 178mm; 12pp text.
Grey cloth titled in dark blue; 24 illustrations.

524. St Andrews. Two poems specially contributed by Rudyard Kipling and Walter de la Mare. May 4 1926 (book dated February 1926). 3,000 copies; published at 2s 6d.

226 × 154mm; 16 illustrations by Malcolm Patterson from pencil drawings and etchings similar to those of the Artists' Sketch Book series.

Fawn cloth, no illustration on front.

Reprinted 1926.

Note: The book was published by arrangement with the University of St Andrews; profits were devoted to the university's Student Welfare Scheme.

525. St Malo: St Servan, Dinard, Dinan and St Michel by Jasper Salwey. March 15 1927; 3,000 copies; published at 3s 6d.

241 × 178mm; 23pp text; map.

Grey cloth titled in dark blue; 21 illustrations including front; map.

526. South Africa: A Series of Pencil Sketches by William M. Timlin; with an introduction by Gilbert E. Chittenden. May 12 1927; 3,350 copies; published at 3s 6d. 241 × 178mm; 16pp text.

Light brown cloth, titled in brown; 24 illustrations.

527. Stratford upon Avon: A Series of Pencil Sketches by Joseph Pike; with an introduction by Frederick C. Wellstood. April 26 1929; 3,000 copies; published at 3s 6d.

241 × 178mm; 20pp text.

Grey cloth titled in black; 24 illustrations.

528. A Winter Sport Book by Reginald Cleaver; with an introduction by Rev. Hon. Edward Lyttleton. Nov 17 1911; 3,000 copies; published at 5s.

241 × 178mm; viii, 62pp.

Blue grey pictorial cloth.

21 illustrations in black and white tipped on grey mounts captioned on the interleaf versos and 21 smaller captioned sketches on the interleaf rectos.

The Charm Series

531. The Charm of Cambridge by S. C. Roberts; illustrated by W. G. Blackall. Nov 10 1927; 3,000 copies; published at £1 1s.

285 × 215mm; x, 142pp.

Blue pictorial cloth; pictorial endpapers; titled in gilt on the front and spine; 24 full page illustrations from pencil drawings captioned on the tissues.

Reprinted 1933 (2,000 copies; 260 × 191mm; 10s 6d).

Note: The book is in the same style as *The Charm of Oxford*, published by Simpkin Marshall in 1920. This did not appear under the A & C Black imprint.

532. The Charm of Lancashire by J. Cuming Walters; illustrated by Frank Greenwood. Oct 31 1929; 3,000 copies; published at 7s 6d.
260 × 191mm; ix, 158pp +2; index.
Blue pictorial cloth; titled in gilt on the spine; 24 full page illustrations from pencil drawings.
Reprinted 1930 (3,000 copies).

533. The Charm of the Scott Country by Rev. James Baikie; illustrated by Gordon Home. Sept 14 1927; 3,000 copies; published at 7s 6d.
260 × 191mm; viii, 128pp; index.
Blue pictorial cloth; titling blocked in gilt on the spine; 24 full page illustrations from pencil drawings.

534. The Charm of Surrey by Gordon Home. May 23 1929; 3,000 copies; published at 7s 6d.
260 × 191mm; viii, 136pp; index.
Blue pictorial cloth; titling blocked in gilt on the spine; 24 full page illustrations from pencil drawings.

535. Edinburgh: Mine Own Romantic Town by Gordon Home. Sept 30 1927; 3,000 copies; published at 7s 6d.
260 × 191mm; viii, 140pp; index.
Blue pictorial cloth; titled in gilt on the spine; 24 full page illustrations from pencil drawings and 2 in the text.

536. New York by Ethel Fleming; illustrated by Herbert S. Kates. Sept 11 1929; 3,000 copies; published at £1 1s.
285 × 215mm; xii, 139pp; index.
Black pictorial cloth; pictorial endpapers; titling blocked in gilt on the front and spine; 24 full page illustrations from pencil drawings captioned on the tissues.

Black's Popular Series of Colour Books

210 × 140mm.
Blue cloth with a repeated design of shields within double ruled boxes blocked in blind on the front and spine: publisher's monogram blocked in blind on the back; titling blocked in black on the front and in gilt on the spine. White dust wrapper with an illustration in colour on the front and spine.
32 full page illustrations in colour, except where stated. Published at 7s 6d.
Most books in these series comprise text and illustrations from earlier colour books, mostly the 20s series. Titles containing all or partly new material, either text or illustrations, are indicated with an asterisk.

541. Australia by Frank Fox; painted by Percy F. Spence. 1927; 3,000 copies.
xiii, 219pp; index; double page map.

542. Belgium by G.W.T. Omond; painted by A. Forestier. Feb 10 1928; 3,000 copies.
ix, 250pp +2; index; double page map.

543. Buckinghamshire and Berkshire by G.E. Mitton; painted by Sutton Palmer. Nov 15 1929; 3,000 copies.
viii, 232pp; index; folding map.

544. Cambridge by M.A.R. Tuker; painted by William Matthison. Nov 16 1922; 5,200 copies.
x, 220pp; index; town plan.
The text has been reduced from 85,000 words in the 20s *Cambridge* to 53,600 words.

545. The Channel Islands by Edith F. Carey; painted by Henry B. Wimbush. May 30 1924; 3,000 copies.
xii, 226pp + 2; index; map.

*546. Cornwall by G.E. Mitton; painted by G.F. Nicholls. April 7 1925; 3,000 copies.
viii, 180pp; index; double page map.
The 7s 6d series book of which this is a reprint contains only 20 illustrations. The extra 12 were specially commissioned for this volume. The book also contains an extra chapter, on the Scilly Islands.

*547. Dalmatia by Horatio F. Brown; painted by Walter Tyndale. April 7 1925; 3,000 copies.
xii, 187pp; index; map; 24 illustrations in colour and one in black and white.

*548. Denmark by Clive Holland; painted by A. Heaton Cooper. Oct 4 1928; 3,000 copies.
x, 228pp; index; map.

*549. Derbyshire by A.R. Hope Moncrieff; painted by W. Biscombe Gardner and A. Heaton Cooper. June 16 1927; 3,000 copies.
viii, 239pp; index; map.

*550. Devon by V.C. Clinton-Baddeley; painted by Sutton Palmer. Dec 10 1925; 3,000 copies.
xi, 248pp; index; double page map.

*551. Dorset by Major H.O. Lock; painted by Walter Tyndale and A. Heaton Cooper. 1925; 3,000 copies.
xi, 200pp; index; double page map.

*552. The County of Durham by G. E. Mitton; painted by A. Heaton Cooper. Oct 1 1924; 3,000 copies.
viii, 234pp; index; map; 24 illustrations.

553. Egypt painted and described by R. Talbot Kelly. Nov 15 1923; 3,250 copies.
xiv, 240pp; index; map.

554. The English Lakes by W. T. Palmer; painted by A. Heaton Cooper. April 7 1925; 3,430 copies.
xi, 192pp +4; index; map.
Text reduced by about one sixth from that of the 20s *The English Lakes*.

555. Essex by A. R. Hope Moncrieff; painted by L. Burleigh Bruhl. Sept 1 1926; 3,000 copies.
xi, 262pp; index; double page map.

*556. Gloucestershire by J. D. Newth; painted by G. F. Nicholls. June 16 1927; 3,000 copies.
x, 208pp +2; index; map; 24 illustrations.

557. Greece by Rev. J. A. McClymont; painted by John Fulleylove. Jan 19 1924; 3,000 copies.
ix, 235pp +4; index; map.

558. Hampshire by Rev. Telford Varley; painted by Wilfrid Ball. Oct 7 1926; 3,050 copies.
xi, 243pp; index; double page map.
Text reduced by about one third from the 20s *Hampshire*.

559. The Highlands and Islands of Scotland by A. R. Hope Moncrieff; painted by William Smith Jr. 1925; 3,000 copies.
xi, 235pp; index; map.

560. The Holy Land by Rev. John Kelman; painted by John Fulleylove. Nov 15 1923; 3,250 copies.
viii, 248pp; index; map.

561. India by Flora A. Steel, revised by H. Clive Barnard; painted by Mortimer Menpes. Nov 15 1923; 3,250 copies.
xi, 220pp; index; map.

*562. Ireland by Harrison Dale; painted by A. Heaton Cooper. Sept 30 1927; 3,000 copies.
xii, 208pp; index; map.
Text newly published; illustrations from *Ireland* (1916) in the 20s series.

563. The Italian Lakes by Richard Bagot; painted by Ella Du Cane. 1925; 3,000 copies.
xi, 196pp; index; double page map.
*Reissued with an extra chapter by Laura M. Ragg and 2 illustrations by C.T.G. Formilli replacing 2 of Ella Du Cane's; Feb 5 1931. xi, 224pp +2.

*564. Japan by Walter Weston; painted by Ella Du Cane and others. Aug 17 1926; 3,000 copies.
xi, 240pp; index; map.
Text newly published; illustrations from various earlier books.

565. Kashmir by Sir Francis Edward Younghusband; painted by Major E. Molyneaux. June 12 1924; 3,620 copies.
xv, 238pp +2; index; double page map.

566. Kent by W. Teignmouth Shore; painted by W. Biscombe Gardner. Sept 1 1924; 3,000 copies.
ix, 238pp; index; double page map.

*567. Wild Lakeland by Mackenzie MacBride; painted by A. Heaton Cooper. Sept 6 1922; 5,000 copies.
viii, 230pp +2; index; map.
Text new; illustrations from the 20s *The English Lakes*.

568. London by A.R. Hope Moncrieff; painted by various artists. Jan 10 1924 (book dated 1923); 3,000 copies.
viii, 267pp; index.
Text of the 20s *London* reduced by about one fifth; illustrations by J.H. Hartley, John Fulleylove, W.L. Wyllie, L. Deller, Herbert Marshall, Gordon Home, Rose Barton, Mima Nixon and Allan Stewart.

569. New Zealand by the Hon W.P. Reeves; painted by F. and W. Wright; May 12 1927. 3,000 copies.
xx, 241pp; index; two maps.

*570. Northumberland by Agnes Herbert; painted by A. Heaton Cooper. Sept 5 1923; 3,000 copies.
viii, 238pp +2; index; 24 illustrations.
Dedicated to 'My friend Adam Black, Publisher ... Up Adam's profession *Hamlet*'.

571. Oxford by Edward Thomas; painted by John Fulleylove. Nov 16 1922; 5,200 copies.
x, 268pp; index; map.

572. Rome by M.A.R. Tuker and Hope Malleson; painted by Alberto Pisa. April 7 1925; 3,425 copies.

viii, 244pp +4; index.
Text of 20s *Rome* reduced by about 5,000 words.

573. Scotland by A.R. Hope Moncrieff; painted by Sutton Palmer. Sept 6 1922; 5,000 copies.
x, 260pp; index; map.
Text from 20s *Bonnie Scotland.*

*574. Somerset by Mrs A. C. Osborn Hann; painted by A. Heaton Cooper (21) and Walter Tyndale (11). June 16 1927; 3,000 copies.
viii, 182pp +2; index; double page map.

*575. Spain by John Lomas; painted by Edgar T. A. Wigram and Trevor Haddon. Dec 14 1925; 3,000 copies.
viii, 283pp; index; map.
Text from *In Spain* (1908), illustrations from *Northern Spain* and *Southern Spain* (20s series).

576. Surrey by A.R. Hope Moncrieff; painted by Sutton Palmer. Sept 6 1922; 5,000 copies.
xi, 255pp; index; double page map.

577. Sussex [by Hilaire Belloc]; painted by Wilfrid Ball. 1925; 3,430 copies.
ix, 197pp; index; map.
Belloc to A & C Black, Oct 24 1924: 'Gentlemen, by all means make any changes you like in the book. I have no say in the matter. I do not acknowledge it. (You know the circumstances under which you got the manuscript at half price). Nor have I any property or interest in it. Very faithfully yours, H. Belloc'.

*578. Sweden by Dudley Heathcote; painted by A. Heaton Cooper. July 1 1927; 3,000 copies.
xii, 228pp; index; map.

579. Wales by Edward Thomas; painted by Robert Fowler. July 1 1924; 3,000 copies.
ix, 203pp; index; map.

580. Warwickshire by Clive Holland; painted by Fred Whitehead.
Nov 16 1922; 5,000 copies.
xii, 260pp; index; map.
Text of 20s *Warwickshire* reduced by about one third.

581. Yorkshire. Painted and described by Gordon Home. April 7 1925; 3,000 copies.
xi, 248pp; index; map.

Black's New Series of Colour Books

In format these books are the same as the Popular series. Most are reprints of the Popular series books and some are exactly the same books issued under the different series title. These are therefore listed here by title only with the relevant Popular series number in parentheses. A few, marked by asterisks, were newly published in this series and are listed fully.

591. Australia (541)

*592. Austria by J. D. Newth; painted by E. Harrison Compton. April 16 1931; 3,000 copies.
x, 208pp +2; index; map; 24 illustrations.

593. Belgium (542)

594. Buckinghamshire and Berkshire (543)

595. Burma. Painted and described by R. Talbot Kelly. March 23 1933; 3,000 copies.
xii, 256pp; index; map.
From the 20s *Burma.*

596. Cambridge (544)

597. The Channel Islands (545) 1930; 3,000 copies.

598. Cornwall (546) 1932; 3,250 copies.

599. Dalmatia (547)

600. Denmark (548)

601. Derbyshire (549)

602. Devon (550) 1928; 3,000 copies.

603. Dorset (551) 1934; 3,000 copies.

604. The County of Durham (552)

605. Egypt (553) 1928; 3,000 copies.

*606. England by Ronald Carton; painted by various artists. 1932; 3,000 copies.
xi, 250pp; index; double page map.
Text newly published; illustrations from a variety of earlier books.
Reprinted 1934 (3,000 copies).

607. The English Lakes (554) 1929; 3,000 copies.
Reprinted May 1936 (3,120 copies).,

608. Essex (555)

*609. Germany by Gerald Bullett, with a chapter on German tourism and mountaineering by Anthony Bertram; painted by E.T. Compton and E. Harrison Compton. March 5 1930; 3,000 copies.
viii, 195pp +2; index; folding map.

610. Gloucestershire (556) 3,000 copies.

611. Greece (557)

612. Hampshire (558)

613. The Highlands and Islands of Scotland (559) Sept 1929; 3,000 copies.

614. The Holy Land (560)

615. India (561) July 1929; 3,000 copies.

616. Ireland (562)

*617. The Italian Lakes by Richard Bagot and Laura M. Ragg; painted by Ella Du Cane and C.T.G. Formilli. May 25 1932; 3,000 copies.
xi, 258pp +2; index; double page map.
Two more chapters have been added to the Popular series book, and Mrs Ragg is presented as joint author; 8 illustrations by Formilli replace 8 by Ella Du Cane.

618. Japan (564)

619. Kashmir (565) 1932; 3,120 copies.

620. Kent (566)

621. Wild Lakeland (567) Sept 20 1928; 3,000 copies.

622. London (568) 1929; 3,000 copies. Text revised by G.E. Mitton.

623. New Zealand (569)

624. Northumberland (570)

*625. Norway by S.C. Hammer; painted by A. Heaton Cooper. July 1928; 3,000 copies.
viii, 196pp +2; index; map.
Text and ??? illustrations newly published; it is interesting that Nico Jungman's illustrations for *Norway* in the 20s series were not used.

626. Oxford (571) 1932; 2,080 copies.

627. Rome (572)

628. Scotland (573) Oct 1927; 3,000 copies.
Reprinted July 1932 (3,300 copies).

629. Somerset (574)

630. Spain (575)

631. Surrey (576) 1934; 3,200 copies.

632. Sussex (577) 1935; 3,425 copies.

633. Sweden (578)

634. Wales (579)

635. Warwickshire (580)

636. Yorkshire (581) 1932; 3,000 copies.

Miscellaneous Books

641. Amid the High Hills by Sir Hugh Fraser; [painted by Finlay Mackinnon, V.R. Balfour-Browne, Philip Stretton, J. Wolf and Frank Wallace]. Aug 9 1923; 3,000 copies; published at 18s.
228 × 159mm; xv, 224pp; index.
Dark blue cloth with a design blocked in gilt on the front and spine; titling blocked in gilt on the front and spine.
16 full page illustrations in colour, 16 in black and white; headings to each chapter in pencil.

Reprinted 1934 (2,000 copies).

642. Ancient Egyptian, Assyrian and Persian Costumes and Decorations by Mary G. Houston and Florence S. Hornblower. Nov 15 1920; 3,000 copies; published at 10s 6d.
238 × 175mm; xii, 83pp +2.
Fawn pictorial cloth, titled in brown.
16 full page illustrations in colour tipped on white mounts, 9 full page in black and white and 60 line illustrations in the text.
Reprinted in the 1930s and still in print in the 1970s.

643. Ancient Greek, Roman and Byzantine Costume by Mary G. Houston. 1931; 3,000 copies; published at 10s 6d.
238 × 175mm; xi, 106pp +2.
Brown pictorial cloth titled in black.
8 full page illustrations in colour, 6 full page in black and white and 93 pen and ink drawings in the text.
The book was still in print in the 1970s.

644. The Basque Country by Katharine Fedden; painted by Romilly Fedden. April 7 1921; 3,000 copies. Published at 20s.
228 × 159mm; xvi, 197pp +2; index; folding map.
Dark blue cloth with a design and titling printed in light brown on the front and spine.
24 full page illustrations in colour captioned on the tissues and 19 in black and white in the text.
Note: The price of the book was reduced to 5s soon after publication, the new price being printed on the dust wrapper.

645. Belgium Past and Present by A. R. Hope Moncrieff; painted by various artists. 1920; published at 20s.
228 × 159mm; xii, 210pp +2; index; folding map.
Red cloth with a design printed in black and fawn on the front and spine; titled in gilt on the spine.
32 full page illustrations in colour.
Note: A reissue from the same stock of the book *The Cockpit of Europe*, also published in 1920.

646. Birds of Britain and their Eggs by J. Lewis Bonhote; painted by H. E. Dresser. 1923; 3,000 copies; published at 10s 6d.
228 × 159mm; viii, 405pp.
Brown cloth with a pictorial design printed on the front and spine; titled in black.
33 full page illustrations in colour.
The book was reissued in 1927 (1,000 copies; 82 illustrations; 10s 6d); this was itself reprinted in 1930 (grey cloth; 3,000 copies). Both versions have their origin in *Birds of Britain* (No. 6).

647. Boulogne: A Base in France being thirty two drawings from the sketch book of Capt. Martin Hardie. Oct 12 1918; 2,000 copies; published at 5s.
241 × 172mm; 32pp.
Cream cloth with a title label including a picture in colour onlaid on the front.
8 illustrations in colour and 24 in black and white tipped on white mounts.

648. The British Bird Book by The Rev. Canon Theodore Wood and W. P. Pycraft.
1930 (book dated 1921); 3,000 copies.
254 × 184mm; xvi, 269pp.
Red cloth with a bird design blocked in blind on the front; titling blocked in gilt on the front and spine.
20 full page illustrations in colour tipped on grey mounts, 24 full page in black and white from photographs and 9 from line drawings; also numerous illustrations in the text.
Note: This book comprises the text and illustrations of *Birds in Flight* (1921) by W. P. Pycraft and *Birds One Should Know* (1925) by Rev. Canon Theodore Wood, both of which were published by Gay & Hancock, who were taken over by A & C Black after World War I. A third Gay & Hancock volume is *Birds and their Young*; all three were illustrated by Roland Green. *Birds in Flight* and *Birds One Should Know* were both reprinted under the A & C Black imprint in 1932 (3,000 copies each) and 1933 (3,000 copies each).

649. California by Mary Hunter Austin; painted by Sutton Palmer. Sept 25 1914; 3,000 copies; published at 18s.
241 × 178mm; viii, 178pp; index; folding map.
Green cloth with a pictorial design printed in blue, orange and yellow on the front and spine; background to titling blocked in gilt on the front and spine; top edge gilt.
32 full page illustrations in colour tipped on white mounts, captioned on the tissues.
The book was issued in a cream coloured box with picture on the lid.

650. The Call of the Open: A little anthology of contemporary and other verse.
Compiled by Leonard Stowell. Nov 6 1914; 2,000 copies; published at 2s 6d.
163 × 104mm; viii, 115pp +4.
White cloth with a floral design printed in pink and green on the front and spine.
12 full page illustrations in colour; decorative endpapers including a colour picture of bluebell woods.
Reprinted 1919; 1932 (3,000 copies).

650a. The Call of the Open: A Nature Anthology. Compiled by Leonard Stowell.
1922; 3,000 copies; published at 5s.
185 × 120mm; viii, 226pp +4.
Cream cloth with a floral design printed in pink and green on the front and spine; decorative endpapers.
16 full page illustrations in colour.
Reprinted 1925.

Note: This book comprises the text and most of the illustrations of *The Call of the Open* and *Nature's Moods* (Nos. 650 and 673), both published in 1914.

651. Oriental Carpets, Runners and Rugs, and some Jacquard Reproductions by Sydney Humphries. Jan 25 1910; 3,000 copies; published at £2 2s.
305 × 216mm; xii, 428pp; index.
White cloth with a design blocked in gilt on the front and spine; titling blocked in gilt on the front and spine; top edge gilt.
24 full page illustrations in colour captioned on the tissues and 8 full page in black and white.

652. A Century of Sea Trading by L. Cope Cornford; painted by W L. Wyllie and J. Spurling. Aug 11 1924; 2,000 copies; published at 10s 6d.
228 × 159mm; x, 182pp.
Blue cloth with a design blocked in gilt on the front; titling blocked in gilt on the front and spine; top edge gilt.
8 full page illustrations in colour, 18 in black and white.

653. The Cockpit of Europe by A.R. Hope Moncrieff; painted by various artists. Jan 6 1920; 3,000 copies; published at 20s.
228 × 159mm; xii, 210pp +2; index; folding map.
Red cloth with a design printed in black and fawn on the front and spine.
32 full page illustrations in colour.
Reissued the same year as *Belgium Past and Present* (No. 645).

654. The Light Side of Egypt painted and described by Lance Thackeray. Oct 16 1908; 3,000 copies; published at 10s.
228 × 298mm.
Beige cloth with a pictorial design blocked in gilt and black and printed in blue and orange on the front; titling blocked in gilt on the front.
36 full page illustrations in colour and notes facing each plate.
Reprinted 1912 (3,000 copies); 1928 (281 × 222mm; 3,000 copies; 24 illustrations tipped on white mounts).

655. Forged Egyptian Antiquities by T.G. Wakeling. Oct 15 1912; 3,000 copies; published at 5s.
202 × 132mm; x, 155pp; index.
Blue green cloth with a picture onlaid on the front and a design blocked in blind on the front and spine; titling blocked in gilt on the spine; top edge gilt.
16 full page illustrations in colour and 12 line drawings.

656. Elementary Watercolour Painting by J. Hullah Brown. Nov 7 1922; 3,000 copies; published at 2s 6d.
220 × 137mm; 24pp.
Dark brown boards quarter bound in fawn cloth; titled in white on the front.
6 full page illustrations in colour.

657. Gainsborough by James Greig; engraved by Mortimer Menpes. Dec 7 1909; 1,000 copies; published at £3 3s.
381 × 280mm; xiii, 187pp.
Blue cloth with a design blocked in gilt on the front; titling blocked in gilt on the front and spine; top edge gilt.
15 full page illustrations in colour by Gainsborough captioned on the tissue versos.

658. Gardens of South Africa by Dorothea Fairbridge; painted by E. Drake and others. Oct 22 1924; 3,000 copies; published at 10s 6d.
210 × 140mm; viii, 213pp; index.
Dark green cloth with a design blocked in gilt on the front and printed in pink on the front and spine; titling blocked in gilt on the front and spine.
16 full page illustrations in colour by Elizabeth Drake, E. Driscoll, E. Struben and E. Barter.
Reprinted 1934 (1,000 copies).
Notes: 1. The title page refers to F. Drake; this is an error. 2. 750 copies of the 3,000 were published with a Maskew Miller (Cape Town) imprint; these copies contain 28 illustrations.

659. Gardens of the Great Mughals coloured and described by Mrs C.M. Villiers-Stuart. Nov 6 1913; 3,000 copies; published at 12s 6d.
228 × 140mm; xvii, 290pp +2; index.
Blue cloth with a design printed in black on the front and spine; titling blocked in gilt on the front and spine; top edge gilt.
16 full page illustrations in colour.

660. The Four Georges by W.M. Thackeray, with a preface by Gordon Home. Oct 20 1910; 2,000 copies; published at 5s.
210 × 140mm; xvi, 160pp; index.
Dark blue cloth with a design blocked in gilt on the front and spine; titling blocked in gilt on the front and spine.
4 portraits in colour and 12 full page illustrations in black and white.

661. Gray's Elegy: An Elegy Written in a Country Churchyard by Thomas Gray; illustrated by G.F. Nicholls. Sept 25 1914; 3,000 copies; published at 5s.
262 × 191mm; 75pp.
Green pictorial cloth with a design printed in light green, mauve and yellow; titling blocked in gilt on the spine; top edge gilt; pictorial endpapers.
8 full page illustrations in colour tipped on grey mounts; text printed in brown on grey paper and set within green pictorial borders.
Brown dust wrapper with a picture in colour on the front within a brown box with a picture in colour on the lid. Designed and printed by W.W. Curtis Ltd, Cheylesmore Press, Coventry.

662. The Annals of Hampstead by Thomas J. Barratt. Dec 6 1912; 550 copies, signed *Thomas J. Barratt*; published at £5 5s (raised to £8 8s in January 1913).

280 × 228mm; blue cloth with a design and crest blocked in gilt and printed in light blue, red and silver on the front and blocked in gilt and printed in light blue on the spine; titling blocked in gilt on the front and spine; top edge gilt.
Vol I: xxii, 306pp; 4 full page illustrations in colour tipped on black mounts and captioned on the tissue rectos, 11 in black and white and many illustrations in the text; 1 map.
Vol II: xix, 299pp; 15 full page illustrations in colour tipped on black mounts and captioned on the tissue rectos, 17 in black and white and many illustrations in the text; 2 maps.
Vol III: xviii, 409pp; 9 full page illustrations in colour tipped on black mounts and captioned on the tissue rectos, 8 in black and white and many illustrations in the text; 3 maps.

The three volumes contain 23 reproductions of paintings by Constable, Cornelius Varley and others; 6 representations of Chatelain's engravings; 27 photogravures from new drawings by A. R. Quinton; around 500 line illustrations and half tones in the text reproducing old prints and engravings, and 6 maps.
Note: The book was published at the author's expense.

663. How to Enjoy Pictures by J. Littlejohns. June 16 1927; 3,000 copies; published at 6s.
260 × 190mm; vi, 81pp +2.
Fawn cloth with a design and titling printed in brown on the front.
8 full page illustrations in colour tipped on white mounts and 43 constructional drawings in the text.

664. The Castles of Italy painted and described by Commendatore C.T.G. Formilli. Nov 21 1933; 2,240 copies; published at 15s.
241 × 178mm; xi, 179pp; index.
Cream cloth with a picture on the front and spine; titling printed in dark red.
24 full page illustrations in colour.

665. The Stones of Italy painted and described by Commendatore C.T.G. Formilli. Sept 30 1927; 3,000 copies; published at 20s.
228 × 159mm; xvi, 247pp; index; map.
Grey cloth with a pictorial design on the front and spine; titling blocked in gilt on the spine.
32 full page illustrations in colour.

666. The Lady of the Lake by Sir Walter Scott; painted by Sutton Palmer; with topography of the poem by Sir George Riddell Airy and notes by Andrew Lang. May 27 1904; 3,000 copies; published at 5s.
203 × 134mm; viii, 159pp; folding map.
Dark blue cloth with a design printed in pink and green on the front and spine; titling blocked in gilt on the spine; top edge gilt.
8 full page illustrations in colour and 42 full page in black and white.

667. Lancashire by F. A. Bruton; painted by A. Wood. Oct 11 1921; 3,000 copies; published at 20s.
228 × 159mm; viii, 242pp +2; index.
Red cloth with a design blocked in gilt and blind on the front and blocked in blind on the spine; titling blocked in gilt on the front and spine.
32 full page illustrations in colour captioned on the tissue versos.

668. The Romance of London by Gordon Home. June 28 1910; 3,000 copies; published at 2s 6d.
244 × 178mm; iv, 60pp; folding map.
Blue cloth with a design printed in grey and a picture in colour onlaid on the front; gilt titling on the front and spine.
16 full page illustrations in colour and line drawings in the text.
Note: Reprinted in 1911 in the Beautiful Britain series.

669. Mediaeval Costume in England and France by Mary G. Houston. Oct 27 1939; 3,000 copies; published at 12s 6d.
238 × 175mm; xi, 228pp.
Orange cloth titled in gilt on the spine.
8 full page illustrations in colour and 350 drawings in the text.

670. Morocco from a Motor by Paul E. Vernon. Sept 14 1927; 3,300 copies; published at 12s 6d.
228 × 159mm; viii, 184pp; index; folding map in colour.
White pictorial cloth; white pictorial wrapper.
48 full page illustrations in colour from photographs.
Note: The book's dedication is 'To my father whose early poems possessed a merry rhythm and whose commercial letters were examples of clearness.'

671. Musical Instruments: Historic, Rare and Unique by A. J. Hipkins; illustrated by William Gibb. Sept 1 1921; 3,000 copies; published at £2 2s.
317 × 228mm; xxiv, 123pp; index.
Red cloth quarter bound in white vellum cloth with a design and titling blocked in gilt on the front and spine; top edge red.
48 full page illustrations in colour.
Note: The illustrations were reproduced by chromo lithography. The book was first published in 1881.

672. Natural History: Animals. An illustrated Who's Who of the Animal World by George Jennison; illustrated by E. H. Fisher. Oct 19 1927; 3,000 copies; published at 12s 6d.
223 × 148mm; xv, 344pp; index.
Dark blue cloth with an elephant's head blocked in gilt on the front and a monkey blocked in gilt on the spine; titling blocked in gilt on the spine.
16 full page illustrations in colour and many in black and white from photographs.
Reprinted 1929 (3,000 copies).

Beautiful Britain and Europe series: (top) examples of the decoration used on the earliest titles and of the 'two tone' cloth where the darker blue is used to cover a previously printed title (see text p 78); (centre) the later decoration used for the bulk of the series and the series dust wrapper; (bottom) a paper board variant used for some reprints and the later design used when the cover picture was dropped.

Above: *A French version of a Peep (*The South Seas*) which appeared in the Contes et Nouvelles series; and a book from the Sportsmen series.* Below: *One of the three Menpes Portrait Biographies flanked by two small nature books:* The Call of the Open *and a reprint of* Highways and Hedges *first published in the 7s 6d series.*

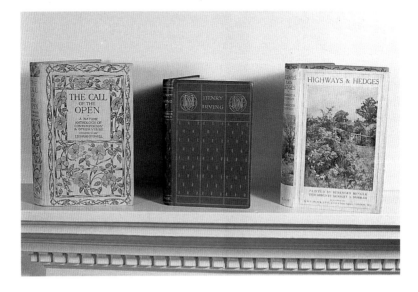

673. Nature's Moods: A little anthology of verse. Compiled by Leonard Stowell. Nov 6 1914; 2,000 copies; published at 2s 6d.
163 × 104mm; vii, 112pp.
White cloth with a floral design printed in pink and green on the front and spine; decorative endpapers with a colour picture of bluebell woods.
12 full page illustrations in colour.
Reprinted 1919.
Note: See also No. 650a.

674. Picturesque Nepal by Percy Brown; [painted by Percy and Muriel Brown].
Dec 15 1912; 2,000 copies; published at 7s 6d.
216 × 152mm; xvi, 205pp +2; index; map.
Brown cloth with a design printed in cream on the front and spine; titling blocked in gilt on the front and spine; top edge gilt.
4 full page illustrations in colour and 40 in black and white from photographs.

675. The New Zealand Shipping Company's Pocket Book by W. P. Reeves. Oct 30 1908; 5,000 copies; published at 2s 6d.
168 × 105mm; x, 159pp plus 20pp for memoranda; 4 maps and plans.
Dark blue cloth with a design blocked in gilt on the front and spine; titling blocked in gilt on the front and spine; top edge gilt.
16 full page illustrations in colour, 6 in black and white.

676. Norfolk and Suffolk by W. G. Clarke; painted by A. Heaton Cooper. April 27 1921; 3,000 copies; published at 25s.
228 × 159mm; x, 275pp; index; folding map.
Blue cloth with a border design blocked in blind on the front and spine; titling blocked in gilt on the front and spine.
40 full page illustrations in colour.

677. The P & O Pocket Book. July 9 1908; 10,000 copies; published at 2s 6d (cloth); 3s 6d (leather).
168 × 105mm; viii, 272pp plus 24pp for memoranda; 29 maps and plans; 3 plates of flags.
Green cloth with a design blocked in gilt on the front; titling blocked in gilt on the front and spine; top edge gilt.
16 full page illustrations in colour.
Note: This is the third impression; the first two had no colour plates.

678. The Pipe Book by Alfred Dunhill. Oct 7 1924; 3,000 copies; published at 18s.
228 × 159mm; x, 262pp +2; index.
Dark blue cloth with a design blocked in gilt on the front and spine; titling blocked in gilt on the front and spine.
4 full page illustrations in colour, 24 full page in black and white and 230 line drawings in the text.

679. A Book of Porcelain by Bernhard Rackham; fine examples in the Victoria and Albert Museum painted by William Gibb. Nov 5 1910; 3,000 copies; published at 12s 6d.
254 × 203mm; xv, 95pp; index.
Green cloth with a design printed in blue and black on the front and a design blocked in gilt on the spine; titling blocked in gilt on the front and spine.
30 full page illustrations in colour tipped on brown mounts, captioned on the tissue versos.

680. The Ramparts of Empire by Frank Fox; painted by Norman L. Wilkinson and Rose Barton. May 26 1910; 3,000 copies; published at 5s.
203 × 140mm; viii, 271pp; index.
Blue cloth with a design and titling printed in olive green on the front and spine.
17 full page illustrations in colour.

681. The Roman Soldier by Amédée Forestier; with an introduction by Ian A. Richmond. 1928; 3,000 copies; published at 10s 6d.
241 × 178mm; 144pp.
Blue cloth titled in black on the front and spine.
15 full page illustrations in colour tipped on white mounts with captions facing and 46 in black and white, 18 of which are photogravures.

682. The Rubáiyát of Omar Khayyam translated by Edward Fitzgerald; painted by Gilbert James; edited and with notes by Reynold Alleyne Nicholson. Sept 24 1909; 3,000 copies; published at 7s 6d.
260 × 190mm; viii, 203pp.
White cloth with an elaborate design printed in blue and green on the front and spine; titling blocked in gilt on the front and spine.
16 full page illustrations in colour with verses facing.
Reprinted Dec 1912 (3,000 copies); Dec 1914 (3,000 copies); 1916 (3,000 copies to sell at 3s 9d); 1917 (3,000 copies); 1922 (190 × 120mm; vii, 136pp; 8 illustrations); 1933 (1922 edition).

683. Stained Glass of the Middle Ages in England and France by Hugh Arnold; painted by Lawrence P. Saint. Aug 9 1913; 3,000 copies; published at 25s.
241 × 172mm; xiv, 269pp; index.
Brown cloth with a design printed in yellow, blue and white on the front and spine; titling blocked in gilt on the spine. 50 full page illustrations in colour captioned on the tissue versos.
Reprinted Oct 1925 (3,400 copies; 224 × 140mm; blue cloth; 48 illustrations, no tissue guards; 12s 6d); 1939 (1,000 copies; 238 × 172mm; red cloth; 15s); also in 1955 and 1956.

684. Hugh Thomson: His art, his letters, his humour and his charm by M.H. Spielmann and Walter Jerrold. Nov 18 1931; 3,282 copies; published at 25s.
228 × 159mm; xx, 269pp; index.

Red cloth; titling printed in black on the spine. Decorated endpapers.
12 full page illustrations in colour captioned on the tissue versos, 16 in black and white and more than 90 in the text.

685. War Posters: Issued by Belligerent and Neutral Nations 1914-19. Selected and edited by Martin Hardie and Arthur K. Sabin. May 18 1920; 3,000 copies; published at 25s.
254 × 203mm; 46pp.
Red cloth with a design printed in black on the front; titling blocked in gilt on the spine.
16 reproductions of posters in colour, 64 in black and white.
Note: The book is also found in fawn cloth with a design printed in black and red on the front; and in green cloth with a design blocked in black and red on the front. Since A & C Black's Historic Library contains no copy, the gilt titling on the spine of the red cloth version is the only possible determinant of precedence.

686. Water-Colour Guidance by Hullah Brown. Sept 17 1931; 3,000 copies; published at 12s 6d.
228 × 140mm; xx, 302pp +2.
Dark blue cloth titled in gilt on the spine.
24 full page illustrations in colour [by Wilfrid Ball, Sutton Palmer, etc].
Reprinted 1947.

687. Whistler as I knew him by Mortimer Menpes. 1904; 2,000 copies; published at £2.
280 × 210mm; xv, 153pp +2.
Light brown cloth with a design and printed in dark brown and orange on the front and spine; top edge gilt.
125 full page illustrations in colour and tint by James McNeill Whistler and Mortimer Menpes, captioned on the tissue rectos.
Note: 1. The book was set in the USA and electros shipped to Britain. 2. The text was issued separately in 1905 at 2s 6d.

Peeps at Many Lands and Cities

197 × 133mm.
Cloth with picture in colour onlaid on the front and decorative designs blocked in blind or printed in black or colours on the front and spine; titled in gilt on the spine.
Later titles (from around 1920) have no picture on the front and no gilt.
Eight, twelve or thirteen full page illustrations in colour, including the cover illustration.
Published at 1s 6d; later 2s, 2s 6d and 3s.
Notes: Artists are named only where they appear on a book's title page [or in the list

of illustrations]. Reprints may show variations in the cloth colour, the picture on the front, the endpapers and the choice and number of illustrations.

701. Alsace-Lorraine by A.W. Holland; painted by E. Harrison Compton, C.E. Flower and Allan Stewart. May 10 1915; 5,000 copies.
viii, 88pp; map.
Light blue cloth; 12 illustrations.
Reprinted 1926 (3,000 copies).

702. Arabia by Sirdar Ikbal Ali Shah. April 16 1931; 3,000 copies.
viii, 87pp; map.
Blue cloth, no picture on front; 8 illustrations.

703. Australia by Sir Frank Fox; painted by Percy F.S. Spence and others. Sept 22 1911; 5,000 copies.
viii, 88pp; double page map.
Red cloth; 13 illustrations.
Reprinted 1914 (5,000 copies); 1920 (3,000 copies); 1924 (5,000 copies); 1933 (3,000 copies).

704. Austria by J.D. Newth. 1930; 5,000 copies.
96pp.
Blue cloth, no picture on front; 4 illustrations in colour, 8 in black and white.

705. The Baltic States by Hebe Spaull. April 16 1931; 5,000 copies.
x, 81pp +2; map.
Light blue cloth, no picture on front; 4 illustrations in colour, 8 in black and white.

706. Belgium by G.W.T. Omond; painted by Amédée Forestier. Sept 15 1909; 5,000 copies.
vii, 87pp; map.
Navy blue cloth; 13 illustrations.
Reprinted 1912 (5,000 copies); 1915 (5,000 copies); 1925 (3,000 copies).

707. Berlin by Edith Siepen; painted by Alois Metz. Sept 22 1911; 5,000 copies.
96pp; map; map on front endpapers.
Green cloth; 12 illustrations.

708. Berlin by E. Siepen-Hetherington; painted by Hans Bastanier. 1929; 3,000 copies.
vii, 88pp; plan on front endpapers.
Blue cloth, no picture on front; 6 illustrations in colour.
Note: The text of No. 707 was completely revised and reset.

709. British North Borneo by L.W.W. Gudgeon; painted by Allan Stewart. Oct 3 1913; 5,000 copies.

viii, 88pp; map.
Blue cloth, no picture on front; 12 illustrations.

710. Burma painted and described by R. Talbot Kelly. Sept 22 1908; 5,000 copies.
viii, 85pp +2; map.
Brown cloth; 13 illustrations.
Reprinted 1909; 1929 (3,000 copies).

711. Canada by J.T. Bealby. Oct 22 1909; 5,000 copies.
viii, 88pp +4; map.
Red cloth; 13 illustrations (12 listed).
Reprinted 1910; 1915 (5,000 copies); 1921 (3,000 copies); 1924 (5,000 copies).

712. Canada by J.H. Cranston. July 24 1935; 5,000 copies.
vi, 90pp; map.
Blue cloth, no picture on front; 4 illustrations in colour, 8 in black and white.

713. Ceylon by Alfred Clark; painted by Allan Stewart and Mrs C. Creyke. Oct 20 1910; 5,000 copies.
vii, 88pp; map.
Brown cloth; 12 illustrations (plus duplicate on front).
Reprinted 1920 (3,000 copies); 1928 (20,000 copies).

714. China by Lena E. Johnston; [painted by Norman H. Hardy and T. Hodgson Liddell]; Oct 22 1909; 5,000 copies.
vi, 88pp; map.
Red cloth; 12 illustrations (plus duplicate on front).
Reprinted 1910; 1911 (5,650 copies); 1913 (2,500 copies); 1915 (5,000 copies); 1922 (3,000 copies); 1929 (3,000 copies).

715. Corsica by Ernest Young; painted by E.A. Norbury. Sept 15 1909; 5,000 copies.
vii, 88pp; map.
Green cloth; 12 illustrations (plus duplicate on front).
Reprinted 1925 (3,000 copies).

716. Cuba by Ford Fairford; painted by Claude Pratt. Oct 3 1913; 5,000 copies.
vii, 88pp; map; shields on front endpapers.
Red cloth; 12 illustrations.
Reprinted 1926 (3,000 copies).

717. Czechoslovakia by Helena C. Schott. June 11 1926; 3,000 copies.
viii, 70pp +; map; shields on front endpapers.
Blue cloth, no picture on front; 4 illustrations in colour, 8 in black and white.
Reprinted 1928 (3,000 copies).

718. Delhi and the Durbar by John Finnemore; painted by Mortimer Menpes. Feb 23 1912; 5,000 copies.
vii, 88pp.
Red cloth; 12 illustrations.

719. Denmark by M. Pearson Thomson; painted by Ingeborg Hyldahl. Oct 7 1910; 5,000 copies.
vii, 88p +4; map.
Green cloth; 12 illustrations (plus duplicate on front).
Reprinted 1924 (3,000 copies; revised by John B. Dano).

720. Edinburgh by Rosaline Masson. Oct 7 1910; 5,000 copies.
96pp; map on front endpapers.
Green cloth; 12 illustrations (plus duplicate on front).
Reprinted 1919 (5,000 copies).

721. Egypt painted and described by R. Talbot Kelly. Sept 22 1908; 5,000 copies.
viii, 87pp +4; map.
Dark green cloth; 13 illustrations.
Reprinted 1909; 1910; 1912 (7,500 copies); 1916 (5,000 copies); 1920 (5,000 copies); 1926 (5,000 copies).

722. England by John Finnemore. Sept 22 1908; 5,000 copies.
viii, 88pp +4; map.
Red cloth; 13 illustrations (12 listed).
Reprinted Sept 1908; Oct 1908; Dec 1909; 1910; 1912 (7,500 copies); 1913 (5,000 copies); 1917 (5,000 copies); 1926 (3,000 copies); 1934 (3,000 copies).

723. Finland by M. Pearson Thomson. Nov 5 1909; 5,000 copies.
viii, 88pp +4; map.
Blue cloth; 12 illustrations (plus duplicate on front).

724. Finland and the Tundra by L. Edna Walter. July 12 1917; 3,000 copies.
vii, 88pp.
Brown cloth; 12 illustrations.
Reprinted 1927 (3,000 copies).
A later issue of the book *Life and Legends of Other Lands: Finn and Samoyad* (No. 777) published in March 1915.

725. Florence by Elizabeth Grierson; painted by Col. R. Goff and others. Oct 15 1912; 5,000 copies.
viii, 88pp; map; double page plan on front endpapers.
Blue cloth; 12 illustrations.
Reprinted 1930 (3,000 copies).

726. France by John Finnemore; painted by Nico Jungman, E. Crescioli, W. Scott and J. Williamson. Sept 17 1907; 5,000 copies.

viii, 86pp +2; map.
Red cloth; 12 illustrations.
Reprinted 1907; 1908; 1910; 1912 (5,000 copies); 1915 (5,000 copies); 1919 (3,000 copies); 1921 (3,000 copies); 1927 (5,000 copies).

727. Germany by Mrs Alfred Sidgwick. Painted by L. Burleigh Bruhl, Arthur G. Bell and Allan Stewart. Oct 22 1909; 5,000 copies.
viii, 88pp.
Red cloth; 12 illustrations (plus duplicate on front).
Reprinted 1910; 1915 (5,000 copies).
Note: Bell's name is given as Arthur C. Bell on the title page.

728. Germany by Agnes Platt. Oct 12 1932; 3,000 copies.
vi; 90pp; map.
Blue cloth, no picture on front; 4 illustrations in colour, 8 in black and white.

729. Greece by Edith A. Browne; painted by E.H. Fitchew and John Fulleylove. Nov 5 1909; 5,000 copies.
viii, 88pp; map.
Blue cloth; 12 illustrations (plus duplicate on front).
Reprinted 1913 (5,000 copies); 1929 (3,000 copies; reset).

730. Holland by Beatrix Jungman; painted by Nico Jungman. Sept 17 1907; 5,000 copies.
viii, 82pp +6; map.
Blue cloth; 13 illustrations (12 listed).
Reprinted 1908; 1909; 1913 (5,000 copies); 1920 (3,000 copies); 1925 (3,000 copies); 1932 (3,000 copies).

731. The Holy Land by John Finnemore; painted by John Fulleylove. Sept 22 1908; 5,000 copies.
viii, 83pp +4; map.
Dark blue cloth; 12 illustrations.
Reprinted 1908; 1911 (5,000 copies); 1917 (5,000 copies); 1921 (3,000 copies); 1928 (3,000 copies).

732. Hungary by H. Tornai de Kover; painted by Adrian and Marianne Stokes. Oct 6 1911; 5,000 copies.
95pp; map.
Red cloth; 12 illustrations.

733. Hungary by J.D. Newth; [painted by Mr and Mrs Adrian Stokes]. Feb 24 1932; 5,000 copies.
vi, 88pp; map.
Blue cloth, no picture on front; 4 illustrations in colour, 8 in black and white from photographs.

734. Iceland by Mrs Disney Leith; painted by M.A. Wemyss and Mrs Disney Leith. Sept 22 1908; 5,000 copies.
viii, 70pp +2; map.
Blue cloth; 12 illustrations (plus duplicate on front).
Reprinted 1911 (5,000 copies).

735. India by John Finnemore; painted by Mortimer Menpes. Sept 17 1907; 5,000 copies.
viii, 87pp; map.
Blue cloth; 13 illustrations (12 listed).
Reprinted Nov 1907; 1908; 1910; 1913 (5,000 copies); 1915 (5,000 copies); 1920 (3,000 copies); 1924 (5,000 copies); 1928 (5,000 copies).

735a. India. A translation into Welsh by David G. Evans.

736. Home Life in India by John Finnemore; painted by Mortimer Menpes. 1917.
iv, 87pp.
Blue cloth, no picture on front; 12 illustrations.
A later issue of the book *Home of Many Lands: India* published in 1912 (No. 776).

737. Ireland by Katherine Tynan; painted by F.S. Walker. Nov 5 1909; 5,000 copies.
vii, 88pp +4; map.
Green cloth; 13 illustrations.
Reprinted 1910; 1911 (5,000 copies); 1914 (5,000 copies); 1926 (3,000 copies).

738. Ireland by Katherine Tynan; painted by A. Heaton Cooper. June 15 1927; 3,000 copies.
vii, 88pp; map.
Blue cloth, no picture on front; 8 illustrations.
Note: Text the same as No. 737 but with changes to Chapter 5 and alterations to the map.

739. Italy by John Finnemore. Sept 17 1907; 5,000 copies.
viii, 87pp; map.
Blue grey cloth; 13 illustrations (12 listed).
Reprinted 1908; 1909; 1911 (5,000 copies); 1915 (5,000 copies); 1916 (10,000 copies); 1920 (3,000 copies); 1926 (5,000 copies).

740. Jamaica by John Henderson; painted by A.S. Forrest. Oct 22 1909; 5,000 copies.
vii, 87pp +4; map.
Blue green cloth; 12 illustrations (duplicate on front).
Reprinted 1924 (3,000 copies).

741. Japan by John Finnemore; painted by Ella Du Cane. Sept 17 1907; 5,000 copies.

viii, 88pp; map.

Blue green cloth; 8 illustrations (plus duplicate on front).

Reprinted Nov 1907; 1908; 1909; 1910; 1913 (5,000 copies); 1917 (5,000 copies); 1919 (5,000 and 3,000 copies); 1924 (7,000 copies); 1930 (5,000 copies, reset).

Note: Reprints from 1907 contain 12 illustrations.

742. Java by J.F. Scheltema; painted by Hugo V. Pedersen. Oct 15 1912; 5,000 copies.

vii, 88pp; map.

Blue cloth; 12 illustrations.

Reprinted 1926 (3,000 copies).

743. Kashmir by The Hon Mrs C.G. Bruce; painted by Major E. Molyneaux. Nov 8 1911; 5,000 copies.

95pp; map; shields on front endpapers.

Blue cloth; 12 illustrations.

Reprinted 1915 (5,000 copies); 1932 (3,000 copies).

744. Korea by Constance J.D. Coulson; painted by Constance J.D. Coulson and E.H. Fitchew. 11 Nov 1910; 5,000 copies.

vii, 85pp +4; map.

Red cloth; 12 illustrations (plus duplicate on front).

745. Korea by Agnes Herbert; painted by C.J.D. Coulson and E.H. Fitchew. Nov 14 1924; 3,000 copies.

vii, 88pp; map.

Red cloth; 8 illustrations.

746. London by G.E. Mitton; painted by Herbert Marshall, Rose Barton, Ralph Hedley and Allan Stewart. Sept 22 1911; 5,000 copies.

viii, 88pp; double page map on front endpapers; double page map of 16th century London on rear endpapers.

Blue cloth; 12 illustrations.

Reprinted 1914 (5,000 copies); 1921 (5,000 copies); 1930 (3,000 copies).

747. Madagascar by Harold A. Ridgwell; painted by native artists; Sept 1 1921; 5,000 copies.

viii, 87pp; map.

Red cloth; 8 illustrations.

748. The Malay States by Philip C. Coote; painted by D.A.H. Aldworth; Dec 5 1923; 5,000 copies.

viii, 87pp; map.

Blue cloth; 8 illustrations.

749. Montenegro by Roy Trevor; painted by Allan Stewart. Oct 3 1913; 5,000 copies.
viii, 88pp; map.
Red cloth; 12 illustrations.

750. Morocco by John Finnemore; painted by A.S. Forrest. Sept 22 1908; 5,000 copies.
viii, 85pp +2; map.
Orange cloth; 12 illustrations.
Reprinted 1910; 1935 (5,000 copies, reset).

751. Newfoundland by Ford Fairford; painted by C.G. Lowther. Oct 15 1912; 5,000 copies.
viii, 88pp; map; shields on front endpapers.
Blue green cloth; 12 illustrations.
Reprinted 1928 (3,000 copies).

752. New York by Hildegarde Hawthorne; painted by Martyn Lewis. Sept 22 1911; 5,000 copies.
vii, 87pp; 'bird's eye' view on front endpapers.
Blue cloth; 12 illustrations.
Reprinted 1923 (3,000 copies).

753. New Zealand by P.A. Vaile; painted by F. and W. Wright. Sept 15 1909; 5,000 copies.
vii, 88pp; map.
Red cloth; 13 illustrations.
Reprinted 1910; 1919 (3,000 copies); 1921 (twice, 5,000 copies each).

754. Norway by Lt. Col. A.F. Mockler-Ferryman; painted by A. Heaton Cooper and Nico Jungman; Sept 15 1909; 5,000 copies.
vii, 88pp; map.
Blue cloth; 13 illustrations.
Reprinted 1910; 1919 (5,000 copies).

755. Norway and the Lapps by L. Edna Walter; painted by Warwick Reynolds and others. July 12 1917.
vii, 88pp.
Brown cloth; 12 illustrations.
A later issue of the book *Life and Legends of Other Lands: Norse and Lapp* (No. 778) published in October 1913.
Reprinted 1929 (5,000 copies; alterations to text).

756. Panama by Edith A. Browne. May 23 1913; 5,000 copies.
viii, 88pp; map; shields on front endpapers.
Red cloth; 8 illustrations in colour, 8 in black and white from photographs.

Reprinted 1923 (5,000 copies).

757. Paris by Margery Williams; painted by Allan Stewart. Nov 11 1910; 5,000 copies.
vii, 88pp; map on front endpapers.
Blue cloth; 12 illustrations (plus duplicate on front).
Reprinted 1916 (3,000 copies); 1932 (5,000 copies, reset).

758. Paris by The Comtesse Jean de Pange; painted by Eleanor Duncan. 1933; 5,000 copies.
viii, 88pp.
Blue cloth, no picture on front; 8 illustrations.

759. Persia. Painted and described by H.F. Haig. Dec 5 1923; 5,000 copies.
vii, 87pp; map; shields on front endpapers.
Blue cloth; 8 illustrations.

760. Poland by Monica M. Gardner; painted by Arthur Grottger and others. Nov 6 1917; 3,000 copies.
viii, 87pp.
Brown cloth; 4 illustrations in colour, 8 in black and white.
Reprinted 1926 (3,000 copies).

761. Portugal painted and described by Agnes M. Goodall. Nov 5 1909; 5,000 copies.
vii, 88pp +4; map.
Green cloth; 12 illustrations (plus duplicate on front).
Reprinted 1919 (3,000 copies).

762. Rome by G.T. Genn. Nov 8 1911; 5,000 copies.
96pp; shields on front endpapers.
Blue cloth; 12 illustrations.
Reprinted 1919 (5,000 copies).

763. Rumania by Hebe Spaull. April 15 1930; 5,000 copies.
x, 96pp; map.
Blue cloth, no picture on cover; 4 illustrations in colour, 8 in black and white.

764. Russia by L. Edna Walter; painted by F. de Haenen and others. Oct 7 1910; 5,000 copies. viii, 88pp; map.
Yellow brown cloth; 13 illustrations (12 listed).
Reprinted 1913 (5,000 copies); 1917 (3,000 copies); 1928 (3,000 copies).

765. Scotland by Elizabeth Grierson. Sept 17 1907; 5,000 copies.
viii, 86pp; map.
Green cloth; 13 illustrations (12 listed).

Reprinted Nov 1907; 1908; 1910; 1918; 1920 (3,000 copies); 1927 (3,000 copies).

766. Siam by Ernest Young; painted by Edwin A. Norbury. Sept 22 1908; 5,000 copies.
viii, 83pp +4; map.
Blue green cloth; 12 illustrations (duplicate on front).
Reprinted 1910; 1927 (5,000 copies).

767. South Africa. Dudley Kidd; painted by A.M. Goodall. Sept 22 1908; 5,000 copies.
viii, 87pp; map.
Grey cloth; 13 illustrations.
Reprinted 1909; 1910; 1919 (5,000 copies); 1927 (3,000 copies, revised by G.E. Chittenden).

768. South America by Edith A. Browne; Dec 29 1915; 5,000 copies.
viii, 88pp; map.
Blue cloth; 12 illustrations.
Reprinted 1928 (3,000 copies).

769. The South Seas (Melanesia) by J.H.M. Abbott; painted by Norman Hardy.
Sept 22 1908; 5,000 copies. viii, 83pp +4; map.
Blue cloth; 13 illustrations.
Reprinted 1926 (3,000 copies).

770. Spain by Edith A. Browne; painted by Trevor Haddon and E.T.A. Wigram.
Oct 7 1910; 5,000 copies.
96pp; map.
Yellow brown cloth; 13 illustrations (12 listed).
Reprinted 1916 (3,000 copies); 1929 (3,000 copies).

771. Sweden by Rev. W. Liddle and Mrs Liddle; painted by Anders Zorn, Carl Larsson and others. Nov 1 1911; 5,000 copies.
viii, 88pp; map; shields on front endpapers.
Red cloth; 12 illustrations.
Reprinted 1922 (3,000 copies).

772. Switzerland by John Finnemore; painted by A.D. McCormick, J. Hardwicke Lewis and others. Sept 22 1908; 5,000 copies.
viii, 86pp +2; map.
Blue cloth; 13 illustrations.
Reprinted 1908; 1911 (5,200 copies); 1915 (5,000 copies); 1920 (3,000 copies); 1926 (5,000 copies); 1928 (3,000 copies).

773. Turkey by Julius R. van Millingen; painted by Warwick Goble. Oct 6 1911; 5,000 copies.

iv, 95pp; map.
Red cloth; 12 illustrations.
Reprinted 1920 (3,000 copies, some new setting and Sirdar Ikbal Ali Shah as joint author); 1931 (3,000 copies).

774. Wales by E.M. Wilmot-Buxton; Sept 22 1911; 5,000 copies.
viii, 88pp; map.
Blue cloth; 12 illustrations.
Reprinted 1921 (3,000 copies).

775. Yugoslavia by Lena A. Yovilchitch; painted by Alfreda Markovitch and others; July 11 1928; 5,000 copies.
vi, 89pp +2; map.
Blue cloth, no picture on cover; 8 illustrations.

Homes of Many Lands Series

776. India. John Finnemore; painted by Mortimer Menpes; Oct 15 1912; 5,000 copies.
viii, 87pp.
Red cloth; 12 illustrations.
Note: This book was later reissued in the Peeps at Many Lands series as *Home Life in India*.

Life and Legends of Other Lands

197 × 133mm.
Cloth with a picture in colour onlaid on the front and designs printed on the front and spine; full page illustrations in colour.

777. Finn and Samoyad: The Bear-Hunters of the North by L. Edna Walter; painted by Guy Lipscombe, Alexander Federley and others. March 16 1915; 5,000 copies.
vii, 88pp.
Red cloth; 12 illustrations in colour.

778. Norse and Lapp by L. Edna Walter; painted by Warwick Reynolds and others. Oct 3 1913; 5,000 copies.
vii, 88pp.
Red cloth; 12 illustrations in colour.
Note: These two books were later reissued in the Peeps at Many Lands and Cities series (Nos. 724, 755).

Larger Peeps at Many Lands

'Larger volumes in the style of the Peeps at Many Lands and Cities series, each containing 32 full page illustrations in colour.'
213 × 140mm; 5,000 copies.
Cloth with picture in colour onlaid on the front and designs blocked in blind on the front and spine; titled in gilt on the spine. Published at 3s 6d.

779. The British Empire by Frank Fox. Oct 6 1911.
xvi, 199pp; double page map.
Red cloth; titling blocked in gilt on the spine; 32 illustrations.
Reprinted 1914 (5,700 copies); 1929 (3,150 copies).

780. The Far East (China, Korea and Japan) by Frank Elias. Nov 17 1911.
viii, 213pp; folding map.
Blue cloth; titling blocked in gilt on the spine; 32 illustrations.
Reprinted 1913.

781. The Gorgeous East (India, Burma, Ceylon and Siam) by Frank Elias. Oct 3 1913.
viii, 221pp +2; folding map.
Red cloth; titling blocked in gilt on the spine; 32 illustrations.

782. Oceania (Australia, New Zealand and South Seas) by Frank Fox. Oct 6 1911.
viii, 204pp; folding map.
Blue cloth; titling blocked in gilt on the spine; 32 illustrations.
Reprinted 1919 (3,000 copies).

783. The World by Ascott R. Hope. Sept 22 1908.
viii, 184pp; folding map.
Green cloth; titling blocked in gilt on the spine; 38 illustrations.
Reprinted 1909; 1915 (5,000 copies).

Peeps at Ancient Lands

197 × 133mm.
Cloth with colour picture onlaid on the cover and designs printed on the front and spine; full-page illustrations in colour and black and white; published at 1s 6d, later 2s 6d.

784. Ancient Assyria by Rev. James Baikie; painted by Constance Baikie. Nov 1 1916; 3,000 copies.
iv, 92pp; map.
Fawn cloth; 8 illustrations in colour, 8 in black and white.
Reprinted 1928 (3,000 copies).

785. Ancient Crete by Rev. James Baikie; painted by Constance Baikie. Oct 7 1924; 5,000 copies.
96pp; map.
Blue cloth, no picture on cover; 4 illustrations in colour, 8 in black and white.

786. Ancient Egypt by Rev. James Baikie; painted by Constance Baikie. Oct 5 1912; 5,000 copies.
viii, 88pp; map.
Blue cloth; 8 illustrations in colour, 8 in black and white.
Reprinted 1916 (12,500 and 5,000 copies); 1932 (3,000 copies).

787. Ancient Greece by Rev. James Baikie; painted by Constance N. Baikie and John Fulleylove. Jan 26 1920; 5,000 copies.
iv, 92pp; map.
Brown cloth; 8 illustrations in colour, 8 in black and white.
Reprinted 1931 (3,000 copies).

788. Ancient Jerusalem by Rev. James Baikie. Sept 10 1920; 3,000 copies.
vi, 90pp; map.
Blue cloth, no picture on cover; 4 illustrations in colour, 8 in black and white.
Reprinted 1930 (3,000 copies).

789. Ancient Palestine by Rev. James Baikie. Feb 23 1927; 3,000 copies.
iv, 92pp; map.
Blue cloth, no picture on cover; 4 illustrations in colour, 8 in black and white.

790. Ancient Rome by Rev. James Baikie; painted by Constance N. Baikie and Alberto Pisa; Jan 8 1918; 3,000 copies.
vii, 88pp; maps.
Fawn cloth, plans on endpapers; 8 illustrations in colour, 8 in black and white.
Reprinted 1925 (3,000 copies); 1932 (3,000 copies).

Peeps at History

197 × 133mm.
Cloth with colour picture onlaid on the front and designs printed on the front and spine; full-page illustrations in colour; published at 1s 6d, later 3s.

791. America by John Finnemore. Oct 15 1912; 3,000 copies.
vii, 88pp.
Navy blue cloth; 8 illustrations in colour, 21 line drawings.
Reprinted 1923 (3,000 copies).

792. The Barbary Rovers by John Finnemore. Oct 15 1912; 3,000 copies.
96pp.
Blue cloth, no picture on cover; 8 illustrations in colour, 21 line drawings.
Note: Some copies, in fawn paper boards, carry an illustration on the front.

793. The British Dominions Beyond the Seas by E.L. Hoskyn. Nov 7 1922; 3,000 copies.
vii, 87pp; double page map.
Red cloth; 4 illustrations in colour, 4 in black and white, 20 line drawings.

794. Canada by Beatrice Home. Oct 8 1911; 3,000 copies.
96pp.
Red cloth; 8 illustrations in colour, 20 line drawings.
Reprinted 1924 (3,000 copies).

795. France by John Finnemore. Oct 3 1913; 3,000 copies.
vii, 88pp.
Red cloth; 8 illustrations in colour, 8 in black and white, 5 line drawings in text.
Reprinted 1925 (3,000 copies).

This book was retitled and reissued as:
795a. A Short History of France by John Finnemore. 1915.
12 illustrations in colour plus line drawings in the text.

796. Germany by John Finnemore; painted by E. Harrison Compton and others.
Oct 3 1913; 3,000 copies.
95pp.
Navy blue cloth; 8 illustrations in colour, 20 line drawings.
Note: Compton's name is printed as E.T. Harrison Compton on the title page.

This book was retitled and reissued with different illustrations as:
796a. A Short History of Germany by John Finnemore. 1915.
95pp.
Black cloth bearing a Prussian eagle in yellow on the front; titled in gilt on the spine, where the author's name is spelt Finnimore; 8 illustrations in colour, 8 in black and white, 20 line drawings (not 5 as stated on the title page).
Note: The final sentences of the book read: 'For the victories of war Germany has exchanged the victories of peace. Her manufactures have grown with wonderful rapidity, her men of science have made striking discoveries, her scholars and thinkers have added greatly to the sum of the world's knowledge. She has known no war since the struggle which saw her born anew as a nation, and in the long interval

which has passed she has steadily risen in power, wealth and authority. 'For a book published in 1915, these words are remarkable!

797. Holland by John Finnemore; painted by Allan Stewart and Mima Nixon. Oct 15 1912; 3,000 copies.
vii, 88pp.
Red cloth; 8 illustrations in colour, 20 line drawings.

798. India by T. H. Manners-Howe; painted by Allan Stewart. Nov 6 1911; 3,000 copies.
96pp.
Blue cloth; 8 illustrations in colour, 26 line drawings.
Reprinted 1920 (3,000 copies).

799. Ireland by Beatrice Home. Sept 25 1914; 3,000 copies.
iv, 92pp.
Green cloth; 8 illustrations in colour, 20 line drawings.

800. Japan by John Finnemore; painted by Miss Wakana Utagawa. Dec 14 1911; 5,000 copies.
95pp.
Blue cloth; 8 illustrations in colour, 20 line drawings.

801. Scotland by G. E. Mitton; painted by J. Jellicoe. Oct 12 1911; 3,000 copies.
iv, 96pp.
Deep blue cloth; 8 illustrations in colour, 24 line drawings.
Reprinted 1912 (3,000 copies).

Peeps at Great Railways

197 × 133mm.
Cloth with colour picture onlaid on the front, which also carries a design of signals; full-page illustrations in colour and line drawings in black and white; maps on front endpapers; published at 1s 6d.

802. The Canadian Pacific Railway by Frederick A. Talbot. Nov 9 1915; 3,000 copies.
96pp.
Blue cloth; 8 illustrations in colour, 21 in black and white.
Reprinted 1922 (3,000 copies).

803. The Great Western Railway by Gordon Home. May 9 1913; 3,000 copies.
92pp.

Blue cloth; 8 illustrations in colour, 21 in black and white.
Reprinted 1926 (3,000 copies).

804. The London and North Western Railway by George Eyre-Todd. Nov 25 1911;
3,000 copies.
96pp.
Blue green cloth; 8 illustrations in colour, 23 in black and white.

The above was revised and reissued as:
805. The London Midland and Scottish Railway by George Eyre-Todd. Nov 15
1926; 3,000 copies.
iv, 92pp.
Blue cloth, no picture on cover; 8 illustrations in colour, 19 in black and white.

806. The North Eastern and Great Northern Railways by G.E. Mitton. Nov 25 1911;
3,000 copies.
96pp +4.
Red cloth; 8 illustrations in colour, 26 in black and white.

The above was revised and reissued as:
807. The London and North Eastern Railway by G.E. Mitton. Nov 16 1925; 3,000
copies.
iv, 92pp.
Blue cloth, no picture on cover; 8 illustrations in colour, 24 in black and white.

808. The South East and Chatham and London, Brighton and South Coast Railways
by G.E. Mitton. Oct 15 1912; 3,000 copies.
vii, 88pp.
Blue cloth; 8 illustrations in colour, 27 black and white.

The above was revised and reissued as:
809. The Southern Railway by G.E. Mitton. Nov 16 1925; 3,000 copies.
iv, 92pp.
Blue cloth, no picture on cover; 8 illustrations in colour, 27 in black and white.

Peeps at Nature

197 × 133mm.
Cloth with picture in colour onlaid on the cover which also carries a design of
flowers; full-page illustrations in colour and black and white and line drawings in
the text; published at 1s 6d, later 2s 6d.

810. Aquaria and Garden Ponds by W. Harold Cotton; Nov 28 1935; 5,000 copies. vi, 90pp.
Blue cloth, no picture on cover; 2 illustrations in colour, 8 in black and white.
Note: The book does not refer to itself as a Peep, but advertisements for it refer to Peeps at Nature as being in the same series; it is therefore listed here.

811. Bees, Wasps and Ants by Rev. Charles A. Hall. June 9 1925; 3,000 copies. viii, 88pp; index.
Navy blue cloth, no picture on cover; 4 illustrations in colour, 10 in black and white (on 8 pages); 5 line drawings.
Reprinted 1932 (3,000 copies).

812. Bird Life of the Seasons by W. Percival Westell. Oct 6 1911; 3,000 copies. viii, 84pp +4; index.
Green cloth; 8 illustrations in colour, 13 in black and white, 1 line drawing.
Reprinted 1912 (3,000 copies); 1917 (3,000 copies); 1920 (3,000 copies); 1923 (3,000 copies); 1926 (5,000 copies); 1930 (5,000 copies); 1935 (3,000 copies); 1939; also 1940; 1944; 1948 and later.

813. Birds, Eggs and Nests by Rev. Charles A. Hall. March 25 1932; 5,000 copies. vii, 88pp; index.
Blue cloth; 8 illustrations in colour, 8 in black and white.
Reprinted 1935 (3,000 copies); 1938.

814. British Butterflies by A.M. Stewart. May 1 1912; 3,000 copies. viii, 88pp; index.
Dark green cloth; 8 illustrations in colour, 8 in black and white.
Reprinted 1916 (3,000 copies); 1919 (3,000 copies); 1922 (3,120 copies); 1926 (3,000 copies); 1934 (3,000 copies).

815. British Ferns, Clubmosses and Horsetails by Daniel Ferguson. Oct 15 1912; 3,000 copies.
viii, 88pp; index.
Green cloth; 8 illustrations in colour, 11 in black and white (on 8 pages), 4 line drawings.'
Reprinted 1922 (3,000 copies).

816. British Land Mammals and their Habits by A. Nicol Simpson; painted by C.F. Newall, W.S. Berridge and others. Oct 6 1911; 5,000 copies. viii, 88pp; index.
Brown cloth; 8 illustrations in colour, 14 in black and white (on 8 pages).
Reprinted 1912 (3,000 copies); 1926 (3,000 copies).
Note: The title page is wrong in referring to 24 illustrations.

817. British Reptiles and Amphibians by A. Nicol Simpson. Nov 5 1913; 3,000 copies.
viii, 86pp +2; index.

Green cloth; 8 illustrations in colour, 12 in black and white (on 8 pages), 6 line drawings.
Reprinted 1924 (3,000 copies).

British Trees (see under Trees)

818. Common British Beetles by Rev. Charles A. Hall. May 1 1914; 3,000 copies. viii, 88pp.
Navy blue cloth; 8 illustrations in colour, 8 in black and white, 5 line drawings.
Reprinted 1924 (3,000 copies).

819. Common British Moths by A.M. Stewart. July 29 1913; 3,000 copies. vii, 88pp; index.
Green cloth; 8 illustrations in colour, 8 in black and white, 2 line drawings.
Reprinted 1923 (3,000 copies); 1930 (3,000 copies).

820. The Natural History of the Garden. W. Percival Westell. Oct 15 1912; 3,000 copies. vii, 88pp; index.
Green cloth; 8 illustrations in colour, 15 in black and white (on 8 pages), 18 line drawings.
Reprinted 1920 (3,000 copies); 1930 (3,000 copies).

821. The Naturalist at the Seashore by Richard Elmhurst. Oct 3 1913; 3,000 copies. viii, 86pp +2; index.
Maroon cloth; 8 illustrations in colour, 13 in black and white (on 8 pages), 16 line drawings.
Reprinted 1920 (3,000 copies); 1921 (3,000 copies); 1932 (3,000 copies); 1936 (3,000 copies).

822. Pond Life by Rev. Charles A. Hall. May 9 1913; 3,000 copies. viii, 88pp; index.
Dark blue cloth; 8 illustrations in colour, 14 in black and white (on 8 pages), 28 line drawings.
Reprinted 1928 (3,000 copies).

823. The Romance of the Rocks by Rev. Charles A. Hall. Oct 15 1912; 3,000 copies. viii, 88pp; map; index.
Brown cloth; 8 illustrations in colour, 16 in black and white (on 8 pages), 33 line drawings.
Reprinted 1919 (3,000 copies).

824. Trees by Rev. Charles A. Hall. March 5 1930; 5,000 copies. viii, 88pp; index.
Blue cloth, no picture on cover; 8 illustrations in colour, 8 in black and white.
Reprinted 1936 (3,000 copies), and later.
Note: Reprints were titled *British Trees*.

825. Wild Flowers and their Wonderful Ways by Rev. Charles A. Hall; Oct 6 1911; 3,000 copies.
viii, 88pp; index.
Navy blue cloth; 8 illustrations in colour (3 by C.F. Newall and 5 from colour photographs by Ernest T. Waltham), 8 in black and white.
Reprinted 1912 (3,000 copies); 1916 (3,000 copies); 1919 (3,000 copies); 1924 (3,000 copies); 1926 (5,000 copies); 1931 (5,000 copies); 1936 (5,000 copies).

Peeps at Great Explorers

197 × 133mm; 3,000 copies.
Blue cloth bearing a design of shields; no picture on front; full-page illustrations in colour and black and white.
Published at 1s 6d.

826. Alexander the Great by Sir George Scott. Nov 7 1928.
vi, 90pp; map.
4 illustrations in colour, 8 in black and white.

827. Columbus by G.E. Mitton. May 25 1927.
vi, 90pp; map.
4 illustrations in colour, 8 in black and white.
Reprinted 1932 (3,000 copies).
Note: *Columbus* and *Vasco da Gama* were published as a joint volume in the 1930s.

828. Captain Cook by G.E. Mitton. Oct 19 1927.
vi, 90pp; map.
8 illustrations in colour, 1 in black and white.

829. David Livingstone by G.E. Mitton. April 17 1929.
vi, 90pp; map.
4 illustrations in colour, 8 in black and white.

830. Mungo Park by Sir George Scott; painted by John Williamson. Jan 9 1930.
vii, 88pp; map.
8 illustrations in colour.

831. Marco Polo by Sir George Scott. Nov 10 1927.
vi, 90pp; map.
4 illustrations in colour, 8 in black and white.
Note: 500 copies were produced to carry the Macmillan imprint.

832. Vasco da Gama by Sir George Scott. April 14 1929.
vi, 90pp; map.
4 illustrations in colour, 8 in black and white.

Peeps at Great Men

197 × 133mm; 3,000 copies.
Blue cloth with decorative designs and titling printed in black; with full-page
illustrations in colour. Published at 1s 6d.

833. Charles Dickens by Samuel Jeans. April 17 1929.
vii, 86pp +2.
4 illustrations in colour, 8 in black and white.

834. Sir Walter Scott by Elizabeth Grierson; Oct 15 1913.
viii, 88pp; index.
12 illustrations; brown cloth with picture on cover.
Reprinted 1930 (3,000 copies).

835. William Shakespeare by Samuel Jeans. Oct 19 1927.
vii, 88pp.
4 illustrations in colour, 8 in black and white.

836. George Washington by Mary Gaunt. April 17 1929.
iv, 92pp.
4 illustrations in colour, 8 in black and white.

Peeps for Little People

197 × 133mm; 5,000 copies. 48pp.
Blue cloth with a pictorial jacket in colour. Each volume contains 2 full-page
illustrations in colour and 8 line illustrations in the text suitable for colouring.
Published at 1s 6d. [Uncle Robert was Robert F. Finch.]

837. Children of the Snow and Ice by Uncle Robert. March 3 1925.
Reprinted 1928 (5,000 copies).

838. Children of the Sunshine by Uncle Robert. March 31 1925.
Reprinted 1928 (5,000 copies).

839. Children of the Field and Forest by Uncle Robert. Nov 16 1925.
Reprinted 1930 (5,000 copies).

840. Children of the Mountain and Plain by Uncle Robert. Nov 16 1925.
Reprinted 1930 (5,000 copies).

Peeps at Nature for Little People

197 × 133mm; 5,000 copies. 48pp.
Grey cloth with a picture in colour onlaid on the front; with full-page illustrations
in colour and black and white.
Published at 1s.

841. Creatures of the Frozen North by June Morton; painted by Winifred Vaizey.
Sept 4 1929.
8 illustrations in colour, 4 in black and white.

842. Creatures of the Night by June Morton; painted by Winifred Vaizey. Sept 4
1929.
8 illustrations in colour, 4 in black and white.

843. Creatures that Climb by June Morton; painted by Winifred Vaizey. Dec 18
1928.
Light brown cloth; 8 illustrations in colour (duplicate on front), 7 in black and
white.

844. Creatures that Fly by June Morton; painted by Winifred Vaizey. Oct 17 1928.
8 illustrations in colour, 7 in black and white.

845. Creatures that Swim painted and described by Winifred Vaizey. Dec 18 1928.
8 illustrations in colour, 5 in black and white.

846. Creatures that Walk by June Morton; painted by Winifred Vaizey. Dec 18
1928.
8 illustrations in colour, 5 in black and white.

Peeps at Industries

197 × 133mm.
Cloth with a photograph onlaid on the front and designs printed on the front and
spine. Illustrated in black and white from photographs. Published at 1s 6d, later 3s.

847. Cocoa by Edith A. Browne. Dec 21 1920; 5,000 copies.
viii, 88pp.
Red cloth; 16 illustrations (duplicate on front).

848. Rubber by Edith A. Browne. May 1 1912; 3,000 copies.
viii, 88pp.
Blue cloth; 24 illustrations.
Reprinted 1920 (3,000 copies).

849. Sugar by Edith A. Browne. Oct 6 1911; 3,000 copies.
vii, 88pp; advertisements on endpapers.
Blue cloth; 26 illustrations (on 24 pages).
Reprinted 1927 (3,000 copies).

850. Tea by Edith A. Browne. Nov 24 1912; 3,000 copies.
viii, 88pp; advertisements on endpapers.
Blue cloth; 28 illustrations (on 24 pages).
Reprinted 1917 (3,000 copies); 1930 (3,000 copies).

851. Vegetable Oils by Edith A. Browne. 1924; 5,000 copies.
viii, 88pp.
Blue cloth; 16 illustrations.

Miscellaneous Peeps

197 × 133mm.
Cloth with picture in colour on the cover and decorative designs printed on the
front and spine. Full-page illustrations in colour and black and white. Published at
1s 6d.

852. Architecture by Phoebe Allen. Oct 3 1913; 3,000 copies.
viii, 88pp; glossary.
Grey green cloth; 8 illustrations in colour, 53 line drawings in the text.
Reprinted 1924 (3,000 copies).

853. The Art of the Potter by Harry Barnard. Feb 24 1932; 5,000 copies.
vi, 89pp.
Blue cloth, no picture on cover; 4 illustrations in colour, 32 in black and white (on
16 pages), 3 line drawings.

854. Arts and Crafts by Gertrude M. Hector. Sept 20 1928; 5,000 copies.
iv, 92pp.
Blue cloth, no picture on cover; 4 illustrations in colour, 8 in black and white.

Note: *Arts and Crafts* and *The Art of the Potter* were combined into a single volume in the 1930s; the books were simply bound together, the page numbering restarting in the middle of the book; brown cloth.

855. The British Army by W.G. Clifford. March 5 1915; 5,000 copies.
96pp.
Brown cloth; 12 illustrations in colour, 35 line drawings in the text.
Reprinted 1916 (3,000 copies); 1917 (3,000 copies).

856. The British Blue Jacket by Patrick Vaux; painted by C.C. Titterton. Jan 26 1920; 5,000 copies.
viii, 88pp.
Brown cloth; 12 illustrations in colour.

857. Children of Long Ago by F.J. Bowman; painted by Alice E. Mockton. May 4 1927; 5,000 copies.
viii, 84pp +4.
Blue cloth, no picture on cover; 4 illustrations in colour, 8 in black and white.

858. English Folk Dances by Violet Alford. Dec 13 1923; 5,000 copies.
viii, 88pp.
Red cloth; 4 illustrations in colour, 8 in black and white.

859. Great Steamship Lines: The P & O by G.E. Mitton; painted by Ella Du Cane and others. Oct 3 1913; 3,000 copies.
vii, 88pp.
Blue cloth; 9 illustrations in colour, 1 in black and white, 22 line drawings in text.

860. The Heavens by Rev. James Baikie; painted by Constance Baikie. Sept 22 1911; 5,000 copies.
96pp; constellations on front endpapers.
Blue cloth; 8 illustrations in colour, 8 in black and white.
Reprinted 1913 (5,000 copies); 1919 (5,000 copies); 1929 (3,000 copies).

861. Heraldry by Phoebe Allen. Oct 5 1912; 3,000 copies.
viii, 88pp.
Maroon cloth; 8 illustrations in colour, 55 line drawings in text.
Reprinted 1926 (3,000 copies).

862. Historical Songs by Enid Leale. Nov 10 1927; 3,000 copies.
vi, 90pp.
Blue cloth, no picture on cover; 8 illustrations in colour.

863. The League of Nations by Hebe Spaull. Nov 9 1927; 3,000 copies.
vi, 90pp.

Blue cloth, no picture on cover; 4 illustrations in colour, 8 in black and white. Reprinted 1928 (5,000 copies).

864. Men of the Old Stone Age by Rev. James Baikie; painted by A. Forestier. Nov 7 1928; 5,000 copies.
v, 90pp.
Blue cloth, no picture on cover; 4 illustrations in colour, 8 in black and white.

865. The Royal Navy by Rev. James Baikie; painted by Norman L. Wilkinson. Oct 3 1913; 5,000 copies.
vii, 88pp.
Blue cloth; 12 illustrations in colour.
Reprinted 1915 (3,000 copies); 1921; 1928 (3,000 copies).

866. Royal Palaces of Great Britain by Beatrice Home. Oct 3 1913; 3,000 copies.
96pp.
Dark green cloth; 8 illustrations in colour and 20 line drawings by Gordon Home.
Reprinted 1921.

867. Postage Stamps by Stanley C. Johnson. Sept 29 1915; 3,000 copies.
iv, 92pp.
Red cloth, no picture on cover; 16 illustrations in black and white.

868. The Union Jack and other Principal Flags of the British Empire by Nora Hewett. May 16 1928; 3,000 copies.
vi, 65pp +2.
Blue cloth, no picture on cover; 8 illustrations in colour.

869. World's Children by L. Edna Walter. Sept 29 1915; 5,000 copies.
viii, 88pp.
Blue cloth; 12 illustrations in colour, 10 in black and white; a pocket at the back contained 11 sketches for colouring.
Reprinted 1915 (5,000 copies); 1921 (5,000 copies); 1925 (5,000 copies); 1931 (3,000 copies).

870. The World's Dolls by H.W. Canning-Wright. Sept 5 1923; 5,000 copies.
viii, 87pp.
Blue cloth; 4 illustrations in colour, 8 in black and white.
Reprinted 1930 (3,000 copies).

871. The 'Zoo' Aquarium by A.E. Hodge. Nov 10 1927; 3,000 copies.
xii, 84pp.
Blue cloth, no picture on cover; 8 illustrations in colour (on 4 pages), 9 in black and white.
Reprinted 1936 (3,000 copies).
This book was sometimes listed by the publisher with the Peeps at Nature series.

Les Beaux Voyages: Peeps in French

'Collection de volumes dans 8vo (20 X 14c) relies toile ormes de 12 planches en couleurs.' Published jointly with Les Arts Graphiques, Rue Diderot, Vincennes, France.

197 X 133mm.
Map; shields on front endpapers.
Blue cloth (except where stated) with picture in colour onlaid on the front and designs blocked in blind on the front and spine; titled in gilt on the spine.
12 full page illustrations in colour including the cover illustration.
Series edited by Jean Aicard of the Académie Française.
Published at 1s 6d, later 2s; 2frs, later 2frs 50.
The books carry a joint Adam et Charles Black and Les Arts Graphiques imprint, with the exception of *En Chine*, which omits any mention of A & C Black.

872. Algérie by Brieux. Aug 3 1912; 5,000 copies.
115pp +2.

873. En Alsace by André Lichtenberger. May 23 1912; 5,000 copies. 118pp.
Blue cloth; 12 illustrations.
Reprinted 1912 (5,000 copies).

874. En Chine: Merveilleuses Histoires by Judith Gautier; preface by Jean Aicard.
Nov 8 1911; 5,000 copies.
116pp +2.
Red cloth.

875. Ecosse by Henri de Noussanne. July 18 1912; 5,000 copies.
115pp +2.

876. Egypte by Jean Bayet; preface by Jean Aicard. Nov 24 1911; 5,000 copies.
118pp.
Reprinted 1912 (5,000 copies).

877. Espagne by V. H. Friedel; preface by Maurice Fauré. May 1 1912; 5,000 copies.
118pp.
Note: The book also appears in red cloth.

878. Aux Indes by Le Capitaine Pionnier. May 16 1912; 5,000 copies.
118pp.

879. Indo-Chine by Myriam Harry. Sept 19 1912; 5,000 copies.
120pp.

880. Le Japon by Judith Gautier; preface by Jean Aicard. Dec 18 1911; 10,000 copies.
116pp +2.

881. Le Maroc by Le Commandant Haillot; preface by Jean Aicard. Nov 20 1911; 5,000 copies.
118pp.

882. Russie by Henri de Noussanne. May 1 1912; 5,000 copies.
113pp +4.
12 full page illustrations in colour and two in black and white from line drawings.
Note: The book also appears in red cloth.

883. Tunisie by Brieux. Sept 19 1912; 5,000 copies.
118pp

Les Alpes, La Palestine and *Siam* were at various times described as in preparation; none appeared.

Viajes Pintorescos: Peeps in Spanish

Publication of this series was also arranged with Les Arts Graphiques, who took half the profits.

884. La China by Judith Gautier; translated by Francisco Vera. Feb 17 1913; 4,000 copies.

885. El Japon by Judith Gautier. Feb 22 1913; 4,000 copies.

886. Marruecos by Le Comt Haillot. 1913; 4,000 copies.

Viagens Piturescos: Peeps in Portuguese

887. Belgium. 1915; 2,000 copies.

888. China. 1914; 1,000 copies.
Reprinted 1920 (1,000 copies)

889. Egypt. 1915; 1,000 copies
Reprinted 1920 (1,000 copies).

890. Franca. April 22 1914; 2,000 copies.

891. Inglaterra. 1917; 1,000 copies.

892. Italy. 1921; 1,000 copies; 12 illustrations.

893. Japao. April 22 1914; 2,000 copies.
Note: 1,500 copies were sold to A. Moura.

894. Portugal. Nov 7 1913; 3,000 copies.
Note: The edition was sold to A. Moura, Rio de Janeiro.

895. Russia. 1916; 1,000 copies.

Cards for Colouring

Picture cards were included in a pocket at the back of some Peeps for a short period during the first world war. The following series were published:

I   World's Children (11)
Ia   World's Children
Ib   World's Children
II   France
III   Canada
IV   China
V   Switzerland
VI   Belgium
VII   Germany
VIII   Italy

The cards were sold separately at 2d a set of 6, 3d for the set of 11.

Contes et Nouvelles

These titles were produced by A & C Black and published on a joint profits basis with Les Arts Graphiques of Vincennes, France, who were also joint publishers of the Beaux Voyages series. The series was intended for children but the titles are listed here because one is a translation of a Peep.
213 × 147mm.
Picture in colour onlaid on the front and border designs printed in yellow and black on the front and spine; titled in gilt on the spine.

Published at 3s 6d; 3frs, 3frs 50 or 4frs.
The books carry a joint Adam et/and Charles Black and Les Arts Graphiques imprint, with the exception of No. 905, which omits any mention of A & C Black.

901. La Case de l'Oncle Tom by Mrs Harriet Beecher Stowe; translated by Madame Louis Hourticq. May 1 1912; 5,000 copies.
226pp +4.
Red cloth; 8 full page illustrations in colour and 16 in black and white from drawings.

902. La Guerre aux Fauves by Le Capitaine Marcel Pionnier. Nov 20 1911; 3,000 copies.
154pp.
Fawn cloth; 12 full page illustrations in colour.

903. Les Petits Aventuriers en Amérique by Ch de Lapré.
April 26 1912 (book dated 1911); 3,000 copies.
161pp +2.
Fawn cloth; 12 full page illustrations in colour.

904. Un Tour en Mélanésie by Fergus MacGrégor. March 18 1912; 3,000 copies.
172pp +2.
Red cloth; 12 full page illustrations in colour.
Note: The text is a translation of *The South Seas* by J. H. M. Abbott in the Peeps at Many Lands series, but with the addition of two extra chapters; the illustrations are by Norman Hardy (first published in *The Savage South Seas.)*

905. Voyages chez Plusiers Nations Eloignées du Monde par Lemuel Gulliver [by Jonathan Swift]. Illustrated by Stephen Baghot de la Bère. June 17 1912; 3,000 copies.
170pp.
Red cloth; 12 illustrations in colour.

Romans du Fond de la Mer was advertised in this series but it was not published.

Tales of English Minsters

195 × 130mm. 2,000 copies. Paper boards with picture in colour on the cover and borders and titling printed in black; with full-page illustrations in colour and black and white; published at 1s.

911. Canterbury by Elizabeth Grierson. Oct 7 1910.
82pp +6.
3 illustrations in colour, 4 in black and white.

912. Durham by Elizabeth Grierson. Oct 7 1910.
48pp.
2 illustrations in colour (duplicate on front), 4 in black and white.

913. Ely by Elizabeth Grierson. Oct 7 1910.
41pp.
2 illustrations in colour (duplicate on front), 4 in black and white.

914. Hereford by Elizabeth Grierson. Sept 14 1911; 3,000 copies.
49pp +2.
3 illustrations in colour, 4 in black and white.

915. Lincoln by Elizabeth Grierson; Oct 7 1910.
50pp.
2 illustrations in colour (duplicate on front), 4 in black and white.

916. St Albans by Elizabeth Grierson. Oct 7 1910.
42pp.
3 illustrations in colour, 4 in black and white.

917. St Paul's by Elizabeth Grierson. Oct 7 1910.
61pp.
2 illustrations in colour (duplicate on front), 4 in black and white.

918. York by Elizabeth Grierson. Oct 7 1910.
37pp.
2 illustrations in colour (duplicate on front), 4 in black and white.

Note: the text and some of the illustrations of the above series were published as:

919. The Children's Book of English Minsters by Elizabeth Grierson. Oct 22 1909;
3,000 copies; published at 6s.
210 × 148mm; xiv, 337pp +2.
Green pictorial cloth, titled in gilt; 12 full page illustrations in colour.

Pictures of Many Lands

248 × 182mm. 64pp. Cloth or paper boards, cloth backed, with a colour picture
onlaid on the front.
Illustrations in colour and black and white from drawings and photographs.
Published at 1s 6d and 2s (prize editions), later at 3s 6d and 5s.

921. Africa in Pictures by H. Clive Barnard. Nov 23 1923; 5,000 copies.
Blue boards; 32 illustrations in colour, 27 in black and white.

922. America in Pictures by H. Clive Barnard. July 5 1916; 10,000 copies.
Red boards; 30 illustrations in colour, 28 in black and white.

923. Asia in Pictures by H. Clive Barnard. Jan 19 1915; 7,500 copies.
Blue cloth; 32 illustrations in colour, 33 in black and white.
Reprinted 1927 (3,000 copies).

924. Australia, New Zealand and Oceania in Pictures by H. Clive Barnard. June 1
1923; 5,000 copies.
Red boards; 32 illustrations in colour, 27 in black and white.

925. Beasts and Birds by C. von Wyss. Nov 24 1910; 5,000 copies.
Green cloth; 31 illustrations in colour, 24 in black and white.

926. The British Empire in Pictures by H. Clive Barnard. Oct 21 1910; 10,000
copies.
Red cloth; 32 illustrations in colour, 26 in black and white.
Reprinted 1915 (10,000 copies); Nov 1924 (5,000 copies, new edition to sell at 3s).

927. Pictures of British History by E. L. Hoskyn. Nov 9 1911; 10,000 copies.
Brown cloth; 32 illustrations in colour, 28 in black and white.
Reprinted 1915 (7,500 copies; red boards); 1919 (6,000 copies; brown cloth).

928. More Pictures of British History by E. L. Hoskyn. Jan 20 1914; 10,000 copies.
Red boards; 32 illustrations in colour, 26 in black and white.

929. The British Isles in Pictures by H. Clive Barnard. Oct 28 1910; 7,500 copies.
Blue cloth; 32 illustrations in colour, 26 in black and white.
Reprinted 1915 (10,000 copies); 1920 (5,000 copies); 1923; 1929 (3,000 copies).
Note: The book was also produced with a pictorial cover, showing a village scene
with stream, bridge and children.

930. The Child's World in Pictures by C. von Wyss. Dec 6 1909;
5,000 copies.
Pictorial cover, blue spine; 32 illustrations in colour, 30 in black and white.
Note: The same illustrations as *The World in Pictures* (No. 938) but with a more
elementary text.

931. The Children's World by S. Shenessy. March 29 1912; 5,000 copies.
Blue cloth; 32 illustrations in colour, 30 in black and white.
Reprinted 1914 (7,500 copies); 1920 (7,500 copies).

932. Europe in Pictures by H. Clive Barnard. June 6 1911; 10,000 copies.
Blue cloth; 32 illustrations in colour, 25 in black and white.
Reprinted 1914 (10,000 copies); 1920 (7,500 copies).

Above: *Books from the Brush Pen and Pencil series: the first impression* (left) *shows a coloured background to the cover design; this is absent in the 1930 reprint.* Below: New York, *an example of the* Charm *series published during the late 1920s, and* Rembrandt, *one of four books on artists published at 12s 6d.*

Artists' Sketch Book series. Above: *copies in cloth (left) and paper boards (right) and in soft covers (front); at the back is an example of the later series of sketch books with fewer illustrations but expanded captions.* Below: *Artists' Sketch Books in the rarely found boxes: plain and greetings styles are shown. Some books in the Beautiful Britain, Water-Colour and Brush Pen and Pencil series were also issued in boxes during 1913–15.*

933. Pictures of Famous Travel by H. Clive Barnard. Nov 26 1913; 7,500 copies.
Blue cloth; 31 illustrations in colour, 28 in black and white.

934. Gardens in their Seasons: A Nature Book for Boys and Girls by C. von Wyss.
March 6 1912; 10,000 copies.
Grey cloth; 32 illustrations in colour, 25 in black and white.

935. How other people live by H. Clive Barnard. Dec 21 1911; 10,000 copies.
Light brown cloth; 32 illustrations in colour, 28 in black and white.
Reprinted 1927 (5,200 copies).

936. India in Pictures by H. Clive Barnard. June 21 1922; 5,000 copies.
Red cloth; 32 illustrations in colour, 21 in black and white.

937. The Motherland in Pictures by V. A. S. Stow and H. Clive Barnard. Nov 10
1920; 5,000 copies.
80pp; two maps.
Red boards; 30 illustrations in colour, 34 in black and white.
Reprinted 1920 (5,000 copies).

938. The World in Pictures by C. von Wyss. June 24 1910; 7,500 copies.
Blue cloth; 32 illustrations in colour, 30 in black and white.
Note: This was a prize edition published at 2s; also published in red cloth at 1s 6d.
Reprinted 1912 (7,500 copies); 1914 (7,000 copies); 1920 (5,000 copies); 1927
(5,000 copies).

A similar volume is:
939. Lectures Illustrées (Elements de Grammaire) by E. Magee and M. Anceau.
Nov 29 1913; 5,000 copies.
Dark red pictorial cloth; 32 illustrations in colour, 26 in black and white.

What to See

178 × 147mm; 5,000 copies. 32pp. Published at 2s 6d.

941. What to see in the Channel Islands by Gordon Home. March 13 1925; 5,000
copies.
Grey cloth; 15 illustrations in colour.

942. What to see in the English Lakes by Gordon Home; painted by A. Heaton
Cooper. 1925; 3,200 copies.
Grey decorated cloth; 15 illustrations in colour.

Travel Pictures

These sets of 24 illustrations in colour and 24 in black and white were selected and edited by Robert J. Finch, and published as 'detachable file portfolios', 280 × 228mm, at 10d a set. The sets comprised a mixture of illustrations previously used in the colour books and reproductions of photographs. They were bound by metal staples in putty coloured folders bearing the contents on the front; problems and exercises inside front cover; map inside back cover; advertisements on back. The following titles were published:

951. Africa
952. Asia
953. Australasia
954. The British Empire
955. The British Isles
956. Central and South America
957. Countries of the Great War
958. Europe
959. Land Forms and Cities
960. The Mediterranean
961. North America and The West Indies

One was also published as a book
962. Countries of the Great War Dec 17 1914 (book dated 1915); 10,000 copies; published at 1s.
Grey-green decorated cloth; 24 illustrations in colour, 26 in black and white.

Black's Beautiful Postcards
Of British Design and Manufacture

Price 9d net per packet of six cards
'The subjects have been selected, in most cases, from volumes in "Black's Beautiful Books" and the "Artist's Sketch Book" series, and they meet the demand, often expressed by possessors of these volumes, for separate pictures to be framed or sent away to friends.'

In colour

Series	Title	Artist
1	The Royal Navy	Norman Wilkinson [and Allan Stewart]
2	The Channel Islands	H.B. Wimbush
3	The Channel Islands	H.B. Wimbush
4	The Channel Islands	H.B. Wimbush
5	The English Lakes	A. Heaton Cooper
6	The English Lakes	A. Heaton Cooper
6A	The English Lakes	A. Heaton Cooper
7	The English Lakes	A. Heaton Cooper
7A	The English Lakes	A. Heaton Cooper
8	Belgium	A. Forestier
9	Belgium	A. Forestier
10	Banks of the Nile	Ella Du Cane
11	Banks of the Nile	Ella Du Cane
12	The People of Egypt	Lance Thackeray
13	The People of Egypt	Lance Thackeray
14	Edinburgh	John Fulleylove
14A	Around Edinburgh	Sutton Palmer
15	Canterbury	W. Biscombe Gardner
16	The Broads	A. Heaton Cooper
17	The Trossachs	Sutton Palmer
18	English Gardens	George S. Elgood
19	English Gardens	Beatrice Parsons and Isabelle Forrest
20	British Dogs	G. Vernon Stokes
21	Our Indian Armies	Col A.C. Lovett
22	Our Indian Armies	Col A.C. Lovett
23	Our Indian Armies	Col. A.C. Lovett
24	The People of India	Mortimer Menpes
25	Alpine Flowers	G. Flemwell
26	Italian Lakes	Ella Du Cane
27	The Rubaiyat of Omar Khayyam	Gilbert James
28	Jerusalem	John Fulleylove
29	Cornwall	G.F. Nicholls
30	Cornwall	G.F. Nicholls
31	Russia	F. de Haenen
32	South Devon	Sutton Palmer
32A	North Devon	Sutton Palmer
33	Japan	Mortimer Menpes
34	Japan	Ella Du Cane
35	Japan	Ella Du Cane
36	Devon	Sutton Palmer
37	Surrey	Sutton Palmer
38	Surrey	Sutton Palmer

Series	Title	Artist
39	Surrey	Sutton Palmer
40	The Wye	Sutton Palmer
41	Sussex	Wilfrid Ball
42	Sussex	Wilfrid Ball
43	English Nursery Rhymes (with music)	Dorothy Wheeler and Charles Folkard
44	English Nursery Rhymes (with music)	[Dorothy Wheeler and Charles Folkard]
44A	English Nursery Rhymes (with music)	Dorothy M. Wheeler
45	English Nursery Rhymes (with music)	[Dorothy Wheeler and Charles Folkard]
45A	English Nursery Rhymes (with music)	Dorothy Wheeler and Charles Folkard
46	Birds of Britain	[H.E. Dresser]
46A	Birds of Britain	[H.E. Dresser]
47	Birds of Britain	[H.E. Dresser]
48	Gardens of England	Beatrice Parsons
49	Flowers and Gardens of Madeira	Ella Du Cane
50	Flowers and Gardens of Madeira	Ella Du Cane
71	Elves and Fairies	Ida Rentoul Outhwaite
71A	Elves and Fairies	Ida Rentoul Outhwaite
72	Elves and Fairies	Ida Rentoul Outhwaite
73	Elves and Fairies	Ida Rentoul Outhwaite
74	Elves and Fairies	Ida Rentoul Outhwaite
75	Elves and Fairies	Ida Rentoul Outhwaite
76	Elves and Fairies	Ida R. Outhwaite
77	The Highlands	William Smith
78	The Cotswolds	G.F. Nicholls
79	Elves and Fairies	Ida Rentoul Outhwaite
80	Alice in Wonderland	Charles Folkard
81	London	[Various artists]
82	Animals	E.H. Fisher
83	Animals	E.H. Fisher
84	British Wild Flowers	C.F. Newall
85	British Wild Flowers	C.F. Newall
86	Teneriffe	Ella Du Cane
87	Birds and their Young	[George Rankin and Roland Green]
88	Pheasants	[Various artists]

Series	Title	Artist
89	British Birds	Roland Green
90	Scripture: The New Testament	J.H. Hartley
91	Nursery Rhymes and Tales	

In pencil and tint

Series	Title	Artist
51	Oxford	Fred Richards
52	Cambridge	Walter M. Keesey
53	Windsor and Eton	Fred Richards
54	Harrow	Walter M. Keesey
55	Harrow	Walter M. Keesey
56	Canterbury	Walter M. Keesey
57	Stratford-on-Avon	Gordon Home
58	London	Dorothy E.G. Woollard
59	Cambridge	Walter M. Keesey
60	The Zoo	A.W. Peters
61	London	Dorothy E.G. Woollard
62	Bournemouth	Dorothy E.G. Woollard
63	Chester	Joseph Pike
64	Chester	Joseph Pike
65	Norwich	E.V. Cole
66	Rome	Fred Richards
67	Venice	Fred Richards
68	St Andrews	Malcolm Patterson
69	Cambridge	W.G. Blackall
70	Cambridge	W.G. Blackall

Other publishers:

A & C Black provided illustrations from many books for use by other postcard publishers.

RAPHAEL TUCK
Apart from the series listed below, Tuck also issued postcards taken from *Oxford*. Most series consisted of six cards.
(*WWW* = Wide Wide World cards; *BS* = Bonnie Scotland).

Series	Title		Artist
7109	*WWW*	Strassburg	
7047	*WWW*	The West Indies I	A.S. Forrest
7048	*WWW*	The West Indies II	A.S. Forrest
7049	*WWW*	Jamaica	A.S. Forrest
7050	*WWW*	Barbadoes [sic]	A.S. Forrest

Series	Title	Artist
7105	*WWW* Switzerland I	A.D. McCormick
7106	*WWW* Switzerland II	A.D. McCormick
7107	*WWW* Switzerland III	A.D. McCormick
7308	*WWW* The Holy Land I	John Fulleylove
7309	*WWW* The Holy Land II	John Fulleylove
7310	*WWW* The Holy Land III	John Fulleylove
7311	*WWW* The Holy Land IV	John Fulleylove
7317	Guernsey I	H.B. Wimbush
7318	Guernsey II	H.B. Wimbush
7319	Jersey	H.B. Wimbush
7320	Alderney and Sark	H.B. Wimbush
7321	Edinburgh I	John Fulleylove
7322	Edinburgh II	John Fulleylove
7327	*WWW* Tibet	A.H. Savage Landor
7344	*BS* Perthshire	Sutton Palmer
7345	*BS* Argyllshire	Sutton Palmer
7349	*BS* The Highlands	Sutton Palmer
7350	*BS* The Trossachs	Sutton Palmer
7351	*BS* The Lowlands	Sutton Palmer
7372	*WWW* Naples	Augustine FitzGerald
7373	*WWW* The Bay of Naples	Augustine FitzGerald
7374	*WWW* Florence	[Col. R.C. Goff]
7411	Westminster Abbey	John Fulleylove
7427	*WWW* Morocco	A.S. Forrest
7514	Father Thames I	W.L. Wyllie
7515	Father Thames II	W.L. Wyllie
7516	Father Thames III	W.L. Wyllie
7554	*WWW* Rome II	Alberto Pisa
7555	*WWW* Rome III	Alberto Pisa
7556	*WWW* Holland	Nico Jungman
7557	Picturesque Yorkshire: The North-East Coast	Gordon Home
7558	The Yorkshire Moors	Gordon Home
7559	The New Forest	Mrs Rawnsley
7560	Scott's Country III	Wm Smith Jr
7660	*BS* The Highlands	Wm Smith Jr
7661	*BS* The Highlands	Wm Smith Jr
7662	*BS* The Islands	Wm Smith Jr
7731	Shakespeare's Country VI	Fred Whitehead
7732	Shakespeare's Country VII	Fred Whitehead
7733	Shakespeare's Country VIII	Fred Whitehead
7734	Shakespeare's Country IX	Fred Whitehead
7785	*WWW* The Holy Land V	[John Fulleylove]
7786	*WWW* The Holy Land VI	[John Fulleylove]
7801	Cambridge I	W. Matthison

Series	Title	Artist
7802	Cambridge II	W. Matthison
7803	Cambridge III	W. Matthison
7804	Cambridge IV	W. Matthison
7857	London	
7866	*WWW* Burma II	R. Talbot Kelly
7867	*WWW* Burma III	R. Talbot Kelly
7901	Cambridge IV	W. Matthison
7902	Cambridge V	W. Matthison
7908	Fair Japan I	Mortimer Menpes
7909	Fair Japan II	Mortimer Menpes
7910	Fair Japan III	Mortimer Menpes
7911	Fair Japan IV	Mortimer Menpes
7912	Fair Japan V	Mortimer Menpes
7913	Fair Japan VI	Mortimer Menpes
7914	Fair Japan VII	Mortimer Menpes
7915	Fair Japan VIII	Mortimer Menpes
7916	Flowers and Gardens of Japan I	Ella Du Cane
7917	Flowers and Gardens of Japan II	Ella Du Cane
7918	Flowers and Gardens of Japan III	Ella Du Cane
7919	Flowers and Gardens of Japan IV	Ella Du Cane
7926	*WWW* Brussels	A. Forestier
7927	*WWW* Bruges	A. Forestier
7928	*WWW* Antwerp	A. Forestier
7929	*WWW* Ghent	A. Forestier
7930	*WWW* Liège	A. Forestier
7937	Flowers and Gardens of Madeira	Ella Du Cane
7943	*WWW* Picturesque Egypt XIV	R. Talbot Kelly
7944	*WWW* Picturesque Egypt XV	R. Talbot Kelly
7955	*WWW* Burma	R. Talbot Kelly
7956	*WWW* Burma	R. Talbot Kelly
7962	*WWW* Australian Life I	Percy Spence
7963	*WWW* Australian Life II	Percy Spence
8978	*WWW* The Holy Land (12)	John Fulleylove
8979	*WWW* The Holy Land (12)	John Fulleylove
8980	*WWW* The Holy Land	John Fulleylove

(above three series comprise the same pictures as 7308-11)

| 9271 | Scottish Life and Character I | H.J. Dobson |

Series	Title	Artist
9272	Scottish Life and Character II	H. J. Dobson
9343	Scottish Life and Character III	H. J. Dobson
9479	Scottish Life and Character IV	H. J. Dobson
9769	Scottish Life and Character	H. J. Dobson
(framed versions of 9343 and 9479)		
9965	Scottish Life and Character VII	H. J. Dobson
9966	*WWW* Native Life in India	Mortimer Menpes
9967	*WWW* Native Life in India IV	Mortimer Menpes
9995	Scottish Life and Character VI	H. J. Dobson

J. SALMON

Card	Title	Artist
1676-1687	Surrey	Sutton Palmer
1688-1723	Bonnie Scotland	Sutton Palmer
(probably plus 1724)		
1725-1738	Rivers and Streams	Sutton Palmer
(plus others up to 1760, some of which are by W. W. Quatremain)		

J. HENDERSON & SONS LTD

Series	Cards	Title and book title	Artist
A2	3001-3006	Beautiful Gardens (*Gardens of England*)	Beatrice Parsons
A1	3007-3012	Through the Woods (*Surrey*)	Sutton Palmer
A4	3013-3018	By River and Stream (*Rivers and Streams*)	Sutton Palmer
A3	3019-3024	Rural Scenes (*Sussex*)	Wilfrid Ball
A5	3025-3030	Picturesque Old Villages (*Sussex, Wessex*)	Wilfrid Ball and Walter Tyndale
A6	3031-3036		
A7	3037-3042	Cottage Homes (*Surrey, Worcestershire*)	Sutton Palmer and Thomas Tyndale
A8	3043-3048		

Series	Cards	Title and book title	Artist
A9	3049-3054	*(Flowers and Gardens of Madeira)*	Ella Du Cane
A10	3055-3060	Evening Glow *(Rivers and Streams)*	Sutton Palmer
A11	3061-3066	Country Charms *(Sussex)*	Wilfrid Ball
A12	3067-3072	*(Alpine Flowers and Gardens)*	George Flemwell

PICTOGRAPH PUBLISHING CO.

Card	Title and book title	Artist
621	Japanese Gardens (*Flowers and Gardens of Japan*)	Ella Du Cane
624	Japanese Gardens (*Flowers and Gardens of Japan*)	Ella Du Cane
625	St Paul's Cathedral	
626	London (*London to the the Nore*)	W. L. Wyllie
716	Beauty Spots of England (*Surrey*)	Sutton Palmer
717	Beauty Spots of England (*Surrey*)	Sutton Palmer

ROBERT PEEL POSTCARD COMPANY, OXFORD

Cards:

1-23 plus	Oxford	John Fulleylove

G. AJELLI & CO.

Series	Title	Artist
330		
631	Flowers and Gardens of Japan	Ella Du Cane

WRENCH

Cards from *World's Children* by Mortimer Menpes:

Card	Title
8498	One of our New Allies
8500	May Blossoms
8501	A Bargee Girl
8507	The Salmon Gown
8508	A Chinese Girl
8509	Standing at Attention
8510	Phoebe

E. F. ROCHAT

Cards from *Constantinople* by Warwick Goble:

Card	Title
503	A Cemetery by the Bosphorus
505	Grand Bazaar, Stamboul
544	Tomb in Scutari

From the numbering of the cards, it is obvious that many more were issued.

Inter-Relationships

Belgium (1908; 20s) comprises the text and illustrations of *Brabant and East Flanders* (7s 6d), *Bruges and West Flanders* (10s) and *Liège and the Ardennes* (7s 6d), published in 1906-08.

English Costume (1907; 20s) combines the text and illustrations of four books in the 7s 6d series published in 1906: *Early English*; *The Middle Ages*; *Tudor and Stuart*; *Georgian*.

The Lake of Geneva (1909; 20s) is the combined text and illustrations of three books in the 7s 6d series published in 1908: *Geneva, Lausanne* and *Montreux*.

Hampshire (1908; 20s) contains the abridged text and all the illustrations of *Winchester* published in 1910 at 7s 6d.
Winchester was written first and its text cut down for *Hampshire*.

Ireland (1906; 20s) was reissued with identical text but with only 32 illustrations in the 6s series in 1907. Existing stock of the larger book was used for this.

Kent (1907; 20s) includes the whole text and illustrations of *Canterbury* (1907; 7s 6d).
Russia (1913; 20s) combines the text and illustrations of three books in the 7s 6d series: *Moscow* (1912), *Provincial Russia* (1913) and *St Petersburg* (1910).

The West Indies (1905; 20s) includes the whole text and illustrations later published in the 6s series as *Jamaica* (1907).

Yorkshire (1908; 20s) combines the text and illustrations of three 7s 6d series books: *Yorkshire: Coast and Moorland* (1904); *Yorkshire: Dales and Fells* (1906); *Yorkshire: Vales and Wolds* (1908). The illustrations of A Typical Yorkshire Farmer facing p 120 of *Coast and Moorland* was not included in the 20s volume.

Rivers and Streams of England (1909; 20s) includes some of the text and illustrations later published as *The Wye* (1910; 7s 6d).

Biographies of
Artists and Authors

This list includes all the named artists and authors referred to in the bibliography. Well known figures (Scott, Kipling, etc.) whose lives are fully chronicled elsewhere have been given dates-only entries with references. A number of other artists and authors, even of the major series, have proved resistant to research: this applies particularly to the women, who were often ignored by the reference books of the day.

The books written and illustrated by a particular author or artist are listed in the same order as the bibliography. Square brackets are used where a book is known to be the work of a listed artist, but where no name is mentioned. This applies to most of the artists in the Beautiful Britain series.

In the case of books in different series but bearing the same title, that title has not been repeated where the artists are concerned, since all the material in smaller series was first published in one of the larger series. In the case of writers, however, the title is often repeated because the text for the later book differed from that of the earlier.

Abbreviations

b	born
d	died; daughter
DSO	Distinguished Service Order
CB	Companion of the Order of the Bath
CVO	Commander of the Royal Victorian Order
ed	educated
FAS	Fine Art Society
fl	flourished
GBE	(Knight or Dame) Grand Cross of the British Empire
GCMG	(Knight) Grand Cross of the Order of St Michael and St George
ILN	Illustrated London News
JP	Justice of the Peace
KCB	Knight Commander of the Bath

KCIE	Knight Commander of the Indian Empire
KCMG	Knight Commander of the Order of St Michael and St George
KCSI	Knight Commander of the Star of India
KCVO	Knight Commander of the Royal Victorian Order
LCC	London County Council
m	married
MBE	Member of the Order of the British Empire
MP	Member of Parliament
MVO	Member of the Royal Victorian Order
NEA	New English Art Club
OBE	Officer of the Order of the British Empire
OWS	Old Watercolour Society (later RWS)
RA	Royal Academy
RAS	Royal Astronomical Society
RASC	Royal Army Service Corps
RBA	Royal Society of British Artists
RCA	Royal College of Art
RE	Royal Society of Painter-Etchers and Engravers
RGS	Royal Geographical Society
RHA	Royal Hibernian Academy
RI	Royal Institute of Painters in Water Colours
RM	Resident Magistrate
RMA	Royal Military Academy, Woolwich
RMC	Royal Military College, Sandhurst
RMS	Royal Society of Miniature Painters Sculptors and Gravers
RN	Royal Navy
RNVR	Royal Naval Volunteer Reserve
ROI	Royal Institute of Oil Painters
RSA	Royal Scottish Academy; Royal Society of Arts
RSE	Royal Society of Edinburgh
RSW	Royal Scottish Water-Colour Society
RWS	Royal Society of Painters in Water Colours
s	son
SWA	Society of Women Artists
TLS	Times Literary Supplement

REFERENCES

ADB   *Australian Dictionary of Biography* (Melbourne University Press)

Archibald *Dictionary of Sea Painters* by E.H.H. Archibald (Antique Collectors Club, 1980)

AWWW   *Authors and Writers' Who's Who*

Bénézit   *Dictionnaire des Peintres, Sculptures, Dessinateurs et Graveurs* by E. Bénézit (Librairie Grund, 1976)

BMC	*Book and Magazine Collector*
Burke	*Burke's Peerage*
Caw	*Scottish Painting Past and Present* by James L. Caw (T.C. & E.C. Jack, 1908)
CBD	*Chambers' Biographical Dictionary*
Coysh	*Dictionary of Picture Postcards in Britain* by A.W. Coysh (Antique Collectors Club, 1984)
CWWW	*Canadian Who Was Who*
DAB	*Dictionary of American Biography* (Humphrey Milford/OUP)
DAustB	*Dictionary of Australian Biography* (Angus and Robertson)
DBF	*Dictionnaire de Biographie française* (Librairie Letouzey et Ane, 1951-1985)
Desmond	*Dictionary of British and Irish Botanists and Horticulturalists* by Ray Desmond (Taylor & Francis, 1977)
DNB	*Dictionary of National Biography* (Smith Elder/OUP)
DNZB	*Dictionary of New Zealand Biography*
Graves	*Dictionary of Artists* (Graves, 1895)
Houfe	*Dictionary of British Book Illustrators and Caricaturists* by Simon Houfe (Antique Collectors Club, 1978)
Kunitz	*Twentieth Century Authors* edited by Stanley J. Kunitz (H.W. Wilson, 1955)
LWW	*Literary Who's Who*
LYB	*Literary Year Book*
Maas	*Victorian Painters* by J. Maas (1970)
Mallalieu	*Dictionary of British Water Colour Artists* by Huon Mallalieu (Antique Collectors Club, 1976)
MDCB	*Macmillan Dictionary of Canadian Biography*
Newth	*Adam & Charles Black 1807-57: Some Chapters in the History of a Publishing House* [by J. D. Newth] (A & C Black, 1957)
Peppin	*Dictionary of British Book Illustrators* by Brigid Peppin and Lucy Micklethwait (John Murray, 1983)
SADNB	*Southern African Dictionary of National Biography* (Frederick Warne)
TB	*Allgemeine Lexikon der Bildenden Kunstler von der Antike bis zur Gegenwart* by Ulrich Thieme and Felix Becker (Engelmann/Seeman, 1907-50)
Waters	*Dictionary of British Artists Working 1900-1950* by Grant M. Waters (Eastbourne Fine Art, 1975)
Wood	*Dictionary of Victorian Painters* by Christopher Wood (Antique Collectors Club, 1971)
WW	*Who's Who* (A & C Black)
WWA	*Who's Who in Art*
WWL	*Who's Who in Literature*
WWW	*Who Was Who* (A & C Black)
WrWW	*Writers' Who's Who*

KEY

20s	20 shilling series	1-92
12/6	12s 6d series	101-104
10s	10 shilling series	111-114
7/6	7s 6d series	121-193
	2nd impression	201-206
Fasc	Fascination of Europe	211-216
Ltd	Limited editions	221-264
6s	6 shilling series	271-283
MR	Motor Routes	291-294
People	People series	301-303
Crown	Menpes Crown	304
BB	Beautiful Britain	311-338
BE	Beautiful Europe	339-345
WC	Water-Colour	351-395
WCV	Water-Colour Views	401-402
GA	British/Great Artists	411-415
QP	Quotation and Picture	421-425
BPP	Brush, Pen and Pencil	431-436
WF	War Front	441-444
Sport	Books for Sportsmen	451-457
Port	Portrait Biographies	461-463
ASB	Artists' Sketch Book	471-515
NASB	New Artists' Sketch Book	516-522
MSB	Miscellaneous sketch books	523-528
Charm	Charm series	531-536
Pop	Popular series	541-581
New	New series	591-636
Misc	Miscellaneous books	641-687
PML	Peeps at Many Lands and Cities	701-775
HML	Homes of Many Lands	776
LL	Life and Legends of Other Lands	777-778
LPML	Larger Peeps at Many Lands	779-783
PAL	Peeps at Ancient Lands	784-790
PH	Peeps at History	791-801
PGR	Peeps at Great Railways	802-809
PN	Peeps at Nature	810-825
PGE	Peeps at Great Explorers	826-832
PGM	Peeps at Great Men	833-836
PLP	Peeps for Little People	837-840
PNLP	Peeps at Nature for Little People	841-846
PI	Peeps at Industries	847-851
MP	Miscellaneous Peeps	852-871
BV	Les Beaux Voyages	872-883
PS	Peeps in Spanish	884-886

Artists and Authors

ABBOTT, John Henry Macartney *The South Seas (Melanesia)* (PML); *Un Tour en Mélanésie* (Contes)
1874-1953. Australian soldier and writer; served in Boer War. Wrote *Tommy Cornstalk* (1902), *Plain and Veldt* (1903).
Refs: SADNB.

AICARD, Jean Editor, Les Beaux Voyages series
1848-May 1921; *b* Toulon; *ed* Lycée de Mâcon; Lycée de Nimes. Member of the Académie Française; officer of the Legion of Honour. Poet, novelist and playwright, the author of many books. Lived 40 rue de Luxembourg, Paris; Villa les Lauriers-roses, Var, France; Solliès-le-Vieux, Var, France.
Refs: WWW.

AIRY, Sir George Riddell *The Lady of the Lake* (Misc; topography of the poem)

ALDWORTH, D. A. H. *The Malay States* (PML)

ALFLALO, F. G. *Fisherman's Weather* (Sport)

ALFORD, Violet *English Folk Dances* (MP)

ALLEN, Phoebe *Architecture; Heraldry* (MP)

ALLEN, Herbert Warner *Our Italian Front* (WF)
March 8 1881-Jan 12 1968; *s* Capt George Woronzow Allen; *m* Ethel Pemberton; one *s*; *ed* Charterhouse; University College, Oxford. Paris Correspondent of *The Morning Post* 1908-14. Attached to British, French and Italian General Headquarters in WWI as correspondent for *The Morning Post* and other London newspapers. Foreign Editor of *The Morning Post* 1925-28; London Editor of *Yorkshire Post* 1928-30; Assistant Deputy Director, Foreign Division, Ministry of Information 1940-41; Chevalier de la Légion d'Honneur. Wrote many books on wines and spirits and novels, including *The Unbroken Line* (1916), *The Wines of France* (1924), *Gentlemen, I give you Wine* (1930), *Rum, the Englishman's Spirit*

(1931), *Mr Clerihew, Wine Merchant* (1933), *Trent's Own Case* (with E.C. Bentley, 1936), *Death Fungus* (1937), *The Timeless Moment* (1946), *Number Three St James's Street* (1950), *White Wine and Cognac* (1952), *History of Great Vintage Wines from Homer to the Present Day* (1961). Lived Iden House, Sotwell, Wallingford, Berkshire. Refs: WWW.

ALLINGHAM, Helen *Happy England* (20s, Ltd); *The Homes of Tennyson* (7/6); *Cottages of England* (WC)
Sept 26 1848-Sept 28 1926; *b* Barton-on-Trent; *d* A. Henry Paterson, MD; *m* 1874 William Allingham, the Irish Poet; two *s*, one *d*; studied at Royal Academy schools. Drew extensively for magazines such as *Graphic, Cornhill*, ILN, *Cassells* (including illustrations for *Far from the Madding Crowd*; *Cornhill* 1874). AWRS 1875, RWS 1890; principally known for cottage and rural subjects; exhibited widely, mainly at FAS. Illustrated *A Flat Iron for a Farthing* (Mrs Ewing, 1873), *Jan of the Windmill* (1876), *Gentle and Simple* (M.A. Paul, 1897), *The Cottage Homes of England* by Stewart Dick (Edward Arnold, 1909); also edited William Allingham's diaries and letters. Lived Eldon House, Lyndhurst Road, Hampstead.
Refs: WWW; Houfe; Maas; TB; Wood.

AMHERST, Hon. Florence Margaret *The Herb Garden* (7/6)
d Aug 9 1946; 3rd *d* 1st Baron Amherst of Hackney; unmarried; Lady of the Order of St John of Jerusalem. Lived 1 Kinnerton Studios, Studio Place, Kinnerton Street, London SW1.
Refs: Burke.

ANCEAU, M. *Lectures Illustrées* (PIX)
A teacher at Edgbaston High School for Girls, Birmingham.

ANDERSON, Miss A. *Aucassin and Nicolete* (7/6)
b 1874; parents Scottish; spent childhood in Argentina; *m* Alan Wright, writer and illustrator. Etcher, watercolourist and greetings card designer, she also illustrated *The Funny Bunny ABC* (1912), *The Water Babies* (1924), *Heidi* (1924), volumes of fairy tales and books written by Alan Wright. Lived Berkshire.
Refs: Peppin.

ANDERSON, Robert *Deeside* (7/6)
'An Aberdonian and a great walker.'

ANDREWS, Douglas Sharpus *Bath and Wells*; *Cardiff* (ASB)
Nov 4 1885-1944; *b* Brighton; studied at RCA. Served in Royal Artillery on Western Front in WWI. Landscape and town painter, illustrator and illuminator; successively head of Bath School of Art, principal of Derby School of Arts and Crafts and principal of Leeds and Sheffield Colleges of Art.
Refs: Waters.

ARNOLD, Hugh *Stained Glass of the Middle Ages in England and France* (Misc)
'Secretary of the Guild', 1906

ASHDOWN, Charles H. *British Castles* (7/6)

AUSTIN, Alfred *The Garden that I Love* (7/6, Ltd); *Haunts of Ancient Peace* (7/6); *Lamia's Winter Quarters* (7/6, Ltd)
May 30 1835-June 2 1913; 2nd *s* Joseph Austin; *m* Hester; *ed* Stonyhurst; Oscott; London University. Called to bar Inner Temple 1857; on death of father devoted himself to travel and literature; Editor *National Review* 1883-93; Poet Laureate 1896-1913. Wrote large number of prose and poetry works. Lived Herefordshie and Swinton Old Manor, Ashford, Kent.
Refs: WWW; DNB; *Autobiography* (Macmillan, 1911); N.B. Crowell *Alfred Austin, Victorian* (Weidenfeld and Nicholson, 1955).

AUSTIN, Mary Hunter *California* (Misc)
Sept 9 1868-August 13 1934; *b* Carlinville, Illinois; *d* Capt George Hunter and Susanna Savilla Graham; *m* 1891 Stafford Wallace Austin, rancher and teacher; one *d*, who was mentally afflicted and placed in an institution; *ed* Blackburn College. On death of father was strongly influenced by her mother who was devoted to 'causes'. On marriage settled at Lone Pine, Inyo County. Later separated and visited Italy to study prayer and mysticism; influenced by Fabian socialism and became interested in women's rights. Spent 17 years in Mojave Desert studying Indians and desert life and fighting for the preservation of Indian and Spanish arts and handicrafts. First book published 1903, followed by large number of publications; helped found literary colony at Carmel. Settled in Santa Fe, New Mexico in 1924. 'An inquiring intellectual frontierswoman steeped in Transcendentalism' (DAB)
Refs: WWW; DAB; Kunitz; *Earth Horizon* (autobiography) 1932; Helen M. Doyle *Mary Austin, Woman of Genius* (1939); T.M. Pearce *The Beloved House* (1940).

AUSTIN, Robin Sargent *Surrey; Warwick, Leamington and Kenilworth* (ASB)
June 23 1895-Sept 18 1973; *b* Leicester; *s* Robert Austin and Elizabeth Smith and brother of F.G. Austin; *m* 1924 Ada Harrison (*d* 1958); one *s*, two *d*; *ed* Leicester School of Art; Royal College of Art, South Kensington, studying under Frank Short. Served in Royal Artillery 1916-19; studied in Rome 1922-23; taught engraving at RCA 1927-44; Professor of Graphic Design 1948-55; RA 1949; RWS 1934 (President 1956); RE 1928 (President 1962). Illustrated *Some Umbrian Cities* (1925), *The Ballad of the White Horse* (1928), *There and Back* (1932), *Northanger Abbey* (1948), *The Doubling Rod* (1957). Designed the title page in the Popular and New series. Lived Lingard House, Chiswick Mall, London W4.
Refs: WWW; Peppin; Waters.

BAGHOT DE LA BERE, Stephen *Voyages chez Plusiers Nations Eloignées du Monde* (Contes)
Dec 1877-July 29 1927; *s* Kinard Baghot de la Bère of Burbage Hall, Leicestershire and Catherine Leahy; unmarried; *ed* Ilkley College, Yorkshire; studied in London and France. Exhibited at RA, etc. Illustrated a number of children's books for A & C Black and contributed black and white work to magazines and periodicals. 2nd

Lt in Royal Garrison Artillery; served in France 1917. Member of the London Sketch Club. Lived 52 Sydney Buildings, Bath.
Refs: WWW.

BAGOT, Richard *The Italian Lakes* (20s, Pop, New)
Nov 8 1860-Dec 11 1921; *s* Col Charles Bagot and Sophy Louisa Percy; succeeded to Levans and Kilburn estates; *ed* privately. Novelist and Roman catholic well known as a controversialist attacking methods of the priesthood in securing converts, as in novel *Casting of Nets* (1901); prolific writer, much honoured in Italy. Lived Levens Hall, Westmorland; Tripalle, Crespina, Italy.
Refs: WWW; WWL; LYB

BAIKIE, Constance N. *Ancient Assyria; Ancient Crete; Ancient Egypt; Ancient Greece; Ancient Rome* (PAL); *The Heavens* (MP) Wife of James Baikie (see below).

BAIKIE, Rev James *The Charm of the Scott Country* (Charm); *Ancient Assyria; Ancient Crete; Ancient Egypt; Ancient Greece; Ancient Jerusalem; Ancient Palestine; Ancient Rome* (PAL); *The Heavens; Men of the Old Stone Age; The Royal Navy* (MP)
Nov 25 1866-Nov 5 1931; *s* Hugh Baikie; *m* 1903 Constance, *d* of E. Turner Smith; two *s; ed* George Watson's College, Edinburgh Univ and New College, Edinburgh. FRAS 1892; Minister of Ancrum, Roxburghshire 1892; Minister of Wardie Free Church, Edinburgh 1912-22; Minister of St John's, Torphichen 1922-31. Lived The Cottage, Broomieknowe, Lasswade, Midlothian.
Refs: WWW

BAILLIE-GROHMAN, W. A. *Tyrol* (6s)
April 1 1851-Nov 27 1921; *m* 1887 Florence Nicholls; one *s,* one *d; ed* Austria, England, France. Author of many publications on hunting, rifle shooting and the Alps; noted collector of books on hunting and shooting; sometime Justice of the Peace in British Columbia. Lived Schloss Matzen, Brixlcgg, Tyrol.
Refs: WWW; LYB.

BAKER, Olaf *The Beautiful Birthday Book* (7/6)

BALFOUR-BROWNE, V. R. *Amid the High Hills* (Misc).

BALL, Wilfrid *Hampshire* (20s, WC, Pop, New); *Sussex* (20s, WC, [QP], PC, Pop, New); *Winchester* (7/6, [BB]).
Jan 4 1853-Feb 14 1917; *m* 1895 Florence Brock-Hollinshead; *ed* Hackney Grammar School and at Heatherley's. Began working life as public accountant in London; became professional painter 1877; exhibited at RA from 1876; elected RE; won London Athletic Club challenge cup for walking 1876. Also illustrated *English Country Life* (Foulis, 1910). Died in Khartoum of heat stroke while working as an accountant for the army. Lived Sunnerset, Lymington, Hampshire.
Refs: WWW; Houfe; TB; Waters; *The Studio,* Vol 70.

BARDSWELL, Frances A. *The Herb Garden* (7/6)
Lived at Meadow House, Mundesley, Norfolk. Probably the wife of Charles William Bardswell.

BARNARD, Harry *The Art of the Potter* (MP)

BARNARD, H. Clive *Africa in Pictures*; *America in Pictures*; *Asia in Pictures*; *Australia, New Zealand and Oceania in Pictures*; *The British Empire in Pictures*; *The British Isles in Pictures*; *Europe in Pictures*; *Pictures of Famous Travel*; *How Other People Live*; *India in Pictures*; *The Motherland in Pictures* (all PIX)
b June 7 1884; *b* London; *s* Howard Barnard; *m* Edith Gwendolen Wish (*d* 1956); one *s*; one *d*; *ed* University College School, London; Brasenose College, Oxford; London School of Economics; King's College, London; and in France and Germany. Taught in Manchester, Bradford and Gillingham, Kent; examiner to many universities; Professor of Education, Reading University 1937-51; Professor Emeritus from 1951; Freeman of the City of London. Wrote a number of books on education in France and England, and on teaching and geography, as well as numerous school books. Lived 54 Grosvenor Road, Caversham, Reading, Berkshire.
Refs: WWW.

BARRATT, Thomas J. *The Annals of Hampstead* (Misc)

BARTER, E. *Gardens of South Africa* (Misc)

BARTON, Rose *Familiar London* (20s, Ltd); *London* (WC, PML); *The Ramparts of Empire* (Misc)
1856-Oct 10 1929; *d* Augustine Barton, an Irish lawyer, and his wife Emily, *d* of James Martin; *ed* privately; studied in Paris under Henri Gervex. Worked and exhibited in Dublin and London; ARWS 1893; RWS 1911; moved to London around 1904. Also illustrated *Picturesque Dublin Old and New* (1898, grey-wash drawings). Lived 79 Park Mansions, Knightsbridge.
Refs: WWW; Houfe; TB; Waters; Rose Barton Exhibition Catalogue (Christie's, 1987).

BASTANIER, Hans *Berlin* (PML)
German-born artist who lived in Berlin.

BAYET, Jean *Egypte* (BV)
Jan 25 1882-April 7 1915; *b* Lyon; studied literature and politics. Wrote extensively on the history of art; joined French infantry in 1914 and died in Alsace.
Refs: DBF.

BEALBY, Contributor to *Encyclopaedia Britannica* who retired to farm in Canada. Lived Wellard Ranch, Nelson, B.C.

BEJOT, Eugène *Paris* (ASB)
Aug 31 1867-Feb 28 1931; *ed* Paris; studied with Jules Lefebvre and Benjamin-Constant. Painter and engraver; RE 1908; Chevalier de la Légion d'Honneur 1912; member of the Société Nationale des Beaux Arts, Paris; FRSE; worked in France and Britain. Lived 8 quai de la Megisserie, Paris.
Refs: WWW; Bénézit; DBF; TB.

BELL, Arthur George *Nuremberg* (7/6); *Germany* (PML)
1849-Sept 24 1916; *b* City of London; *s* George Bell, publisher; *m* 1882 Nancy Meugens (see below); two *s*, one *d*; *ed* Slade School; Ecole des Beaux Arts, Paris, under Gerome. RI; ROI; exhibited RA, RI. Also illustrated *Picturesque Brittany*, *Skirts of the Great City*, *The Royal Manor of Richmond*, *From Harbour to Harbour*, etc. Lived York House, Portugal Street, London; Rastgarth, Southbourne-on-Sea, Hampshire.
Refs: WWW; Waters; Wood.

BELL, MRS A.G. *Nuremberg* (7/6)
1850?-Aug 30 1933; maiden name Nancy Meugens; *m* 1882 A.G. Bell (see above). Worked for a time on staff of *The Studio*. Very prolific author, she used the pseudonym N. D'Anvers up to 1882; wrote many books on art, artists, travel, topography, religion and translations from French and German. Lived Southbourne (see above).
Refs: LYB; WWL.

BELLOC, Hilaire [*Sussex* (20s, Pop, New)]
July 27 1870-July 16 1953; *b* Saint-Cloud, France; *s* Louis Belloc, a French barrister, and his English wife; *m* 1896 Elodie Agnes Hogan (*d* 1914); one *s*, two *d*; *ed* Oratory School; Balliol College, Oxford. Military service in French army; Liberal MP 1906-10; Knight Commander of the Order of St Gregory 1934. An immensely prolific author whose work range from nonsense verse for children to travel books, historical studies and religious books; his name does not appear on *Sussex*. Lived King's Land, Shipley, Sussex.
Refs: WWW; CBD; DNB; Biographies by J.B. Morton (1955), R. Speight (1957), A.N. Wilson (Hamish Hamilton, 1984; Penguin 1986).

BENGER, Berenger *Highways and Hedges* (7/6)
March 14 1868-March 5 1935; *b* Tetbury, Glos; *ed* Royal Academy schools and in Antwerp under Verlat. Painted in oils and watercolour; frequent exhibitor at RA from 1890; travelled widely in US and Europe. Lived The Grange, Fittleworth, Sussex (1910); Hillside, Pulborough, Sussex.
Refs: WWW; Waters; Wood.

BENSUSAN, Samuel Levy *Morocco* (20s, Ltd)
Sept 29 1872-Dec 11 1958; *b* Dulwich; *m* Marian Prichard; *ed* City of London School; Great Ealing School. Editor of Jewish World 1897-98; special correspondent in Morocco, Spain, Portugal, Italy, Germany and Canada; music critic

ILN, *Sketch* and *Vanity Fair*; adviser to publications branch of Agriculture and Transport ministries 1919-21; editor *Theosophical Review* 1925-28. Wrote large number of books (*Morocco* being the first) on travel, topography, art and country matters. Lived 21 Holland Park, London; Godfrey's, Langham, Colchester, Essex. Refs: WWW; LYB; WrWW.

BERRIDGE, W. S. *British Land Mammals and their Habits* (PN)

BERTRAM, Anthony *Germany* (New)
Nov 19 1897-Aug 2 1978; *s* Ernest Bertram; *m* 1929 Barbara Randolph; two *s*; *ed* Douai Abbey; Pembroke College, Oxford. Author and lecturer; served in both world wars; art critic for *Spectator* and *Saturday Review*; lecturer on fine arts at the National Portrait Gallery, Queen's University, Belfast, etc. Wrote many books on the arts and design as well as novels. Lived Coates Castle, Fittleworth, Sussex. Refs: WWW.

BERTRAM, Robert J.S. *Durham; Newcastle-upon-Tyne* (ASB)

BLACKALL, W.G. *The Charm of Cambridge* (Charm); *Cambridge* (PC)

BLAKE, Sir Henry Arthur *China* (Crown)
Jan 18 1840-Feb 23 1918; *b* Limerick; *s* Peter Blake, County Inspector of Irish Constabulary; *m* 1st 1862 Jeannie Irwin (*d* 1866), 2nd 1874 Edith Osborne; two *s*, one *d*. Cadet Irish Constabulary 1859; RM 1876; Special RM 1882; Governor of the Bahamas 1884-87; of Newfoundland 1887-88; Captain General and Governor-in-Chief Jamaica 1889-97; Governor of Hong Kong 1897-1903; of Ceylon 1903-07; GCMG 1897; KCMG 1888; Knight of Justice of the Order of St John of Jerusalem. Also wrote *Pictures from Ireland*. Lived Myrtle Grove, Youghal, Co. Cork. Refs: WWW.

BONHOTE, J. Lewis *Birds of Britain* (20s); *Birds of Britain and their Eggs* (Misc)
Lived Gadespring Lodge, Hemel Hempstead, Herts (1906).

BORON, Vittorio *Malta* (7/6)
Lived Piazza San Martino 5, Turin, Italy (1910).

BOWMAN, F.P. *Children of Long Ago* (MP)

BOXER, P.N. *Riverside London* (ASB)

BRADLEY, Arthur Granville *The Rivers and Streams of England* (20s); *The Wye* (7/6, BB); *Worcestershire* (7/6)
Nov 11 1850-Jan 25 1943; *s* George Granville Bradley, Dean of Westminster, and Marian, *d* Archdeacon Philpot; brother of Mrs A. Murray Smith *qv*; *m* Florence Rackham (*d* 1925); one *d*; *ed* Marlborough; Trinity College, Cambridge. Wrote large number of books, mostly topographical and including several in the High-

ways and Byways series. Lived Red Cottage, Rye, Sussex (1912); West Watch, Rye.
Refs: WWW; LYB.

BRIEUX, Eugène *Algérie*; *Tunisie* (BV)
Jan 19 1858-Dec 6 1932; *b* Paris; left school at 14 to earn a living. Became a writer
on political and social subjects; long list of books to his credit between 1896 and
1926; member of the Académie Française 1910. Lived 26 rue Victor Masse, Paris,
and 205 Promenade des Anglais, Nice.
Refs: WWW; DBF.

BRINTON, Edith Danvers *Eton* (7/6, WC); [*Windsor and Eton* (BB)]
July 4 1861-after 1941; *d* Dr William Brinton, a physician (1823-67), who on his
early death left a large family and no money, and Mary Danvers. Cousins came to
the rescue, but Edith had to earn her own living. She probably received professional
training. Exhibited 1885-1900 at RA, RBA. Her brother Hubert taught at Eton
1887-1924.
Refs: Wood; personal information.

BROWN, Horatio Robert Forbes *Dalmatia* (Pop, New)
Feb 16 1854-Aug 19 1926; *b* Nice; *s* Hugh Horatio Brown and Gulielmina
Macdonell; *ed* Clifton College; New College, Oxford; unmarried. Hon LLD
Edinburgh 1900; historian of Venice, where he lived from 1879; member of Ateneo
Veneto and other Italian institutions. Responsible for calendaring Venetian state
papers with regard to British history. Author of large number of publications on
history and translations from Italian, including *Life on the Lagoons* (1884),
Venetian Studies (1887), *The Venetian Printing Press* (1891), *John Addington
Symonds: a biography* (1895). Lived 560 Campiello Incurabili, Zattere, Venice.
Refs: WWW; DNB; LYB; *The Times* Aug 21 1926.

BROWN, J. Hullah (in later life indexed as **J. Hullah-Brown**) *Elementary Water-
colour Painting*; *Water-Colour Guidance* (Misc)
Oct 8 1875-Feb 17 1973; *s* James Conway Brown; *m* 1923 Hilda May Chatfield; one
d; *ed* Farnham; privately (self-taught in music and art). Organist and choirmaster
Cobham, Surrey, Parish Church 1899-1906; Music and Art Master, Sandroyd Prep
School, Cobham; served in WWI. Wrote books on art and music including
Technique of the Fiddle Bow, *Violin Glissando*, *Peter Pan Class Violin Tutor*, Bow-
Craft Series; author of the Violinda method and books. Lived 52 Linton Street,
Palmerston North, New Zealand.
Refs: WWW.

BROWN, Samuel John Milton *Liverpool* (ASB)
b April 13 1873; *b* Wavertree, Liverpool; *ed* Liverpool School of Art under John
Finnie. Exhibited RI, etc; president Liverpool Academy of Arts and Liver Sketching Club. Lived in Liverpool and later at Upton, Chester.
Refs: Waters.

BROWN, Percy *Picturesque Nepal* (Misc)
1872-March 22 1955; *b* Birmingham; *m* 1st 1908 Muriel Talbot, *d* 1943; one *d*;
2nd 1948 Genevieve Le Play; *ed* Edward VI Grammar School and School of Art,
Birmingham; Royal College of Art. Indian Educational Service from 1899;
Principal, Mayo School of Art, Lahore 1899-1909; Principal, Government School
of Art, Calcutta 1909-27; Secretary and Curator, Victoria Memorial Hall, Calcutta
to 1947; Assistant Director Art Exhibition Delhi Durbar 1902-3; MBE 1941;
ARCA 1898. Also wrote/illustrated *Tours in Sikkim* (1917), *Indian Painting* (1918),
Indian Painting under the Mughals (1924), *Indian Architecture* (1942). Lived Victoria
Memorial Hall, Calcutta.
Refs: WWW.

BROWN, Mrs Percy *Picturesque Nepal* (Misc)
The wife of Percy Brown (see above).

BROWNE, Edith A. *Greece*; *Panama*; *South America*; *Spain* (PML); *Cocoa*;
Rubber; *Sugar*; *Tea*; *Vegetable Oils* (PI)
Nov 21 1874-March 15 1963; *b* Norwich; *ed* Surrey House School, Norwich. Civil
Service 1893-1903. Involved with sugar cane industry in West Indies and British
Guiana; rubber industry in Asia and South America; cocoa and other tropical
industries in Africa; lectured widely on tropical industries; FRGS; cookery expert
and exhibition organiser; edited *Social Guide* annual and *Black's Domestic Diction-
ary*. Author of many books on trade, architecture and travel. Lived Bramble
Cottage, Haslemere, Surrey.
Refs: WWW; LYB.

BROWN, Thomas Arthur *Tom Browne* (BPP)
Dec 8 1872-March 16 1910; *b* Nottingham; left school at eleven, worked in lace
trade; apprenticed to firm of lithographers; *m* 1892 Lucy Pares; one *s*; two *d*.
Moved to London 1893 and started career as comic illustrator and strip cartoon
artist; also produced caricatures, greetings cards and advertisements. Later
founded lithographic firm in Nottingham. RBA 1898; RI 1901; Member of London
Sketch Club. Illustrated *Tom Browne's Clyde Sketchbook* (1897), *Tom Browne's
Annual* (1904-5), *The One Before* (1902); contributed to numerous periodicals.
Lived Wollaton, Hardy Road, Blackheath, London.
Refs: WWW; DNB; Houfe; Peppin; TB; Waters; *The Times* March 17 1910.

BRUCE, Hon Mrs C.G. *Kashmir* (PML)
A Brigadier-General C.G. Bruce served with the Gurkhas in various parts of Asia
from 1889 onwards and wrote a book about the Himalayas; the author of *Kashmir*
in the Peeps series was probably his wife.

BRUHL, L. Burleigh *Essex* (20s, WC, Pop, New); *Germany* (PML)
July 29 1861-Jan 29 1942; *b* Baghdad; *m* 1st 1890 Alice With; 2nd 1940 Maud May;
ed Vienna. RBA 1897; ARCA 1909; RCA 1929; President, British Water Colour
Society 1914; President Old Dudley Art Society 1905. Author of *A China Dish*

(farce), *Landscape Painting, The Wye and I, The Other Vagabond*. Lived Glen Rothes, Watford.
Refs: WWW; Houfe; TB; Waters; Wood; WWA.

BRUTON, F.A. *Lancashire* (Misc)

BULLETT, Gerald *Germany* (New)
Dec 30 1893-Jan 3 1958; *b* London; *s* Robert Bullett; *m* 1921 Rosalind Gould; one *d*; *ed* Jesus College, Cambridge. Prolific author of fiction, criticism, etc.; first book published 1914.
Refs: WWW; AWWW; WWL.

BUTLER, Lady Elizabeth Southerden *From Sketch Book and Diary* (10s); *Letters from the Holy Land* (7/6; Ltd)
Nov 3 1846-Oct 2 1933; *b* Lausanne; *d* T. J. Thompson; *sister* Alice Meynell; *m* 1877 Lt-Gen Sir William Francis Butler (*d* 1910); three *s*; two *d*; *ed* Female School of Art, South Kensington, Florence and Rome. Exhibited at RA from 1873; specialised in military and equestrian subjects; lived and worked for a time in South Africa. Also illustrated *Poems* (Alice Meynell), *Ballads* (Thackeray), *Campaigns of the Cataracts* (W.F. Butler). Lived Bansha Castle, Co. Tipperary.
Refs: WWW; DNB; Houfe; TB; Waters; Wood; *An Autobiography* (Constable, 1922)

CAINE, William Ralph Hall *Isle of Man* (7/6)
1869-Jan 14 1939; brother of Hall Caine; *m* 1904 Mary Elizabeth Levy (*d* 1929). Started journalistic career with *Liverpool Mercury*; editor *Court Circular, Family Churchman, Household Words*; for some time director and manager Sir Isaac Pitman & Sons. Author of books on travel and history including *Love Songs of England* (1893), *The Courting of Kitty the Water-Wheel* (1923). Lived The Farm House, Ken Wood, London NW3.
Refs: WWW; LYB.

CALLOW, WILLIAM *William Callow* (7/6); [*Belgium* (BE, 2 illustrations)]
July 28 1812-Feb 20 1908; *b* Greenwich; *s* Robert Callow; *m* 1st 1846 Harriet Anne Smart (*d* 1883); 2nd 1884 Mary Louisa Jefferay. Studied with Theodore and Thales Fielding in London and with Newton Fielding in Paris; taught painting to family of King Louis Philippe; made long walking and sketching tours in France, Switzerland and Italy; settled in London 1841; among his pupils were Lady Amherst and her six daughters (see *The Herb Garden*); RWS 1848; FRGS. Lived The Firs, Great Missenden, Bucks.
Refs: WWW; Houfe; DNB; TB; Wood.

CALTHROP, Dion Clayton *English Costume* (20s); *Royal Palaces and Gardens* (20s, Ltd [introductory essay]); *English Costume: I Early English; II Middle Ages; III Tudor and Stuart; IV Georgian* (all 7/6); *The Charm of Gardens* (7/6)
May 2 1878-March 7 1937; *b* London; *s* John Clayton, actor, and Eve Boucicault;

m 1898 Mary Violet Marsden; *ed* St Paul's School; St John's Wood Art Schools; Julian's and Colarossi's in Paris. Exhibited RA and RI; RNVR in World War I. Worked as graphic artist, illustrator, writer and playwright. Author and illustrator of large number of books, including *Guide to Fairyland* (1905), *The Dance of Love*, *Tinsel and Gold*, *Bread and Butterflies*; also many plays.
Refs: WWW; Houfe; LYB; Peppin; TB; *My Own Trumpet* (autobiography, Hutchinson, 1928).

CALVERT, Albert Frederick *Southern Spain* (20s)
20 July 1872-27 June 1946; *s* Frederick Calvert; *m* Florence Holcombe. Explorer; travelled extensively in Australia and later in Spain; Knight Grand Cross of the Royal Order of Alfonso XII. Author of books on Australian history and resources, aborigines, etc. and on Spanish history and topography; also *Salt in Cheshire* (1914), *The German African Empire* (1915) and books on Brazil and The Cameroons. Lived Royston, Eton Avenue, London NW3.
Refs: WWW; LYB.

CAMPBELL, William Wilfred *Canada* (20s)
June 1 1861-Jan 1 1919; *b* Berlin, Canada; *s* Rev Thos Swainston and Matilda Francis Campbell; *m* Mary Louisa Dibble; *ed* privately; Upper Canada College; University of Toronto; Cambridge, Mass. Studied for church; became rector of St Stephen, New Brunswick; retired to enter Canadian Civil Service and devote life to literature 1891; bibliographer of the Dominion Archives and Records Office; LLD Aberdeen 1906. Edited *Oxford Book of Canadian Verse*; writer of verse and poetical dramas. Also wrote *Lake Lyrics* (1889), *Collected Verse* (1906), *Ian of the Orcades* (1906), *Poetical Tragedies* (1908), *Scotsman in Canada* (1911). Lived The Archives, Ottawa.
Refs: WW; CWWW; MDCB; C. F. Klinck *Wilfred Campbell* (1942).

CANNING-WRIGHT, H. W. *The World's Dolls* (MP)

CAREY, Edith F. *The Channel Islands* (20s, Ltd, Pop, New)
Possibly *d* of Maj-Gen George Jackson Carey of Rozel, Guernsey. Lived Le Vallon, Guernsey.

CARTER, Frederick *London at Night* (ASB)
1885-1967; *b* nr Bradford; studied engineering and surveying; later attended Académie des Beaux Arts, Paris, and studied art in Antwerp. Worked for poster printers in England; exhibited oils and watercolours at RA etc; studied etching under Sir Frank Short. ARE 1910. Illustrated many books including *Manfred* (1929), *Florentine Nights* (1933), *The Wandering Jew*, *D. H. Lawrence and the Body Mystical*, *Manfred*, *Cafe Royal Cocktail Book* (1937), etc. Lived 66 Abbey Road, St John's Wood, London.
Refs: WWW; Houfe; Peppin; Waters.

CARTON, Ronald Lewis *England* (New)
1888-July 9 1960; *b* London; *m* 1927 Jane Lamb; one *s*; one *d*. Author and

journalist; on editorial staff of *The Times* 1910-37; managing editor Country Life Publications 1937-40; served in World War I. Also wrote *Steel and Flowers, The English Scene, This Our London, The Gentle Adventure*. Lived 2 Canonbury Place, London N1.
Refs: WWW.

CHEESMAN, Edith *Mesopotamia* (WC)
b Westwell, Kent; *ed* King's College of Art and Chelsea School of Art. *fl* 1920s; landscape and animal painter in oil and watercolour; exhibited RA and abroad; worked in the Gold Coast, Southern Rhodesia and Iraq.
Refs: Waters.

CHILD, Harold Hannyngton *Aucassin and Nicolete* (translation) (7/6)
June 20 1869-Nov 8 1945; *b* Gloucester; *s* Rev T.H.I. Child and Florence Crossman; *m* 1st Drusilla May Cutler (*d* 1918); 2nd 1934 Helen Mary Wilkinson; *ed* Winchester; Brasenose College, Oxford. Abandoned law training to become an actor; sec RSE 1902-05; Assistant Editor, *The Academy* 1905-07 and *The Burlington Magazine*; writer for the *Times* and TLS from 1902; *Observer* drama critic 1912-20. Contributed to the *Cambridge History of English Literature* and the DNB; wrote novels, books of literary criticism, the libretto for *Hugh the Drover* (Vaughan Williams) and translations; also *A Poor Player* (1939), a record of his acting years. Lived 17 Aberdare Gardens, London NW6.
Refs: WWW; DNB; LYB; *The Times* Nov 9 and 10 1945.

CHITTENDEN, Gilbert E. *South Africa: A Record in Pen and Pencil* (MSB)

CHRISTMAS, E.W. *Argentina Past and Present* (20s)
d July 30 1918; *b* South Australia; *s* John S. Christmas; *ed* Adelaide, Sydney, London. Exhibited RI, RA etc. Painted Andes and mountains from Argentina to Chile 1910; Southern Andes 1911.
Refs: WWW; Waters.

CLARK, Alfred *Ceylon (PML)*

CLARKE, Mary Gavin *Girton College* (BB)
Dec 29 1881-Feb 12 1976; *d* John Clarke; unmarried; *ed* Aberdeen High School; Aberdeen University; Girton College, Cambridge. Taught at Roedean and schools in Scotland; Headmistress Edinburgh Ladies College 1912-24 and Manchester High School for Girls 1924-45. Lecturer and examiner Manchester University from 1948. Lived 3 Gordon Road, Corstorphine, Edinburgh.
Refs: WWW; *A Short Life of Ninety Years* (autobiography)

CLARKE, W.G. *Norfolk and Suffolk* (Misc)

CLEAVER, Reginald Thomas *Alpine Sports* (ASB); *A Winter Sport Book* (MSB)
d Dec 15 1954. On staff of *Graphic* 1893-1910; contributed to *Punch* and *Black and*

White. Also illustrated *Humorous Tales from Rudyard Kipling* (1931).
Refs: WWW; Houfe; Peppin; M.H. Spielmann *The History of Punch* (1895).

CLIFFORD, W.G. *The British Army* (MP)

CLINTON-BADDELEY, V.C. *Devon* (Pop, New)

COLE, Elsie Vera *Norwich* (ASB, NASB, PC)
July 27 1885-1968; *b* Braintree, Essex; *ed* Norwich and Chelmsford art schools. *fl*
1920s; exhibited at RI, SWA, etc; landscape and animal painter in oil, watercolour
and pastel; art mistress at Norwich School of Art 1919-41. Lived Norwich.
Refs: Waters.

COMPTON, Edward Harrison *Germany* (20s, New; PH); *The Dolomites* (7/6);
Chester (7/6, WC); *Tyrol* (6s); *Austria* (New); *Alsace-Lorraine* (PML).
b Oct 11 1881; *s* E. T. Compton (see below); *b* Feldafing, Bavaria; studied with his
father and at London County Council School of Arts and Crafts. Exhibited at
Munich Kunstverein 1907 and elsewhere.
Refs: TB; Waters; *Art Journal* 1905.

COMPTON, Edward Theodore *Germany* (20s, New)
b 27 July 1849; *b* London; *ed* English art schools. Moved to Darmstadt, in 1869 to
Munich and in 1874 to Feldafing. Painter in oils and watercolour and alpinist, he
travelled widely in Switzerland, Spain, Corsica, N. Africa and Norway; one of the
first painters of Alpine heights; climbed the Grossglockner when over 70; briefly
interned in WWI. Also illustrated *A Mendip Valley* (1892), *The Picturesque
Mediterranean* (1891) and publications of the German and Austrian Alpine Clubs.
Lived Feldafing, Bavaria and London.
Refs: Mallalieu; Wood; Graves; TB; *Art Journal*, 1907.

CONWAY, Sir William Martin (later **Lord Conway of Allington**) *The Alps* (20s; Ltd)
April 12 1856-April 19 1937; *b* Rochester; *s* Rev William Conway, Canon of
Westminster; *m* 1st 1894 Katrina Lambard (*d* 1933); one *d*; 2nd 1934 Iva Lawson;
ed Repton; Trinity College, Cambridge. Professor of Art, University College,
Liverpool 1885-88; travelled widely in Europe, Egypt and the East; led expedition
in Himalayas 1892; traversed Alps 1894; explored in Spitsbergen, Bolivian Andes
and Chile; Slade Professor of Fine Arts, Cambridge 1901-04; MP for Combined
Universities 1918-31; knighted 1895; created 1st Baron 1931. Author of many
books on art and exploration, including *Woodcutters of the Netherlands in the
Fifteenth Century* (1884), *Climbing and Exploration in the Karakoram Himalayas*
(1894), *The Alps from End to End* (1895), *The Sport of Collecting* (1914), *Mountain
Memories* (1920), Lived Allington Castle, Maidstone.
Refs: WWW; DNB; LYB; *Episodes in a Varied Life* (autobiography, Country Life,
1932). Joan Evans *The Conways: A History of Three Generations* (Museum Press,
1966).

COOK, Ernest Thomas *Gardens of England* (7/6)
1870-May 5 1915; unmarried; *ed* privately; studied at RHS gardens at Chiswick. Worked for *Gardeners' Magazine*; edited *Gardening Illustrated*; later became editor of *The Garden* magazine and Garden Editor of *Country Life*. Emigrated to Canada *c* 1911. Also wrote *Gardening for Beginners* (1901), *Trees and Shrubs for English Gardens* (1902), *Sweet Violets and Pansies*, *Carnations and Pinks*, *Rock and Wall Gardening* (ed). Lived 761 Crawford St, Toronto.
Refs: WWW; Desmond.

COOPER, Alfred Heaton. As artist: *The English Lakes* (20s, Ltd, [BB], Pop, New, PC); *Ireland* (20s, Pop, New, PML); *Isle of Man*; *Isle of Wight* (7/6, [BB], WC); *English Lakes, Suffolk*; *Norfolk* (WC); *Dorset*; *Somerset* (WC, Pop, New); *The English Lake District* (QP). *Denmark*; *Derbyshire*; *Durham*; *Northumberland*; *Sweden*; *Wild Lakeland* (Pop, New); *Norway* (New, PML); *Norfolk and Suffolk* (Misc); *What to See in the English Lakes* (WTS); *The Broads* (PC); As artist and author: *The Norwegian Fjords* (6s); *Norwegian Fjords* (BE)
June 14 1864-July 21 1929; *b* Halliwell, Bolton, Lancashire; *m* Mathilde Marie Valentinsen; three *s*; two *d*; *ed* privately; Westminster School of Art. Worked in Morocco, Gibraltar, Scotland and Norway; settled in the Lake District at Coniston, later moving to Ulverston, finally to Ambleside; exhibited in London at the RA, in Stockholm and at his studio. Apart from prolific output for A & C Black, he illustrated two books of reminiscences by A. Holden Illingworth. Lived Cross Brow, Ambleside; buried at Ambleside.
Refs: WWW; TB; Waters; Wood; W. Heaton Cooper *Mountain Painter* (Frank Peters Publishing, 1984).

COOTE, Philip C. *The Malay States* (PML)

CORNFORD, Leslie Cope *A Century of Sea Trading* (Misc)
March 20 1867-Aug 4 1927; *s* Rev James and Emily Cornford; *m* 1898 Christabel Lawrence; two *s*; *ed* privately. Naval Correspondent to *The Morning Post* during 1914-18 war. Also wrote *R. L. Stevenson* (1899), *W. E. Henley* (1913), *The Merchant Seaman in War* (1918) etc. Lived 9 Stone Buildings, Lincoln's Inn, London.
Refs: WWW; LYB.

COTTON, W. Harold *Aquaria and Garden Ponds* (PN)

COULSON, Constance J.D. *Korea* (PML)
Maiden name Miss C. Taylor

CRAIK, Mrs (Dinah Maria Mulock) *John Halifax Gentleman* (7/6), Ltd)
April 20 1826-Dec 12 1887; *d* Thomas and Dinah Mulock; *m* 1864 George Lillie Craik, a partner in Macmillan. Came to London 1846; at first wrote children's books, followed by three volume novels such as *The Ogilvies* (1849); established as a successful author she 'became the ornament of a wide social circle' while living at

Wildwood, North End, Hampstead; on marriage moved to Shortlands near Bromley, Kent.
Refs: DNB.

CRANSTON, J.H. *Canada* (PML)

CRESCIOLI, E. *France* (PML)

CREYKE, Mrs C. *Ceylon* (PML)

CROCKETT, Rev William Shillinglaw *Abbotsford* (7/6); [*Abbotsford* (BB)]
June 24 1866-June 25 1945; *b* Earlston, Berwickshire; *s* William Crockett and Margaret Wood; *m* 1894 Mary Ross (*d* 1944); *ed* Edinburgh University. Ordained Church of Scotland minister 1894; Minister of Tweedsmuir from 1894. Wrote profusely on the Borders, Walter Scott, Burns and church matters. Lived The Manse, Tweedsmuir.
Refs: WWW; LYB.

CRUIKSHANK, George *Cruikshank's Water-Colours* (20s, Ltd)
Sept 27 1792-Feb 1 1878; *s* Isaac Cruikshank. Well known artist, caricaturist and polemicist; illustrated works of Dickens and Thackeray among others.
Refs: DNB; Houfe; TB; Wood; R. McLean *George Cruikshank, His Life and Work as a Book Illustrator* (1949); Michael Wynn-Jones *George Cruikshank, His Life and London* (Macmillan, 1978).

CUMING, Edward William Dirom *George Morland* (20s, Ltd); *George Morland* (GA)
May 4 1862-Dec 3 1941; *s* Col E.W. Cuming; *m* 1892 Ethel Maud Locock; *ed* privately. In Burma 1880-87 before returning to England and adopting literature as a career. Books include *With the Jungle Folk* (1897), *The Arcadian Calendar* (1903), *British Sport, Past and Present* (1909), *Robert S. Surtees* (1924) and other books on Surtees, *A Vendor of Dreams* (1923); also wrote novels as Evelyn Tempest. Lived The Orchard House, Appleford, Berkshire.
Refs: WWW; LYB.

CUNDALL, Herbert Minton *Birket Foster* (20s, Ltd); *Birket Foster* (GA); *William Callow* (7/6)
Aug 25 1848-May 25 1940; *s* Joseph Cundall; *m* 1878 Ursula Mary Ewer (*d* 1932); one *s*, one *d*; *ed* King's College School, London. Joined South Kensington Museum (now Victoria and Albert Museum) 1869; keeper 1891; senior keeper 1905; retired 1910. Books include *A History of British Water-Colour Painting* (1908), *The Norwich School* (1920), *Bygone Richmond* (1925); compiled several Murray's Handbooks. Lived 4 Richmond Gardens, Richmond, Surrey.
Refs: WWW.

DALE, Harrison *Ireland* (Pop, New)

DAVIES, Randall (Robert Henry) *Reynolds*; *Romney*; *Velasquez* (12/6)
1866-Jan 24 1946; *s* Rev R.H. Davies, Chelsea Old Church; *m* 1910 Gladys
Margaret Miles; two *s*; *ed* Bradfield; Scoones. At times art critic for *The Academy*,
Westminster Gazette, *New Statesman*, *Queen*; solicitor from 1898. Also wrote
Chelsea Old Church (1904), *Stories of the English Artists* (1908), *Black's Dictionary
of Pictures* (1921), *A Lyttel Book of Nonsense* (1912, 1925), *The Railway Centenary*
(1925), *Less Eminent Victorians* (1927). Lived 1 Cheyne Gardens, Chelsea.
Refs: WWW.

DAY, Hilda G. *A Few Flowers of the Italian Riviera* (QP)

DE HAENEN, F. *Russia* (20s, PML, PC); *Moscow*; *Provincial Russia*; *St Petersburg*
(7/6)
A Frenchman who worked for the magazine *L'Illustration*; contributed to ILN;
went to South Africa as correspondent for *Graphic* in 1900. Lived 3 St Paul's
Studios, West Kensington.
Refs: Houfe.

DE KOVER, H. Tornai *Hungary* (PML)

DE LAMBERT, Maurice *The Spirit of Paris* (7/6)
b Feb 9 1873; *b* Paris; studied under G. Moreau. Executed theatrical designs for the
Paris Odeon and became known as a painter of actors and actresses; also painted
urban scenes.
Refs: TB.

DE LA MARE, Walter *St Andrews* (MSB)
1873-1956. English writer and poet; retired from employment with the Anglo-
Iranian Oil Company in 1908 to devote himself to writing. His life is described in
Walter de la Mare by David Cecil (1973).

DE LAPRE, Ch *Les Petits Aventuriers en Amérique* (Contes)

DE NOUSSANNE, Henri *Ecosse; Russie* (BV)
Pseudonym of **Henri de Rossignol.**

DE PANGE, Comtesse Jean *Paris* (PML)

DELLER, Lawrence *[Galloway* (BB)]

DEWAR, George A.B. *The Book of the Dry Fly* (Sport)
Nov 3 1862-March 20 1934; *s* Capt Dewar of Doles, Hampshire; *ed* privately;
Pembroke College, Oxford; *m* Ida Beatrice Robinson (*d* 1922). Editor of *Saturday
Review* 1914-17; of the *Nineteenth Century* 1919-25; visited the British, French and
Italian armies in 1916 and 1917. Publications include *Nature: The Supreme
Problem*, *The Leaning Spire*, *This Realm, This England*, *Dreams*, *The Airy Way*, *The*

Faery Year, Wild Life in Hampshire Highlands, Life and Sport in Hampshire, The Great Munition Feat 1914-18, Sir Douglas Haig's Command. Lived Brook Cottage, Abbotts Inn, Andover, Hampshire.
Refs: WWW.

DICKIE, Rev James *Germany* (20s)
Nov 13 1845-May 28 1933; *b* Kilmarnock; *s* Francis and Susan McLelland Dickie; *m* Grace Mackenzie Wood; *ed* Edinburgh University. Pastor, St Andrew's Church, Berlin, Canada 1871-79; Pastor, Central Presbyterian Church, Detroit 1879-84; Chief Pastor, American and British Church, Berlin 1894-1914. Also wrote *In the Kaiser's Capital, Germany Described, Detroit of Fifty Years Ago, Seven Christmas Trees.*
Refs: WWW.

DOBSON, G. *Russia* (20s); *St Petersburg* (7/6)
d Oct 13 1938; *m* one *d. The Times* correspondent for 25 years in St Petersburg and elsewhere in Russia; his *Who's Who* entry is notable for including almost every detail of an incident-packed life. Also wrote *Russia's Railway Advance into Central Asia* (1890), *Russia under the Red Terror* in Harmsworth's *History of the Great War* (1919). Lived 61 St Quintin Avenue, London W10.
Refs: WWW.

DOBSON, Henry John *Scottish Life and Character* (7/6)
1858-July 1928; *b* Peeblesshire; *s* Thomas and Rebecca Dobson; *m* 1890 Jeanie Charlotte Hannah Cowan; three *s*, one *d*; *ed* Innerleithen, Edinburgh; School of Design and Royal Scottish Academy, Edinburgh. Painter of Scottish character and interiors; exhibited RA and elsewhere; visited USA and Canada 1911. Also contributed to *Scottish Art.* Lived 5 Merchiston Place, Edinburgh, and in Kirkcudbrightshire.
Refs: WWW; Wood.

DRAKE, Elizabeth *Gardens of South Africa* (Misc)
b Oct 14 1866; *b* Chatham, Kent; *ed* Rochester and Westminster art schools and Colarossi's, Paris. Specialised in landscapes and flowers; exhibited at RA, RI, etc; worked in South Africa and painted cathedrals in England and France and the rivers Thames and Medway. Lived Wokingham, Berkshire.
Refs: Waters.

DRESSER, Henry Eeles *Birds of Britain* (20s, [PC]); *Birds of Britain and Their Eggs* (Misc)
May 9 1838-Dec 5 1915; *b* Thirsk, Yorkshire; *m* 1878; one *s*; one *d*; ed Bromley, Kent; Ahrensburg, Germany; Gefle and Upsala, Sweden. Joined British Ornithologists Union 1865; secretary 1882-88. Started business as iron and steel merchant in London 1869. Amassed a large collection of bird skins, ornithological books and eggs, which were later in the keeping of Owens College Museum. Wrote and illustrated *A History of the Birds of Europe including all the Species inhabiting*

the Western Palearctic Region (eight volumes plus supplement, 1871-96); contributed to *The Ibis*.
Refs: WWW.

DRISCOLL, E. *Gardens of South Africa* (Misc)

DU CANE, Ella *The Italian Lakes* (20s, Pop, New, PC); *The Flowers and Gardens of Japan* (20s); *Banks of the Nile* (20s, PC); *The Canary Islands* (7/6); *The Flowers and Gardens of Madeira* (7/6, PC); [*The Lake of Como* (BE)]; *Egypt*; *The Nile* (WC); *Japan* (Pop, New, PML, PC); *Great Steamship Lines: The P & O* (MP); *Teneriffe* (PC)
Sister of Florence Du Cane; active 1890-1930. Exhibited at FAS. Lived 41 Eaton Place, London SW1.
Refs: Peppin; Wood.

DU CANE, Florence *The Flowers and Gardens of Japan* (20s); *The Canary Islands*; *The Flowers and Gardens of Madeira* (7/6)
Sister of Ella Du Cane.

DUCKWORTH, Francis Robinson Gladstone *Chester* (7/6); *The Cotswolds* (6s); *Chester*; *The Cotswolds* (BB)
Aug 2 1881-Sept 21 1964; *b* Llanfairfechan; *s* Henry and Mary Duckworth; *m* Ethelwyn Compton; no *c*; *ed* Rossall School; Trinity College, Oxford. Taught at Dover College, Cheltenham and Eton; war service 1915-19; from 1920 HM Inspector of Schools; later Senior Chief Inspector, Board of Education. Also wrote *From a Pedagogue's Sketch Book*, *Swiss Fantasy*. Lived Lebanon, Itchenor, Chichester, Sussex.
Refs: WWW.

DUNCAN, Eleanor *Paris* (PML)

DUNHILL, Alfred *The Pipe Book* (Misc)
Sept 30 1872-Jan 2 1959; *s* Henry Dunhill; *m* 1895 Alice Mary Stapleton; two *s*, one *d*; *ed* private school, Hampstead; privately. Founded Dunhills Ltd (Dunhill's Motorities); severed connection with firm and started in tobacco business; produced the Dunhill Pipe for Alfred Dunhill Ltd; bought third motor car that came to England; took part in first motor run to Brighton; FRSA. The above was his only book. Lived Lynsters, Fourth Avenue, Charmandean, Worthing, Sussex.
Refs: WWW.

EALAND, C. A. *Insect Life* (20s [published at 25s])

ELGOOD, George S. *The Garden that I Love; Lamia's Winter Quarters* (7/6d, Ltd); *English Gardens* (PC)
Feb 26 1851-Oct 21 1943; *s* Samuel and Jane Elgood; *m* Mary Clephan (*d* 1925); *ed* Bloxham; privately; the brother-in-law of John Fulleylove *qv*. Best known for

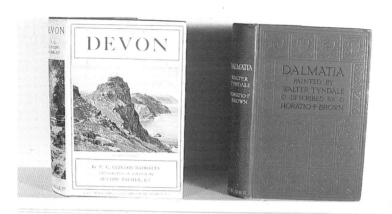

Above: *Popular series books with and without wrapper; this wrapper design was used widely in various series from the early 1920s onwards.* Below left: *A Travel Pictures portfolio of illustrations intended as an educational aid for children.* Below right: India *from the Pictures of Many Lands series in a binding similar to that of the Beautiful Britain series; most Pictures books carry a design of columns and borders.*

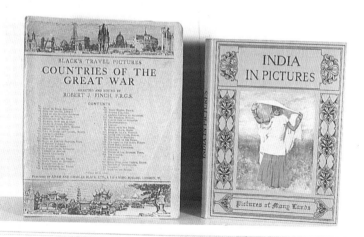

The Peeps: (top) China *in English and French versions and* Home Life in India; (centre) Belgium *in two styles and a railway Peep;* (bottom left and centre) *the same book as issued in the Life and Legends of Other Lands series and later in the Peeps at Many Lands and Cities series;* (bottom right) The Barbary Rovers (*Peeps at History*) *in a paper board binding used for many Peeps reprints.*

paintings of gardens and architecture in England, Italy and Spain; RI 1881; ROI 1883; exhibited at RI and FAS. Also illustrated *Some English Gardens* (1904), *Italian Gardens* (1907). Lived Knockwood, Tenterden, Kent, and Barnclose, Markfield, Leics.
Refs: WWW; Houfe; TB; Waters; Wood; WWA; *The Studio,* Vol 5, Vol 31.

ELIAS, Frank. *The Far East; The Gorgeous East* (LPML)

ELKINGTON, E. Way. *The Savage South Seas* (20s)
b 1872; *b* London; *s* Surg-Gen A. G. Elkington; *ed* St Paul's School; *m* 1902 Agnes Mary Young; two *s.* Studied medicine but went to Stock Exchange; 'getting tired of fogs and figures' sailed for New Zealand 1891, tried gold and gum digging, cattle driving and journalism. Moved to San Francisco 1897, travelled across US, returned to London; edited *King's Jester* 1900-02, various other publications later; travelled in Canada 1908-11. Also wrote *The Lucky Shot* (1902), *The Squatter's Stud* (1903), *Adrift in New Zealand* (1906), *Canada: The Land of Hope* (1910).
Refs: WW.

ELLIOTT, Ernest C. *A Short History of the Church of England (7/6)*

ELMHURST, Richard. *The Naturalist at the Seashore* (PN).

EVANS, David G. *India* (PML, Welsh translation).

EYRE-TODD, George *The London and North Western Railway; The London Midland and Scottish Railway* (PGR).
June 2 1862-July 10 1937; *b* Glasgow; *s* Henry Todd and Elizabeth Lees; *m* 1895 Jean Laing Lees; one *s;* two *d; ed* Glasgow High School; Glasgow University. Became editor of *Scottish Country Life;* president Glasgow St Andrew Society; lecturer on English Literature and Scottish History in Glasgow Athenaeum; editor of *Scottish Field* 1908-13; commanded 3rd City of Glasgow Cadets 1916-19. Author of many publications on Scottish history, traditions and literature. Lived Auchenlarich, by Balloch, Dumbartonshire.
Refs: WWW; LYB.

FAED, James Jr *Galloway* (6s, WC)
*c*1847-Feb 17 1920; *s* James Faed. Landscape painter and illustrator. Lived Edinburgh and London.
Refs: TB; Waters; Wood.

FAIRBRIDGE, Dorothea *Gardens of South Africa* (Misc)

FAIRFORD, Ford *Cuba; Newfoundland* (PML).

FARQUHARSON, Joseph *Salmon Fishing* (Sport)
May 4 1846-April 15 1935; *b* Edinburgh; *s* Francis Farquharson; *m* 1914 Violet

Hay. Exhibited at RA, RI, etc. RA 1915. Lived Finzean, Banchory, Scotland.
Refs: WWW.

FARRER, Reginald John *The Dolomites* (7/6)
Feb 17 1880-Oct 16 1920; *s* James and Elizabeth Farrer of Inglesborough; *ed*
privately; Balliol College, Oxford. Plant collector, traveller, horticultural writer;
made yearly journeys of botanical exploration in the Alps, Ceylon, Greece, Turkey,
China and Tibet; unfit for military service; employed by Foreign Office; died
during expedition to Burma with E. H. M. Cox. Also wrote *My Rock Garden*
(1909), *Alpines and Bog Plants* (1908), *In a Yorkshire Garden* (1909), *The Rock
Garden* (1912), *On the Eaves of the World* (1917), *English Rock Gardens* (1919) and a
number of novels and plays. Lived Ingleborough, Yorkshire, where the results of
his explorations can be seen in the Reginald Farrer Nature Trail; also at 50
Ennismore Gardens, London SW7.
Refs: WWW; Desmond; LYB.

FEDDEN, A. Romilly *The Basque Country* (Misc)
Feb 5 1875-March 30 1939; *b* Stoke Bishop; *s* Henry Fedden of Henbury, Glos; *m*
1907 Katharine Douglas (see above); one *s*; studied with Professor Herkomer and
at the Académie Julian in France and in Spain; travelled in France, Germany and
the Far East. Served in 1st World War; RBA 1903. Also wrote/illustrated *Modern
Water Colour Painting* (1918), *Golden Days from the Fishing Log of a Painter in
Brittany* (1919). Lived France and 32a Pembroke Square, London.
Refs: WWW; TB.

FEDDEN, Katharine Waldo Douglas *The Basque Country* (Misc)
d April 7 1939; *d* Mr Douglas of New York; *m* 1907 Romilly Fedden; one *s*. Hon
Organiser and Chairman of Belgravia War Hospital Supply Depot 1915-19. Also
wrote *The Sign* (1912), *The Spare Room* (1913), *The Rock* (1914), *The Peacock's Tail*
(1926), *Old Manor Life in France* (1932). Lived in France.
Refs: WWW; LYB.

FEDERLEY, Alexander *Finn and Samoyad* (LL)

FELTON, Robert Forester British Floral Decoration (7/6)
Florist to King Edward VIII; Fellow of the Royal Horticultural Society; Fellow of
the Zoological Society, etc.

FERGUSON, Daniel *British Ferns, Clubmosses and Horsetails* (PN)

FINCH, Robert J. (Uncle Robert) *Children of the Snow and Ice; Children of the
Sunshine; Children of the Field and Forest; Children of the Mountain and Plain* (PLP);
Travel Pictures (editor)

FINNEMORE, John *Delhi and the Durbar; England; France; The Holy Land; India;
Home Life in India; Italy; Japan; Morocco; Switzerland* (PML); *America; The*

Barbary Rovers; France; A Short History of France; Germany; A Short History of Germany; Holland; Japan (PH).
Author of many of A & C Black's children's books. His offer of a book called *A Barbary Corsair* was turned down in 1905 because ... 'for some time we have been careful to eliminate all love interest from the books in the series'. Lived Ty Cnwc, Llanilar, Aberystwyth.

FISHER, E. H. *Natural History: Animals* (Misc); *Animals* (PC)

FITCHEW, E. H. *Greece; Korea* (PML)
Portraitist and illustrator.
Refs: Houfe.

FITZGERALD, Augustine *Naples* (20s, Ltd)
Married to Sybil FitzGerald (see below). Lived 11 Avenue Hoche, Paris.
Refs: Waters.

FITZGERALD, Edward *The Rubaiyat of Omar Khayyam* (7/6)
1809-1883. *Ed* Bury St Edmunds and Trinity College, Cambridge; English man of letters, poet and translator famous for his free rendition of the *Rubaiyat;* a friend of Carlyle, Thackeray and Tennyson. Also wrote a life of Bernard Barton (1849) appended to an edition of his poems, *Euphranor* (1851), *Polonius* (1852), English versions of *The Agamemnon* and plays by Sophocles. Lived Suffolk.
Refs: DNB.

FITZGERALD, Sybil *Naples* (20s, Ltd)
Wife of Augustine FitzGerald (see above).

FLEMING, Ethel *New York* (Charm)

FLEMWELL, George Jackson *Alpine Flowers and Gardens* (7/6); *Alpine Flowers* (PC)
May 29 1865-May 5 1928; *s* John and Anne Flemwell of Mitcham, Surrey; *m* 1912 Grace Priddle; *ed* Thanet College, Margate; private tutor; studied with W. P. Frith, with Prof Rosier in Antwerp and in Nuremberg and Munich. Settled in Switzerland and devoted himself to painting and studying the Alps and Alpine wild life. Also wrote/illustrated *The Flower Fields of Alpine Switzerland* (1911), *Sur l'Alpe Fleurie, Beautiful Switzerland, Lucerne, Locarno, Lugano, Lausanne, Villars and Champery, Chamonix, Zermatt;* also the plates for H. Stuart Thomson's *Sub-Alpine Plants of Swiss Wood and Meadows* (1912). Lived Lugano, Switzerland.
Refs: WWW; Desmond; Waters; Wood; *Gardeners Chronicle* 1928; *Journal of Botany* 1928, 1930.

FLOWER, Charles Edwin *Alsace-Lorraine* (PML)
April 4 1871-1957; *b* Merton, Surrey; *m* Alice Perry; one *s*; *ed* Royal College of Art. Worked as draughtsman; travelled in North and South America and Europe,

especially Germany; principally known as a prolific postcard artist. Lived
Wallingford, Oxfordshire.
Refs: Coysh; Waters.

FOLKARD, Charles James *Alice in Wonderland; English Nursery Rhymes* (PC); also
a number of books for children which are outside the scope of this volume.
1878-Feb 25 1963; *m;* one *s,* two *d; ed* Colfe's School, Lewisham. Joined *Daily Mail*
as an artist; left to become a book illustrator; invented Teddy Tail cartoon
character 1915; for a time a professional conjuror. Illustrated many books
including *Swiss Family Robinson* (1910), *Pinocchio* (1911), *Grimm's Fairy Tales*
(1911), *Aesop's Fables* (1912), *Arabian Nights* (1913), *Mother Goose Nursery Rhymes*
(1919), *Songs from Alice in Wonderland* (1921), *The Troubles of a Gnome* (1928),
Tales of the Taunus Mountains (1937), *The Book of Nonsense* (1956). Lived Gowans,
Sandy Cross, Heathfield, Sussex.
Refs: WWW; Coysh; Houfe; Waters.

FORESTIER, Amédée *Belgium* (20s, Pop, New, [BE], PML, PC); *Bruges and West
Flanders* (10s); *Brabant and East Flanders; Liège and the Ardennes* (7/6); *The
Cockpit of Europe; Belgium Past and Present* (Misc); *Men of the Old Stone Age* (MP)
1854-Nov 14 1930; *b* probably Belgium. Came to England 1882; worked
extensively for ILN; sent by Queen Victoria to Moscow in 1896 to paint the
coronation of Tsar Nicholas II; illustrated other royal occasions; later studied and
illustrated archaeology. RA, ROI. Illustrated *Blind Love* (1890), *The Romantic
History of Robin Hood* (1898) and books on Shakespeare, Tennyson and
Wordsworth; also illustrated novels by Besant, Seton Merriman, Anthony Hope,
Q, Robert Hichens and others. Also contributed to *The Girls' Own Paper, Strand,
Pearson's, Windsor Magazine, Lady's Pictorial.* Lived 7 Alleyn Park, West Dulwich,
London.
Refs: WWW; Houfe; Peppin.

FORMILLI, Cesare T. G. *The Stones of Italy; The Italian Lakes* (Pop, New); *The
Castles of Italy* (Misc)
d Dec 8 1942; *b* Rome; *m* Alice Eleanor Morgans; two *s,* one *d; ed* privately; Royal
Academy of Arts, Rome.
Architect-contractor to British section of Turin Exhibition 1911; Italian section of
Panama Exhibition 1915; lectured on art in California and London; painted ceiling
of throne room at Italian Embassy in London; decorative artist of Brompton
Oratory, London, and Middlesbrough and Leeds Cathedrals. Lived 6 Tregunter
Road, The Boltons, London SW10.
Refs: WWW.

FORREST, Archibald Stevenson *Morocco* (20s, Ltd, PML); *South America; The
West Indies* (20s); *Jamaica* (6s, PML)
1869-Jan 3 1963; *b* Greenwich, London; *s* James Forrest, of Yett, Carluke, Lanark;
m 1913 Marion Douglas; *ed* Roan School, Greenwich; Edinburgh; Westminster
School of Art; City and Guilds College; Edinburgh Art School. Specialised in

black and white in the 1890s, colour in 1900s, landscape from 1910. Also illustrated *Picturesque Normandy* (1905), *Stories of Robin Hood* (1905), *A Tour through Portugal* (1907), *Our Island Story* (1909), *A Tour through Old Provence* (1911), *Uncle Tom's Cabin, Adam Bede* (1933); also contributed to periodicals. Lived Silver Birches, Shermanbury, Sussex.
Refs: WWW; Caw; Houfe; Peppin; Waters.

FORREST, Isabelle *The Herb Garden* (7/6); *English Gardens* (PC)
Also provided the frontispiece to *Twelve Moons* by F. A. Bardswell (1912).

FOSTER, Myles Birket *Birket Foster* (20s, Ltd, WC, GA)
Feb 4 1825-March 27 1899; *b* North Shields; *s* Myles Birket Foster and Ann King; *m* 1st 1850 Ann Spence (*d* 1859); three *s*, two *d;* 2nd 1864 Frances Watson; *ed* Tottenham; Hitchin. Pupil of E. Landells, wood engraver, 1841; illustrated many books with wood engravings before turning to watercolours 1858; RWS 1861. Lived Braeside, Weybridge, Surrey.
Refs: WWW; CBD; DNB; Houfe; TB; Wood.

FOWLER, Robert *Beautiful Wales* (20s) *North Wales* ([BB], WC); *Wales* (Pop, New, PML).
Jan 15 1853-Oct 28 1926; *ed* Liverpool College; Heatherley's. Worked in Liverpool until 1904, then in London. Exhibited at RA from 1876 and in Paris, Munich, Berlin, Brussels, Venice and Vienna; RI 1891.
Refs: WWW; Waters; Wood.

FOX, Sir Frank Ignatius *Australia* (20s, Pop, New); *England; Italy; Switzerland* (20s, Fasc); *Bulgaria* (Fasc); *The Ramparts of Empire* (Misc); *Australia* (PML); *The British Empire*; *Oceania* (LPML).
Aug 12 1874-March 4 1960; *b* Kensington, Adelaide, Australia; *s* Charles James and Mary Ann Fox; *m* Helen Clint (*d* 1958); one *s*, two *d; ed* Christ's College, Hobart, Tasmania. Edited Australian publications; became bankrupt in 1898 as result of wife's illness; came to London 1909; urged preparation against menace of European war; joined *The Morning Post*, becoming Assistant Editor 1909, News Editor 1910; war correspondent during Balkan war, with Bulgarian army; with Belgian army during first part of World War I; commissioned in Royal Field Artillery 1914; wounded twice in battle of Somme; on General Staff, War Office 1917-18; awarded OBE; returned to journalism and charitable work after the war; Knighted 1926. Also wrote *Mastery of the Pacific, Our English Land Muddle, GHQ,* histories of the Inniskillings (1928 and 1951), *The Agony of Belgium* (1915), *The British Army at War* (1917), *Beneath an Ardent Sun* (1923), *The English, Finland To-day, Italy To-day.* Lived Broom Cottage, West Wittering, Sussex.
Refs: WWW; ADB.

FRAIPONT, Gustave *The Spirit of Paris* (7/6)
b May 9 1849 in Brussels; studied with Hendrick and H. de Hem. Worked in Paris and became a naturalised Frenchman; exhibited oil paintings of Paris and Britain;

contributed to books and magazines; Chevalier de la Légion d'Honneur 1896. Also illustrated *Environs de Paris* (1886), *Les Bêtes à Paris* (1886), *Les Environs de Rouen* (1889); wrote *L'Art de peindre les animaux, L'Art de prendre le croquis, L'Eventail, l'Ecran et le Paravent* (1892), *La Plante* (1893).
Refs: Bénézit; DBF; TB.

FRASER, Sir Hugh *Amid the High Hills* (Misc)
d July 8 1927; *s* Thomas Fraser; *ed* Charterhouse; Trinity Hall, Cambridge; *m* 1888 Ethel Mary Hamilton; two *s*, three *d*. Reader and Examiner in Common Law to the Inns of Court; JP County of Ross and Cromarty; knighted 1917; from 1924 Judge in the King's Bench Division of the High Court. Wrote a number of books on tort, libel, slander and the law of parliamentary elections. Lived 48 Linden Gardens, London W2, and Stromeferry House, Ross-shire.
Refs: WWW.

FRIEDEL, Viktor Henri *Espagne* (BV)
b Sept 19 1867 at Bischwiller near Strasbourg; studied at Bischwiller; Strasbourg; University of Bonn; and in Paris; studied philology with Paul Meyer.
Refs: Bénézit.

FULLEYLOVE, John *Greece* (20s, Pop, New, PML); *The Holy Land* (20s, Ltd, Pop, New, WC, PML); *Oxford* (20s, Ltd, Pop, New, [BB], WC); *Edinburgh* (7/6, Ltd, WC, PC); *The Tower of London* (7/6, [BB]); *Middlesex* (7/6); *Westminster Abbey* (7/6, Ltd, [BB]); *Scott Country* (WC); *Ancient Greece* (PAL); *Jerusalem* (PC)
Aug 18 1844-May 22 1908; *b* Leicester; *s* John and Elizabeth Fulleylove; *m* 1878 Elizabeth Sara Elgood (sister of George S. Elgood *qv*); one *s*, two *d*; *ed* Leicester; articled to firm of architects. Exhibited from 1871, particularly at the FAS; travelled widely abroad and made tours in Italy; elected RI 1878; ROI; he regarded his black and white sketches more highly than his colour work. Also illustrated *Pictures and Sketches of Greek Landscape* (1897), *In the Footsteps of Charles Lamb* (1905), *The Pageant of London* (1906); also contributed to numerous magazines. Lived 21 Church Row, Hampstead, London.
Refs: WWW; DNB; Graves; Houfe; TB; Waters; Wood; *The Studio*, Vol 7.

GARDNER, Monica M. *Poland* (PML)

GARDNER, William Biscombe *Kent* (20s, Pop, New, WC); *Canterbury (7/6,* [BB], PC); *The Peak Country* (6s, [BB]); *Dickens Country* (WC); *Derbyshire* (Pop, New)
c 1849-Feb 23 1919. Landscape painter, wood engraver and etcher; engraved for ILN and *Graphic;* worked in London and Surrey and finally settled in Tunbridge Wells. Lived Hillsborough, Prospect Road, Tunbridge Wells (1908).
Refs: Houfe; Peppin; TB; Waters; Wood.

GAUNT, Mary *George Washington* (PGM)
d 1942; *d* Judge Gaunt of Melbourne; *m* 1894 Hubert Lindsay Miller; no *c*; *ed*

Grenville College, Ballarat; Melbourne University. 'At her husband's death, finding herself with very small means, she came to England to make her living by her pen; after many vicissitudes she at last succeeded in making enough money to travel to West Africa' (*Who's Who*). Among the large number of books she wrote is one called *Joan of the Pilchard;* also *The Uncounted Cost,* published by A & C Black, 'which brought me in more money than any book I ever wrote ...' Lived Villa Camilla, Bordighera, Italy.
Refs: WWW; LYB.

GAUTIER, Judith *En Chine; Le Japon* (BV); *La China; El Japon* (PS)
d Dec 1917; *d* Théophile Gautier. Member Goncourt Academy; Chevalier de la Légion d'Honneur. Author of novels, plays, translations and poetry. Lived 30 rue Washington, Paris; Pre' des Oiseaux, Dinard, Ill-et-Vilaine, France.
Refs: WWW.

GAUTIER, Lucien Marcelin *The Spirit of Paris* (7/6)
b Jan 8 1850 in Aix en Provence; studied with Marius Reynaud and Leon Gaucherel. Painted town scenes in Paris, Rome and London. Lived Montrouge.
Refs: Bénézit; TB.

GENN, G. T. *Rome* (PML)

GIBB, William *A Book of Porcelain; Musical Instruments: Historic Rare and Unique* (Misc)
1839-1929; *b* Scotland; brother of Robert Gibb. Lithographer and painter in watercolour of works of art. Lived London.
Refs: Waters; Wood.

GILBEY, Sir Walter *George Morland* (20s, Ltd)
May 2 1831-Nov 12 1914; *b* Bishop's Stortford; *s* Henry and Elizabeth Gilbey; *m* 1858 Ellen (*d* 1896); four *s,* four *d.* First worked for an estate agent and in the parliamentary agent's office at Westminster; founded W & A Gilbey, wine merchants; president Shire Horse Society 1883, 1897; president Hackney Horse Society 1889-1904; created baronet 1893. Author of many books on horses and art including *Life of George Stubbs;* also books on early carriages, poultry, alcohol, pigs, cock-fighting. Lived Elsenham Hall, Essex.
Refs: WWW.

GOBLE, Warwick *Constantinople* (20s); *Turkey* (PML)
Nov 22 1862-Jan 22 1943; *d* Dalston, London; *s* Burkitt and Mary Goble; *ed* City of London School; Westminster School of Art. Worked on staff of *Pall Mall Gazette* and *Westminster Gazette;* became accomplished black and white illustrator; worked in drawing office at Woolwich Arsenal during World War I and for British Red Cross Society afterwards. Also illustrated *The War of the Worlds* (1898), *The Greater Abbeys of England* (1908), *The Water Babies* (1909), *Green Willow and other Japanese Fairy Tales* (1910), *Folk Tales of Bengal* (1912), *Indian Myth and Legend*

(1913), *The Fairy Book* (1913), *Treasure Island* (1923). Lived The Glade, Beech Road, Shepherd's Hill, Merstham, Surrey.
Refs: WWW; Houfe; Peppin; TB; Waters; Wood; BMC Feb 1988.

GOFF, Colonel Robert Charles *Florence and some Tuscan Cities; Italy* (20s); *Florence* (PML)
July 28 1837-1 July 1922; *m* Clarissa, *d* of Baron de Hochpied. Entered army at 18, fought in Crimea; retired from Coldstream Guards in 1878 with rank of honorary Colonel; then devoted his time to art; moved to Hove 1889 and painted Brighton, Shoreham, etc; settled in Florence 1903; also worked in Italy and Egypt; lived in Switzerland during WW1; FRSE. Lived Wick Studio, Holland Road, Hove, Sussex; Villa dell'Ombrellino, Via della Piazzola, Florence.
Refs: WWW; TB; Waters; Wood.

GOFF, Clarissa Catherine *Florence and some Tuscan Cities* (20s). Married to Colonel Goff (see above).

GOLDSMITH, Oliver *The Vicar of Wakefield* (7/6, Ltd)
1728-74. Irish born poet, playwright and man of letters. His eventful life is fully chronicled in the DNB and other literary reference works. Biographies by John Forster and others.

GOODALL, Agnes M. *Portugal; South Africa* (PML)
Lived Pine Ridge, Farnham, Surrey.

GORGES, Mary *Killarney* (BB)

GRAY, Thomas *Gray's Elegy* (Misc)
1716-71. English poet, whose life is described in *Thomas Gray* by M. Golden (1964) and elsewhere.

GREEN, Roland [*The British Bird Book* (Misc)]; *British Birds* (PC)
Jan 9 1895-Dec 18 1972; *b* Rainham, Kent; *ed* Sir Joseph Williamson's School, Rochester. Unmarried. Bird and wildlife painter in oil and watercolour; lectured on bird watching and the drawing of birds. Also illustrated *Birds in Flight* (Pycraft). Known as the hermit artist, he lived alone at The Studio, Hickling Broad, Norfolk.
Refs: WWW; Waters.

GREENAWAY, Catherine or **Kate** *Kate Greenaway* (20s, Ltd, GA)
March 17 1846-Nov 6 1901; *d* John and Elizabeth Greenaway; studied at the art school at South Kensington, where she was a contemporary of Elizabeth Thompson (later Butler) and Helen Paterson (later Allingham) and at Heatherley's and the Slade. RI 1889. Miss Greenaway's life is extensively described in Spielmann and Layard's book and in Rodney Engen's biography *Kate Greenaway* (Macdonald Futura, 1981). Lived 39 Frognal, Hampstead.
Refs: WWW; DNB; TB; Waters; Wood.

GREENWOOD, Frank *Scarborough and Whitby* (ASB); *The Charm of Lancashire* (Charm)

GREGO, Joseph *Cruikshank's Water-Colours* (20s, Ltd); *The Vicar of Wakefield* (7/6; Ltd [Introduction])
Sept 23 1843-Jan 24 1908; *b* Clerkenwell, London; *s* Joseph and Louisa Grego; unmarried; *ed* privately. Worked for a time at Lloyd's; drifted into collecting, dealing, art journalism and authorship; authority on Gillray, Rowlandson, Morland and Cruikshank; also organised exhibitions and designed theatrical costumes. He was a director of Carl Hentschel Ltd, the photo-engravers, 1899-1908, and a substantial shareholder in Kegan Paul & Co. Edited volumes on Rowlandson, Gillray, Thackeray and Dickens. Lived 23 Granville Square, London.
Refs: WWW; DNB; obituaries in *The Times, Athenaeum, Graphic.*

GREIG, James *Gainsborough* (Misc)
1861-Oct 13 1941; *b* Arbroath; *s* Alexander Greig. Moved to London 1891; Paris 1895; for many years art critic of *The Morning Post;* RBA 1898. Contributed drawings to magazines including *Punch, Cassell's, Black and White,* etc; also wrote *Raeburn, Farrington's Diary, Diaries of a Duchess.* Lived 189 Denmark Hill, London.
Refs: WWW; Houfe; Waters; Wood.

GRIBBLE, Francis Henry *The Lake of Geneva* (20s); *Geneva; Lausanne; Montreux* (7/6)
July 15 1862-Oct 10 1946; *b* Barnstaple, Devon; *s* Henry Gribble; *m* 1st Maria Evertje Aleida Schanze (*d* 1928); 2nd 1937 Minnie Maud Battell; *ed* privately; Exeter College, Oxford. Classics master, Warwick Grammar School; moved to London 1887 to write for newspapers; original editor of *Phil May's Annual.* A prolific author, his works include *The Red Spell* (1895), *The Early Mountaineers* (1899), *The Story of Alpine Climbing* (1904), *George Sand and her Lovers* (1907), *The Romance of the Oxford Colleges* (1910), *The Royal House of Portugal* (1915), *Dumas, Father and Son* (1930), *What America Owes Europe* (1932). Lived 76 West Bay Road, Bridport, Dorset.
Refs: WWW; LYB.

GRIERSON, Elizabeth *Florence; Scotland* (PML); *Sir Walter Scott* (PGM); *Canterbury, Durham, Ely, Hereford, Lincoln, St Albans, St Paul's, York* (TEM)
Author of many of A & C Black's children's books. Lived Whitchester, Hawick, North Britain (Scotland).

GROTTGER, Arthur *Poland* (PML)

GROVE, Henry Montgomery *Russia* (20s); *Moscow* (7/6)
Feb 27 1867-April 1 1942; *s* Maj-Gen H. L. Grove; *m* 1906 Lilian Mabel Hall; four *s; ed* Clifton College; RMC, Sandhurst. Served in Devonshire Regiment and Indian

Army until 1897; British Consul in Moscow 1901-13; Consul at Warsaw 1913-15; Helsingfors, Finland 1915-18; Gothenburg, Sweden 1919-20; Consul-General Moscow 1921-23; Reval, Estonia 1923-28; later employed in Foreign Office. Lived Wayside Cottage, Brasted Chart, Kent.
Refs: WWW.

GUDGEON, L. W. W. *British North Borneo* (PML)

HADDON, Arthur Trevor *Southern Spain* (20s); *Spain* (Pop, New, PML)
1864-Dec 13 1941; studied at Slade School under Legros 1883-86. Travelled in Spain 1886-87; worked with Sir Hubert Herkomer 1888-90; also worked in Rome and Venezuela; RBA 1896; painted principally portraits and Venetian and Spanish subjects. Also illustrated *The Old Venetian Palaces.* Lived 67a St Andrews St, Cambridge.
Refs: WWW; Houfe; TB; Waters; Wood.

HAIG, H. F. *Persia* (PML)

HAILLOT, Le Comt *Le Maroc* (BV); *Marruecos* (PS)
'Attaché au Corps Expeditionaire'.

HALL, Rev Charles Albert *Plant Life* (20s); *The Isle of Arran* (BB); *Bees, Wasps and Ants; Birds, Eggs and Nests; Common British Beetles; Pond Life; The Romance of the Rocks; Trees; Wild Flowers and their Wonderful Ways* (PN)
July 11 1872-Aug 27 1965; *b* Eastfield, Peterborough; *s* Henry James and Christina Hall; *m* 1896 Annie Unwin; two *s; ed* Deacon's School, Peterborough; New Church College, London. Commercial work in Sheffield 1891-96; New Church ministry 1896; pastorates at Hull, Bristol, Paisley, Southport and London 1896-1935; editorial and journalistic work from 1890. Long list of works includes *Art of Being Happy, Art of Being Healthy, The Lordship of Jesus, The Friendliness of Things,* Pocket Books of *British Birds, Wild Flowers, Butterflies and Moths, Birds.* Lived Gables, Sleepy Hollow, Storrington, Sussex.
Refs: WWW; LYB.

HAMMER, S. C. *Norway* (New)
Official historian of Oslo.

HAMMOND, Gertrude E. Demain *The Beautiful Birthday Book* (7/6)
1862-July 21 1952; *b* Brixton, London; *d* Horatio Demain and Eliza Mary Hammond; *m* 1898 Henry Going McMurdie; *ed* Lambeth Art School; RA Schools. RI 1896; exhibited RI 1886-1940. Also illustrated *A Girl of To-day* (1898), *The Virginians* (1902), *Martin Chuzzlewit* and *Our Mutual Friend* (1903), US edition of George Eliot (1907), US edition of Shakespeare (1902-3), *The Pilgrim's Progress* (1904), *The Faerie Queene* (1909), *David Copperfield* (1920), and books by Dorita F. Bruce and Mrs Molesworth. Lived Gracemere, 53 Richmond Road, Worthing, Sussex.

Refs: WWW; Houfe; Peppin; TB; Waters; Wood.

HAMPTON, H. G. *Brighton & Environs; Hastings & Environs* (ASB)

HANN, Mrs A. C. Osborn *Somerset* (Pop, New)

HANNAFORD, Charles E. *South Devon* (6s)
1863-Oct 21 1955; *m* 1st Helen Lean; two *s*; 2nd Margery Wright; *ed* Paris; studied under Stanhope Forbes. Exhibited RA, RI, RBA. Lived 7 Boulton Road, Thorpe, Norwich.
Refs: WWW; Mallalieu; Waters.

HAPPERFIELD, Laura *Bath and Bristol* (7/6)
Exhibited 1904-33; flower and watercolour painter. Lived Bristol and London.
Refs: Waters.

HARDIE, Martin *John Pettie* (20s); *John Pettie* (GA); *The Italian Front* (WF); *Boulogne: A Base in France; War Posters* (Misc)
Dec 15 1875-Jan 20 1952; *b* London; *s* James Hardie and nephew of Charles Martin Hardie and of John Pettie; *m* 1903 Madeline Pattisson; two *s*; *ed* St Paul's School; Trinity College, Cambridge. Joined Victoria and Albert Museum 1898; Keeper 1921-35 in charge of departments of paintings and engraving, illustration and design; war service 1915-19; RE 1920; RSW 1933; CBE 1935; Hon RWS 1942. Books include *English Coloured Books* (1906), *The British School of Etching* (1920), *Samuel Palmer* (1928), *J. S. Sargent* (1930), *English Water-Colours of the XVIII Century* (1949), *Water-Colour Painting in Britain* (1966-68); contributor to DNB. Lived Rodbourne, Yardley Park Road, Tonbridge, Kent.
Refs: WWW; DNB; TB; Waters.

HARDY, Dudley *Dudley Hardy* (BPP)
Jan 15 1867-Aug 11 1922; *s* T. B. Hardy, marine painter; *m* 1st 1899 Mrs Burnside (*d* 1906); 2nd 1907 Annie Morrison; one *s*, one *d*; *ed* Boulogne School; University College School, London; Dusseldorf; Antwerp; Paris. RI 1897; RMS. Worked as magazine and book illustrator and poster designer. Illustrated *The Humour of Holland* (1894), *Lays for the Little Ones* (1898), *The Stock Exchange in the Year 1900* (1900), *Sensations of Paris* (1912). Contributed widely to magazines including ILN, *Punch, Black and White*.
Refs: WWW; Houfe; Peppin; TB; Wood; *The Studio*, Vol 8

HARDY, Norman H. *The Savage South Seas* (20s); *The South Seas* (Melanesia) (PML)
C 1864-1914. Illustrator and etcher; worked most of his life in London; attached to *Sydney Herald* 1896; archaeological drawings for ILN 1889-90.
Refs: Houfe.

HARPER, Charles G. *Wessex* (BB)
1863-Dec 8 1943. Magazine and book illustrator; 'An enthusiastic pedestrian, cyclist and lover of the countryside'. Wrote and illustrated a large number of books, mostly on topographical subjects, including volumes in A & C Black's Pilgrimage series; a substantial collection could be built up of this author's works alone. Lived Rockwood, Hazel Road, Petersham, Surrey.
Refs: WWW; Houfe.

HARRY, Myriam *Indo-Chine* (BV)

HARTLEY, J.H. *Scripture: The New Testament* (PC)

HASSALL, John *John Hassall* (BPP)
May 25 1868-March 8 1948; *b* Walmer, Kent; *s* Christopher Clark and Louisa Hassall, RN; *m* 1st 1893 Isobel Dingwall; one *s*, two *d*; 2nd 1903 Constance Maud Webb (*d* 1950); one *s* (Christopher), one *d* (Joan); *ed* Newton Abbot College; Neuenheim College, Heidelberg. On failing army entrance exams was sent with his brother Owen to farm in Manitoba; acted for a time as pathfinder to a tribe of Sioux Indians; on return to Europe studied in Antwerp and Paris; RI 1901; RMS 1901; member of the London Sketch Club; founded and ran the New Art School. Produced posters, illustrations, book covers, etc. Helped Baden-Powell design the Boy Scouts' uniform. Illustrated *Grimm's Fairy Tales* (1902), *Through the Wood* (1907), *The Princess and the Dragon* (1908), *Gulliver's Travels*, *Robinson Crusoe*, *The Swiss Family Robinson*, books by Walter Emanuel and G. E. Farrow and books of fairy tales and nursery rhymes. Lived 88 Kensington Park Road, London.
Refs: WWW; DNB; Houfe; Peppin; TB; Waters; Wood; *The Studio*, Vol 36; David Cuppleditch *The John Hassall Lifestyle* (Dilke Press, 1980)

HAWTHORNE, Hildegarde *New York* (PML)

HAY, J. Hamilton *Liverpool* (6s, WC)
1874-1916; *s* Scottish architect. Trained as architect; studied painting with J. Finnie; worked in Liverpool until 1912, then in London; exhibited with Camden Town Group; painted at St Ives with Julius Olsson.
Refs: Houfe; TB; Waters; Wood.

HEADLAM, Cecil *Inns of Court* (7/6)
Sept 19 1872-Aug 12 1934; *s* Edward and Mary Headlam; *m* 1913 Mary May Elles Fraser; *ed* Rugby; Magdalen College, Oxford. Editor of *State Papers, Colonial Series*; played cricket for Oxfordshire and Middlesex; toured India with Oxford University Authentics 1902. Wrote extensively, mainly on travel, including *India and Burma* (1903), *Naples, Nuremberg, Chartres, Oxford, Provence, Languedoc*; novels and anthologies. Lived Broadmead, Charing, Kent.
Refs: WWW; LYB

HEATHCOTE, Dudley *Sweden* (Pop, New)

HECHT, Henry J. *The Motor Routes of Germany* (MR)

HECTOR, Gertrude M. *Arts and Crafts* (MP)

HEDLEY, Ralph *London* (PML)
1848-June 12 1913; *b* Richmond, Yorkshire; studied at Newcastle Art School. Genre, landscape and portrait painter; president Bewick Art Club and Northumberland Art Institute. Exhibited at RA etc. from 1879.
Refs: WWW; TB; Waters.

HENDERSON, John *The West Indies* (20s); *Jamaica* (6s); *Jamaica* (PML)

HENTON, George W. Moore *Windsor* (7/6, WC); [*Windsor and Eton* (BB)]
1861-April 21 1924. *b* Leicester; *ed* Leicester School of Art under Wilmot Pilsbury. Landscape and architecture painter. Exhibited RA from 1884. Lived Leicester.
Refs: TB; Waters; Wood.

HERBERT, Agnes *Northumberland* (Pop, New); *Korea* (PML)
d Feb 6 1960; *d* Helena Agnes and James Bateman Thorpe; *m* 1st W.G.H.Y. Field; one *d* (Bradda Field, whose *Who's Who* entry is a particular delight); 2nd 1913 Cdr A.M. Stewart, RN; *ed*: home. Edited *Writers' and Artists' Yearbook* 1922-29; OBE 1931. Also wrote *Two Dianas in Somaliland, Two Dianas in Alaska, The Isle of Man, Life Story of the Lion; The Moose* (A & C Black).
Refs: WWW; LYB.

HEWETT, Nora *The Union Jack and other Principal Flags of the British Empire* (MP)

HIND, C. Lewis *Adventures among Pictures*; *Days with Velasquez* (7/6); *Rembrandt* (12/6); *Rembrandt* (GA)
1862-Aug 31 1927; *s* Charles Hind; *m* 1907 Henrietta Richardson Hitchcock; *ed* privately; Christ's Hospital. Editor *Pall Mall Budget* 1893-95; founder of *The Studio* 1893; Editor of *The Academy* 1896-1903. A prolific writer on art and artists, author of over 30 books. Lived 24 Queen Anne's Gate, London SW1.
Refs: WWW; LYB.

HIPKINS, Alfred James *Musical Instruments: Historic, Rare and Unique* (Misc)
June 17 1826-June 3 1903; *ed* privately; *m* 1850 Jane Souter Black. Joined Broadwood piano makers 1840; studied piano and organ; lectured on musical instruments from 1883; read papers on acoustics to the Royal Society; assisted with the Vienna Exhibition 1892; Paris Exhibition 1900; became Member of Council and Hon. Curator of the Royal College of Music. Contributor to Grove's *Dictionary of Music and Musicians* and to the *Encyclopaedia Britannica*. Wrote *A Description and History of the Pianoforte* (1896). Lived 100 Warwick Gardens, Kensington, London.
Refs: WWW.

HODGE, A.E. *The 'Zoo' Aquarium* (MP)

HODGSON, W. Earl *Salmon Fishing*; *Trout Fishing* (Sport)
d Feb 15 1910; *b* Anstruther, Fifeshire; *s* William Hodgson; *m* 1905 Violet Neave; one *d*. Leader writer, reviewer and essayist. For many years A & C Black's principal Reader; for a time employed by the firm, he 'worked successfully in a back room at Soho Square in charge of a large and expanding fishing list until he died of an excess of nicotine'. Also wrote *Unrest, Haunted by Posterity, How to Fish* (A & C Black). Lived Oakbank, Aberfeldy, Perthshire.
Refs: WWW; Newth.

HOLLAND, A.W. *Alsace-Lorraine* (PML)

HOLLAND, Clive (Charles James HANKINSON) *Warwickshire* (20s, Pop, New); *Wessex* (20s); *Denmark* (Pop, New)
April 23 1866-Feb 14 1959; *b* Bournemouth; *m* 1894 Violet Downs (*d* 1945); four *s*; three *d*; *ed* Mill Hill School; privately. Trained for the law; worked on staff of several London papers; contributed to British and foreign newspapers and magazines; MBE 1920; JP; honoured in Denmark and Belgium. Wrote profusely on travel and literary subjects as well as novels and plays over a period of more than 50 years. His relations with A & C Black were clouded by plagiarism accusations made against him over *Egypt*. Lived 10 Woodville Gardens, London W5.
Refs: WWW.

HOLMES, Sir Richard Rivington *Windsor* (7/6)
Nov 16 1835-March 22 1911; *b* London; *s* John Holmes (of the British Museum) and Mary Anne Rivington; *m* 1880 Evelyn Gee; two *d*; *ed* Highgate School. Joined British Museum 1854; archaeologist to Abyssinian expedition 1868; Librarian Windsor Castle 1870-1906; an accomplished watercolour painter and designer. MVO 1897; CVO 1901; KCVO 1905. Also wrote *Naval and Military Tropies* (1879), *Queen Victoria* (1897), *The Queen's Pictures* (1897); illustrated Mrs Oliphant's *Makers of Venice*. Lived Ann Foord's House, Windsor.
Refs: WWW; DNB.

HOME, Beatrice *Windsor and Eton* (BB); *Canada*; *Ireland* (PH); *Royal Palaces of Great Britain* (MP)

HOME, Gordon Cochrane. As author and illustrator: *Yorkshire* (20s, Pop, New); *France* (20s, Fasc); *Yorkshire: Coast and Moorland Scenes* (7/6, Ltd); *Yorkshire: Dales and Fells*; *Yorkshire: Vales and Wolds* (7/6); *Yorkshire: Coast and Moorland* (BB); *Edinburgh*; *Mine own Romantic Town*; *The Charm of Surrey* (Charm). As author: *The Motor Routes of England: Southern Section*; *The Motor Routes of England: Western Section and Wales* (MR); *The Motor Routes of France* (MR [some illustrations by GH]); *The People of Egypt*; *The People of Holland* (People [introductions]); *Cambridge*; *Canterbury*; *The English Lakes* (BB); *The Romance of London* (Misc, BB); *The Great Western Railway* (PGR); *London* (QP); *The Four*

Georges (Misc [preface]); *What to see in the Channel Islands*; *What to see in the English Lakes* (WTS). As artist: *Yorkshire* (WC); *The English Lakes* ; *Malta*; *Stratford-upon-Avon* (ASB, PC); *Winchester* (ASB, NASB); *York* (ASB); *Edinburgh* (NASB); *The Charm of the Scott Country* (Charm)
July 25 1878-Dec 13 1969; *b* London; *s* Erskine Sandilands Home; *m* 1926 Violet Chapman (*d* 1944); one *s*; one *d*. Art editor of *The Tatler* 1901; *The King* 1902-03; worked as an editor for A & C Black; Major RASC 1914-20; exhibited RA. Also wrote/illustrated books on Farnham, Epsom, The Riviera, Normandy, The Chilterns, London, Surrey, Cyprus; also edited many historical and topographical works. Lived Malt House Cottage, Fittleworth, Sussex.
Refs: WWW; LYB; TB; Waters.

HOPE, Ascott R. *The World* (LPML)
See under **MONCRIEFF, A. R. Hope**

HORNBLOWER, Florence G. *Ancient Egyptian, Assyrian and Persian Costume and Decoration* (Misc)

HORNBY, Lester George *Edinburgh* (ASB); *London* (ASB)
b March 27 1882 in Lowell, Massachusetts; studied under Eric Pape at School of Art, Boston, and at New York Art Students' League and in Paris. Travelled in the US, Europe and N. Africa.
Refs: TB; *The Studio* Vol 36.

HOSKYN, E.L. *The British Dominions beyond the Seas* (PH); *Pictures of British History*; *More Pictures of British History* (PIX)

HOUSTON, George *Ayshire Idylls* (7/6); *The Burns Country* (WC)
Feb 20 1869-Oct 5 1947; *b* Dalry, Ayrshire. Prolific painter in oils and watercolour; RSA 1909; exhibited in Canada, Australia, New Zealand, the US, etc; worked mainly in Ayrshire and Argyllshire. Lived Dalry, Ayrshire.
Refs: WWW; Caw; TB; Waters.

HOUSTON, Mary G. *Ancient Egyptian, Assyrian and Persian Costume and Decorations*; *Ancient Greek, Roman and Byzantine Costume*; *Mediaeval Costume in England and France* (Misc)

HUISH, Marcus Bourne *British Water-Colour Art*; *Happy England* (20s, Ltd)
1845-May 4 1921; *s* Marcus Huish and Margaret Bourne; *m* Catherine Winslow; one *s*. Barrister, Inner Temple; editor *Art Journal* 1881-93; director Fine Art Society. Also wrote *Japan and its Art* (1889), *Greek Terra Cotta Statuettes* (1900), *Year's Art*, *The Seine and the Loire*, *Samplers and Tapestry Embroideries* (1900), *American Pilgrims Way* (1907). Lived 21 Essex Villas, London W8.
Refs: WWW; LYB.

HUMPHRIES, Sydney *Oriental Carpets, Runners and Rugs, and Some Jacquard Reproductions* (Misc)
Aug 7 1862-Feb 16 1941; *s* John Humphries; *m* Mary Elizabeth Rankine; *ed* privately. Developed interests in printing, publishing, books, illuminated manuscripts, music, painting, sculpture and architecture. Wrote extensively on Shakespeare, Milton, Sir Philip Sydney, Bacon, Agincourt, Waterloo, etc; many of his books were privately printed in limited editions. Lived Thirlestaine Court, Cheltenham, Glos.
Refs: WWW; LYB.

HUNTER, John Young *The Clyde* (20s, Ltd)
Oct 29 1874-Aug 9 1955; *b* Glasgow; *s* Colin Hunter; *m* Mary 1899 (see below); studied RA Schools, London. RBA 1914; travelled in Germany and Belgium; went to US around 1925; lived for a time in Suffolk; painted in oils and watercolour; later in life signed paintings J. Young-Hunter. Lived (1907) Gifford's Hall, Wickhambrook, Newmarket.
Refs: Caw; Houfe; TB; Waters; Wood; *The Studio* Vol 28.

HUNTER, Mary Y. (Mary Ethel HUNTER) *The Clyde* (20s, Ltd)
1878-1936; studied at Newlyn, Cornwall and in Paris. Portrait and flower painter. Exhibited RA from 1900. Wife of John Young Hunter. ASWA 1901; worked in Kensington 1902-14.
Refs: Houfe; TB; Waters; Wood; *The Studio* Vol 28.

HUTTON, Stanley *Bath and Bristol* (7/6)
A pseudonym of A. E. Tilling of Kingsdown, Bristol.

HYLDALL, Ingeborn *Denmark* (PML)

JAMES, Gilbert *The Rubaiyat of Omar Khayyam* (7/6, PC)
Active 1886-1926; *b* Liverpool. Figure and still life painter and illustrator; worked first in commerce; moved to London; contributed drawings to journals, mostly on Eastern themes. Also illustrated *Faust* (1904), *Aucassin and Nicolete* (1905), *The Book of Ruth and Esther* (1905), *Contes de Grimm* (1908), *Tristian and Iseulte* (1911), *Mind your own Buzziness* (1912), *Contes de Andersen*, etc. Lived Fitzroy Street, London.
Refs: WWW; Houfe; Peppin.

JEANS, Samuel *Charles Dickens*; *William Shakespeare* (PGM)

JELLICOE, John *The Royal Navy* (20s); *Scotland* (PH)
Figure painter and illustrator. Illustrated *Queen of Beauty* (1894), *Cherry and Violet* (1897), *Jack Haydon's Quest* (A & C Black); contributed to ILN, *Good Words, Lady's Pictorial, Windsor Magazine*.
Refs: Houfe.

JENNISON, George *Natural History: Animals* (Misc)

JERROLD, Walter Copeland *Hugh Thomson* (Misc)
May 3 1865-Oct 27 1929; *b* Liverpool; *s* Thomas Jerrold and Jane Copeland; *m* 1895 Clara Armstrong; five *d*. Began life in city warehouse; sub-editor for the *Observer* 1892-1905; then worked on literary staff of the *Daily Telegraph*, *Amalgamated Press* and *Glasgow Evening News*. Wrote numerous books, including 'popular' biographies of Faraday, Gladstone, etc; and contributed to the Highways and Byways series; also, as Walter Copeland, books for children; also edited large number of series of the classics. Lived 6 Warwick Avenue, London W2. Refs: WWW.

JOHNSON, A.E. *Tom Browne*; *Dudley Hardy*; *John Hassall*; *Frank Reynolds*; *W. Heath Robinson*; *Lawson Wood* (BPP).
An artists' agent who started his own business in 1906.

JOHNSON, Stanley C. *Postage Stamps* (MP)

JOHNSTON, Lena E. *China* (PML)

JONES, E.E. Constance *Girton College* (BB)
d April 17 1922; *d* Dr J. and Emily Edith Jones; *ed* privately; Miss Robinson's, Cheltenham; Girton College, Cambridge. Lecturer at Girton from 1884; Vice-Mistress 1896-1903; Mistress 1903-16. Author of a number of works on logic and ethics. Lived Meldon House, Weston-super-Mare, Somerset; Ar-y-Bryn, Llandewi Skyrrid, Abergavenny.
Refs: WWW; *As I Remember: An Autobiographical Ramble* (A & C Black, 1922).

JUNGMAN, Beatrix (Beatrice) *Holland* (20s, Ltd); *Norway* (20s); *Holland* (PML)
c 1883-1942; the English wife of the Dutch-born painter Nico Jungman (see below), who she married in 1901; one *s*; two *d*. Divorced from Nico Jungman, she married Richard Guinness; referred to as Gloomy Beatrice or Gloomy Guinness, she became known as a hostess and talent spotter (Noel Coward, Cecil Beaton). The Jungmans' daughter Teresa 'Baby' Jungman was a 'bright young thing' and friend of Evelyn Waugh, who reportedly wanted to marry her.
Refs: Elizabeth Longford *The Pebbled Shore* (Weidenfeld and Nicholson, 1986); *Diaries of Evelyn Waugh* (Weidenfeld and Nicholson, 1976).

JUNGMAN, Nico *Holland* (20s, Ltd, PML); *Norway* (20s, PML); *Normandy* (10s); *The People of Holland* (People); *France* (PML)
Feb 5 1872-Aug 14 1935; *b* Amsterdam; *m* 1901 Beatrice (see above); one *s*; two *d*; apprenticed at 12 to church decorator; attended Academy of Plastic Art, Amsterdam; won scholarship to London. Later became a British subject; lived in London but continued to paint Dutch scenes, often chalk drawings with pastel colours. An account of his internment in Ruhleben prison camp in 1916-18 appeared in *The Studio*, Vol 73.

Refs: Houfe; TB; Wood; *The Studio*, Vol 13.

JUTA, Réné *The Cape Peninsula* (7/6)
1887-1940; *b* Cape Town; *d* Jan Carel Juta; *m* Luke Hansard, a British diplomat.
She also wrote *The Tavern* (1920, a novel of the early Cape) and a book about
Corsica. Lived in Europe after her marriage.
Refs: SADNB.

KATES, Herbert S. *New York* (Charm)

KEESEY, Walter Monckton *Cambridge* (ASB, NASB, PC); *Canterbury* (ASB, PC);
Harrow (ASB, NASB, PC)
June 16 1887-Dec 4 1970; *s* Rev G. W. Keesey; *m* J. H. Swinglehurst (*d* 1963); one *d*;
ed Caterham; St Olave's; Royal College of Art. Architect, etcher and watercolour
painter; on staff of Architectural Association 1913-25; Royal Engineers 1914-19;
inspector for Ministry of Education; OBE. Also drew postcards for Trust Houses,
published by Radermacher Aldous. Lived Yew Tree Cottage, Epperstone, Notts.
Refs: WWW; TB; Waters.

KELLY, Robert George Talbot *Burma* (20s, Ltd, New); *Egypt* (20s, Ltd, Pop, New);
Burma (PML); *Egypt* (PML)
Jan 18 1861-Dec 30 1934; *b* Birkenhead; *s* Robert George and Mary Kelly; *m* 1894
Lilias Lindsay (*d* 1917); *ed* Birkenhead School; studied art under his father.
Worked abroad from 1882, mainly in Morocco, Egypt and Burma; specialised in
oriental work; RI 1907. Lived 3 St John's Wood Studios, Queens Terrace, London
NW8.
Refs: WWW; TB; Waters; Wood.

KELMAN, Rev John *From Damascus to Palmyra* (20s); *The Holy Land* (20s, Ltd,
Pop, New)
June 20 1864-May 3 1929; *s* Rev J. and Margaret Kelman; *m* Ellen Runcorn; one *d*;
ed Royal High School, University and New College, Edinburgh. Assistant to Rev
(later Sir) George Adam Smith in Aberdeen; Minister New North Church (United
Free Presbyterian), Edinburgh, 1897-1907; served with YMCA in France during
war, awarded OBE; pastor of Fifth Avenue Presbyterian Church, New York, 1919-
24. Also wrote *The Faith of Robert Louis Stevenson, The Light that Saves, The War
and Preaching, The Foundations of Faith*. Lived 7 Inverleith Place, Edinburgh.
Refs: WWW.

KENDALL, Rev John Francis *A Short History of the Church of England* (7/6)
March 21 1862-Aug 8 1931; *m* 1888 Julia Augusta Angerstein; two *s*, two *d*; *ed*
London University. Vicar of Little Tew 1889-95; Great Tew 1891-95; Rector of
Hempstead with Lessingham, Norfolk, 1895-1904; incumbent of St Germans,
Blackheath 1904-17; Vicar of Richmond 1917-28; Canon Residentiary, Norwich
Cathedral from 1928. Lived The Close, Norwich.
Refs: WWW.

KIDD, Dudley *South Africa* (PML)
Also wrote *The Essential Kafir* (1904), similar in format to the 20s series but illustrated by black and white photographs.

KIMBALL, Katharine *Rochester* (ASB)
1866-March 19 1949; *b* New Hampshire; *ed* Jersey Ladies College, St Helier; National Academy of Design, New York; RCA, London. ARE. Also illustrated Thomas Okey's *Paris* (1904), Gilliat Smith's *Brussels* (1906), Sterling Taylor's *Canterbury* (1912); contributed to *The Century, The Studio, Queen*, etc.
Refs: WWW; Houfe; TB; Waters.

KIPLING, Rudyard *St Andrews* (MSB)
1865-1936. English writer. His life and works are described in a number of biographies, notably those by Carrington (1955), Angus Wilson (1977), R.T. Hopkins (1977) and Lord Birkenhead (1978).

KIRCHNER, Raphael *The Spirit of Paris* (7/6)
1876-Aug 2 1917; *b* Vienna. Worked as portait painter and illustrator in Austria, France and the USA, where he moved on the outbreak of WWI; well known as postcard artist 1900-17. Contributed to magazines, especially *La Vie parisienne* and *The Sketch* and to books.
Refs: Bénézit; DPC.

KOEBEL, W.H. *Argentina Past and Present*; *South America* (20s)
1872-June 20 1923; *s* Oscar Koebel; *m* Eleanor Garstin; one *d*; *ed* privately and in France, Switzerland, Germany. Joined staff of *The Times* 1918; sent on special mission to South America by the War Council 1921. Wrote extensively, mainly on the countries of South America; founded *Anglo South American Handbook*. Lived 23 Gilston Road, The Boltons, London SW.
Refs: WWW; LWW; LYB.

LANDOR, Arnold Henry Savage *Tibet and Nepal* (20s)
June 2 1865-Dec 26 1924; *b* Florence; *s* Charles Savage Landor and *gs* Walter Savage Landor; *ed* Liceo Dante, Istituto Technico, Florence; and in Paris. Started mountaineering career at 13, painting career in his early 20s; travelled widely through the world's less hospitable regions in Japan, Korea, Tibet, Nepal, China, achieving numerous exploration firsts, some of which were disputed by other explorers; he was imprisoned and tortured in Tibet; later he travelled across Africa and South America. He also claimed to have invented an improved armoured car, a rigid airship and a device for destroying barbed-wire entanglements. Savage Landor's exploits are vividly chronicled in his books: *Alone with the Hairy Ainu* (1893), *Corea* (1895), *In the Forbidden Land* (1898), *China and the Allies* (1901), *Across Coveted Lands* (1902), *The Gems of the East* (1904), *Across Widest Africa* (1908)*, Across Unknown South America* (1913). Lived Calappiano, Empoli per Vinci; 10 Via Farini, Florence, Italy.
Refs: WWW; LYB; BMC March 1985; *Everywhere, The Memoirs of an Explorer* (1924).

LANG, Andrew *The Lady of the Lake* (Misc [notes])
March 31 1844-July 20 1912; *s* John Lang and Jane Sellar; *m* 1875 Leonora
Alleyne; *ed* Edinburgh Academy; St Andrews University; Balliol College, Oxford.
Author of many books on history, ballads, folklore, fairy tales, etc. Lived 1
Marloes Road, London.
Refs: WWW.

LARSSON, Carl Olof *Sweden* (PML)
May 28 1953-Jan 22 1919; *b* Stockholm. Painter and illustrator, he contributed to
many books.
Refs: TB.

LAWLEY, Lady (Later Lady WENLOCK) *Southern India* (20s)
d April 29 1944; *b* Annie Allen Cunard; *d* Sir Edward Cunard; *m* 1885 Arthur
Lawley; two *d*. Hon Sir Arthur Lawley was Governor of Madras 1906-11 and later
inherited the title Baron Wenlock (*d* 1932). Lady Lawley became GBE in 1917;
Hon Sec Queen Mary's Needlework Guild; a Dame of Grace of the Order of St
John of Jerusalem; one daughter married Geoffrey Dawson, Editor of *The Times*,
the other Baron Wraxall. Lived Tyntesfield, Bristol.
Refs: WWW.

LAYARD, George Somes *Kate Greenaway* (20s, Ltd)
Feb 4 1857-May 30 1925; *s* Rev C. C. Layard; *m* Eleanor Byng Gribble; one *s*, one *d*;
ed Harrow; Trinity College, Cambridge. Barrister; member of Inner Temple; contributor to DNB and Times Supplement of *Encyclopaedia Britannica*. Author and
reviewer; wrote books on Charles Keene, Cruikshank, Tennyson, book lending;
novels; and *Suppressed Plates* 1907 (A & C Black). Lived 5 Pelham Place, London
SW7.
Refs: WWW; LYB.

LEALE, Enid *Historical Songs* (MP)

LEITH, Mrs Disney *Iceland* (PML)

LEWIS, John Hardwicke *The Lake of Geneva* (20s); *Switzerland (20s, Fasc, PML);*
Geneva; Lausanne; Montreux; La Côte d'Emeraude/Around St Malo; Our Life in the
Swiss Highlands (7/6); *The Upper Engadine* (6s); [*The Engadine; The Lake of*
Geneva; The Lake of Lucerne (BE)]
1840-Oct 3 1927; *b* Hyderabad; *s* Frederic Christian ('Indian') Lewis; *m* 1st Ellen
Andrews; 2nd Elizabeth Eugenie Steele; two *s*, two *d*; *ed* Kensington Grammar
School; privately; in Paris under Thomas Couture. Lived in California 1885-89 and
in Switzerland from 1889; an artist member of the Alpine Club. Lived Veytaux,
Switzerland.
Refs: WWW; TB; Wood.

LEWIS, Martyn *New York* (PML)

LEWIS, May Hardwicke *The Lake of Geneva* (20s); *Switzerland* (20s, Fasc); *Geneva*; *Lausanne*; *Montreux* (7/6); [*The Lake of Geneva*; *The Lake of Lucerne* (BE)]
The daughter of J. Hardwicke Lewis (see above).

LICHTENBERGER, A. *En Alsace* (BV)
Possibly Adam Lichtenberger, father of Rt Rev Arthur Carl Lichtenberger (1900-68). Also wrote *La Morte de Corinthe, Père, Portraits a' Aieules, Rédemption.*

LIDDLE, Rev W. and Mrs LIDDLE *Sweden* (PML)

LIPSCOMBE, Guy *Finn and Samoyad* (LL)

LITTLEJOHNS, J. *How to Enjoy Pictures* (Misc)

LOCK, Major H. O. *Dorset* (Pop, New)

LOCKE, Agnes *Haunts of Ancient Peace* (7/6)
fl 1905-25; a cousin of Alfred Austin (qv); in 1909 A & C Black declined her offer to illustrate Gilbert White's *Natural History of Selborne.* Lived at various times at Great Ayton, Yorkshire; Derby; and Frencham, Surrey.
Refs: Houfe.

LOMAS, John *Spain* (Pop, New)
Nov 2 1846-Mar 1 1927; *s* George Lomas; *m* 1875 Maria Thurston Gabriel; three *s* two *d*; *ed* Manchester Grammar School; Victoria University, Manchester. Described in *Who's Who* (presumably by himself) as a 'prominent Anglican Churchman in the jurisdiction of North and Central Europe, and estate owner in Switzerland.' Wrote on Spain, church music, communion offices, etc. Lived St Jean, Territet, Switzerland.
Refs: WWW.

LOVETT, Major Alfred Crowdy *Armies of India* (20s, Ltd); *Our Indian Armies* (PC)
Nov 22 1862-May 27 1919; *m* 1903 Fannie Rumsey. Gloucestershire Regiment 1883; Colonel 1915; CB 1915.
Refs: WWW.

LOWTHER, C. G. *Newfoundland* (PML)

LUXMOORE, Henry Elford *Eton from a Backwater* (7/6)
Feb 28 1841-Nov 11 1926; *s* Rev Henry Luxmoore of Barnstaple; *ed* Stoke Poges; Eton; Pembroke College, Oxford. Unmarried. Assistant Master at Eton 1864; Housemaster 1871; retired 1908; Bucks county councillor; member of Oxford Diocesan Board. Much influenced by Ruskin; wrote pamphlets on a variety of subjects from gardening to church matters; created Luxmoore's Garden at Eton. Lived Baldwin's End, Eton, Bucks.

Refs: WWW; Waters; *The Times* Nov 12 1926; *Letters of H. E. Luxmoore* (Cambridge, 1929); Michael Cox *M. R. James: An Informal Portrait* (OUP, 1983).

LYALL, Sophie *Dutch Bulbs and Gardens* (7/6)

LYTTLETON, Rev Hon Edward *An Alpine Sports Book* (MSB)
July 23 1855-Jan 26 1942; *b* London; *s* 4th Lord Lyttleton; *m* 1888 Caroline West (*d* 1919); two *d*; *ed* Eton; Trinity College, Cambridge. Taught at Wellington and Eton; headmaster of Haileybury 1890-1905 and of Eton 1905-16; Rector of Sidestrand, Norfolk 1918-20; Dean of Whitelands College, Chelsea; Hon Canon of Norwich from 1931. Wrote *Cricket* (1890), *Are we to go on with Latin Verses?* (1897), *Training for the Young in the Laws of Sex* (1900), *Character and Religion* (1912), *Memories and Hopes* (1925), *The Christian and Birth Control* (1929), etc. Lived Grangegorman, Overstrand, Norfolk.
Refs: WWW.

MacBRIDE, Mackenzie *The Firth of Clyde* (BB); *Wild Lakeland* (Pop, New)
Journalist; lecturer on English literature and language; worked on *Citizen, City Express, Westminster Gazette, Weekly Dispatch, Oban Times*; edited *London Scotsman*. Wrote *Arran of the Bens, the Glens and the Brave, Wonderful Weans, With Napoleon at Waterloo, For Those We Love at Home*, etc. Lived London.
Refs: LYB

McCLYMONT, Right Rev James Alexander *Greece* (20s, Pop, New)
May 26 1848-Sept 19 1927; *b* Girvan, Ayrshire; *s* Samuel McClymont; *m* Agnes Smith; *ed* Girvan Grammar School; Ayr Academy; Edinburgh University; Tübingen. Minister of Holburn, Aberdeen; Moderator of General Assembly of Church of Scotland 1921-22. Author of theological works, especially on the New Testament. Lived 22 Murrayfield Drive, Edinburgh.
Refs: WWW.

McCORMICK, Arthur David *The Alps*; *Switzerland* (20s, Ltd, Fasc, PML)
Oct 14 1860-March 12 1943; *b* Coleraine, Ireland; *s* Arthur McCormick; *m* 1st Helen Woods (*d* 1899); 2nd 1906 Nellie Laker; *ed* Coleraine and Belfast; South Kensington Art Schools 1883-86. Artist with Sir Martin Conway's expedition to Karakoram, Himalayas 1892-93; with Clinton T. Dent in Central Caucasus 1895; FRGS 1895; SRBA 1897; ROI 1905; RI 1906. Also illustrated *Climbing and Exploration in the Karakoram Himalayas* (1894), *The Alps from End to End* (1895), *The Kafirs of Hindu Kush* (1896), *Climbs in the New Zealand Alps* (1896), *New Climbs in Norway* (1898), *From the Cape to Cairo* (1900), *Tales of Mystery and Imagination* (1905), *The Netherlands* (1907), *New Zealand* (1908), *India* (1909), *Drake's Drum* (1914); wrote *An Artist in the Himalayas* (1895). Lived 53 Colet Gardens, Barons Court, London W14.
Refs: WWW; Houfe; Peppin; TB; Waters; wood.

MacGREGOR, Fergus *Un Tour en Mélanésie* (Contes)

MACKENZIE, W. W. *Pompeii* (7/6)

MACKINNON, Finlay *Amid the High Hills* (Misc)

MacMUNN, Major George Fletcher *Armies of India* (20s, Ltd)
Aug 14 1869-Aug 23 1952; *s* J. A. and Charlotte Edith MacMunn; *m* 1st 1893 Alice
Emily Watson (*d* 1934); one *s*, one *d*, 2nd 1937 Kathleen; *ed* Kensington School.
Joined RA 1888; served in Burma, India, South Africa and in Europe; DSO 1893;
CB 1916; KCB 1917; KCSI 1919; promoted to Major-General; Quartermaster-
General in India 1920-24; retired 1925; colonel Commandant RA 1927-39; Warden
Sackville College, East Grinstead. Also wrote *Pike and Carronade* (1912), *A Free
Lance in Kashmir* (1915), *Behind the Scenes in Many Wars* (1930), *The Indian Mutiny
in Perspective* (1931), *Kipling Women* (1933), *Always into Battle* (1952).
Refs: WWW.

MAGEE, E. *Lectures Illustrées* (PIX)
A teacher at Edgbaston High School for Girls, Birmingham.

MALCOLM, George *Grouse and Grouse Moors* (Sport)

MALLESON, Hope *Rome* (20s, Ltd, Pop, New)
A female friend of Miss M. A. R. Tuker *qv.* Also wrote (with Miss Tuker) *Handbook
to Christian and Ecclesiastical Rome* (A & C Black).

MANN, A. J. *The Salonika Front* (WF)
An officer in the Salonika Balloon Company.

MANNERS-HOWE, T. H. *The Thames* (BB); *India* (PH)

MARCEL-CLEMENT, Amédée Julian *The Spirit of Paris* (7/6)
b Sept 15 1873 in Paris. Landscape, marine and animal painter who lived in Paris;
his paintings were bought by galleries in Paris, Nimes, Strasbourg and Tokyo.
Refs: Bénézit; TB.

MARKOVITCH, Alfreda *Yugoslavia* (PML)

MARSHALL, Herbert Menzies *The Scenery of London* (20s); *London* (WC, PML)
Aug 1 1841-March 2 1913; *b* Leeds; *s* Thomas H. and Maria Marshall; *m* Amy Dee;
one *s*, two *d*; *ed* Westminster School; Trinity College, Cambridge. Studied architecture at Atelier Questel, Paris; Travelling Studentship for Architecture at Royal
Academy 1868; Professor of Landscape Painting, Queen's College, London. Also
illustrated *The Cathedral Cities of France*. Lived 83 Philbeach Gardens, London.
Refs: WWW; Waters; Wood; *The Studio* Vol 58.

MARTIN, T. Mower *Canada* (20s); *Kew Gardens* (6s)
1839-1934; *b* London; lived at Kew; died in Canada.

Member of the Royal Canadian Academy.

MASSON, Rosaline *Edinburgh* (7/6, Ltd); *Edinburgh* (PML)
d Dec 7 1949; *d* Prof David and Emily Rosaline Masson. Author and historian, her work included books on Wordsworth, Stevenson, Shakespeare and Scottish subjects. Lived 20 Ann Street, Edinburgh.
Refs: WWW; LYB

MATHEW, Frank *Ireland* (20s, 6s)
1865-Oct 25 1924; *b* Bombay; *s* Frank Mathew; *m* 1899 Agnes Woodroffe; two *s*; *ed* Beaumont College; King's College School; London University. Novelist and barrister, his output consisted largely of historical novels. Lived 1 Hernes Road, Oxford.
Refs: WWW; LYB

MATTHISON, William *Cambridge* (20s, Pop, New, [BB], WC)
fl 1883-1923; lived in Banbury 1885-1902, Oxford from 1905. Exhibited at RA, RI. Also provided postcards of Oxford and Whitby for Robert Peel.
Refs: Houfe; Waters.

MAXWELL, Capt Aymer (later **Major-General Sir Aymer Maxwell**) *Grouse and Grouse Moors*; *Partridges and Partridge Manors*; *Pheasants and Covert Shooting* (Sport)
Dec 27 1891-Oct 16 1971; *s* Wellwood Maxwell of Kirkennan; *m* 1915 Isobel Shaw; *ed* Cheltenham; RMA, Woolwich. Commissioned in Royal Artillery 1911; served in both world wars; member of Queen's Body Guard for Scotland; Vice-Lieutenant of Stewartry of Kirkcudbright from 1957. Lived Kirkennan, Dalbeattie, Kirkcudbrightshire.
Refs: WWW

MAXWELL, Donald *The Naval Front* (WF)
1877-July 25 1936; *b* London; *s* Dr Frederick Charles Maxwell; *m* Fanny Morgan; two *d*; *ed* Manor House school, Clapham Common; South Kensington and Slade schools. Oil and watercolour marine and landscape artist; for 20 years naval artist-correspondent for *Graphic*; Lieutenant in RNVR during World War I and official artist to the Admiralty; visited Palestine and Mesopotamia for the Imperial War Museum; accompanied the Prince of Wales to India. Illustrated and wrote a large number of travel and topographical books including illustrations for books by Kipling, Belloc and Hardy; also *The Enchanted Road, A Detective in Kent, Surrey and Essex, Unknown Kent, Surrey, Sussex, Essex, Suffolk, Norfolk, Dorset, Somerset, A Painter in Palestine, The London River, Aquatints in Colour, Adventures with a Sketchbook.* Lived East Farleigh House, Maidstone, Kent.
Refs: WWW; Houfe; Waters.

MAXWELL, Gordon S. *The Naval Front* (WF)

MENPES, Dorothy Whistler *Brittany*; *The Durbar*; *Japan* (20s, Ltd); *Paris* (20s, Ltd, 6s); *Venice*; *War Impressions*; *World's Children*; *World Pictures* (20s, Ltd); Sept 14 1883-July 12 1973; younger daughter of Mortimer Menpes; *m* Ivan Charles Glower, stockbroker; one *s*, one *d*. Lived 31 Blenheim Road, Minehead, Somerset.
Refs: Personal information.

MENPES, Mortimer *Brittany*; *The Durbar* (20s, Ltd); *France* (20s); *India* (20s, Pop, New, PML); *Japan* (20s, Ltd, PC); *Paris* (20s, Ltd, 6s); *The Thames* (20s); *Venice* (20s, Ltd, [BE]); *War Impressions*; *World's Children*; *World Pictures* (20s, Ltd); *Rembrandt* (12/6d); *China* (Crown); *The People of India* (People, PC); *London* (WC); *Sir Henry Irving*; *Lord Kitchener*; *Lord Roberts* (Port); *Gainsborough* (Misc); *Whistler as I Knew Him* (Misc, Ltd); *Delhi and the Durbar*; *India*; *Home Life in India* (PML); *India* (HML)
[Feb 22] 1856-April 1 1938; *b* Australia; *ed* Port Adelaide Grammar School; *m* 1875 Rosa Mary Grosse; four *s*, two *d*. Moved to England in 1870s; studio assistant to Whistler in 1880s; travelled extensively and held large number of one-man exhibitions; RE 1881; RBA 1885; RI 1897; FRGS; war artist for *Black and White* in South Africa 1900. Founder of the Menpes Press; originator of the Menpes Great Masters reproductions; managing director of the Menpes Fruit Farms, Pangbourne. The 'founder' of the 20s series, his life and work are dealt with in detail in the text of this book. Also illustrated *Madame Prune* (1919), *The Grey River*. Lived at various times at 25 Cadogan Gardens, London SW1; 13 Shelley Court, Tite St, London SW; finally Iris Court, Pangbourne, Berks.
Refs: WWW; Houfe; Peppin; TB; Waters; *The Studio* Vol 17; *The Times*, April 5 1938; personal information.

METZ, Alois *Berlin* (PML)
b Nov 27 1869; *b* Klein-Steinheim am Main; studied at Hanau Academy. Lived 1900-03 in Rome, then in Berlin until 1923, Karlsruhe until 1928. Painted figures, landscapes, still lifes, etc.
Refs: Bénézit; TB.

MITTON, G. E. *Buckinghamshire and Berkshire* (20s [published at 25s], Pop, New); *The Scenery of London*; *The Thames* (20s); *Normandy* (10s); *Austria-Hungary* (Fasc); *Cornwall* (7/6, Pop, New); *The People of India* (People [introduction]); *Isle of Wight*; *St Paul's Cathedral*; *The Trossachs* (BB); *The County of Durham* (Pop, New); *London* (PML); *Scotland* (PH); *The London and North Eastern Railway*; *The North Eastern and Great Northern Railways*; The South East and Chatham and London, Brighton and South Coast Railways; The Southern Railway (PGR); *Columbus*; *Captain Cook*; *David Livingstone* (PGE); *Great Steamship Lines: The P & O* (MP)
d April 25 1955; *d* Rev H. A. and Annie Eliza Mitton; *m* 1920 Sir George Scott *qv* (*d* 1935); *ed* home; Durham High School. Came to London 1896; worked under Sir Walter Besant on the *Survey of London*; joined staff of A & C Black 1899; editor *Englishwoman's Year Book* 1907-16; *Writers' and Artists' Year Book* 1907-20; worked on *Who's Who* 1899-1920; wrote large number of guide books and books

on travel; also books for children and novels, between 1903 and 1932. Lived
Thereaway, Graffham, Sussex.
Refs: WWW; LYB; Newth.

MOCKLER-FERRYMAN, Lt Col Augustus Ferryman *Norway* (PML)
1856-May 26 1930; *s* Edward Mockler and Julia Ferryman; *m* Evelyn Whitehead;
one *s*; *ed* Cheltenham; Sandhurst. Joined Oxfordshire Light Infantry; Lt Col 1900;
held many military posts; barrister Inner Temple 1899. Wrote extensively on travel
and military matters. Lived St John's House, Tavistock, Devon.
Refs: WWW; LYB.

MOCKTON, Alice E. *Children of Long Ago* (MP)

MOLYNEAUX, Major Edward Mary Joseph *Kashmir* (20s, Pop, New, PML)
March 13 1866-Jan 29 1913; *s* Henry Molyneaux; *m* 1902 Mary Alison Knolles;
ed Stonyhurst College. Served in 3rd Dragoon Guards; Indian Staff Corps 1891;
Viceroy's gold medal for best picture painted in India, 1895, 1898; DSO in Boer
War 1900. Lived Punjab, India.
Refs: WWW.

MONCRIEFF, Ascott Robert Hope [also Ascott R. HOPE] *Essex* (20s, Pop, New);
London (20s, 7/6, Pop, New); *Bonnie Scotland* (20s, Ltd); *Surrey* (20s, Pop, New);
The Highlands and Islands of Scotland (10s, Pop, New); *Isle of Wight*; *Middlesex*;
The Heart of Scotland (7/6); *The Cockpit of Europe/Belgium Past and Present*
(Misc); *Kew Gardens*; *The Peak Country* (6s); *Derbyshire*; *Scotland* (Pop, New)
1846-Aug 1927; *b* Edinburgh; *ed* Edinburgh and privately in England. 'Took some
steps towards the Scottish bar, but "penned a stanza", etc. at an early age, and
served a time as a school teacher'. Wrote some 200 volumes of history, fiction,
travel, school books, guidebooks, under various names, usually Ascott R. Hope
and many of them for A & C Black.
Refs: WWW.

MO-NO-YUKI [*Ancient Tales and Folklore of Japan* (20s).]

MORLAND, George *George Morland* (20s, Ltd, GA)
June 26 1763-Oct 29 1804; *s* Henry Robert Morland. In the words of the DNB he
'early developed a taste for dissipation'.
Refs: DNB; TB; art reference books.

MORRAH, Herbert A. *Highways and Hedges* (7/6)
1870-March 29 1939; *b* Winchester; *s* Col James Arthur and Mary Elizabeth
Morrah; *m* Alice Elise Macgregor; two *s*; two *d*; *ed* Canterbury, Hastings,
Highgate; France and Germany; St John's College, Oxford. Professional author of
verse, novels and short stories; editor of the Literary Year Book and other
publications.
Refs: WWW; LYB.

MORRIS, Joseph E. *The Channel Islands*; *The Isle of Man*; *North Wales*; *Oxford*; *The Peak Country*; *Westminster Abbey* (BB); *Belgium*; *The Lake of Como*; *The Lake of Geneva*; *The Lake of Lucerne*; *Venice* (BE)

MORTON, June *Creatures of the Frozen North*; *Creatures of the Night*; *Creatures that Climb*; *Creatures that Fly*; *Creatures that Swim*; *Creatures that Walk* (PNLP).

MOSER, Robert Oswald *John Halifax Gentleman* (7/6, Ltd)
1874-March 31 1953; *m* 1911 Margot Murray; *ed* Skelmsmergh House School, Highgate; St John's Wood Art Schools. 'Many things, then artist.' Worked in London until 1925, then in Rye; ROI 1908; RI 1909. Lived 33 Canfield Gardens, Hampstead, London.
Refs: WWW; Houfe; Waters.

MRKVITCHKA, Jan V. *Bulgaria* (Fasc)
b April 24 1856 in Vidin, Czechoslovakia; studied with Lhota in Prague and Seitz at the Munich School of Fine Arts. Became professor of drawing at the Lycée in Philippopolis, Bulgaria; later professor of drawing at the Sofia Lycée; first director of School of Fine Arts in Sofia, founded in 1906; gold medal at Paris Exhibition 1900.
Refs: TB; *The Studio,* Vol 57.

MULOCK, Dinah Maria See **Mrs CRAIK**

MUNRO, Neil *The Clyde* (20s, Ltd); *Ayrshire Idylls* (7/6)
June 3 1864-Dec 22 1930; *b* Inverary. Journalist and novelist. Wrote *John Splendid* (1898), *Gillian the Dreamer* (1899), *Doom Castle* (1901), *The New Road* (1914); journalism under the pseudonym Mr Incognito. Lived Cromalt, Helensburgh, Dumbartonshire.
Refs: WWW; LYB.

MUSSON, Spencer C. *Sicily* (20s); *La Côte d'Emeraude/Around St Malo* (7/6); *The Upper Engadine* (6s); *The Engadine* (BE)
'The author visited Sicily to gather information for this book at the time of the Messina earthquake, and there are many interesting allusions to that dire catastrophe in his text.' (Publisher's leaflet). A clergyman, he lived at La Chapelle, Aigle, Switzerland (1906).

NESBITT, Frances E. *Algeria and Tunis* (20s)
1864-Jan 12 1934. ASWA 1899; lived London 1886, 1903; Ilfracombe 1900; Louth, Lincolnshire 1901; Abinger Hatch 1906; King's Langley 1926.
Refs: Houfe; Waters; Wood.

NEWALL, C. F. *Plant Life* (20s); *British Land Mammals and their Habits; Wild Flowers and their Wonderful Ways* (PN); *British Wild Flowers* (PC).

NEWTH, J. D. *Austria* (New); *Gloucestershire* (Pop, New); *Austria*; *Hungary* (PML)
Joined A & C Black in 1925; appointed a director 1935; president of the Publishers Association 1949-51. Wrote the history of the firm: *Adam and Charles Black 1807-1957.*

NICHOLLS, George F. *Cornwall* (7/6, Pop, New, WC, PC); *John Halifax Gentleman* (7/6, Ltd); *Cotswolds* (6s, [BB], WC, PC); *Gloucestershire* (Pop, New); *Grey's Elegy* (Misc)
Exhibited 1885-1937; watercolour, landscape and flower painter. Lived Liverpool, Cheshire, Oxford and Worcestershire.
Refs: Waters.

NICHOLSON, Reynold Alleyne *The Rubaiyat of Omar Khayyam* (Misc [notes])
Aug 19 1868-Aug 27 1945; *s* Henry Alleyne Nicholson; *m* 1903 Cecilia Varty; *ed* University of Aberdeen; Trinity College, Cambridge (Fellow 1893). Studied Arabic and Persian; held various lectureships and professorships in Arabic and Persian studies and wrote extensively on these subjects. Lived 52 Bateman Street, Cambridge.
Refs: WWW.

NISBET, John *Glasgow* (ASB)

NIXON, Mima *Royal Palaces and Gardens* (20s, Ltd); *Dutch Bulbs and Gardens* (7/6); *Holland* (PH)
Exhibited 1894-1918; lived Ballybrack 1894; Wimbledon 1896; St Ives, Cornwall, 1909.

NORBURY, Edwin Arthur *Corsica*; *Siam* (PML)
1849-Oct 16 1918; *b* Liverpool; *s* Richard Norbury; *m* 1873 Elvira Browne; two *d*; *ed* Dr Wand's School, Liverpool. Contributed to ILN and *Illustrated News* from age of 15; joined *Graphic* as artist correspondent; lived in Wales 1875-90; visited Siam 1892-96; director of the Norbury Sketching School and St James's Life School; principal of Henry Blackburn Studio; founder member of Royal Cambrian Academy. Illustrated *The Kingdom of the Yellow Robe* (1898), *The Romance of Animal Arts and Crafts* (1907), *Corsica* (1909), *Greek Wonder Tales* (1913). Lived 241 King's Road, Chelsea.
Refs: WWW; Houfe; Peppin; Waters.

NORMAN, Philip *London Vanished and Vanishing* (20s, Ltd)
c 1843-May 17 1931; *b* Bromley Common, Kent; *s* George Ward Norman, director of Bank of England; a widower by 1913; *ed* Eton; Slade School. Artist and antiquary who made study of old London buildings. Illustrator and part author of *The Inns of Old Southwark* (1888); wrote *London Signs and Inscriptions* (1893), *The Ancient Halls of the City Guilds* (1903). Lived 45 Evelyn Gardens, South Kensington.

Refs: WWW; Houfe; LYB; TB; Waters; Wood.

OMOND, George William Thomson *Belgium* (20s, Pop, New); *Bruges and West Flanders* (10s); *Brabant and East Flanders*; *Liège and the Ardennes* (7/6); *Belgium* (PML)
Sept 13 1846-June 18 1929; *b* Craigentor, Perthshire; *s* Rev J. R. Omond; *m* 1878 Margaret Wright; one *s*; three *d*; *ed* Edinburgh; Heidelberg. Called to bar in Scotland 1871; Advocate-Depute 1885. Wrote many books, mostly on historical subjects and the law. Lived Laddingford House, Yalding, Kent.
Refs: WWW; LYB.

OUTHWAITE, Ida Rentoul *Elves and Fairies* (PC)
Australian artist who illustrated a number of books for children which are outside the scope of this volume.

PALMER, Harry Sutton *Buckinghamshire and Berkshire* (20s [published at 25s], Pop, New); *The Rivers and Streams of England*; Bonnie Scotland (20s, Ltd); *Surrey* (20s, Pop, New, WC, PC); *California*; *The Lady of the Lake* (Misc); *The Heart of Scotland* (7/6); *The Wye* (7/6, [BB], WC, PC); *Berkshire*; *Buckinghamshire*; *Kent*; *Scott Country*; *Scottish Highlands* (WC); [*North Wales*; *The Thames* (BB)]; *The Trossachs* ([BB], PC); [*Sussex* (QP)]; *Devon* (Pop, New, WC, PC); *Scotland* (Pop, New); *Wales* (PML); *Around Edinburgh*; *North Devon*; *South Devon* (PC)
1854-May 8 1933; *b* Plymouth; *m* Maud Moore of California; one *d*; *ed* Camden Town High School; South Kensington Art School. Began as still-life painter; changed to landscape painting; RBA 1892; RI 1920; painted several hundred watercolours for A & C Black colour books. Lived Burlington Cottage, Heathfield Terrace, Chiswick, London W4.
Refs: WWW; Houfe; Peppin; TB; Waters; Wood; Martin Hardie *Water-Colour Painting in Britain* (Batsford, 1966-68).

PALMER, William Thomas *The English Lakes* (20s, Ltd, Pop, New)
b 1877. Editor of the *Journal of the Fell and Rock Climbing Club* 1910-19; on staff of *Liverpool Courier*. Also wrote *Lake Country Rambles* (1902), *In Lakeland Dales and Fells* (1903), *Odd Corners in England Lakeland* (1913), *Odd Yarns of English Lakeland* (1914), *Rock Climbing in Cumberland* (1914); edited several popular guides. Lived Liverpool.
Refs: LYB

PARSONS, Beatrice *Gardens of England* (7/6, PC); *English Gardens* (PC)
1870-Feb 17 1955; *d* Arthur W. Parsons; *ed* King's College, London; Royal Academy Schools. Painted chiefly garden subjects; held '22 one man shows of garden pictures . . .'! Queen Mary owned a number of her pictures. Lived 63 Kingsfield Road, Watford, Herts.
Refs: WWW; Waters.

PATERSON, Arthur Henry *The Homes of Tennyson* (7/6)
July 15 1862-Jan 16 1928; *s* Alexander Paterson; *brother* of Helen Allingham; *m* Helen Allingham; *m* 1894 Mary McCallum; one *s*; *ed* University College School, London. Sheep rancher New Mexico 1877-79; farmer Western Kansas 1879-80; merchant's office Birkenhead 1881-84; later held posts with charity organisations. Wrote novels and books on historical and social topics. Lived 6 Thurlow Road, Hampstead, London.
Refs: WWW; LYB.

PATTERSON, Malcolm *St Andrews* (MSB, PC)

PEDERSEN, Hugo Vildfred *Java* (PML)
b Jan 25 1870; *b* Copenhagen. Painter and illustrator, he lived for 20 years in India.

PENNY, Fanny Emily *Southern India* (20s)
d Dec 22 1939; *d* Rev John and Emily Caroline Farr; *m* 1877 Rev Frank Penny, Madras Chaplain, retired; one *s*, one *d*; *ed* Queen's College, Harley St, London. Wrote novels about India including *Romance of a Nautch Girl, A Mixed Marriage, A Love Tangle* (1917), *Swami's Curse* (1922). Lived 3 Park Hill, Ealing, London.
Refs: WWW; LYB.

PETERS, A. W. *The Zoo* (ASB, PC)

PETTIE, John *John Pettie* (20s, GA)
March 17 1839-Feb 23 1893. Pettie's life is described in this book, written by his nephew Martin Hardie. Lived The Lothians, Fitzjohn's Avenue, Hampstead.
Refs: WWW ; Houfe ; TB

PIKE, Joseph C. M. *Chester* (ASB, PC) ; *Ampleforth* ; *Bruges* (ASB) ; *Stratford on Avon*; *Rugby* (MSB)
b March 6 1883 ; *ed* Ampleforth College. *Fl* 1895-1910 ; watercolour painter of architectural subjects; exhibited RA, etc. Lived 14 Gerrard Road, London SW13 (1929); Addison Studios, Kensington.
Refs: WWW; Waters.

PIONNIER, Le Capitaine Marcel *Aux Indes* (BV); *La Guerre aux Fauves* (Contes)
'Chargé de Missions de Gouvernement Français'.

PISA, Alberto *Italy* (20s); *Rome* (20s, Ltd, Pop, New); *Sicily* (20s); *Pompeii* (7/6); *Ancient Rome* (PAL)
b March 1864; *b* Ferrara; studied at Florence Academy. Watercolour landscape and figure painter; exhibited 1892-1919. Lived 21 Campden Road, London NW.
Refs: TB.

PLATT, Agnes *Germany* (PML)
Later editions of this book were written by Mrs Alfred Sidgwick (Cecily Sidgwick).

POCOCK, Noel *Bulgaria* (Fasc)

POYSER, Arthur Horatio *The Tower of London* (7/6); *The Tower of London* (BB)
Jan 21 1849-June 6 1923; *s* Charles Poyser; *m* 1872 Alice Whytehead; one *s*, four *d*;
ed Shrewsbury; Christ Church, Oxford. Called to Bar 1873. Lived Burneston,
Sydenham, London. Refs: WWW.

PRATT, Claude *Cuba* (PML)
b Jan 11 1860; *b* Leicester; *s* Jonathan Pratt; *ed* Birmingham School of Art and in
Antwerp and Paris. Genre painter in oil and watercolour; exhibited in Midlands.
Lived Birmingham.
Refs: Waters.

PYCRAFT, W. P. *The British Bird Book* (Misc)
1868-May 1 1942; *b* Great Yarmouth; *m* 1899 Lucy Agnes Shee; two *d*. Assistant
Keeper in charge of Osteological Collections, British Museum. Wrote numerous
books on ornithology and animals. Lived Little Paddock, Longcross, Chertsey,
Surrey.
Refs: WWW.

QUINTON, Alfred Robert *The Thames* (BB); *Annals of Hampstead* (Misc)
Oct 28 1853-1934; *ed* Hornsey School; Heatherley's; *m* Elizabeth Crompton.
Travelled widely in Europe; exhibited RA; contributed to ILN; became well known
as a postcard artist particularly for J. Salmon. Illustrated *Cycling in the Alps* (1900),
The Historic Thames (Belloc, 1907), *The Avon and Shakespeare's Country* (1910),
A Book of the Wye (1911) *The Cottages of Rural England* (1912). Lived Finchley,
London.
Refs: Houfe; TB; Waters; Wood.

RACKHAM, Bernard *A Book of Porcelain* (Misc)
July 26 1876-Feb 13 1964; *s* Alfred Thomas Rackham; *m* Ruth Adams (*d* 1963);
one *s,* one *d*; *ed* City of London School; Pembroke College, Cambridge. Employed
at Victoria and Albert Museum 1898-1938; retired as Keeper of Department of
Ceramics. Wrote extensively on pottery, tiles, stained glass and porcelain. Lived
26 Fort Road, Guildford.
Refs: WWW

RAGG, Rev Canon Lonsdale *Venice* (20s)
Oct 23 1866-July 31 1945; *b* Wellington, Shropshire; *s* Rev Thomas Ragg; *m* 1902
Laura Roberts; one *d*; *ed* Newport School; Christ Church, Oxford; Cuddesdon
Theological College. Held various church posts in Lincoln, Bologna, Venice,
Bangor, Rome and Bordighera during 1895-1943; archdeacon of Gibraltar from
1934. Wrote a number of books chiefly on church matters but also on Dante,
Venice and trees. Lived 5 St James's Square, Bath.
Refs: WWW.

RAGG, Laura *Venice* (20s); *The Italian Lakes* (Pop, New). Wife of Lonsdale Ragg (see above); born Laura Roberts. Wrote *The Women Artists of Bologna, Things Seen in Venice, Crises in Venetian History.*

RANKIN, George *Partridges and Partridge Manors*; *Pheasants and Covert Shooting* (Sport); [*Birds and their Young* (PC)]
A popular postcard painter, who specialised in pictures of animals and birds.

RAWNSLEY, Mrs Willingham (Alice Julia RAWNSLEY) *Country Sketches for City Dwellers*; *The New Forest* (7/6, Ltd), *The New Forest* (BB)
Probably related to Canon Rawnsley, who married an Edith and an Eleanor; his mother was the daughter of Sir Willingham Franklin. Lived (1903) Loughrigg House, Ambleside.

REEVES, Hon William Pember *New Zealand* (20s, Pop, New); *The New Zealand Shipping Company's Pocket Book* (Misc)
Feb 10 1857-1932; *b* Lyttleton, Canterbury, New Zealand; *s* Hon William and Ellen Reeves, pioneer colonists; *m* Magdalen Stuart Robison; two *d*; *ed* Christ's College Grammar School, Christchurch. Barrister but preferred journalism; member of NZ parliament 1887-1896; Minister of Education, Labour and Justice 1891-96; Agent-general for New Zealand in London 1986-1909; 'not rich enough' to enter British politics but influenced Liberal and Labour policies; director London School of Economics 1908-17. Best known for *The Long White Cloud*, a history of New Zealand; also wrote verse and contributed to the DNB and *Encyclopaedia Britannica.* Lived 48 Cornwall Gardens, South Kensington, London.
Refs: WWW; DNZB.

REMBRANDT (Rembrandt Harmenszoon van Rijn) *Rembrandt* (12/6, GA)
1609-69. Dutch painter, whose life and work are described in numerous art reference books.

REYNOLDS, Frank *Frank Reynolds* (BPP)
Feb 13 1876-April 18 1953; *s* W. G. Reynolds; *m* 1905 Winifred Milne; one *s*, two *d*; studied at Heatherley's and at Académie Julian, Paris. Black and white artist and illustrator; worked for ILN and *The Sketch*; joined *Punch* 1919; Art Editor 1920-30; RI 1903. Illustrated *By the Way Ballads* (1901), *The Smiths of Surbiton* (1906), *Pictures of Paris and some Parisians* (1908) and several books by Dickens; illustrated and wrote *Golf Book (1932), Off to the Pictures* (1937), *Hamish McDuff* (1937), *Humorous Drawing for the Press* (1947). Lived Nyren, Giggs Hill Green, Thames Ditton, Surrey.
Refs: WWW; Peppin; TB; Waters; biography in book.

REYNOLDS, J. B. Editor, Quotation and Picture series.

REYNOLDS, Warwick *Norse and Lapp* (LL); *Norway and the Lapps* (PML)
1880-Dec 15 1926; *b* Islington; *s* Warwick and Martha Reynolds; *m* 1906 Mary

More Peeps: (top) *early and later versions of* Hungary, *and a Miscellaneous Peep;* (centre) *examples of generic and dedicated Peeps wrappers and a Peep at Nature;* (bottom) *examples of other Peeps series: Ancient Lands, English Ministers, Industry.*

A selection of Black's postcards using illustrations from the colour books; several other publishers also issued postcards based on A & C Black illustrations.

Kincaid; two *d*; *ed* Stroud Green; Grosvenor Studio; St John's Wood; Julian's, Paris. Studied animals at Zoological Society 1895-1901. Contributed to many magazines. Lived 26 West Princes Street, Glasgow.
Refs: WWW; Houfe; TB.

RICHARDS, Frederick Charles *Florence* (ASB); *Oxford* (ASB, NASB, PC); *Rome*; *Venice*; *Windsor and Eton* (ASB, PC).
Dec 1 1878-March 27 1932; *b* Newport, Mon; studied architecture at RCA and abroad. Etcher, watercolour and black and white artist; travelled widely in England, France and Italy; RE 1921; lectured at RCA 1922-27. Lived 28 Hereford Buildings, Church Street, Chelsea.
Refs: WWW; TB; Waters.

RIDGEWELL, Harold A. *Madagascar* (PML)

RIOM, G. *The Spirit of Paris* (7/6)

ROBERT, Uncle (Robert F. Finch) *Children of the Snow and Ice*; *Children of the Sunshine*; *Children of the Field and Forest*; *Children of the Mountain and Plain* (PLP)

ROBERTS, Sir Sydney (Castle) *The Charm of Cambridge* (Charm)
April 3 1887-July 21 1966; *b* Birkenhead; *s* Frank Roberts; *m* 1st Irene Wallis (*d* 1932); one *s*, two *d*; 2nd 1938 Marjorie Swann; *ed* Brighton College; Pembroke College, Cambridge. Fellow Pembroke College 1929; Bursar 1935-36; Master 1948-58; Secretary, Cambridge University Press 1922-48; Vice-Chancellor, Cambridge University 1949-51. Held many public and educational offices. Wrote extensively on education, religion, Dr Johnson, Cambridge, etc. Lived The Loke House, 21 West Street, Cambridge.
Refs: WWW.

ROBINSON, William Heath *Heath Robinson* (BPP)
May 31 1872-Sept 13 1944; *s* Thomas Robinson and *brother* Charles and Thomas Heath Robinson; *m* Josephine Lacey; four *s*, one *d*; *ed* Islington; Royal Academy Schools. Artist and illustrator who became a household name; his life is described in the book and in *The Illustrations of W. Heath Robinson* by Geoffrey Beare (Werner Shaw, 1983). Lived 25 Southwood Avenue, Highgate, London N6.
Refs: WWW; Houfe; TB; Waters.

ROLFE, H. L. *Trout Fishing* (Sport [frontispiece])

ROWE, Charles R. *South Devon* (6s)

RYAN, Frederick W. *Malta* (7/6)

SABIN, Arthur Knowles *War Posters* (Misc)
April 3 1879-Oct 19 1959; *b* Rotherham; *s* Thomas Sabin; *m* 1st 1903 Elizabeth

Thompson; one *s*; 2nd 1919 Alma Kuher (*d* 1954); one *d*; 3rd 1959 Rose Wallace. Writer, poet and printer; printed books for the Samurai Press 1907-09, for the Pear Tree Press 1908-16 and the Temple Sheen Press, which he owned from 1911. Worked in the Victoria and Albert Museum from 1909; Keeper 1935; Officer-in-Charge of the Bethnal Green Museum 1922-40. Wrote *Typhon and other Poems* (1902), *The Wayfarers* (1907), *Dante and Beatrice* (1908), *War Harvest* (1914), *East London Poems* (1931). Lived 26 Mountney Drive, Beachlands, Pevensey Bay, Sussex.
Refs: WWW.

SAINT, Lawrence Bradford *Stained Glass of the Middle Ages in England and France* (Misc)
Jan 29 1885-June 1961; *b* Sharpsburg, Pennsylvania, USA; *s* Joseph Alexander and Jennie Bradford Saint; *m* 1910 Katharine Wright Proctor; seven *s*; one *d*; *ed* Pennsylvania Academy of Fine Arts, Philadelphia; also studied in England, France and Spain. Worked in designing and painting stained glass; Director, Department of Stained Glass, Washington Cathedral 1928-35; established glass-making factory. Painted large number of representations of stained glass for museums and other institutions; wrote and illustrated *A Knight of the Cross*; wrote *Ponderin' Pete*. Lived Huntingdon Valley, Montgomery County, Near Philadelphia.
Refs: WWW.

ST LEGER, Captain Stratford Edward *War Sketches in Colour* (20s, Ltd)
1878-1935; *s* Frederick York St Leger; *m*; *ed* Tonbridge School. Served with Mounted Infantry in South African War; World War I; DSO, CMG, CVO; retired with rank of Colonel 1924.
Refs: WWW.

SALWEY, Jasper *Cornwall* (ASB); *Lincoln* (ASB, NASB); *St Malo* (MSB)

SANDERSON, William *Scottish Life and Character* (7/6)
Some time Editor of the Border Magazine.

SCHELTEMA, J. F. *Java* (PML)

SCHOTT, Helena C. *Czechoslovakia* (PML)

SCOTT, Dixon (Walter SCOTT) *Liverpool* (6s); *Stratford, Leamington and Warwick* (BB)
1882-Oct 23 1915. Leader writer on *Liverpool Courier* in his 20s; correspondent for *The Studio, Manchester Guardian, The Bookman, Country Life*, etc; regarded as a writer of great promise; joined Royal Field Artillery in World War II; landed with his regiment in Gallipoli; died of dysentery on board a hospital ship. Also wrote *Art and Democracy* (1908). Lived Marston Trussel, Market Harborough, Leics.
Refs: *The Bookman*, Dec 1915.

SCOTT, Sir James George *France* (PML); *Alexander the Great*; *Mungo Park*; *Marco Polo*; *Vasco da Gama* (all PGE)
Dec 25 1851-April 4 1935; *s* Rev George Scott; *m* 1910 G. E. Mitton *qv*; one *d*; *ed* Stuttgart; Württemberg; King's College School, London; Edinburgh University; Lincoln College, Oxford. Held a number of administrative posts in Asia from 1875 to 1910; Superintendent and Political Officer, Shan States 1902-10. Wrote a number of books on Burma and Indochina. Lived Thereaway, Graffham, Sussex. Refs: WWW.

SCOTT, Sir Walter *The Lady of the Lake* (Misc)
1771-1832. Scottish writer, the subject of numerous biographies. A & C Black held the copyright of his works for many years during the 19th and early 20th centuries, and for a long time these formed a significant part of the publisher's output.

SCOTT, William *The Riviera* (20s); *Lamia's Winter Quarters* (7/6; head and tail pieces); *France* (PML)
b 1848. Articled to an architect and later elected to one of first Whitworth exhibitions; ARIBA 1870; silver medal of RIBA 1875, Soane Medallion 1877, travelling studentship 1878; RE 1881; lived mostly in Italy: Rome 1882, Venice 1884, Bordighera 1896. Wrote *Rock Villages of the Riviera*.
Refs: Houfe; Wood; *The Studio* Vol 22.

SHAH, Sirdar Ikbal Ali *Arabia* (PML)

SHARPLEY, R. *Harrogate*; The Thames (ASB)
Ed Heatherley's; studied to be a civil engineer but turned to art instead. Watercolour painter and wood engraver; exhibited RA, etc. Lived Campden, Glos. Refs: Waters.

SHELDON-WILLIAMS, Inglis *The Canadian Front in France and Flanders* (WF)
1871-1940; *s* Alfred Sheldon-Williams; *m* 1904 Maud Thomson. Farmed in Canada 1887-91; returned to Europe; studied at the Slade; Ecole des Beaux Arts, Paris; and with Sir Thomas Brock; appointed Special Artist to *The Sphere* to cover the Boer War; covered Russo-Japanese war 1903 and the Delhi Durbar for the FAS 1902-3. Later worked in Gloucestershire and Bedfordshire; commissioned by the Canadian government to portray Canada's part in World War I. Also illustrated *After Pretoria, The Guerilla War* (1902).
Refs: Houfe; *The Studio* Vol 41.

SHELDON-WILLIAMS, Ralf Frederic Lardy *The Canadian Front in France and Flanders* (WF)
Brother of Inglis (see above); served with Canadian Machine-Gun Battalion in World War I.

SHENESSY, S. *The Children's World* (PIX)

SHORE, W. Teignmouth *Kent* (20s, Pop, New); *Canterbury* (7/6)
27 April 1865-Jan 3 1932; *s* Canon Teignmouth and Eleanor Shore; *ed* Westminster; Oxford. Journalist and novelist, he worked for Cassell for many years and for the Encyclopaedia Britannica department of *The Times*; editor of *The Academy and Literature* 1903-05; did marketing and advertising work. Wrote many books including *The Talking Master, Dickens, Charles Dickens and his Friends, Westminster School, Shakespeare's Self, My Cook Book, The Trials of Neill Cream*. Lived 18 Templar's Avenue, Golders Green, London.
Refs: WWW; LYB.

SIDGWICK, Mrs Alfred [Cecily SIDGWICK] *Germany* (PML)
d Aug 10 1934; *b* London; *s* David and Wilhelmine Ullmann; *m* 1883 Alfred Sidgwick. Wrote many novels between 1889 and 1932. Lived Trewoofe Orchard, St Buryan, Cornwall.
Refs: WWW; LYB.

SIEPEN, Edith *Berlin* (PML)
Later known as E. Siepen-Hetherington.

SILBERRAD, Una *Dutch Bulbs and Gardens* (7/6)
May 1872-Sept 1 1955; *b* Buckhurst Hill, Essex. Wrote large number of novels from *The Enchanter* (1897) to *The Three Men who went to Ardath* (1944). Lived The Wick House, Burnham-on-Crouch, Essex.
Refs: WWW; LYB.

SIMPSON, A. Nicol *British Land Mammals and their Habits*; *British Reptiles and Amphibians* (PN)

SLOAN, John MacGavin *Galloway* (6s)
d Nov 13 1926; *b* Scotland; *m* 1880 Mary Jane Helm; one *d*; *ed* privately; Glasgow University. Withdrew from ministry to become a litterateur; editor Dumfries and Galloway Courier and Herald 1897-1900; settled in London. Wrote on socialism, Carlyle, Burns, Scott etc. Lived 9 Bonham Road, Brixton Hill, London.
Refs: WWW.

SMITH, A. Croxton *British Dogs at Work* (7/6)
Dec 3 1865-Aug 27 1952; *s* William Croxton Smith; *m* 1892 Ada Frances Stimpson; one *s*; one *d*; *ed* privately. Entered journalism but left in 1909 to take up article writing, specialising in dogs; director of publicity to Ministry of Food in World War I; dog show judge; held Kennel Club posts; an active sportsman. Wrote a number of books on dogs. Lived Kipling House, 43 Villiers Street, London WC2.
Refs: WWW.

SMITH, Mrs A. Murray (E.T. BRADLEY) *Westminster Abbey* (7/6, Ltd)
One of five *d* of George Granville Bradley, Dean of Westminster, and Marian, *d* of Archdeacon Philpot; *sister* of A. G. Bradley *qv* and of Margaret L. Woods, poet

and novelist. Historian of Westminster Abbey. Author of the *Annals of Westminster Abbey: its Story and Associations* and the *Roll Call of Westminster Abbey.* Refs: *The Studio* Vol 33.

SMITH, Richard Gordon *Ancient Tales and Folklore of Japan* (20s)
April 20 1858-Nov 8 1918; *b* Urswick, Barrow-in-Furness; *s* John Bridson and Elizabeth Anne Smith; *ed* Cheltenham College; *m* 1879 Ethel Newcomb; one *s*; three *d* (also two children who died in infancy); *ed* Cheltenham. Moved to Canada in 1877, where he married; returned to England 1889 after death of son; left his family and travelled to Japan, where he spent the next 20 years; held 4th class Order of Rising Sun, Japan; in collecting objects of interest for the British Museum he picked up the tales that made up his diaries. He seems not to have minded when his name was spelt with a hyphen, and therefore appears in most reference books under **G.**
Refs: WWW; Victoria Manthorpe *The Japan Diaries of Richard Gordon Smith* (Viking/Rainbird, 1986).

SMITH, William Jr *The Highlands and Islands of Scotland* (10s, Pop, New); *Abbotsford* (7/6, [BB]); *Deeside* (7/6, [BB], WC); *The Scott Country* (WC); *Scottish Highlands* (WC); *The Highlands* (PC)
Lived (1905) 18 Diamond St, Aberdeen.

SNELL, F. J. *North Devon* (6s)

SOMMERVILLE, Frankfort [A. M. Sommerville STORY] *The Spirit of Paris* (7/6)
d after 1966; *b* Frankfort-am-Main; *s* A. T. Story; *m* 1st 1903 Alice Loughton; one *s*; one *d*; 2nd 1924 Thelma Thomas; *ed* Brussels, Lancashire, London, Bonn, Fleet Street. Editor *Belgian Times and News*; *Continental Daily Mail*; *Paris Evening Telegraph,* etc; contributor to English, French and American journals and magazines. Also wrote *The Face of Pan* (1907), *A Parisian Princess* (1911), *Paris in Ten Days, a Little Guide for Tommy and the Yank* (1919), *The Battlefields of France* (1919-20), *Paris à la Carte* (1922), *The Tales of my Study* (1928), *Tales of France* (1931), *Auguste Rodin* (1939), *France and the French* (1951). Lived 92 Talbot Road, London W2.
Refs: WWW.

SPAULL, Hebe *The Baltic States* (PML); *Rumania* (PML); *The League of Nations* (MP).

SPENCE, Percy Frederick Seaton *Australia* (20s, Pop, New, PML)
1868-Aug 1933; *b* Sydney. Early career in Australia and Fiji; came to London 1895, working there for the rest of his life; represented in National Gallery, Sydney, and in National Portrait Gallery (R. L. Stevenson, whom he knew while in the South Seas, and Phil May). Also illustrated *Black Beauty* (published by A & C Black); contributed to *Graphic, Punch,* ILN, etc. Lived 28 Fitzjames Avenue, West Kensington.

Refs: Houfe; DAustB; TB.

SPIELMANN, Marion Harry Alexander *Kate Greenaway* (20s, Ltd); *Kate Greenaway* (GA); *Hugh Thomson* (Misc)
May 22 1858-Oct 2 1948; *b* London; *s* Adam Spielmann; *m* 1880 Mabel Henrietta Yates; one *s*; *ed* University College School; University College; Lycée, France. Art writer for *Pall Mall Gazette* and other magazines; editor of *Magazine of Art*. Wrote extensively on many aspects of art and artists including books on Ruskin, sculpture, Watts, Velasquez, Chaucer, Shakespeare; contributed to DNB and *Encyclopaedia Britannica*. Lived 107 Banbury Road, Oxford; Uplands, Folkestone.
Refs: WWW; LYB.

SPURLING, J. *A Century of Sea Trading* (Misc)

STEEL, Flora Annie *India* (20s. Pop, New)
April 2 1847-April 12 1929; *b* Harrow; *d* George and Isabella Webster; *m* 1867 Henry Steel; *ed* home. Lived in India until 1889; provincial inspectress of government and aided schools in Punjab; member Educational Committee. Wrote novels about India, the best known of which is *On the Face of the Waters,* an account of the Indian Mutiny. Lived Springfield, Minchinhampton, Glos.
Refs: WWW; DNB; Violet Powell *Flora Annie Steel: Novelist of India* (Heinemann, 1981)

STEWART, Allan [*The Isle of Arran (BB)*]; *Alsace-Lorraine*; *British North Borneo*; *Ceylon*; *Germany*; *London*; *Montenegro* (all PML); *Paris* (PML); *Holland*; *India* (PH); *The Royal Navy* [PC]
Feb 11 1865-Jan 29 1951; *b* Edinburgh; *s* James Stewart; *m* Jane Ramsay; two *d*; *ed* Edinburgh Institution; RSA Schools. On staff of ILN for some years; Captain in RE during World War I; specialised in military and historical paintings; worked at Kenley, Surrey until 1925, then at Castle Douglas. Also illustrated many children's books for A & C Black. Lived Rose Cottage, Dalry, Castle Douglas, Kirkcudbrightshire.
Refs: WWW; Caw; Houfe; TB; Waters.

STEWART, A. M. *British Butterflies*; *Common British Moths* (PN)

STEWART, Hugh *Russia* (20s); *Provincial Russia* (7/6)

STOKES, Adrian Scott *Hungary* (20s, PML); *Austria-Hungary* (Fasc)
Dec 23 1854-Nov 30 1935; *b* Southport; *s* S. N. Stokes; *m* 1884 Marianne Preindlsberger (see below) whom he met in Brittany; *ed* Liverpool Institute; RA schools; Paris. Oil and watercolour painter; ROI 1888; ARA 1910; RA 1919; RWS 1926. Wrote *Pansy's Flour-Bin* (1880), *Landscape Painting* (1925); illustrated *The Three Brides, The Clever Woman of the Family* (both Charlotte Yonge), *Tyrol and its People* (C. Holland). Lived 7a Grantham Place, London W1.
Refs: WWW; Houfe; TB; Waters; Wood; *Art Journal* (1900).

STOKES, George Vernon *British Dogs at Work* (7/6); *British Dogs* (PC)
Jan 1 1873-Jan 4 1954; *s* George Edward Stokes; *ed* privately. Animal painter and etcher; RBA 1929; member of the Lake Artists' Society. Wrote *Colour Etchings in Two Printings, How to Paint and Draw Dogs.* Lived Byways, Great Mongeham, Deal, Kent.
Refs: WWW; Houfe.

STOKES, Marianne *Hungary* (20s, PML); *Austria-Hungary* (Fasc)
1855-1927; *b* Marianne Preindlsberger in Southern Austria; *m* Adrian Stokes (see above); studied under Lindenschmidt in Munich and in Paris. Genre and portrait painter in oil and watercolour; NEA, ASWA 1887; ARWS 1923; worked at St Ives during the 1890s.
Refs: Houfe; TB; Waters.

STONE, Christopher Reynolds *Eton* (7/6)
Sept 19 1882-May 22 1965; *b* Eton; *s* Rev E. D. Stone, who wrote two chapters of reminiscences in his son's book; *m* 1908 Alice Chinnery (*d* 1945); *ed* Eton, where his tutor was H. E. Luxmoore *qv*; Christ Church, Oxford. Royal Fusiliers during World War I; DSO 1918; joint founder of *The Gramophone*. Wrote *Lusus Pueriles* (1901), *Scars* (1908), *Lusus* (1909), *They Also Serve* (1910), books on Eton; edited books of verse. Lived 6-7 Turks Head Court, Eton.
Refs: WWW; LYB; DNB.

STOW, Vincent Aubrey Stewart *The Motherland in Pictures* (PIX)
July 27 1883-April 21 1968; *s* Stewart Smith Stow; *m* 1912 Marie Elinor Morler; two *d*; *ed* Winchester; Exeter College, Oxford. Taught at Marlborough; The Daly College, Indore; Rajkumar College, Raipur (Principal 1912 and 1919-31); The Mayo College, Ajmer (Principal 1931-43). Wrote on education, history and geography. Lived The Grange, Goring-on-Thames, Oxon.
Refs: WWW.

STOWE, Harriet Elizabeth Beecher *La Case de l'Oncle Tom* (Contes)
1811-96. American novelist best known for *Uncle Tom's Cabin* (which appears among A & C Black's children's books, the above title being a translation into French). Her life is described in biographies by F. Wilson (1941) and N. B. Gerson (1979).

STOWELL, Leonard H. *The Call of the Open*; *Nature's Moods* (Misc)

STRETTON, Philip Eustace *Amid the High Hills* (Misc)
fl 1884-1919. Animal and landscape painter in oil and watercolour.
Refs: Waters.

STRUBEN, Edith Frances Mary *Gardens of South Africa* (Misc)
1869-1936; *b* Pretoria; *d* H. W. Struben; *ed* Bloemfontein and In Europe. Studied at Crystal Palace Art School; exhibited in London and South Africa; one of the first

women to do colour filming; settled at the Cape; vice-president South African
Society of Arts; member Botanical Society of South Africa.
Refs: SADNB.

SWIFT, Jonathan [*Voyages chez Plusiers Nations Eloignées du Monde par Lemuel
Gulliver* (Contes)]
1667-1745. English author and satirist born in Dublin. All his works were
published anonymously. Biography by J. M. Murry (1955) and bibliography by
J. J. Stathis (1967) describe his life and work.

SWINBURNE, H. Lawrence *The Royal Navy* (20s)
Lived Weybridge, Surrey.

SYMONDS, John Addington *Our Life in the Swiss Highlands* (7/6)
1840-93; *s* John Addington Symonds, physician; *ed* Harrow; Balliol College,
Oxford. Settled at Davos Platz because of his health. Wrote *History of the Italian
Renaissance* (1875-86), books of poems, *Sketches in Italy and Greece* (1874), *Walt
Whitman* (1893), and translations.
Refs: DNB; biography by Horatio Forbes Brown.

SYMONDS, Margaret *Our Life in the Swiss Highlands* (7/6)
Jan 15 1869-Nov 4 1925; *b* Clifton; *d* John Addington Symonds (see above) and
Janet North; *m* 1898 W. Wyamar Vaughan, a master at Wellington College.
Also wrote *Days Spent on a Doge's Farm, The Story of Perugia* (1898), *A Child of the
Alps* (1920), *Out of the Past* (1925). Lived The School House, Rugby.
Refs: WWW.

TALBOT, Frederick A. *The Canadian Pacific Railway* (PGR)

TEMPLAR, H. B. *Manchester* (ASB)

THACKERAY, Lance *The Light Side of Egypt* (Misc); *The People of Egypt* (People,
PC).
d Aug 11 1916. Painter and illustrator best known for comic drawings; member of
London Sketch Club; spent several winters in Egypt producing paintings which
were exhibited at the FAS and Walker galleries; RBA 1899; a prolific postcard
painter, mainly for Tuck; enlisted as private in Artists Rifles on outbreak of war but
he suffered from health problems and was admitted to the Canadian Military
Hospital in 1916; he died of anaemia in Brighton. Also illustrated *The XYZ of
Bridge* (1906); contributed to *The Sphere, Graphic, Punch,* etc.
Refs: WWW; Houfe; Peppin; TB; Waters; *The Morning Post* Aug 12 1916.

THACKERAY, William Makepeace *The Four Georges* (Misc)
1811-63. English writer, whose life and work are described in numerous biographies.

THOMAS, Edward Philip *Oxford* (20s, Ltd, Pop, New); *Beautiful Wales* (20s); *Wales* (Pop, New)
March 3 1878-April 9 1917; *s* Philip Henry and Elizabeth Thomas; *m* 1899 Helen Noble; one *s*, two *d*; *ed* St Paul's School; Lincoln College, Oxford. A poet who found himself among the A & C Black authors as the result of financial necessity, Thomas's life has been portrayed by his widow in *As It Was* and *World Without End;* by Eleanor Farjeon in *ET: The Last Four Years;* by John Moore in *The Life and Letters of ET;* by Robert P. Eckert *ET: A Biography and a Bibliography* (1937); and most recently by R. George Thomas *ET: A Portrait* (1985). Lived Steep, Petersfield, Hants.
Refs: WWW; biographies.

THOMAS, Margaret *From Damascus to Palmyra* (20s)
d Dec 24 1929; *b* Croydon; emigrated with parents to Australia; *ed* RA Schools; Paris. Artist, author, and sculptor, she travelled extensively, particularly around the Mediterranean coast; exhibited at RA from 1868. Her books include *A Hero of the Workshop* (1880), *A Scamper through Spain and Tangier* (1882), *Denmark Past and Present* (1901), *How to Judge Pictures* (1906). Lived Countryside, Croft Lane, Norton, Letchworth, Herts.
Refs: WWW; Houfe; TB; Waters.

THOMSON, Hugh *Hugh Thomson* (Misc)
June 1 1860-May 7 1920; *b* Coleraine, Ireland; *m* 1884; one *s*. Worked for linen manufacturer before joining Marcus Ward, printers and Christmas card publishers; attended Belfast School of Art; moved to London 1883, worked for *English Illustrated Magazine;* became well known as a book illustrator; awarded a civil list pension 1918. Member of the London Sketch Club; RI 1897 (resigned 1907). Illustrated a large number of books, including works by Jane Austen, J. M. Barrie, Charles Dickens, Austin Dobson, George Eliot, Mrs Gaskell, Oliver Goldsmith, Thomas Hughes, Shakespeare, Thackeray, etc; and worked for a number of periodicals. Lived 8 Patten Road, Wandsworth Common, London.
Refs: WWW; DNB; Houfe; Peppin; TB; Waters.

THOMSON, M. Pearson *Denmark* (PML); *Finland* (PML)

TIMLIN, William Mitcheson *South Africa: A Record in Pen and Pencil* (MSB)
1896-1943. South African artist; qualified as an architect; produced landscapes and fanciful works such as *The Ship that Sailed to Mars* and *The Building of a Fairy City.* Lived Kimberley.
Refs: SADNB.

TITTERTON, C. C. *The British Blue Jacket* (MP)

TODD, Professor John Aiton *The Banks of the Nile* (20s)
July 5 1875-July 1954; *b* Glasgow; *m*; two *s*, one *d*; *ed* Hutchesons' Grammar School, Glasgow; Glasgow University. Solicitor in Glasgow 1896-1907; lecturer on

economics at the Khedivial School, Cairo 1907-12; professor of economics at Nottingham 1912-19; lecturer in economics Balliol College, Oxford 1918-23; principal City School of Commerce, Liverpool 1923-40. Also wrote a number of books on economics, cotton and shipping.
Refs: WWW.

TREVOR, Roy *Montenegro* (PML)

TUKER, Miss M. A. R. *Cambridge* (20s, Pop, New); *Rome* (20s, Ltd, Pop, New). Also wrote (with Hope Malleson *qv*) *Handbook to Christian and Ecclesiastical Rome* (A & C Black). Lived at various times in Guernsey; Winchcombe, Glos; and Henfield, Sussex.

TURBAYNE, Albert Angus Designer.
1866-April 29 1940; *b* Boston, USA; *s* David and Jessie Turbayne; *m* 1st 1906 Christiana Owens; two *s*; 2nd Millicent Tavener (*d* 1954); *ed* Boston; Cobourg, Canada. Specialised in book design; headed the Carlton Studio and was demonstrator of design at the LCC School of Photoengraving and Lithography. Lived 11 Fairfax Road, Chiswick, London.
Refs: WWW; Houfe.

TYNAN, Katharine (Mrs Katharine Tynan HINKSON) *Ireland* (PML)
d April 2 1931; *d* Andrew C. Tynan; *m* 1893 H. A. Hinkson; two *s*; one *d*; *ed* Sienna Convent, Drogheda. Irish novelist and poet with an enormous output of books from 1885 to after 1918. Her recreations included 'talking to a good listener'. Lived Herbert Lodge, Blackrock, Co Dublin.
Refs: WWW; LYB.

TYNDALE, Thomas *Worcestershire* (7/6, WC)
Exhibited 1902-11. Lived 55 Woodhurst Road, Acton, London.

TYNDALE, Walter Frederick Roofe *Wessex* (20s, [BB]); *Hardy Country* (WC); *Dalmatia* (Pop, New); *Dorset*; *Somerset* (Pop, New, WC).
Aug 1855-Dec 16 1943; *b* Bruges of English parents; *m* Evelyn Barnard (*d* 1933); three *s*; *ed* Bruges, Antwerp Academy and in Paris. Moved to England 1871; began as oil painter but later decided to specialise in watercolours; travelled in Morocco, Egypt, Lebanon, Syria and Japan; RI 1911; appointed to Censor staff during World War I; Head Censor at Boulogne. Also illustrated *The New Forest* (1904), *Japanese Gardens* (1912); wrote and illustrated *Japan and the Japanese* (1910), *An Artist in Egypt* (1912), *An Artist in Italy* (1913), *An Artist on the Riviera* (1916). Lived 29 Brunswick Gardens, London.
Refs: WWW; Houfe; Peppin; Waters; Wood; *The Studio* Vol 38.

UTAGAWA, Miss Wakana *Japan* (PML; PH).

VAILE, P. A. *New Zealand* (PML)

VAIZEY, Winifred *Creatures of the Frozen North; Creatures of the Night; Creatures that Climb; Creatures that Fly; Creatures that Swim; Creatures that Walk* (all PNLP)

VAN MILLINGEN, Professor Alexander *Constantinople* (20s)
Dec 31 1840-Sept 15 1915; *s* Dr Julius M. van Millingen; *m* 1st 1879 Cora Welch; 2nd Frances Mackenzie; two *s*, one *d*; *ed* Malta Protestant College; Blair Lodge Academy, Polmont; Edinburgh University; New College, Edinburgh. Pastor Free Church of Scotland church, Genoa; Pastor Union Church, Pera, Constantinople; Professor of History, Robert College, Constantinople. Also wrote *Byzantine Constantinople* (1899), *Byzantine Churches in Constantinople* (1912); contributed to *Encyclopaedia Britannica*. Lived Robert College.
Refs: WWW.

VAN MILLINGEN, Julius R. *Turkey* (PML)
Presumed to be the son of Alexander van Millingen.

VARLEY, Rev Telford *Hampshire* (20s, Pop, New); *Winchester* (7/6); *Winchester* (BB).
A teacher at Peter Symonds School, Winchester, he also wrote books on chemistry for A & C Black.

VAUX, Patrick *The British Blue Jacket* (MP)

VERNON, Paul E. *Morocco from a Motor* (Misc)

VILLIERS-STUART, Mrs Constance Mary *Gardens of the Great Mughals* (Misc)
d J. Fielden and Mrs Fielden of Beachamwell Hall, Norfolk; *m* 1908 Major Patrick Villiers-Stuart; one *d*. Lived Beachamwell Hall.

VON WYSS, Clothilde *Beasts and Birds; The Child's World in Pictures; Gardens in their Seasons; The World in Pictures* (all PIX).

WAKELING, T.G. *Forged Egyptian Antiquities* (Misc)

WALKER, Francis S. *Ireland* (20s, 6s, PML); [*Killarney* (BB)]
1848-April 17 1916; *s* Thomas Walker; *ed* Catholic University; Royal Dublin Society; Royal Hibernian Academy. Painter and etcher; came to London 1868, exhibiting at the Dudley Gallery; worked for Dalziel brothers; contributed illustrations to books and magazines, including *Graphic*, ILN, etc.; RHA; RE; exhibited at RA most years from 1871 to 1913. Also illustrated *The Thames from Oxford to the Tower, Rivers of the West of England, Poet's Country* (T. C. & E. C. Jack). *Lived The Firs, Mill Hill, London.*
Refs: WWW; Houfe; Waters; Wood.

WALLACE, Harold Frank *Amid the High Hills* (Misc)
March 21 1881-Sept 16 1962; *b* Richmond, Yorkshire; *s* Edward and Constance Wallace; *m* 1912 Elizabeth Macpherson; one *s*; one *d*; *ed* Eton; Christ Church, Oxford; called to bar 1908. 'Has travelled extensively and shot in many parts of the world'; landscape and sporting painter; lawyer in Pelsall, Staffs. Wrote extensively on hunting and shooting in Britain and abroad. 'Recreations: deer-stalking, shooting, fishing, natural history, and archery.' Lived Little Wyrley Hall, Pelsall, Staffs, and Old Corriemony, Glen Urquhart, Inverness.
Refs: WWW; TB; WWA.

WALTER, L. Edna *Finland and the Tundra*; *Norway and the Lapps*; *Russia* (PML); *Finn and Samoyad*; *Norse and Lapp* (LL); *World's Children* (MP)

WALTERS, J. Cuming *The Charm of Lancashire* (Charm)
d July 16 1933; *s* John and C. E. Cuming Walters; *ed* King Edward's Grammar School, Birmingham. Sub-editor *Birmingham Daily Gazette,* later assistant editor and leader writer; editor *Manchester City News* for 25 years. Wrote extensively on Tennyson, Shakespeare, Dickens, topography and social and religious matters. Lived Sledmere, Egerton Road, Chorlton cum Hardy, Lancashire.
Refs: WWW.

WALTHAM, Ernest T. *Wild Flowers and their Wonderful Ways* (PN)

WEMYSS, M. A. C. *Iceland* (PML)

WESTELL, W. Percival *Bird Life of the Seasons*; *The Natural History of the Garden* (PN)
Dec 21 1874-Nov 1 1943; *s* W. T. Westell; *m* 1896 Alice Moules; one *s*; *ed* St Albans Grammar School. Author of many books on nature; lecturer to schools and institutions; curator of Letchworth Museum from its opening in 1914. Books include *The All-Round Nature Books, The Boy's Own Nature Book, Poems of Bonnie Scotland, My Life as a Naturalist, Yesterdays: An Autobiography.* Lived The Museum, Letchworth, Herts.
Refs: WWW; LYB.

WESTHOFEN, William *The Cape Peninsula* (7/6)
1842-1925; *b* Cape Town of Dutch descent. Qualified as civil engineer; joined Public Works Department of Cape Government 1892; frequent exhibitor of watercolours.
Refs: SADNB, which spells his name **Westhoven.**

WESTON, Reverend Walter *Japan* (Pop, New)
Dec 25 1861-March 27 1940; *s* John Weston; *m* 1902 Frances Fox (*d* 1937); *ed* Derby School; Clare College, Cambridge. British Chaplain, Kobe, Japan, 1889-95; held church posts alternately in England and Japan until 1915; explored in the Japanese Alps 1917; first honorary member of the Japanese Alpine Club.

Also wrote *Mountaineering and Exploration in the Japanese Alps* (1896), *The Playground of the Far East* (1918), *A Wayfarer in Unfamiliar Japan* (1925). Lived 57 Iverna Court, London W8.
Refs: WWW.

WHEELER, Dorothy *English Nursery Rhymes* (PC)
1891-1966; watercolour painter and illustrator; worked in Plumstead, Kent, and Esher, Surrey.
Refs: Houfe; Waters.

WHITEHEAD, Frederick William Newton *Warwickshire* (20s, Pop, New, WC); [*Stratford, Leamington and Warwick* (BB)]
1853-Feb 12 1938; *b* Leamington; *m* 1893 Beatrice Case of Dorchester. Studied with John Burgess. Moved to Paris 1880; worked at Académie Julian under Boulanger and Jules Lefebvre. Returned to England, became acquainted with Thomas Hardy and specialised in painting Dorset; spent summer months in caravan and tent in Wessex; painted mostly in oils. Lived 174 Belsize Road, South Hampstead, London.
Refs: WWW; TB; Waters; Wood; *The Studio* Vol 32.

WHYMPER, Charles *Egyptian Birds* (20s, Ltd); *Fisherman's Weather; Grouse and Grouse Moors* (Sport)
Aug 31 1853-April 25 1941; *b* London; *s* J. W. Whymper and brother of Edward Whymper; *ed* RA Schools; studied under Joseph Wolf. Illustrated books on travel, sport and natural history including *Wild Sports in the Highlands* (1878), *The Game-Keeper at Home* (Jefferies, 1880), *Siberia in Europe* (Seebohm, 1880), *Matabele Land* (1881), *Birds of Wave and Woodland* (1894), *Big Game Shooting* (1895), *The Pilgrim Fathers of New England* (1895), *Off to Klondyke* (1898), *Bird Life in a Southern County* (1899); contributed to ILN, *Good Words,* etc. Lived Houghton, Huntingdonshire.
Refs: WWW; Houfe; Peppin; TB; Waters; Wood.

WIGRAM, Edgar Thomas Ainger *Northern Spain* (20s); *Spain* (Pop, New, PML)
Nov 23 1864-March 15 1935; *s* Rev Woolmore and Harriet Mary Wigram; *ed* King's School, Canterbury; Trinity Hall, Cambridge; unmarried. Inherited baronetcy 1920; ARIBA; Mayor of St Albans 1926-27. Also illustrated *The Cradle of Mankind* (1914). Lived Green Acres, Wells, Somerset.
Refs: WWW; Houfe.

WILKINSON, Norman L. *The Royal Navy* (20s, MP, PC); *The Ramparts of Empire* (Misc)
Nov 24 1878-May 30 1971; *b* Cambridge; *m* 1st 1918 Evelyn Mackenzie (*d* 1967); one *s,* one *d*; 2nd 1968 (when he was 90) Joyce Jarvis; *ed* Berkhamsted; St Paul's Cathedral Choir School; Portsmouth and Southsea School of Art; studied at St Ives. Worked for ILN during 1901-15; became well known as marine painter and

etcher; entered RNVR 1914; originator of dazzle painting for protection of merchant vessels which was adopted by allied nations in WWI; OBE 1918; adviser on camouflage to Air Ministry during WWII; CBE 1948; RBA (1902); RI 1906 (president 1937); ROI (1908); Hon RWS; Marine Painter to Royal Yacht Squadron. Also wrote/illustrated *Tales from Hakluyt* (A & C Black), *An Angler's Anthology* (1913), *The Dardanelles, Colour Sketches from Gallipoli* (1915), *A Summer on the Test* (1924); *Ships in Pictures* (1945), *Water Colour Sketching out of doors* (1953). Lived The Studio, Winchfield, Basingstoke, Hants; Seaview House, Seaview, Isle of Wight.
Refs: WWW; Archibald; Houfe; Peppin; TB; Waters; *A Brush with Life* (memoirs, Seeley Service, 1969).

WILLIAMS, Margery [Mrs BIANCO] Paris (PML)

WILLIAMSON, John *France* (PML); *Mungo Park* (PGE)

WILMOT-BUXTON, E. M. *Wales* (PML)

WIMBUSH, Henry B. *The Channel Islands* (20s, Ltd, [BB], WC, Pop, New, PC, WCV); *North Devon* ([6s], PC); *Guernsey*; *Jersey* (WCV); [*What to see in the Channel Islands* (WTS)]
fl 1880-1908. Landscape and topographical painter; lived in London from 1887 at least until 1903; a prolific postcard artist, especially for Raphael Tuck. Lived (1903) Avonhouse Studios, Steeles Road, London NW.
Refs: Waters; Houfe.

WOLF, J. *Amid the High Hills* (Misc)

WOOD, A. *Lancashire* (Misc)

WOOD, Clarence Lawson. *Lawson Wood* (BPP)
1878-Oct 26 1957; *b* Highgate, London; *s* Pinhorn Wood; *m* 1903 Charlotte Forge; two *s*; one *d*; *ed* Slade School; Heatherley's; Frank Calderon's School of Animal Painting. Worked as artist for publisher Arthur Pearson; member of London Sketch Club; friend of Tom Browne; served as balloonist in Royal Flying Corps in WWI, decorated by the French; later founded factory to make wooden toys. RI. Also illustrated *The Red Men of the Dusk* (A & C Black, 1899), *The Bow-Wow Book* (1912), *Two Boys in War-time* (A & C Black), *The Old Nursery Rhymes* (1933); wrote and illustrated The 'Mr' and 'Mrs' books, *Rummy Tales* (1920), *The Scot 'Scotched'* (1927), etc. Lived Downlands, Salcombe Hill, Sidmouth, Devon.
Refs: WWW; Houfe; Peppin; TB; Waters.

WOOD, Rev Canon Theodore *The British Bird Book* (Misc)
Aug 6 1862-before 1934; *s* Rev J. G. Wood; *m* 1898 Helen Louisa Clarke. Deacon 1889; priest 1890; vicar of St Mary Magdalene, Wandsworth Common from 1902.

Wrote a number of books on insects and birds; his recreations were cycling and collecting British beetles. Lived The Vicarage, Lyford Road, Wandsworth Common, London.
Refs: WWW.

WOOD, William Thomas *The Salonika Front* (WF)
June 17 1877-June 2 1958; *b* Ipswich; *s* Thomas and Annie Wood; *m* Berenice Knowles; one *s*, one *d*; *ed* Regent Street Polytechnic School of Art; Italy. Landscape and war artist; RWS 1918; ROI 1927; in WWI an Observer, Kite-Balloons (RFC); British Official War Artist (Balkans) 1918; Home Guard 1941. Lived 61 Glebe Place, London SW3.
Refs: WWW; TB; Waters; Wood; WWA.

WOOLLARD, Dorothy E. G. *Bournemouth* (ASB, PC); *Brighton & its Environs* (ASB); *Bristol*; *The Isle of Wight* (ASB); *London* (ASB, PC); *Riverside London* (ASB).
Portrait painter and etcher; *fl* 1915-55; exhibited RA, RE, etc.; RE 1925; ARWA. Lived London.
Refs: Waters.

WRIGHT, Frank *New Zealand* (20s, Pop, New, PML)
1860-1923; *b* Nottingham; *ed* Nottingham School of Art; apprenticed to lace manufacturers but moved with family to New Zealand on death of his father; studied in England 1894-97 at Heatherley's. Watercolour painter; he and his brother (see below) were influenced by the Newlyn school. They travelled in New Zealand and were the first artists to exploit the west coast of Auckland and Urewera. Also illustrated a book of New Zealand fairy tales.
Refs: DNZB; TB; *The Studio* Vol 36.

WRIGHT, J. Massey *The Vicar of Wakefield* (7/6, Ltd)
Oct 14 1777-May 13 1866; *b* Pentonville; *s* of an organ builder. Moved to Lambeth on marriage in 1810; watercolour painter; worked as piano tuner for Broadwood; later painted scenery for Strand Panorama and Covent Garden; OWS 1824; set up drawing master's practice in London. Illustrated Shakespeare and other poets.
Refs: DNB; Mallalieu; TB; Wood (which spell his middle name Masey); Houfe.

WRIGHT, Walter *New Zealand* (20s, Pop, New, PML)
1866-Jan 11 1933; *b* Nottingham, moved to New Zealand with his parents 1877; studied in England 1894-97. Oil and watercolour painter; most ambitious work 'Massacre of the Boyd' (Auckland Art Gallery); taught painting until his sight failed:
Refs: DNZB.

WYLLIE, Marian Amy *London to the Nore* (20s, Ltd)
The wife of William Wyllie (see below) whom she married in 1897.

WYLLIE, William Lionel *London to the Nore* (20s, Ltd); *London* (WC); *A Century of Sea Trading* (Misc).
5 July 1851-6 April 1931; *b* London; *s* William Morison and Katherine Wyllie; *brother* of Lionel Smythe and Charles Wyllie; *m* 1879 Marion Amy Carew; five *s* (two of whom died in WWI), two *d*; *ed* Heatherley's; RA Schools (1866); Turner Gold Medal 1869. Marine watercolour and oil painter, illustrator, etcher, aquatint and drypoint artist; boat designer and yachtsman; on staff of *Graphic* for some years as marine illustrator; Marine Painter to Royal Yacht Squadron; did much work for the White Star shipping line and for the navy; NEA 1887; ARA 1889; RA 1907. Also wrote/illustrated *The Tidal Thames* (1884), *Marine Painting in Water-Colour* (1901), *Nature's Laws and the Making of Pictures* (1903), *J. M. W. Turner* (1905), *Sketchbook* (1908). *Norway and its Fjords* (1909), *Sea Fights of the Great War* (1918), *More Sea Fights of the Great War* (1919), *Lionel P. Smythe* (1923), *The Old Portsmouth and the New Southsea* (1923). Lived Tower House, Tower Street, Portsmouth.
Refs: WWW; Archibald; Houfe; DNB; TB; Waters; Wood; WWA; F. Dolman *William L. Wyllie and his Work* (1899); M. A. Wyllie *We Were One – A Life of W. L. Wyllie* (G. Bell, 1935).

YOUNG, Ernest *Corsica* (PML); *Siam* (PML)
1869-Feb 10 1952; *m* May Josephine Norbury (*d* 1925) *d* of Edwin A. Norbury *qv*. Headmaster John Lyon School, Harrow 1899; Inspector of Anglo-Vernacular Schools, Siam; Assistant Secretary for Higher Education, Middlesex; Middle Temple 1915. Wrote large number of books on geography, including textbooks.
Refs: WWW; LYB.

YOUNGHUSBAND, Sir Frances Edward *Kashmir* (20s, Pop, New)
May 31 1863-July 31 1942; *b* Murree, India; *s* Maj. Gen. John William and Clara Jane Younghusband; *m* 1897 Helen Augusta Magniac; one *s* who died in infancy, one *d*; *ed* Clifton; RMC, Sandhurst. 1st Dragoon Guards 1882; Captain 1889; Indian Political Department 1890; explored extensively in India and China; discovered route from Kashgar into India via the Mustagh Pass; Political Officer, Hunza 1892; Chitral 1893-94; Transvaal and Rhodesia 1896-97; Political Agent, Haraoti and Tonk 1898; Resident, Indore 1902-03; British Commissioner to Tibet 1902-04; Resident, Kashmir 1906-09; President RGS 1919; KCIE 1904; KCSI 1917; founded World Congress of Faiths 1936. Wrote extensively about India, Central Asia and Africa and later in life on religion. Books include: *The Heart of A Continent* (1896), *South Africa of To-day* (1898), *India and Tibet* (1910), *The Epic of Mount Everest* (1926), *Everest: The Challenge* (1936), *Life in the Stars* (1927), *The Living Universe* (1933).
Refs: WWW; LYB; CBD, DNB; *The Times,* Aug 3, 4, 26 1942; George Seaver, *Francis Younghusband* (1952).

YOVILCHITCH, Lena *Yugoslavia* (PML)

ZORN, Anders Leonard *Sweden* (PML)
Feb 18 1860-Aug 22 1920; *b* Mora, Dalarne province, Sweden; *s* of peasants; *m* Emma Lamm, Stockhold; no *c*; *ed* School of Enkoping, Stockholm; Academy of Fine Arts, Stockholm. Travelled in Spain, Italy and England painting watercolours; studied etching under Axel Haig. Painted first oil in 1888; self-portrait for Uffizi Gallery 1889; Gold Medal Paris Exhibition 1889. Visited the USA to paint portraits; also painted most of the Swedish Royal Family. Lived Mora, Dalarne, Sweden.
Refs: WWW; TB.

Index

The index is word-by-word: New York comes before Newall. Only the definite and indefinite articles have been inverted: thus *The Scenery of London* is indexed under S with a cross reference under London (in Roman type); *Wild Lakeland* is indexed under W, with a cross reference under Lake District. The entry under Lake District thus refers to all relevant books *except* those titled *(The) Lake District*.

Book titles are printed in italics. References to the Bibliography are indexed by serial number in bold type and are printed first.

References to postcards in the Bibliography, also in bold type, follow the book entries and are preceded by the letters **pc**. Square brackets round the numbers that follow show that the postcards are taken from the book referred to but that the postcard series has a different title. As an example, postcards from the 20s series *Naples* are indexed **pc** [7373] under *Naples and* **pc7373** under *The Bay of Naples*, which is the title of the postcard series.

Text page numbers are in roman type and illustration page numbers in italics.

The final entry after an author or artist's name refers to the biographical entry in the list of authors and artists.

The expression (2) has been used to denote two separate references on a page.

295